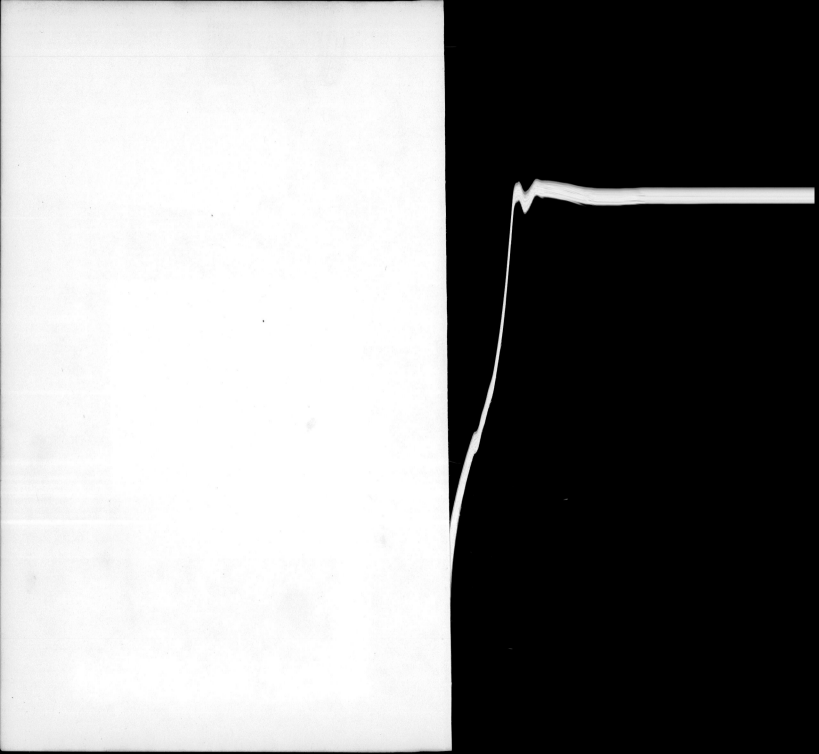

THE VARIETIES OF ECONOMICS | VOLUME ONE

The Varieties of Economics

DOCUMENTS

EXAMPLES

AND MANIFESTOES

in two volumes

Volume One

Edited and with an Introduction by ROBERT LEKACHMAN

Meridian Books

THE WORLD PUBLISHING COMPANY

CLEVELAND AND NEW YORK

ROBERT LEKACHMAN was born in New York City on
May 12, 1920. He took his B.A. and Ph.D. degrees
at Columbia University and has been teaching since
1947, most recently at Barnard College, where he is
Associate Professor of Economics. Mr. Lekachman
edited *National Policy for Economic Welfare* and is
the author of *A History of Economic Ideas* and of
numerous articles in periodicals, among them *Commentary, New Republic, Political Science Quarterly,
New Leader,* and *Harper's.*

AN ORIGINAL MERIDIAN BOOK

Published by The World Publishing Company
2231 West 110th Street, Cleveland 2, Ohio
Published simultaneously in Canada by
Nelson, Foster & Scott Ltd.
First printing June 1962
Library of Congress Catalog Card Number: 62-13385
Designed by Jack Jaget
Printed in the United States of America

In memory of my teacher

in the History of Economic Ideas

ROBERT L. CAREY

CONTENTS: Volume One

PREFACE   11

INTRODUCTION   13

Part I Economics and Salvation

ST. THOMAS AQUINAS ON USURY AND JUST PRICE   47

NICHOLAS ORESME ON COUNTERFEITING   59

MARTIN LUTHER ON TRADING AND USURY   63

JOHN CALVIN ON RULES FOR CHRISTIAN LIVING   68

RICHARD BAXTER ON BUYING AND SELLING   71

LEO XIII ON WORKING-CLASS ACTION   90

THE OXFORD CONFERENCE ON ETHICS AND ECONOMICS   105

REINHOLD NIEBUHR ON MORALITY IN ECONOMICS   108

Part II The Heroic Statesman

THE STATUTE OF ARTIFICERS   115

THE NAVIGATION ACT OF 1651   126

THE FRENCH WOOLENS REGULATION OF 1669   131

THOMAS MUN ON ENGLAND'S WAY TO WEALTH   139

SIR JAMES STEUART ON THE VIRTUES OF THE STATESMAN   142

ALEXANDER HAMILTON ON MANUFACTURING   147

FRIEDRICH LIST ON INFANT INDUSTRIES   156

JOHN MAYNARD KEYNES ON MERCANTILISM   167
GUNNAR MYRDAL ON ECONOMIC PLANNING   175

Part III The Age of Laissez-Faire

A. Theory

SIR DUDLEY NORTH ON FREE TRADE   185
DAVID HUME ON THE MERCHANT   188
ADAM SMITH ON TARIFFS   192
JEREMY BENTHAM ON MORAL CALCULATION   200
THOMAS ROBERT MALTHUS ON THE POOR LAWS   219
HARRIET MARTINEAU ON THE MECHANISM OF TRADE   226
JAMES MILL ON RENT   235
DAVID RICARDO ON VALUE AND COMPARATIVE
    ADVANTAGE   242
JOHN STUART MILL ON THE LIMITS OF LAISSEZ-FAIRE   252
FRIEDRICH A. HAYEK ON PLANNING   264

B. Applications

RICHARD COBDEN ON THE CORN LAWS   273
NASSAU SENIOR ON THE FACTORY ACTS   277
CHARLES DICKENS ON THE WORKHOUSE   289
JOHN STRACHEY ON IMPERIALISM IN BENGAL   293

Part IV The Economics of Utopia

PLATO ON THE PARABLE OF THE METALS   301
WILLIAM GODWIN ON PROPERTY   305
ROBERT OWEN ON EDUCATION AND HAPPINESS   320
HENRI COMTE DE SAINT-SIMON ON SOCIAL ORGANIZATION   341
KARL MARX ON THE GOTHA PROGRAMME   348
EDWARD BELLAMY ON THE INDUSTRIAL ARMY   353
SAMUEL BUTLER ON THE MUSICAL BANKS   361
ALDOUS HUXLEY ON HIGH CONSUMPTION   370
C. A. R. CROSLAND ON GAIETY UNDER SOCIALISM   376

VOLUME TWO CONTAINS:

  V *Economic Reform*
 VI *The Economics of Revolution*
VII *The Techniques of Economics: Theory,
     Measurement, History*

PREFACE

The two volumes of this book claim as their single major objective the illustration of the proposition that the economic view of life has had a rich and varied history. Although not even an economist would presume to claim that making a living and talking about making a living have been the only themes of human action and reflection, it is fair to say that no society has been able to ignore its material foundations either in action or theory. That concern has had diversified expression in the formal, full-dress exposition by the professional economist, the polemical pamphlet frequently by an interested party, the document of state, the statutes of the land, and even the novel and the satire. This is to say that economics has been and still is a matter of applications, of attempts to make sense out of the pressing public problems of the age, of efforts to transform or at least reform society, and of anxious reconciliations of material and ethical objectives. All of these, of course, in addition to the more familiar characterization of economics as primarily a particular mode of intellectual investigation, wedded to an identifiable set of statistical, historical, and analytical tools.

In an effort to exemplify these manifestations of the economic spirit, I have divided the seventy selections that are to be found in these volumes into seven major topics. The order within each topic is roughly chronological. A glance at the Table of Contents reveals one of the consequences of this plan: the varying emphasis and message economics has had over time. Thus, the first four topics— Economics and Salvation, The Heroic Statesman, The Age of Laissez-Faire, and The Economics of Utopia—inevitably contain much nineteenth- and twentieth-century matter, particularly in the instance of the third of these titles. But with equal appropriateness, the first, second, and fourth of these headings also include a great deal that testifies to intense economic discussion even when the tools of economics as we know them now were in primitive condition. These four topics comprise Volume One. Volume Two, on the other hand, devotes itself, with three exceptions only, to nineteenth- and twentieth-century selections. Why the difference? The answer is to be found in the circumstance that, unlike history, philosophy, and theology, economics as a formal intellectual discipline is a comparative late-comer. Thus the long section on economic techniques is almost exclusively filled with examples less than a century old, because these techniques themselves are young. Reform and revolution, good nineteenth- and twentieth-century preoccupations, have been closely affiliated with the growing intellectual power of the weapons of political economy.

I try to tell something more of this story in the Introduction (which appears only in Volume One). Sections 1 and 2 of the Introduction concentrate upon the nineteenth-century advance to glory of political economy. From that vantage point, I take occasional glances back to the past and forward to the present. Section 2 comments as well on economic technique, the complex relation of economic theory and economic problem, and the application of economics to social and political issues.

Section 3 of the Introduction starts with a fuller explanation of why these selections are organized in the manner before us. It continues with some pages of introduction to each of the seven major topics.

As for the selections themselves, I have sought to make each one self-contained. I have refrained from the violence of internal deletion as well as from combining passages from different portions of a given work. There is a brief introduction to each passage which places each selection within a context of time and place and identifies each author. In making my selections, I have tried wherever possible to choose the entertaining rather than the dull, the short rather than the long, and the graceful rather than the clumsy. Always, as an economist ought to say, other things equal.

It is a pleasure to express my gratitude to Arthur A. Cohen, who encouraged me to undertake this project, to Aaron Asher, who smoothed its progress from manuscript to book, to Jo Ann Lieb, who amiably copy-edited all the material, and to Mary Louise Vincent, who cheerfully handled the wearisome details of securing the essential permissions to include extracts. As publishers, all four fulfill an author's largest hopes. I am also indebted to Mrs. Stephanie Kaplowitt, who admirably typed the entire manuscript, in spite of a decided preference for literary over economic subjects. I hope that she did find occasional examples of the alliance between literature and economics which can exist.

                                                          ROBERT LEKACHMAN

INTRODUCTION

1

As a systematic subject of study, economics is a comparatively recent phenomenon. This is not to say that men of affairs and closeted scholars alike did not have much to write about currency, prices, wages, rent, and population long before Malthus became England's first professor of political economy at Haileybury in 1805. But economists as a separate sect, separate both from moral philosophers and politicians, were the consequence of the transforming industrial and intellectual changes of the nineteenth century.

Indeed, the nineteenth century in England is the century of political economy. As never before, political economy acquired a powerful reputation as the custodian of important truths about the natural universe, the guardian of a potent technique of investigation, and the authorized adviser of statesmen. Without doubt the political economist's position was the stronger because competing interpreters of the social world—sociologists, anthropologists, and psychiatrists—did not divide the attention of the economist's audience. As is usually the case, calm certainty about permanent truth was most notable not in the originators of nineteenth-century political economy but in the epigoni and the popularizers, the James Mills and the J. R. McCullochs. Still, the educated citizen who drank the wisdom of the *Edinburgh Review*, the leading Whig organ, or the *Westminster Review*, the chosen voice of the Philosophical Radicals, could scarcely avoid the conclusion that political economy was a settled subject whose conclusions were no longer open to important debate.

The range of these conclusions was impressive. Some of them pertained to the nature of human motives and human behavior. Here Jeremy Bentham was the official philosopher of classical economics.

The Benthamite calculus of pleasures and pains—the felicific calculus —assumed that human beings were primarily organisms that sought pleasure and avoided pain. How well they succeeded depended upon how accurately they calculated. Hence Bentham's *Introduction to the Principles of Morals and Legislation,* which he published in 1789, was a dedicated attempt to identify and apply these principles of calculation. Bentham's analysis came at the end of a long spell of utilitarian speculation, but his line of procedure differed from his predecessors' in its precision and its clarity. The full prescription is worth quotation as the epitome of a whole way of thought. This is the Benthamite set of steps in an accurate measurement of pleasure and pain:

> Begin with any one person . . . take an account
> 1. Of the value of each distinguishable *pleasure* which appears to be produced by it in the *first* instance.
> 2. Of the value of each *pain* which appears to be produced by it in the *first* instance.
> 3. Of the value of each pleasure which appears to be produced by it *after* the first. This constitutes the *fecundity* of the first *pleasure* and the *impurity* of the first *pain.*
> 4. Of the value of each *pain* which appears to be produced by it after the first. This constitutes the *fecundity* of the first *pain* and the *impurity* of the first pleasure.
> 5. Sum up all the values of all the *pleasures* on the one side and those of all the pains on the other. The balance, if it be on the side of pleasure, will give the *good* tendency of the act . . . with respect to the interests of that *individual* person; if on the side of pain, the *bad* tendency. . . .
> 6. Take an account of the *number* of persons whose interests appeared to be concerned; and repeat the above process with respect to each. *Sum up* the numbers expressive of the degrees of good tendency . . . do this again with respect to each individual to whom the tendency of it is *bad.* . . .*

At a time when the proposition was far from automatic, Bentham counted each individual as one. And as the directions imply, Bentham knew what the dimensions of pleasure and pain were: purity, fecundity, propinquity, intensity, certainty or uncertainty, duration, and extent. Even though he never completed a measurement himself, he left an abundance of instructions to his followers.

The Benthamite man, the calculator par excellence of political economy, is that economic man whom critics early and late have held

---

* Jeremy Bentham, *Introduction to the Principles of Morality and Legislation,* 1789 (Hafner edition), p. 182.

up to ridicule. Did such a man really exist, they derisively asked? A man who guided his actions by reason rather than passion, who calculated rather than yielded to his impulses, who was the product exclusively of his associations and education and not at all of his heredity? If he did exist, should he? Bentham, of course, had never claimed that England was populated by felicific calculators, but he had maintained that better calculation was a major objective of enlightened education. Naturally, the economic man pure and simple is a fiction, an ideal type. One may still wonder whether as an ideal type the economic man departs further from human conduct than other ideal types who have won twentieth-century favor, such as psychological man, psychiatric man, bureaucratic man, or organization man.

Political economy offered the cultivated Englishman of the early nineteenth century a conception of the physical universe in addition to this simplification of human behavior. In fact the pessimistic tone which permeates Malthus's *Essay on Population* (1798) and Ricardo's *Principles of Political Economy and Taxation* (1817), two of the central texts of classical political economy, was the consequence of two doctrines about the physical universe: nature was grudging, and man was prolific. Since the supply of arable land was finite, man at best might hope generation by generation to expand the output of food by some constant quantity. This was Malthus's arithmetic ratio. But population, as a consequence of the unchanging state of the passion between the sexes, threatened to increase geometrically. If we were conservative, argued Malthus, and assumed no more than a doubling of population every twenty-five years (which was only to generalize from the American experience), then two million people in 1800 will produce four million in 1825, eight million in 1850, sixteen million in 1875, thirty-two million in 1900, and so on and on. The land to feed these hordes did not exist. Even worse, the Ricardian theory of differential rent made it inevitable that less and less fertile land must be put into cultivation and a larger and larger share of society's proceeds must be paid to unproductive landlords in the shape of rent.

What was the answer? Human prudence promised one exit from the Malthusian trap. If men married late and procreated few children, the pressure of population might be alleviated. But, sighed Malthus, the poor especially were so prone to yield to their passions that little hope lay in this direction. The check that was likeliest to operate made grim reading. Malthus's positive check summarized nature's response to the pressure of population. Included in it were

unwholesome occupations, severe labor and exposure, bad and insufficient food and clothing, bad nursing of children, excesses of all
kinds, great towns and manufactures, common diseases and epi-
demics, wars, infanticide, plague, and famine. The list was somewhat
more impressive than the logic, for while famine was indeed
"natural," wars and great towns were human arrangements. In truth,
Malthus appeared to take a certain delight in his own gloom. The
rhetoric of the passage that follows is a fair example:

> Famine seems to be the last, the most dreadful resource of nature.
> The power of population is so superior to the power of the earth
> to produce subsistence for man, that premature death must in some
> shape or other visit the human race. The vices of mankind are
> active and able ministers of depopulation. They are the precursors
> in the great army of destruction; and they often finish the dreadful
> work themselves. But should they fail in this war of extermination,
> sickly seasons, epidemics, pestilence, and plague, advance in ter-
> rific array, and sweep off their thousands and ten thousands.
> Should success be still incomplete; gigantic famine stalks in the
> rear, and with one mighty blow, levels the population with the
> food of the world.*

These words had momentous semantic consequences. Thomas
Carlyle, perhaps envious that he had encountered a worthy rival
to the patent of pessimism, read Malthus's words and labeled political
economy the "dismal science." It is a name that has stuck.

As a clergyman turned political economist, Malthus was in fact
made to order for lampoon, whether gentle or savage. In his elegant
satirical novel *Melincourt,* Thomas Love Peacock makes Mr. Fax, the
character intended to represent Malthus, say solemnly, "Bachelors
and spinsters I decidedly venerate. The world is overstocked with
featherless bipeds. More men than corn, is a fearful pre-eminence,
the sole and fruitful cause of penury, disease, and war, plague, pesti-
lence, and famine." In a similarly agreeable fashion the wit Sydney
Smith recorded in a letter that ". . . Philosopher Malthus came here
last week. I got an agreeable party for him of unmarried people.
There was only one lady who had had a child; but he is a good-na-
tured man, and if there are no appearances of approaching fertility,
is civil to every lady."

The critics were not always gentle and they did not always give
Malthus credit for benevolent intentions. In his usual declamatory
style, William Cobbett had this to say: "Parson! I have, during my

* Thomas Robert Malthus, *Essay on Population,* 2nd ed., 1803 (Everyman edition), pp. 69-70.

life, detested many men; but never any one so much as you. . . .
No assemblage of words can give an appropriate designation of you;
and, therefore, as being the single word which best suits the character of such a man, I call you *Parson*, which amongst other meanings,
includes that of Borough-monger Tool." It was Cobbett's *Political
Register* which expressed popular indignation at Malthus in some
execrable doggerel:

SQUIRE THIMBLE

Pray, young folks, of procreation
   Of breeding children, shun the woes;
Check the surplus population;
   Restraint that's moral interpose.

DICK

Of children full that I my quiver
   Might have, you heard the parson pray;
Can you then, where God's the giver,
   Behold the gift and turn away?

BETSY

Didn't he pray for God to bless me,
   And make me fruitful on the vine;
And charge my Richard to caress me,
   And sick or well, not to repine?

ALL THE YOUNG MEN AND GIRLS

Hang that Thimble, what can he know?
   The Bible bids us to increase:
Back to London, then, may he go;
   And let us live and love in peace.

Like the Benthamite, the Malthusian is a popular figure of literary
ridicule. Dickens's schoolmaster in *Hard Times* is a Benthamite and a
political economist.

Vituperation and ridicule are both testimonials to the prominence
of that which is vituperated and ridiculed. Certainly in the first half
of the nineteenth century political economy was the queen of the
social sciences. Fashionable mothers insisted that the governesses
whom they hired be qualified to instruct their young charges in political economy. Mrs. Marcet's *Conversations on Political Economy*
and Miss Martineau's *Illustrations of Political Economy* were designed
to instruct helpless young people in the moral meanings and economic
mechanisms of political economy. Malthus himself praised Harriet
Martineau's popularization of his doctrine in *Weal and Woe in Garveloch*. The pre-eminence of the political economists was founded on

much more than their theories of human behavior, diminishing returns from land, differential rent, and population increase. It was the practical policies which appeared to flow inevitably from the theoretical generalizations that suited the times and the economic interests of the rate-paying classes. If, as Malthus had said, ". . . to prevent the recurrence of misery, is, alas! beyond the power of man," if there are ". . . unhappy persons, who, in the great lottery of life, have drawn a blank," if at nature's table there was no place set for some, then it was clear that no human contrivance and especially no governmental contrivance could amend the truths of nature's decree that many must suffer poverty, illness, and deprivation. What could man do against the inexorable limitations upon the supply of food, and the implacable sexual drive which forever threatened to overpopulate the world?

The great lessons of political economy seemed one and all addressed to the limitation of government interference and the encouragement of individual action. From the middle of the eighteenth century on, David Hume and Adam Smith had demonstrated as a matter of theory that the free movement of men and capital from less remunerated to better remunerated employments benefited the entire community as well as the individuals who responded to their own economic advantage. Adam Smith's "invisible hand" was a glorification of the proposition that the clash of naked egotisms in the market for goods and labor services somehow resulted in the social good of all. Did a merchant seek to increase his profits? Did a laborer search for higher wages? The first could achieve his goal only by offering a finished product for which consumers would pay a profitable price. The second could earn higher wages only by selling his services to an employer who desired the special skill that he possessed. Thus the royal road to economic improvement for both merchant and wage earner was better satisfaction of the consumer's wishes. Adam Smith's great lesson of freedom and his great attack upon those who interfered with its attainment were reinforced by his French popularizer, Jean-Baptiste Say. Say's law of markets, often summarized in the phrase "supply creates its own demand," was a proof that general unemployment—general "glut," in the language of the time—of men and resources was impossible when competition was unhampered. The free market made the adjustments which speedily rectified momentary situations of oversupply or shortage in specific industries.

From freedom Smith expected a great deal. Indeed, all the colors on his economic canvas were bright. If only the foolish apprenticeship acts, the silly laws of settlement, the ridiculous network of bounties, drawbacks, and tariffs, could be repealed, human beings in avid pursuit of their self-interest could improve their lot amazingly in short order. It was not true, as Smith argued in opposition to conventional mercantilist opinions, that workmen were lazy. On the contrary, give them a chance to enlarge their incomes and the danger is one of overwork, not malingering. Walter Bagehot's comment a century after Smith that Smith assumed a small Scotsman resident inside each of us was just. The simple and obvious system of natural liberty of which Smith sang promised enormous economic rewards to those who were sensible enough to grasp them. In Smith's own hands, political economy was the science of abundance, not the pitiful geometry of scarcity.

The Malthusian and the Ricardian revelations did in truth transform political economics into the study of scarcity. We have seen how constricted their universe was and how cheerless human prospects in it were. All the more did their dark forebodings lead them to endorse the laissez-faire preachments of their great predecessor. The public policies that Malthusian population doctrine implied were crystal-clear. If food were naturally scarce, then any governmental action that attempted to increase the supply that was vouchsafed to some must inevitably decrease the amount that remained for others. Hence the unreformed poor laws that granted an exiguous provision to the poor in their own homes—"outdoor relief"—were worse than ineffectual, they were actively harmful. For easy relief could only encourage the poor to marry early and breed large families. No doubt the Berkshire justices of Speenhamland who in 1795 tied poor relief to the price of bread meant well, but they and those who emulated them could have the effect only of increasing population and depriving the industrious of provision in favor of the imprudent.

It followed that Malthus and his disciples were earnest proponents of radical revision of the English system of poor relief. True benevolence to the poor discouraged their marriage and reduced the number of births. True benevolence also implied that poor relief be withheld from the imprudent or at most extended only on the severest and most discouraging of terms. How else could the community encourage those who postponed marriage until they could afford a family? The great monument to this attitude was the New Poor Law Act of 1834. This artifact from the workshop of the political economists altered the basic concept upon which relief had long been extended. It proposed to terminate outdoor relief and substitute in its place workhouse care. The workhouse was to be no abode of luxury.

In it the sexes were to be separated (lest paupers breed on the dole), the diet was to be sparse, and the employment monotonous and routine, much in the manner of the penal regimen of oakum-picking. When Oliver Twist raised his voice bravely to ask for more, the officials whom his unprecedented request horrified were in charge of a New Poor Law workhouse, in all truth a house of terror. But, as always in English administrative practice, inertia tempered logic. Outdoor relief did not vanish nor did adequate numbers of workhouses rise. Nevertheless, this important administrative reform testified to the power and influence of the political economists.

Political economy had much to say also on the subject of factory regulation and union activity. Laissez-faire as a principle emphasized the right of free contract. In theory at least, the wage of the laborer was the price that individual bargaining determined. The laborer chose among alternative job offers, and the employer chose among alternative workers. To interfere with the higgling of the market implied that a governmental agent knew what a proper wage was better than the very parties whose self-interest was most clearly at stake. To the nineteenth-century political economist, this was patently ridiculous. Hence parliamentary attempts to limit working hours, improve safety conditions in factories, and otherwise substitute the judgment of legislators for that of contractually free individuals were based upon a wrong principle. The results were necessarily harmful.

This conclusion applied with least qualification to adult male laborers. When in 1848 John Stuart Mill came to examine the reality of the bargaining freedom that women and children possessed, he was willing to distinguish their situation from that of their husbands and fathers. No doubt, especially in the judgment of a feminist like Mill, women should bargain just as freely as men. But a society that discriminated against women, limited their education, and subordinated them legally to men created artificial inferiorities. So long as these inferiorities continued, women's capacity to bargain intelligently was closer to that of their children than it was to that of their husbands. This was the point. Women and children deserved and required legislative protection because they lacked the training and experience to protect themselves.

What of unions? In Mill's *Principles of Political Economy*, union activity appeared as one of the false remedies for low wages. For this conclusion another doctrine of classical economics was responsible. The wages-fund theory which Ricardo had proposed and Mill had amplified proved that at a given time there was no more than a fixed fund of capital available for the employment of labor. If some workers got higher wages, arithmetic taught that others must get lower wages or even lose their jobs entirely. While unions were mistaken in their basic economic attitudes, Mill defended on general libertarian grounds their right to exist.

Now it is easy enough to see why doctrines of this order had an enormous appeal to the commercial and manufacturing classes of England. In the first part of the nineteenth century, England's industrial pre-eminence made free trade a natural and obvious principle, as continental economists acidly noted. The culmination of the free-trade agitation, the repeal of the Corn Laws in 1846 which had so long protected English agriculture, testified to the general realization that English manufacturers had nothing to lose from foreign competition and much to gain from cheap food. At home political economists criticized unions, opposed expensive poor relief, and sympathized with the claims of free enterprise. No wonder that merchants and manufacturers were instinctive political economists. No more gratifying set of notions could have been invented. No wonder also that political economy became ever more vulgarized and formularized. Why investigate further when present truth was so satisfactory, and so profitable?

Unfortunately, it is the vulgarizations of ideas rather than the ideas themselves which often live on after their sources are lost to memory. While the vulgarizations did extend genuine tendencies in political economy, the most original of the classical economists were not unmitigated advocates of laissez-faire, nor did they present a monolithic front to their opponents. Ricardo favored the postponement of free trade until the English tax system was reformed. Malthus advocated continued agricultural protection and argued that general glut was a real danger. Many of the classical economists, including Nassau Senior who is often thought the most doctrinaire of the group, recognized that Ireland was a special case to which English conceptions of land tenure and individual contract imperfectly applied. And Mill proposed worker ownership of the factories in which they worked, as well as virtually confiscatory taxation of inheritances.

Unlike their popularizers, they were much more tentative and much more experimental than general opinion ever seemed to recognize. Ricardo horrified his admirer James Ramsey McCulloch by his admission, in response to a criticism of John Barton, that machinery in the short run at least might displace workers and increase unemployment. All his life Mill wrestled with the dilemma presented to his mind and his conscience by his double attachment to laissez-faire and human welfare. Even Malthus took anxious note of his critics in successive editions of his famous *Essay*.

Nor did the entire group accept the label of pessimism. In his autobiography, John Stuart Mill described how as a young man, fresh from a Benthamite education, he and his young band of utilitarians interpreted Malthus in a cheerful sense: "Malthus's population principle was quite as much a banner and a point of union among us, as any opinion specially belonging to Bentham. This great doctrine originally brought forward as an argument against the indefinite improvability of human affairs, we took up with ardent zeal in the contrary sense as indicating the sole means of realizing that improvability by securing full employment at high wages to the whole labouring population through a voluntary restriction of their numbers." *
Here at last was the true hope. If only human beings could be educated properly then they would voluntarily restrict their numbers. In pursuit of this goal, John Stuart Mill as an adolescent may have been arrested for distributing birth-control literature. The account is quite possibly apocryphal.

In fact, for a Mill, Benthamite psychology, with its emphasis upon environment, and Malthusian population doctrine, with its hope for economic improvement when population was brought under control, merged to constitute a whole program of social and economic improvement. This program—much of the content of Philosophical Radicalism—included free education, repeal of those taxes on knowledge which made newspapers and periodicals too expensive for the poor, repeal of the Corn Laws so that workers might enjoy the benefits of higher living standards and be encouraged to preserve them, and the gradual extension of the franchise to those whom education had prepared to exercise it responsibly.

2

Even today economics—no longer political economy—bears the imprint of its nineteenth-century past. This is not only a matter of the general opinion that economics is a technical subject whose practitioners are addicted to mathematical puzzles, Delphic comments about the turns of the business cycle, and unromantic conceptions of human behavior. It is also the belief of many economists that economics proper begins in the nineteenth century, or, most generously, in 1776 with the publication of *The Wealth of Nations*. Implicit in this

* John Stuart Mill, *Autobiography* (New York: Oxford University Press, 1924), pp. 88-9.

belief is another, the notion that economics defines itself according to its technique. And again, before the nineteenth century economics could boast very little in the way of scientific technique. As technique, economic theory owes much to David Ricardo whose masterpiece, *Principles of Political Economy and Taxation,* displayed many of the characteristic stigmata of later theory. It is, to begin with, highly abstract. What Ricardo looked for were the laws of economic behavior, those regularities in the movements of large numbers of human beings which were susceptible of generalization. In the course of the voluminous correspondence that he conducted with Malthus, he observed that ". . . our differences may in some respect, I think, be ascribed to your considering my book as more practical than I intended it to be. My object was to elucidate principles, and to do this I imagined strong cases that I might show the operation of those principles." * Strong cases are not likely to be real cases. But like Ricardo, later economists have often found it necessary to sacrifice factual resemblance to theoretical rigor. Ricardo was much more interested in the long run, "the permanent state of things," than in the short run where accident tended to distort principle. The step-by-step method culminating in the equilibrium position is another contribution of Ricardo's to later analysis. And finally, Ricardo was implicitly mathematical, even though he personally used nothing grander than arithmetic. The mathematical road is one which economists have found to be increasingly attractive. The lures of abstraction, mathematical analysis, equilibrium goals, diagrammatic presentation, and strong cases are powerful. And all but the diagrams are to be found in Ricardo.

Nothing is easier, therefore, than to tell the story of economics as the gradual growth and refinement of analytical techniques. Such, in fact, was the organizing principle of Joseph Schumpeter's massive *History of Economic Analysis.* Using the single but powerful standard of technical acuity, Schumpeter gave low marks to Adam Smith and awarded supreme honors to Léon Walras, the inventor in the 1870's of a mathematical theory of general equilibrium. By this standard still, Schumpeter favored economists who rigorously separated analysis from policy and criticized economists who too readily mixed their theories with practical recommendations. Schumpeter himself provided an example of the scientific detachment that he advocated. Although a romantic admirer of an idealized version of capitalism, he argued that socialism was nevertheless inevitable. His *Capitalism,*

---

* David Ricardo, *The Works and Correspondence,* ed. Piero Sraffa (Cambridge, Eng.: Cambridge University Press, 1951-5), VIII, 184.

Socialism and Democracy conveys all the sadness of a man who, as a surgeon, dissects the corpse of his beloved.

There are other ways to trace the development of economics. The record of the subject is the record also of the responses of economic writers—a group much larger than economists—to the particular distresses of their own time. Examples are many. The mercantilist predecessors of classical economics concentrated primarily upon the flow of the precious metals, the balance of trade, the power of the sovereign, and the control of the domestic economy. Their choice of topic was the natural selection of men whose lives were bound up in commerce and statecraft. Their dominant solutions—low wages, subsidization of exports, curtailment of imports, and promotion of domestic merchant shipping—represented their conception of the national interest and the advantages of their own class. Their tendency to confuse the two had many parallels before them and since their time.

Abstract as the theory of the classical political economy was, its applications ranged over a wide variety of nineteenth-century dilemmas: poor laws and corn laws, the rights of trade unions, factory acts, free public education, Irish policy, taxes on knowledge, colonial administration, and population control. On each of these topics the political economists had something to say, by no means always a unanimous opinion. The connections between theory and events were very tight. The striking contrast between Smithian optimism about improvement in the condition of the ordinary Englishmen and Ricardian despondency on the same topic can scarcely be traced to any theoretical transformation in the forty-one years between 1776 and 1817. The germ of Malthusian doctrine is to be found in Hume and Smith, but in the theory of neither was it allowed to take an important place. However, it is hard to avoid the conclusion that the sudden spurt in population that the first English censuses disclosed, the economic distress that followed the Napoleonic Wars, and the currency inflation that accompanied the suspension of specie payments combined to make the English prospect much less promising. It was a world dominated by intricate complications in its currency, trade, population, and agriculture. As much as anything else certainly, these problems explain the contrast between Smith and Ricardo.

A last illustration of the perennial relation between economic problem and economic theory should suffice. This is the contemporary case of Keynesian economics. John Maynard Keynes was the son of a Cambridge don, John Neville Keynes, who was himself an economist of note and, as his son was to be after him, Bursar of Kings College. At this same Cambridge college, the younger Keynes studied with the great Alfred Marshall and learned from the venerable sage the pure doctrine of neoclassical economics. Marshall conceived himself as in the direct line of English economics, running from Smith, through Malthus and Ricardo, to Mill, and finally to himself. Although Keynes had a lively public career whose early triumph was that *succès de scandale*, the sensational *Economic Consequences of the Peace*, and enjoyed a reputation among his peers as the proponent of heterodox ideas about central banking and the gold standard, he also taught neoclassical price theory right out of Book V of Marshall's *Principles* to successive classes of Cambridge youths. And he showed little disposition to doubt the applicability of Marshall's theories to contemporary Britain. In this area at least, he was simply Alfred Marshall's best student, the most subtle wielder of Marshall's analytical tools.

At the center of Marshallian theory was price in particular markets and single industries. What induced Keynes to discard the tacit assumption which ran through Marshall's economics that Say's law of markets still described the self-adjusting propensities of competitive markets, and that, therefore, aggregate employment and total demand could take care of themselves? What brought Keynes to write in *The General Theory of Employment, Interest and Money*, ". . . a study of the forces which determine changes in the scale of output and employment as a whole"? The date of Keynes's treatise suggests the answers to the questions. In 1935 only the blind could have avoided recognition of tremendous unemployment, enormous quantities of idle resources, and a manifest failure of Say's durable generalization to describe the principal contours of economic reality. The "unfamiliar paths" upon which Keynes set out were those which economic disruption had revealed to him. Or to put the matter more simply, an economist needs a theory of what determines total output when there is something distressing about the manner in which total output is behaving, much as the physician is impelled to comprehend illness rather than health. No one can know that the *General Theory* would never have been written if the Great Depression had not blighted the 1930's, but the record of Keynes's own intellectual development, his repeated grapplings with successive economic problems, and his continuous effort to make theory applicable to current contingency strongly imply that the timing, at the least, of his new theory depended upon the overriding fact of severe economic crisis.

Nor does this end the list of ways in which the history of economic ideas can be recorded. Economics does truly boast a technique of its own. It is indeed at many key points in its evolution a response to the economic problems of specific places and times. But economics is also a part of a more general history of ideas. From the intellectual milieu that surrounds it, economics picks up a great deal, and to this milieu it contributes something in return. Consider the economics of St. Thomas Aquinas. In the Thomist world view, economics too had a place. Christians were enjoined to shun usury and to charge each other prices no higher than the canons of justice dictated. No small a part of St. Thomas's genius was his ability to translate such ethical precepts into concrete cases. It does not exaggerate to regard his passages on usury and just price as explicit investigations of market organization and business practice, designed to put realistic flesh on the bones of general theory. What persuaded St. Thomas to reflect on matters as mundane as these? It was the belief that economic life was a part of the whole life of the Christian. What the Christian did in the market place influenced his behavior in this world and his prospects in the world to come. In his own system of value judgments (as we might now call them), St. Thomas assigned economic values a necessary but subordinate place. As a later scholastic writer, Nicholas Oresme, put it, "There are some occupations which cannot be carried on without sin; for there are menial tasks which soil the body, such as cleaning sewers or chimneys, and others which stain the soul, like those now in question." Oresme's soul-staining occupation was pre-eminently usury.

If in the Middle Ages economic opinion naturally rested itself upon solid theological foundations, economic writers in the sixteenth, seventeenth, and eighteenth centuries came from the ranks of commerce and public officialdom rather than the roster of theologians, and allied themselves with new heroes and new ideas. The new hero was the statesman, who alone in the mercantilist conception of things could be counted upon to act in the public interest, subordinate his own ambitions, and employ the ambitions of others to promote the general welfare. And with the passage of time welfare itself came to mean not the salvation of souls but a series of temporal gains—power to the monarch, prosperity to the mercantile classes, gold and silver to the royal exchequer, and damage to commercial rivals. Religious values, once at the apex of men's desires, were relegated to instrumental tools of the ruler, well suited to a docile labor force and an aggressive mercantile class.

The economist as the adviser of statesmen and the servant of objectives which transcend the economic has reappeared in the employ of the planned societies of the Soviet bloc and the developing lands of Africa and Asia. The critical role that a Gunnar Myrdal assigns to the state in the underdeveloped countries echoes over the centuries the sentiments of a Sir James Steuart who sets a similarly high valuation upon the efforts of the mercantilist ruler.

Examples of the alliance between economics and other intellectual conceptions are easy to discover. Thus, the social Darwinism of Herbert Spencer combined classical emphases upon free competition with the notion of natural selection. From Darwin's great principle of natural selection, Spencer drew support for the notion that within a community the poor reflected an inferior biological strain to be selected out and the well-to-do a superior racial strain to be cherished and perpetuated. Competition which had served the purposes of economic efficiency in the eyes of the classical economists was now saddled by Spencer with the additional task of eliminating the unfit and improving the breed. The super-Malthusianism of Spencer's position is evident in passages like this one:

> . . . the well-being of existing humanity and the unfolding of it into this ultimate perfection, are both secured by that same beneficial though severe discipline, to which the animate creation at large is subject. It seems hard that an unskilfulness which with all his efforts he cannot overcome, should entail hunger upon the artizan. It seems hard that a labourer incapacitated by sickness from competing with his stronger fellows, should have to bear the resulting privations. It seems hard that widows and orphans should be left to struggle for life or death. Nevertheless, when regarded not separately but in connexion with the interests of universal humanity, these harsh fatalities are seen to be full of beneficence—the same beneficence which brings to early graves the children of diseased parents, and singles out the intemperate and the debilitated as the victims of an epidemic.[*]

But there were other ways of combining economics and evolution. To Spencer the obvious alliance joined laissez-faire theory and natural selection. In Thorstein Veblen, however, a consideration of natural selection evoked a demonstration that classical economics, neoclassical economics, and even Marxian economics (itself tainted by the classical errors) were inaccurate modes of reasoning. Why, asked Veblen in a famous essay, was not economics itself an evolutionary science? Why did not economists comprehend that economic

[*] Herbert Spencer, *Social Statics and Man Versus the State* (London, 1884); reprinted in *Introduction to Contemporary Civilization in the West* (New York: Columbia University Press, 1954), II, 739.

institutions, which Veblen defined as habits of thought, changed in response to the necessities of change in the realm of biology, industry, and society at large? Above all, when would economists realize that from the standpoint of evolutionary theory everything that is, is wrong? Thus, in Veblen's hands evolution became a handy club with which to beat contemporary economic theory.

Not always to their mutual advantage, economics and history have formed numerous alliances. Conceivably the most famous single generalization about American history was Frederick Jackson Turner's thesis that the frontier is at the center of American historical development and any theory of American exceptionalism. Turner's frontier hypothesis reappears in the doctrine of secular stagnation which American followers of Keynes advanced during the Great Depression. When Alvin Hansen in his presidential address to the American Economic Association in 1938 came to enumerate the changes in American life that slowed economic growth, dampened prosperities, and intensified depressions, one of the three major changes in American life that he emphasized was the delayed impact of the closing of the frontier. For as the frontier vanished, so also vanished the major opportunities for new investment which the construction of new houses, new roads, new schools, and new railroad links had in the past meant.

The Marxist affiliation of history and economics was indispensable to their vision of the future. Marx's and Engels's prediction of capitalist breakdown and socialist victory was constructed out of diverse materials. From English classical economics, especially in their Ricardian version, Marx borrowed the labor theory of value, amplified the tacit opposition between worker and employer implied but not stressed by Ricardo, and expanded the classical emphasis upon abstract reasoning. From Hegel, Marx borrowed and revised the dialectical mode of thought. Change can be described in dialectical triads. All phenomena are complex, none is stable, development not stability is the law of human experience.

Armed with such weapons, Marx and Engels took a long view of history. As the future and the past looked to them in 1848 when they issued the *Communist Manifesto,* ". . . the history of all hitherto existing society is the history of class struggles. Freeman and slave, patrician and plebeian, lord and serf, guildmaster and journeyman, in a word, oppressor and oppressed, stood in constant opposition to one another, carried on an uninterrupted, now hidden, now open, fight, a fight that each time ended, either in a revolutionary reconstitution of society at large, or in the common ruin of the contending classes." Of the consequences, intellectual and political, of the view of history and economics here expressed, we will not see the end in our life-time. Although Marx and Engels were certainly not the first men to see history as the clash of material interest, theirs was the completest and the weightiest exemplification of the doctrine. Even the opponents of Marxism write history differently because Marx and Engels united English classical economics, Hegelian metaphysics, and the materialist conception of history.

3

There are at least as many ways of constructing a useful book of readings in the history of economic ideas as there are fruitful modes of recounting the subject's history. A set of selections that pursued Schumpeter's austere definition of economics as the growth of an increasingly subtle technique could start with the fumbling efforts of the mercantilists to grasp the principles of international trade and the quantity theory of money; progress to the refinements of the English classical school; trace the origins of the marginalist mode in France (Cournot and Dupuit), England (Bentham, Senior, and Longfield), and Germany (von Thünen and Gossen); continue with marginalism itself; examine the rocky passage to Keynesian aggregative economics; and conclude with some samples of the work of contemporary econometricians who bid fair to construct new syntheses of mathematics, statistics, and deductive logic. The result might be an interesting, even an exciting, picture of the growth in power and clarity of a social science. Indeed, by judicious use of the selections that have been made for these volumes such a sequence can be arranged.

A very different but equally provocative result might flow from selections organized around the notion that economics is primarily a set of responses to the particular problems of identifiable times and places. One need not adopt the Marxist version of ideology to identify the congruities between mercantilist economics and the necessities of statecraft in an age of warring sovereignties, between classical English economics and the Industrial Revolution of 1760-1832, and between Keynesian economics and the Great Depression of the 1930's. Once more, any reader especially interested in tracing the evolution of economics from this special vantage point can readily rearrange the selections to his taste.

The uses of economics constitute still a third organizing thread. In its time, economic doctrine has served to justify a great many policies: high tariffs and no tariffs; price and wage control and glorious laissez-faire; heroic statesmen and self-effacing, almost invisible officials; large roles for government and small ones; encouragement to businessmen and encouragement to consumers. The antinomies are fascinating and all the more so because the proponents of special interests frequently advance several of these positions in the same historic period.

The easiest organizational device of all centers around the perennial topics of economics. The constituent elements of income—wages, profits, rent, and interest—comprise the grand topic of income distribution. Price levels and the value of money are a second topic. A third is price determination in individual markets. And the fourth and most recent is the manner in which aggregate income is determined by the interplay of a few great variables: interest rates and the marginal efficiency of capital, the supply of money and the propensity to consume. So organized a book of readings would conform closely to the usual sequence of topics included in today's elementary textbooks.

In fact, I have followed no one of these principles by itself. My justifications are to be found in my conception of the nature and history of economics. That history is characterized above all by its variety. Economists, economic writers, theologians, reformers, revolutionists, statesmen, and even novelists had stimulating and original comments to make on the problems of economics and the material life of man. To confine economics to the professional economist is to ignore a great deal that the amateur in economics has contributed. It is in fact to cut off all that was said before the nineteenth century fostered the creation of the professional guild of economists. To treat economics only as the development of a technique is to ignore the reasons why so many men entered economics, the hopes that they reposed in their subject, the manner in which their hopes led them to select their topics of investigation, and the uses to which they put economics. Alfred Marshall was not the only economist, and the Victorian era was not the only time when neophytes studied economics in the hope of doing good to their society.

Therefore, the selections in these volumes are designed to serve several purposes rather than a single objective. Some display the progress of economic technique. Others either exemplify the uses to which economics has been put, illustrate the problems that thorny times have inflicted upon economic writers, or indicate the alliances into which economists have entered.

Let us see how the seven divisions into which the selections have been placed serve these ends. The first, "Economics and Salvation," starts with the realization that the compartmentalization of life and the consequent separation of economic activity from other varieties of behavior are of comparatively recent origin. Even now the small-loan laws and the resentment felt by buyers against sellers whose prices are judged too high testify to a stubborn, lingering belief that ethics and economics really have something to do with each other. The view that moral values and economic behavior are separate is especially abhorrent to the Christian. What "Economics and Salvation" examines, then, is the manner in which theologians have struggled to reconcile men's economic needs and selfish propensities with what the theologian assumes to be man's equally great yearning for salvation. Both Catholic and Protestant viewpoints are included. I would have added a Jewish statement if I had been able to discover a brief and representative passage.

The arrangement of this Part, and of the ones to follow as well, is chronological. In most respects, these passages make their meanings plain and the short introductions aim mainly to supply chronology and specific context. Perhaps this is the place for one or two general observations. It is accurate to say of both the Catholic and the Protestant judgments on economic behavior that the tendency is a movement from the simple to the complex and from the dogmatic to the speculative. Oresme was much less firm about the meanings and implications of usury in the fifteenth-century world than was St. Thomas two centuries earlier, even though Oresme is equally vehement in his condemnation of whatever may be defined as usury. Oresme was even inclined to evaluate counterfeiting as a crime worse than usury. Pope Leo XIII's nineteenth-century parish contained such puzzling organizational phenomena as labor unions, co-operatives, trusts, and strong central governments. As his encyclicals demonstrated, the rule of individual conduct became infinitely harder to render concretely in a world of large units tied to each other by impersonal markets than in a society of craftsmen, small masters, subsistence farmers, and manorial regimes. When the face-to-face tenor of economic life yield to division of labor, specialization of function, social separation of buyer from seller, and substitution of the cash nexus for more human relationships, it is more than simply difficult for the Christian to do his duty, it is exceedingly difficult for him to discover where that duty lies.

So it has also been for Protestants. John Calvin knew what to tell the substantial merchants of Geneva. His definition of business as a secular calling, his high valuation of material prosperity as the stewardship of the Lord, and his careful modification of Catholic prohibitions against usury combined dogmatic theology and realistic grasp of commercial affairs. How different it was for the good Protestants of the Oxford Conference on Church, Community, and State when they sat down together in 1937 to commit to paper their recommendations to fellow Christians on ethical conduct in economic affairs. Baffled by the complexity of economic life, they retreated to the safe ground of abstract generalization. The most sensitive of businessmen could not learn from them how to reconcile his multiple responsibilities to his government, his customers, his suppliers, his workers, and his stockholders. The Christian rule of love is an imperfect technical implement for use in the world of commerce, for it fails to answer the hard questions: who is to be loved, how is he to be loved, and how much is he to be loved.

In the twentieth century the historical link between economics and theology seems to have snapped. Partly this is the consequence of economics' new independence not only of theology but of any obligation to speak out of ethical concerns. In part, the new separation is the result of the general perception that ethical advice on economic affairs now requires the technical competence of the specialist. Few theologians are also technical economists and few economists are theologians.

The second major division of the selections, "The Heroic Statesman," is an account of a second kind of affiliation into which economists have entered, with the governors of the land. Until the middle or even the last third of the nineteenth century, the very name of our subject, political economy, testified to its intentions. It may signify something that after a century of disuse the term seems quietly to be reappearing frequently in conjunction with discussions of economic development. Certainly the older label emphasized the commitment of economists to guide the politicians, or, as is appropriate to the dignity of the dead, the statesmen. While contemporary economists remain a trifle skittish about addressing their speculations to the direct necessities of their rulers, they have not hesitated as individuals to become members of Councils of Economic Advisers or private mentors to officials.

The readings in this Part fall conveniently into three categories. The first contains several samples of the prize handiwork of mercantilist statesmen. The Statute of Artificers and Apprentices (1563) amounted to a major Elizabethan attempt to regulate price, control wages, prescribe the rules of apprenticeship, and define the terms under which relief to the poor should be administered. Its status as a symbol was such that the repeal of the Statute had to await the nineteenth-century triumph of laissez-faire. The Navigation Act of

1651 is a representative sample of the continuing mercantilist policy of promoting business on behalf of England's merchant marine and seaports. The French Woolens Regulation of 1669 is a reasonably good example of the voluminous regulations that Colbert applied to French commerce and manufacture. In its meticulous definition of quality, it indicates the reach, if not the grasp, of French state regulation.

Mercantilist practice often spoke with a louder voice than mercantilist theory. In an age dominated by practical men, it is appropriate to identify a second category—the practical man rendered articulate. What rendered a busy merchant or a preoccupied administrator articulate was frequently some material exigency. Thus Thomas Mun's own deep involvement in the East India trade stimulated him to write his classic exposition of the advantages of a favorable balance of trade and the necessity of allowing gold and silver to leave the country in order to insure such a favorable balance. Among them, Mun, Petty, and Steuart allude at the least to some of the most eagerly sought mercantilist objectives: a favorable balance of trade, perpetual addition of gold and silver to the monarch's exchequer, a strong central authority, low domestic wages, and high barriers against the import of foreign goods.

The last four readings—Hamilton, List, Keynes, and Myrdal—should be taken to recommend not mercantilist doctrine but attachment, for various reasons, to the role of the statesman as a guide to economic policy, and willingness to emphasize the goals of economic nationalism. Hamilton's advocacy of bounties and other encouragements to domestic manufacture was based on an early recognition of the force of the infant-industry argument for the protection of young industries. Those who share Hamilton's judgment point out that even when a nation has a natural advantage in the production of a given finished item, it is unlikely to develop the enterprises that enable it to enjoy that advantage until it offers these enterprises some shelter in their tender infancy against the icy blasts of competition from older firms in other nations. List, who spent some years of exile in the United States and familiarized himself with American economic conditions, employed rather similar arguments to justify protection for German industry and attack English free-trade doctrines.

The two twentieth-century writers, Keynes and Myrdal, concur in a willingness to depart from the classic freedoms of laissez-faire and the classic assumption that free exchange necessarily maximizes domestic and international welfare. Keynes's expression of such sentiments took the shape in part of a rather romantic re-examination of mercantilism. With his characteristic love of a good paradox, Keynes credited mercantilism with intelligent policies well-designed to promote employment and enlarge national product, even though the mercantilists were frequently unaware of the correct theoretical reasons for their own prescriptions. In his recent writings, Myrdal has concentrated upon economic development. He has argued that the supply of entrepreneurial talent in the poor countries is so scant and the prospect of appropriate employment even of this inadequate supply is so slight that the community must plan its own development centrally, allocate its resources according to this central plan, and closely control the operations of markets. If only from the standpoint of this preference for planning and central allocation, Myrdal represents a neomercantilist position.

The third topic, laissez-faire, has been divided into theory and application. Occasionally this division offers an ironic contrast between the aspirations of the theorists of economic freedom and the social consequences of the freedom they praised. John Strachey's account of the Bengal famine identifies one disgraceful historical incident where unchecked greed caused enormous misery and social disruption. Dickens's evocation of his own memories of a brief stay in the workhouse in unforgettable fictional form reminds any modern reader of the suffering and hardship that unimaginative application of laissez-faire doctrine occasionally imposed.

As doctrine, laissez-faire reached the heights of glory in the nineteenth century, but two of its great names, David Hume and Adam Smith, are eighteenth-century figures, and the intrepid Dudley North harks back to the seventeenth century, when the voices lifted in favor of free trade were few, apprehensive, and anonymous. Smith's common-sense emphasis upon the mechanism of resource allocation in competitive markets; Malthus's population doctrine; Ricardo's exposition of comparative advantage in international trade; Bentham's exaltation of man the calculator; and James Mill's popularization of the Ricardian theory of differential rent amount to a list of major elements in the structure of an economic theory which for a long time satisfied economists and men of affairs in the nineteenth century, especially in England.

The tide of affairs has converted most economists and the bulk of politicians to doctrines more interventionist than the great theorists of laissez-faire ever contemplated. In its embryonic state in this country and at a later stage of growth in Western Europe and Oceania, the welfare state has been the consequence of an altered conception of the extent of individual responsibility for personal misfortune. A vague term in itself, the welfare state at the least implies that sickness, unemployment, accident, and indigence spring from events and relationships that no individual can control and from which, therefore, no individual should suffer the hurt. Social causation is sufficient reason for social protection. And so it is that the scope of individual action narrows as the complexity of economic life increases.

But not all economists have reached conclusions like these. An able group of economists at the University of Chicago looks back to Alfred Marshall, takes direct inspiration from the late Henry Simons and the very present Frank Knight, and numbers in its ranks such talented defenders of free markets, limited government, and individual responsibility as Milton Friedman and George Stigler. In a later Part of Volume Two there is a characteristic excerpt from Professor Stigler and, for good measure, another from Lord Robbins who is on the same side of the issue. Since Part III concentrates essentially on major theories, not the growth of technique per se, I have included an excerpt from Friedrich Hayek's *The Road to Serfdom,* an implacable attack on creeping socialism and an eloquent modern defense of the inseparability of political and economic freedom.

Only infrequently has heaven been the destination of economic theory, whatever may be surmised about the individual destinies of the theorists themselves. With the exceptions of Karl Marx and C. A. R. Crosland, none of the contributors to "The Economics of Utopia"— Part IV of this compilation—was a professional economist. Nevertheless, whatever his professional standing as an economist, no utopian can write of the better world to be without speculating upon its economic arrangements. Marx's own musings on this topic in his *Introduction to the Critique of the Gotha Programme* were a most infrequent lapse into the utopian. Such speculation was in general banned as partaking of the futile indulgences of the utopian socialists whom Engels especially had taken pains to separate from "scientific" socialism. Moreover, the logic of capitalist development, not the shape of things to come, was the great theme that unified and strengthened the voluminous books, articles, and pamphlets that poured from the Marxist pen. Crosland's sober discussions of the human merits of socialism, *à l'anglaise,* may be libeled by this inclusion among portraits of a beautiful future.

I have included such dreamers as Godwin, Saint-Simon, Owen, Bellamy, Butler, and Huxley because their dreams were occasionally economic. It must be added, in fairness to the last of the list, that Huxley's dreams were nightmares, not wish fulfillments. The dreamers had in common an assumption worth identification: they were confident

that in a better or at least a different society specifically economic
problems would vanish. After all, economics' glum reputation derives
partly from its monomaniacal emphasis upon the scarcity of the good
things of life and the propensity of human beings to multiply so rapidly that these good things never are numerous enough to go around.
Now the economic problem whether so stated or not has almost always involved some solution to the difficult tasks of allocating scarce
resources among a large number of competing ends. From the pressing weight of this professional obligation the utopian escapes in one of
two traditional ways: either he assumes some magical end to scarcity
or some equally miraculous diminution of human wants. The tedious
inhabitants of Godwin's and Saint-Simon's utopias develop tastes for
intellectual employments, which, in the case of Godwin, even supersede the taste for sexual enjoyment. Thus at a stroke the problem of
scarcity vanishes: men want less and there are fewer of them to want
anything.

In Bellamy's sober utopia and Huxley's high-spirited anti-utopia, the
second path is followed. Efficiency is so increased, mechanization
works so many marvels, and work organization is so perfected that
incredible quantities of goods flood the population. In its extreme
form, Huxley's *Brave New World,* the old problem of production and
scarcity must yield its place to the new problem of consumption and
glut. As mid-century America seems to indicate, utopian dreams occasionally turn into ironical realities. Bellamy's warehouses with enough
for all have been achieved in the instances of many consumer durable goods and overachieved in the instances of several agricultural
commodities. The problems that linger are Huxleian: we have trouble
distributing all that we can produce to those who might use it.

Economics and social reform have often been friends. Hence the
fifth division of these readings. But the friendship while close is historically rather brief, dating from the nineteenth century. In that
short time, the kind of reform that has been advocated has itself suffered a change of meaning. The nineteenth-century reformer among
economists devoted his energies to the achievement of those social
changes which released individual energies, rewarded personal efforts, and expanded human capacities. The activities of that formidable band of Benthamites, the Philosophical Radicals, who enrolled
such considerable figures as Jeremy Bentham, Francis Place, James
Mill, and John Stuart Mill, covered a wide range of public agitations
which were unified by the pursuit of these common objectives. What
a list of good causes it was! They favored full political rights for Dis-
senters, Catholics, and even Jews, partly on the basis of the greatest

happiness principle, partly also because the community lost when it discriminated against talented members of these sects. They supported radical revision of the poor laws because they had persuaded themselves that the old system of outdoor relief rewarded idleness, encouraged profligacy, and penalized the prudent. On his own behalf, John Stuart Mill argued carefully in favor of extremely high, actually confiscatory inheritance taxes and against progressive personal income taxes, because he wanted to bend the tax system to the encouragement of individual effort and personal self-development. While progressive income taxes discouraged the enterprise of the able, inheritance taxes, falling on the property of the dead, afflicted only those who were incapable of further effort and stimulated the survivors to energy rather than sloth. These militant reformers agitated also for repeal of taxes that retarded the spread of books, periodicals, and newspapers, the very materials of enlightenment and education. Indeed, more consistently than most reformers, the English Philosophical Radicals perceived in economic freedom the opportunity for human freedom and individual gratification. The vigorous thrust of their policies was aimed at dismantling the government controls which lingered on from the dreary centuries of mercantilist meddling.

The twentieth-century economic reformer may favor all the objectives of his nineteenth-century predecessors, but he is prone to believe that a more active role for the state is essential to their realization. Like Galbraith, he may believe that state power should serve as a countervailing force against the excessive strength of giant corporations or mammoth unions. Again like Galbraith, he may be convinced that the amenities that make city life really civilized require state expenditure, state control, and state regulation. As seen by writers of this persuasion, our problems stem not from excessive economic intervention on the part of the state but from insufficient, poorly coordinated, and misguided intervention. Social balance demands a readjustment in the use of economic resources to the end that the state may allocate more of them and private citizens fewer of them. In the spirit of Keynes, the twentieth-century economic reformer tends to distrust the capacity of the private economy to generate an adequate volume of investment, employment, and national output. Hence he may feel inclined, according to individual taste, to recommend remedies so mild as lower interest rates or so drastic as socialized investment. Or, he may conclude that huge economic organizations have come to dominate our lives so completely that old assumptions about the competitive order and the automatic allocations of free markets require drastic re-evaluation. Property, competition, economic freedom itself, these all assume new meanings, and the new meanings entail substantial intervention by the community and its organs of government. Thus it is that economic liberalism is so transformed in meaning that an economist like Milton Friedman who is attached to its nineteenth-century connotations feels compelled in the interests of clarity to describe himself as a New Liberal.

The next division of these readings endeavors to illustrate the relation between economics and revolution. Anarchists, syndicalists, and the Veblenian school of institutional economics have shared a common wish to dismantle the apparatus of government and substitute more sensible guides than the profit motive for the guidance of production and distribution. In the case of Veblen, the cherished standard was serviceability, and the deep human yearning to be gratified was accorded the dignity of instinct—the instinct of workmanship. Implicit in Veblen's conception of a rational organization of production was deep distrust of the meretricious, deep offense at the predecessors of the Buicks and the Edsels which he did not live to see. His remedy, possibly worse than the malady it sought to cure, was to entrust the guidance of production to the engineers and the technicians, men who by habit of thought cherished workmanship, serviceability, and their embodiment in the machine process. In Veblen's judgment, capitalism—business enterprise—perverted all three. As for the capitalists themselves, here is a typical Veblenian comment:

> Many a business man turns by preference to something less dubious than the distilling of whiskey or the sale of deleterious household remedies. They prefer not to use deleterious adulterants, even within the limits of the law. They will rather use wool than shoddy at the same price. The officials of a railway commonly prefer to avoid wrecks and manslaughter, even if there is no pecuniary advantage in choosing the more humane course. More than that it will be found true that the more prosperous of the craft, especially, take pride and pains to make the service of their roads, or the output of their mills as efficient, not simply as the pecuniary advantage of the concern demands, but as the best pecuniary results will admit. Instances are perhaps not frequent, but they are not altogether exceptional, where a prosperous captain of industry will go out of his way to heighten the serviceability of his industry even to a degree that is of doubtful pecuniary expediency for himself. Such aberrations are, of course, not large; and if they are persisted in to any very appreciable extent the result is, of course, disastrous to the enterprise. The enterprise in such a case falls out of the cate-

gory of business management and falls under the imputation of philanthropy.*

As usual with Veblen, the sting was in the tail of the quotation. Perhaps it was a just reprisal on an old ironist that in the depression years of the 1930's, Howard Scott and his crackpot movement, Technocracy, conceived of themselves as disciples of Veblen.

In Veblen, the central opposition within capitalism was defined as conflict between groups whose work conditioned them to contrary conceptions of life: on the one hand serviceability and on the other profitability. "Class" was the consequence of vocation. Thus bank clerks and copywriters share the outlook upon work and reward of corporation directors and Wall Street lawyers. At the center of activity for all of them are paper-shuffling, adjudication of legal rights, promotion of meretricious merchandise, and acquisition of pecuniary profits. And, on the other side, a lavishly rewarded factory superintendent and a production-line worker have in common an attachment to the rationalities of the machine process and a preference for the biologically useful over the merely financially profitable.

Marx drew the class lines in a quite different fashion. The contradictions in capitalism upon which he focused were incompatibilities of attitude and thought only at one remove. At its simplest, shorn of the qualifications and amendments that Marx, Engels, and their disciples have profusely added, class and property ownership were congruent categories. In capitalistic societies, one class, the bourgeoisie, owned the means of production—tools, machines, and factories; and the other, the proletariat, owned nothing save a capacity to work, its own "labor power." "Primitive accumulation," the origin of capitalist property, employed all the techniques of force and fraud to wrest from the artisan the tools that had made him relatively independent, and from the farmer the land that had sheltered him from the full blast of emerging commodity markets. In this painful process, enclosures, troops and spies, child labor, rack rents, and usurious loans were devices helpful to the capitalist class.

The capitalist too will meet the fate that those who fill outmoded economic roles must. But in Marx that fate is the consequence of capitalist failure rather than of conflicting habits of thought. The capitalist drive to accumulate leads to the continuous expansion of factory capacity. The distribution of income within capitalism grants so little to the masses and so much to their capitalist masters that the

* Thorstein Veblen, *The Theory of Business Enterprise* (New York: Scribner, 1904), pp. 42-3.

market for this increasing output narrows rather than widens. As a result, capitalism encounters ever more menacing crises of unemployment, business bankruptcy, and descending rates of profit. As the assurance of capitalists begins to flag, the strength of the proletariat expands. For their own misery, joined to the training in co-operative effort that factory co-ordination imposes, leads workers to organize and ultimately to overthrow their oppressors. Marx permitted himself a rhetorical flight of joy over the prospect:

> Along with the constantly diminishing number of magnates of capital, who usurp and monopolise all advantages of this process of transformation, grows the mass of misery, oppression, slavery, degradation, exploitation; but with this too grows the revolt of the working-class, a class always increasing in number, and disciplined, united, organised by the very mechanism of the process of capitalist production itself. The monopoly of capital becomes a fetter upon the mode of production, which has sprung up and flourished along with it and under it. Centralisation of the means of production and socialisation of labour at last reach a point where they become incompatible with their capitalist integument. This integument is burst asunder. The knell of capitalist private property sounds. The expropriators are expropriated.*

The final selection in this group, Oskar Lange's description of how a free-market mechanism might operate even in a socialist economy, represents an ingenious, theoretically adept blend of Marxist commitment and neoclassical price theory. It illustrates the capacity of sophisticated Marxist economists to absorb the work of their "bourgeois" colleagues. Economists like Joan Robinson in England and Paul Sweezy in the United States have been equally successful in blending Keynesian analyses of income determination and Marxist theories of capitalist development into a subtle, if not entirely convincing, account of later-day capitalism.

The last set of selections, "The Techniques of Economics," is an attempt to trace the development of economic method. In much of what has already been said the assumption just beneath the surface implies that economics is affiliated with a single technique, the abstract analyses that have been seen to depend so heavily on a priori axioms, strong cases, simplifications of reality, and deductive logic. At a guess, most economists now living and a great many Anglo-Saxon economists of the preceding century value analysis more highly than other modes of handling material phenomena. Lord Robbins's influential definition of economics as the ". . . science which

---

* Karl Marx, *Capital,* 1906 (New York: Modern Library), I, 475-6.

studies human behavior as a relationship between ends and scarce means which have alternative uses," implies a conception of scientific subject matter, appropriate modes of investigation, and investigative neutrality which, at their best, characterize economic analysis.

The six passages under the heading "Theory" are themselves examples of economic analysis at its most elegant, as well as efforts to say something about how analysis developed in skill and clarified itself in conception. The contrast between David Ricardo, whom we have encountered earlier, and the towering marginalists—Jevons, Menger, and Walras—is instructive. It is the contrast between the instinctive analyst of genius, working with the clumsy tools of arithmetic and a pain-cost concept of value, and the trained minds of the economic revolutionaries of the 1870's. For many an economist "real" economics begins with the marginalist demonstration that economics was the logic of choice and that the important choosers were ordinary consumers. The economics administered to today's college sophomore owes most to this school. The notion that prices are determined at the margin of choice; the conception of consumers as animals who maximize utility, and producers as beasts who maximize profit; the marginal productivity explanation of wages, rent, and interest; and the grand overarching vision of market equilibrium in many markets and several analytical periods of time—these must all be credited to the marginalists of the last third of the nineteenth century. To them also belong the conventional mathematics of price: the diagram, the algebraic equation, the measures of elasticity, and the like.

Possibly because the technique of analysis sets off economics most clearly from other social disciplines, possibly because economists who write histories of doctrine usually are sympathetic to this definition of their subject, quantitative and historical approaches to economic reality frequently receive less attention than their contributions warrant. Such approaches are grouped here under the headings "Measurement" and "History." Statistical investigation of economic phenomena is quite old. The seventeenth-century worthy Sir William Petty founded political arithmetic (in which Adam Smith later declared his lack of faith) and affirmed his confidence in ringing words:

> The method I take is not yet very usual; for instead of using only comparative and superlative Words, and intellectual arguments, I have taken the course (as a specimen of the Political Arithmetick I have long aimed at) to express myself in terms of *Number, Weight,* or *Measure;* to use only Arguments of Sense, and to consider only such Causes, as have visible Foundations in Nature; leaving those that depend upon the mutable Mind, Opinion, Ap-

petite, and Passion of particular men, to the Consideration of Others: Really professing myself as unable to speak satisfactorily upon those grounds (if they may be call'd grounds) as to fortel the case of a Dye; to play well at Tennis, Billiards or Bowles (without long practice) by virtue of the most elaborate Conceptions that ever have been written De Projecilibus et Missilibus or of the angle of Incidence and Reflection.*

Petty's hopes proved larger than his possibilities. For statistical results depend upon materials much more recalcitrant than the interior reflections of the analyst. The state of statistics a century and more later than Petty was sufficiently confused that two political arithmeticians could violently disagree about whether the population of England had increased or decreased since the Glorious Revolution. If economic analysis was a triumph of the nineteenth century, then statistical investigation must be a twentieth-century achievement. It is fitting that the last selection under "Measurement" is a sober account of the methods of two of this century's most successful students of business cycles, W. C. Mitchell and Arthur F. Burns. Their monumental *Measuring Business Cycles,* from which this excerpt is drawn, is a scientific investigator's notebook.

And finally history has its claims and its right to issue the familiar warning that no set of economic phenomena are eternal. The antecedents and the consequences of today can be grasped only by the historical imagination. The rival claims of economic theory and economic history were vehement enough in late nineteenth-century Germany to spark a *Methodenstreit,* a Battle of Methods. One of the more futile conflicts in intellectual history, it subsided when the contestants exhausted themselves and allowed the realization to enter their minds that the methods were supplementary rather than substitutive. The eight selections that exemplify the genetic comprehension of economic affairs include Arnold Toynbee's investigation of the Industrial Revolution, a pioneer effort at historical identification of the phenomenon itself, by the great-uncle of the present Arnold Toynbee; a brief excerpt from the Webbs' magisterial *History of Trade Unionism*; two representatives of American institutionalism, Commons and Perlman; and the investigations of capitalism's origins made by Weber and Sombart. If proof were required, the last two demonstrate that certainty in economic affairs is as little likely to flow from history as from any other technique. Max Weber's seminal essay identified Calvinism as one of the roots of the special spirit of

* Sir William Petty, *Economic Writings* (Cambridge, 1899), I, lxv.

capitalism. It is a subtle account of the psychological mechanisms that translated theological precept into rational capitalist activity. But Sombart extracted the answers to the same historical puzzle from the special place and contribution of the Jew: his contractual theology, geographical dispersion, vocational specialization, and intellectual qualities.

The methods of economics need never exclude each other. Joseph Schumpeter described his two-volume study of *Business Cycles* as a "Theoretical, Historical, and Statistical Analysis of the Capitalist Process." The great economic theorist Alfred Marshall defined economics itself as a ". . . study of mankind in the ordinary business of life; it examines that part of individual and social action which is most closely connected with the attainment and with the use of the material requisites of well-being." * His own contributions to statistical and historical economics supported his generous view of the subject. Good analysts hope at the least that facts can be found to fill the empty boxes of their categories. And the best economic historians seek to illuminate rather than simply to describe the past.

Since this is not a history of economic ideas but a sample of the labors of those who deserve to appear in such histories, it is time to stop and permit the voices of the professionals and the amateurs, the scientists and the dreamers, the revolutionaries and the reformers, the scholars and the statesmen, to speak for themselves.

* Alfred Marshall, *Principles of Economics*, 8th ed. (London: Macmillan, 1920), p. 1.

Part I | ECONOMICS
AND
SALVATION

St. Thomas Aquinas

1225–1274

The "angelic doctor," Chesterton's "Dumb Ox" of God, occupied the same towering situation in medieval thought that Aristotle, whom he greatly admired, filled in the ancient world. Inevitably in the medieval world the universe of thought and the universe of theology tended to coincide. The unifying institution of the medieval world was the Catholic Church. Spiritually, it was the fount of solace in this world and eternal salvation in the next. Politically, it commanded the attention and, on occasion, the obedience, of kings and nobles. The Church joined to these spiritual and political assets formidable economic power as the owner of rich lands and the collector of huge taxes and tithes.

Man's path in life was a spiritual progress. No one aspect of his existence could properly or safely be separated from the remainder. Economic activity was far from an exception, for if anything a Christian encountered more danger to his soul in buying and selling, in the temptations of avarice, than in most other of life's occupations. To organize life around the quest for unlimited profit was as inconceivable to St. Thomas as the organization of life around the gratification of sexual passion. Nevertheless, even if life in this world were only a preparation for eternal life in the next one, men had to earn their livings. It was appropriate, therefore, to offer them the rules that would protect them from sin while they earned their livelihoods. A merchant could be a good Christian—if he were careful. Care implied above all that he regard each transaction not as an opportunity to make as much money as possible but as an effort to deal justly with the fellow Christian who was his customer. He did not conceal the defects of the item he sold, he did not take advantage of the buyer's necessities, and he did not seek to monopolize a neces-

47

sary commodity. Nor did he seek to enrich himself by lending money at interest. Money, as Aristotle had demonstrated, was barren. A rough guide to a merchant's equity was his ability to maintain himself in his appropriate position. If he grew rich, the prices he charged could not be just. If he grew poor, then his customers were themselves dealing unjustly with him.

St. Thomas dealt in great detail with the complicated questions to which generalizations of this kind led. Need the seller of a one-eyed horse point out the beast's defect? Was a man bound to restore his usurious gains? Could a borrower offer a gift in gratitude to a lender? St. Thomas's characteristic mode of analyzing such issues is exemplified in the selection that follows. He starts with a question, for example, Is it sinful to receive usury for money lent? Next he states the arguments for the affirmative. After them comes a single quotation that entirely negates these arguments. Then he states the position that he regards as consonant with good doctrine. He concludes with an argument-by-argument demolition of the false position.

The selection from St. Thomas's Summa Theologica *is drawn from Arthur Eli Monroe's* Early Economic Thought (*Cambridge, Mass.: Harvard University Press 1924*). *Reprinted by permission of the publisher.*

QUESTION LXXVIII Of the Sin of Usury, Which Is Committed in Loans

Divided into four articles

We next have to discuss the sin of usury, which is committed in loans; and under this head there are four points to be considered: 1. whether it is sinful to receive money as a price for money lent, that is, to receive usury; 2. whether it is lawful in the same case to receive any advantage, as a sort of compensation for the loan; 3. whether a man is bound to restore what he has made as a just profit on usurious gains; 4. whether it is lawful to borrow money upon usury.

FIRST ARTICLE. WHETHER IT IS SINFUL TO RECEIVE USURY FOR MONEY LENT

The first point is analyzed as follows:

1. It seems that it is not sinful to receive usury on money loans. For no one sins in following the example of Christ. But the Lord says of himself (Luke xix, 23): *At my coming I might have exacted it with*

usury, that is, the money lent. Hence it is not sinful to receive usury for a loan of money.

2. Furthermore, as it is written in Psalm xviii, 8, *The law of the Lord is unspotted*, that is, because it prohibits sin. But in the divine law some usury is allowed, according to the passage of Deuteronomy (xxiii, 19): *Thou shalt not lend money to thy brother upon usury, nor corn, nor any other thing, but to the stranger;* and what is more, it is promised as a reward for keeping the law, according to Deuteronomy (xxviii, 12): *Thou shalt lend to many nations, and shalt not borrow of any one.* Hence to receive usury is not sinful.

3. Furthermore, in human affairs justice is determined according to the civil laws. But according to these it is allowed to receive usury. Hence it seems to be lawful.

4. Furthermore, to neglect counsels does not bind to sin. But, among other counsels, is found (Luke, vi): *Lend, hoping for nothing thereby.* Hence it is not sinful to receive usury.

5. Furthermore, to receive a price for what one is not bound to do does not seem to be, in itself, sinful. But in no case is a man who has money bound to lend it to his neighbor. Hence it is lawful for him to receive a price for a loan in some cases.

6. Furthermore, silver made into money does not differ essentially from silver made into vessels. But it is lawful to receive a price for vessels of silver that are lent. Hence it is also lawful to receive a price for the loan of silver in the form of coins. Hence usury is not, in itself, sinful.

7. Furthermore, any man may lawfully receive a thing which the owner gives him voluntarily. But he who receives a loan pays usury voluntarily. Hence he who lends may lawfully receive it.

But opposed to this is the saying of Exodus xxii, 25: *If thou lend money to any of my people that is poor, that dwelleth with thee, thou shalt not be hard upon them as an extortioner, nor oppress them with usuries.*

I answer that to receive usury for money lent is, in itself, unjust, since it is a sale of what does not exist; whereby inequality obviously results, which is contrary to justice.

In proof of this, it should be noted that there are some things the use of which is the consumption of the things themselves; as we consume wine by using it to drink, and consume wheat by using it for food. Hence, in the case of such things, the use should not be reckoned apart from the thing itself; but when the use has been granted to a man, the thing is granted by this very fact; and therefore, in such cases, the act of lending involves a transfer of ownership (*dominium*). Therefore, if a man wished to sell wine and the use of the wine separately, he would be selling the same thing twice, or selling what does not exist; hence he would obviously be guilty of a sin of injustice. For analogous reasons, a man commits injustice who lends wine or wheat, expecting to receive two compensations, one as the restitution of an equivalent thing, the other as a price for the use, which is called *usury*.

There are some things, however, the use of which is not the consumption of the thing itself; thus the use of a house is living in it, not destroying it. Hence, in such cases, both may be granted separately, as in the case of a man who transfers the ownership of a house to another, reserving the use of it for himself for a time; or, conversely, when a man grants someone the use of a house, while retaining the ownership. Therefore a man may lawfully receive a price for the use of a house, and in addition expect to receive back the house lent, as happens in leasing and letting a house.

Now money, according to the Philosopher (*Ethics*, V, 5 and *Polit.*, I, 5, 6) was devised primarily for the purpose of effecting exchanges; and so the proper and principal use of money is the consumption or alienation (*distractio*) of it, whereby it is expended in making purchases. Therefore, in itself, it is unlawful to receive a price for the use of money lent, which is called *usury;* and just as a man is bound to restore other things unjustly acquired, so he is bound to restore money received through usury.

In reply to the first argument above, it is to be said that usury is there used in a figurative sense, to indicate the increase of spiritual goods which God requires of us, wishing us always to increase in the goods received from Him; which is for our advantage, not His.

In reply to the second argument, it is to be said the Jews were forbidden to receive usury from their brothers, that is, from Jews; by which we are given to understand that to receive usury from any man is strictly evil: for we ought to regard every man as a neighbor and brother, especially in the state of the Gospel, to which all are called. Hence it is written in so many words (Psalm xiv, 5): *He that hath not put out his money to usury;* and Ezechiel xvii, 8: *He who hath not taken usury.* The permission to receive usury from strangers was not accorded them as something lawful, but as something allowed with a view to avoiding a greater evil, that is, lest through avarice, to which they were addicted (Isaias lvi), they should take usury from the Jews who worshipped God. In the promise of it as a reward: *Thou shalt lend to many nations,* etc., the word (*feneraberis*) is to be taken in the broad sense of lending (*mutuum*), as in Ecclesiasticus xxix: *Many have not lent (fenerati), not out of wickedness,* that is, they have not lent in the broader sense (*mutuaverunt*). Therefore the Jews are promised an abundance of riches as a reward, whereby they may be able to lend to others.

In reply to the third argument, it is to be said that human laws leave some sins unpunished, on account of the conditions among imperfect men, who would be deprived of many advantages, if all sins were strictly forbidden and penalties provided. Hence human law had allowed usury, not in the sense of considering it to be according to justice, but in order not to prevent the advantage of many. Hence in the civil law itself (Constit., lib. II, tit. 4, *de Usufructu*) it is written that *things which are consumed in use do not receive a usufruct, either according to natural reason or civil law, and that the senate did not create a usufruct in their case (for it could not), but a quasi usufruct,* that is, allowing usury. And the Philosopher, led by natural reason, says (*Polit., I, 7*) *that the acquisition of money by means of usury is especially contrary to nature.*

In reply to the fourth argument, it is to be said that a man is not always bound to lend; hence, to this extent, it is placed among the counsels. But that a man should not seek gain from lending is a matter of precept. It may, however, be called a counsel in comparison with the sayings of the Pharisees, who considered some usury lawful; just as loving our enemies is a counsel. Or he speaks in this passage, not about the hope of usurious gain, but about the hope that is placed in man; for we ought not to lend or do any other good deed on account of hope in man, but on account of hope in God.

In reply to the fifth argument, it is to be said that he who is not bound to lend may receive compensation for what he has done; but he ought not to exact more. He is recompensed, however, according to the equality required by justice, if as much is returned to him as he lent. Hence if he exacts more for the use of a thing which has no use except the consumption of the substance, he exacts a price for what does not exist; and so it is an unjust exaction.

In reply to the sixth argument, it is to be said that the principal use of silver vessels is not the consumption of them; hence the use of them can be sold, though the ownership of the thing be retained. The principal use of coined silver, however, is the alienation (*distractio*) of the money in making purchases; hence it is not lawful to sell the use of it, while desiring the restitution of what was lent. It is to be noted, however, that a secondary use of silver vessels may be exchange; and it is not lawful to sell this use of them. And, similarly, there may be a secondary use of coined silver, as in the case of lending coined money for the purpose of display or for deposit as a pledge; and a man may lawfully sell this use of money.

In reply to the seventh argument, it is to be said that he who pays usury does not really do it voluntarily, but under some compulsion, for he needs to obtain the loan, and the one who has the money will not lend it without usury.

ARTICLE II. WHETHER IT IS LAWFUL TO ASK ANY OTHER CONSIDERATION FOR MONEY LENT

The second point is analyzed as follows:

1. It seems that a man may ask some other consideration for money lent. For every man may lawfully provide against his own loss. But sometimes a man suffers loss through lending money. Hence it is lawful for him to ask or exact something over and above the money lent, to make up for his loss.

2. Furthermore, every man is bound by a kind of requirement of honor to make some recompense to one who has done him a favor; as is stated in *Ethics*, V, 5. But he who lends money to a man in need, does him a favor, for which some expression of gratitude is due. Hence he who receives is bound by natural duty to make some recompense. But it does not seem to be unlawful for a man to bind himself to something to which he is bound by natural law. Hence it does not seem to be unlawful for a man, in lending money to another, to contract for some compensation.

3. Furthermore, just as there are gifts *by the hand*, so also there are gifts *by the tongue* and *by service*, as a gloss says on Isaias xxxiii, 15: *Blessed is he that shaketh his hands from all bribes.* But it is lawful to receive service or even praise from one to whom money has been lent. Hence for analogous reasons it is lawful to receive some other gift.

4. Furthermore, there seems to be the same relation between gift and gift as between loan and loan. But it is lawful to receive money for other money given. Hence it is lawful to receive compensation in the form of another loan for money lent.

5. Furthermore, a man who transfers the ownership of money to another in a loan alienates it more than a man who entrusts it to a merchant or craftsman. But it is lawful to receive gain for money entrusted to a merchant or craftsman. Hence it is also lawful to receive gain from money lent.

6. Furthermore, a man may receive a pledge for money lent, the use of which may be sold for some price; as when the pledge is a field

or a house which is inhabited. Hence it is lawful to make some gain from money lent.

7. Furthermore, it sometimes happens that a man sells his goods dearer in a sort of loan, or buys the property of another cheaper, or even increases the price in proportion to the delay in payment, or lowers it in proportion to the promptness; in all of which cases some compensation seems to be given as if for a loan of money. This, however, does not seem to be obviously unlawful. Hence it seems to be lawful to ask or exact some consideration for money lent.

Opposed to this is the mention (Ezechiel xviii, 17) among other things required in a just man: *If he hath not taken usury and increase;* as also verse 8: *If he hath not taken any increase.*

I answer that, according to the Philosopher (*Ethics,* IV, 1), everything is considered money of which the price can be measured by money. Hence, just as a man who, by a tacit or explicit agreement, receives money for the loan of money or anything else which is consumed by use, sins against justice, as explained in the preceding article, so also anyone who, by tacit or explicit agreement, receives anything else, the price of which can be measured by money, is likewise guilty of sin. If, however, he receives something of this kind, not asking it and not according to any tacit or explicit obligation, but as a free gift, he does not sin; because even before he lent the money, he might lawfully receive a free gift, and he is not put at a disadvantage by the act of lending. Compensation in the form of things which are not measured by money may, however, be exacted lawfully, such as good will and love for the lender, or something similar.

In reply to the first argument, it is to be said that a lender may without sin contract with the borrower for compensation to cover the loss arising from the fact that he gives up something which belongs to him; for this is not selling the use of money, but avoiding loss; and it may be that the borrower avoids greater loss than the lender incurs; so that the borrower makes good the other's loss with advantage to himself. Compensation for loss, however, cannot be stipulated on the ground that the lender makes no profit on his money, because he should not sell what he does not yet possess, and which he may be prevented in various ways from getting.

In reply to the second argument, it is to be said that compensation for a favor may be made in two ways; first, as a requirement of justice, to which a man may be bound by definite agreement; and this obligation depends upon the amount of benefit received. Hence a man who receives a loan of money, or of something similar, the use of which is its consumption, is not bound to pay back more than he received in the loan: so that it is contrary to justice, if he is bound to return more. Secondly, a man is bound to make compensation for a favor as a requirement of friendship; in which more consideration is given to the spirit in which the benefit was conferred than to the extent of it; and to such a debt no civil obligation attaches, whereby a certain element of compulsion is introduced, making the compensation no longer spontaneous.

In reply to the third argument, it is to be said that if a man, by a sort of obligation tacitly or explicitly agreed to, expects or exacts compensation in the form of *service* or of *words*, it is just as if he exacted a gift *from the hand;* because both can be valued in money, as we see in the case of those who offer for hire the work they do with their hands or tongues. If, however, a gift *of service* or *of language* is not given as an obligation, but out of good will, which is not subject to valuation in money, it is lawful to receive, and exact, and expect this.

In reply to the fourth argument, it is to be said that money cannot be sold for more money than the amount lent, which is to be repaid. Nor is anything to be exacted or expected except a feeling of good will, which is not subject to valuation in money; from which a spontaneous loan may arise. The obligation to make a loan later is inconsistent with this, however, because such an obligation can also be valued in money. Hence, it is lawful for a lender to receive another loan in return, at the same time, but it is not lawful to bind the borrower to make a loan later.

In reply to the fifth argument, it is to be said that a lender of money transfers the ownership of the money to the borrower; so that the borrower holds it at his own risk, and is bound to restore it intact: hence the lender should not exact more. But he who entrusts his money to a merchant or craftsman, by means of some kind of partnership, does not transfer the ownership of his money to the latter, but it remains his; so that the merchant trades with it or the craftsman uses it at the owner's risk; hence he may lawfully claim a part of the gain arising therefrom, as being from his own property.

In reply to the sixth argument, it is to be said that if a man, in return for money lent to him, pledges something, the use of which can be valued at a price, the lender ought to count the use of this thing as part of the repayment of the loan; otherwise, if he wishes to have the use of that thing granted him without charge, it is just as if he received money for a loan, which is usury; unless the thing happened to be such as are usually lent without charge among friends, as in the case of a book.

In reply to the seventh argument, it is to be said that if a man wishes to sell his goods for more than their just price, expecting the buyer to pay later, it is plainly a case of usury, because such waiting for payment has the character of a loan. Hence whatever is exacted for such waiting, in excess of the just price, is a kind of price for a loan, which comes under the head of usury. And likewise, if a buyer wishes to buy for less than the just price, on the ground that he pays the money before the thing can be delivered to him, it is a sin of usury, because that paying of money in advance has the character of a loan, the price of which is the amount deducted from the just price of the thing bought. If, however, a man wishes to deduct from the just price, in order to obtain the money sooner, he is not guilty of a sin of usury.

ARTICLE III. WHETHER A MAN IS BOUND TO RESTORE ANYTHING HE MAY HAVE MADE OUT OF USURIOUS GAINS

The third point is analyzed as follows:

1. It seems that a man is bound to restore anything he may have made out of usurious gains. For the Apostle says (Romans xi, 16): *If the root be holy, so are the branches.* Hence by the same reasoning *if the root be tainted, so are the branches.* But the root was usurious. Hence whatever was acquired thereby is usurious. Hence he is bound to make restitution of it.

2. Furthermore, as stated in the Decretal *Cum tu, sicut asseris* (*extrav. de Usuris*): *property acquired by means of usury should be sold, and the price thereof restored to those from whom it was extorted.* Hence by the same reasoning anything else acquired from usurious gains should be restored.

3. Furthermore, what a man buys with usurious gains belongs to him by reason of the money which he paid for it. Hence he has no greater right to the thing acquired than to the money he paid. But he was bound to restore usurious gains. Hence he is also bound to restore what he acquired therewith.

Opposed to this is the principle that a man may lawfully keep what he has legitimately acquired. But what is acquired with usurious gains is sometimes legitimately acquired: hence it may lawfully be retained.

I answer that, as stated above in the first article of this question, there are some things of which the use is the consumption of the things themselves, and which have no usufruct, according to the civil law (Instit. II, tit. 4, *de Usufructu*). Hence, if such things were extorted by usury (for example, money, wheat, wine, or something similar), a man is not bound to make restitution beyond what he has received: because what is acquired by this means is not the fruit of such a thing but of human industry; unless perchance the other man suffer a loss through the withholding of such a good, losing a part of his property; for then he is bound to make compensation for the injury.

There are some things, however, of which the use is not their consumption; and such things have a usufruct; such as a house or a field or something of the kind. Hence, if a man has extorted the house or the field of another by usury, he is bound to restore not only the house or field but also the fruits obtained therefrom, because they are the fruits of things of which another is the owner; and hence they belong to him.

In reply to the first argument, it is to be said that the root not only has the character of material, as in the case of usurious gains, but also has in some degree the character of an active cause, since it furnishes nourishment; hence it is not the same thing.

In reply to the second argument, it is to be said that property acquired by means of usury does not belong to the same persons as the usury, but to those who bought it; those from whom the usury was taken have some claims on it, however, as on the other property of the usurer. Hence it is not prescribed that such property be assigned to those from whom the usury was taken, because it may be worth more than the usury paid; but it is prescribed that the property be sold, and the price restored, that is, up to the amount of the usury received.

In reply to the third argument, it is to be said that what is acquired with usurious gains belongs to the purchaser, not on account of the usurious gains he paid for them, as instrumental cause, but on account of his industry, as principal cause; hence he has more right to a thing acquired with usurious gains than to the usurious gains themselves.

ARTICLE IV. WHETHER IT IS LAWFUL TO BORROW MONEY UPON USURY

The fourth point is analyzed as follows:

1. It seems that it is not lawful to borrow money upon usury. For

the Apostle says (Romans i, 32) that *they are worthy of death, not only they that do these sins, but also they that consent to them that do them.* But he who borrows money upon usury consents to the usurer in his sin, and gives him an occasion for sin. Hence he also sins.

2. Furthermore, for no temporal advantage should one give another any occasion for sin; for this is in the nature of active scandal, which is always sinful, as stated above (quaest. 45, art. 2). But he who seeks a loan from a usurer directly gives him an occasion for sin. Hence he is not excused by reason of any temporal advantage.

3. Furthermore, it seems to be no less necessary to deposit one's money sometimes with a usurer than to borrow from him. But depositing one's money with a usurer seems to be entirely unlawful, just as it would be unlawful to put a sword in the keeping of a madman, a maiden in the keeping of a libertine, or food in the keeping of a glutton. Hence it is not lawful to borrow from a usurer.

Opposed to this is the argument that a man who suffers an injury does not sin, according to the Philosopher (*Ethics*, V, 11); hence justice is not a mean between two vices, as stated in the same place (cap. 5). But the usurer sins, in doing injustice to the one who borrows upon usury. Hence the borrower upon usury does not sin.

I answer that it is in no way lawful to induce a man to commit sin; but it is lawful to use the sin of another for a good end; because even God uses all sins for some good end; for He draws some good out of every evil, as is stated in the *Enchiridion* (August. xi). Hence when Publicola asked whether it was lawful to use the oath of a man swearing by false gods, in which he plainly sins, by paying them divine homage, Augustine answered (Epist. xlvii) that *he who uses the oath of one who swears by false gods, not for evil but for good, does not become a party to his sin in swearing by evil spirits, but to his good faith whereby he kept his word. If, however, he induced him to swear by false gods, he would sin.* So, in the present question, it is also to be said that it is in no way lawful to induce a man to lend upon usury; one may, however, borrow upon usury from a man who is ready to do it and practises usury, provided it be for some good purpose, such as helping oneself or somebody else out of difficulty; just as it is also lawful for one who falls among robbers to point out what goods he has, in order to save his life, though the robbers commit sin in plundering him, like the ten men who said to Ishmael (Jeremiah xli, 8): *Kill us not, for we have stores in the field.*

In reply to the first argument, it is to be said that he who borrows money upon usury does not consent to the sin of the usurer, but uses it; nor does the taking of usury please him, but the loan, which is good.

In reply to the second argument, it is to be said that he who borrows money upon usury does not give the usurer occasion for taking usury, but for making a loan. The usurer, himself, however, takes the occasion for sin from the malice of his heart. Hence, it is a passive scandal on his part, not an active one on the part of the borrower. Nor should the other, on account of such passive scandal, refrain from seeking a loan, if he is in need; because such passive scandal does not arise from infirmity or ignorance, but from malice.

In reply to the third argument, it is to be said that if a man deposited his money with a usurer who had no other with which to practise usury, or with the intention of making greater gains by way of usury, he would provide the material for sin; and so he himself would share the blame; but if a man deposits his money for safe-keeping with a usurer who has other money with which to practise usury, he does not commit a sin, but uses a sinful man for a good end.

Nicholas Oresme
1320–1381

Nicholas Oresme, bishop of Lisieux, was one of the chaplains of Charles V and the translator, at his monarch's request, of Aristotle's Politics and his Ethics. Indeed, his view of the meaning of metallic money is Aristotelian in its confidence that a coin is a fixed weight in precious metal, which is guaranteed by the issuing authority. If this is so, then a prince cannot possess the right to alter the weight or the fineness of the coinage.

Oresme's vehemence against princes who behave unjustly by altering the coinage is in its way evidence of the temptations that princes faced and to which they apparently succumbed. While Oresme is as vehement as St. Thomas in his condemnation of usury, even to the extent of calling usury an occupation that "stains the soul," the focus of his concern is less with the individual act of usury by a money-lender than it is with the collective injustice committed by the prince who cheats all of his subjects by debasing the currency they use. In a typical passage, Oresme observes that ". . . there are three ways in which profit may be made from money, without laying it out for its natural purpose; one is the art of the money-changer . . . another is usury, a third alteration of the coinage." And Oresme leaves no doubt about which is most deplorable: "The first way is contemptible, the second bad and the third worse." The slowly increasing use of money, the growing needs of rulers, and the ease of debasement combined to create a problem of ethics for Oresme which did not face St. Thomas a century earlier.

The selection is taken from The De Moneta, translated by Charles Johnson (New York: Thomas Nelson, 1956), pp. 24-8. Reprinted by permission of Thomas Nelson and Sons Ltd., Edinburgh.

CHAPTER XV   That the Profit Accruing to the
Prince from Alteration of the Coinage Is Unjust

I am of opinion that the main and final cause why the prince pretends
to the power of altering the coinage is the profit or gain which he can
get from it; it would otherwise be vain to make so many and so great
changes. I propose therefore to give fuller proof that such gain is unjust. For every change of money, except in the very rare cases which
I have mentioned, involves forgery and deceit, and cannot be the
right of the prince, as has previously been shown. Therefore, from
the moment when the prince unjustly usurps this essentially unjust
privilege, it is impossible that he can justly take profit from it. Besides, the amount of the prince's profit is necessarily that of the community's loss. But whatever loss the prince inflicts on the community
is injustice and the act of a tyrant and not of a king, as Aristotle* says.
And if he should tell the tyrant's usual lie, that he applies that profit
to the public advantage, he must not be believed, because he
might as well take my coat and say he needed it for the public service. And Saint Paul says that we are not to do evil that good may
come.† Nothing therefore should be extorted on the pretence that it
will be used for good purposes afterwards. Again, if the prince
has the right to make a simple alteration in the coinage and draw
some profit from it, he must also have the right to make a greater
alteration and draw more profit, and to do this more than once and
make still more, and also to make one or more compound alterations,
constantly making more profit in the ways already described. And it
is probable that he or his successors would go on doing this either of
their own motion or by the advice of their council as soon as this was
permitted, because human nature is inclined and prone to heap up
riches when it can do so with ease. And so the prince would be at
length able to draw to himself almost all the money or riches of his
subjects and reduce them to slavery. And this would be tyrannical,
indeed true and absolute tyranny, as it is represented by philosophers
and in ancient history.

CHAPTER XIV   That Such Profit Is Unnatural

Although all injustice is in a way contrary to nature, yet to make a
profit from altering the coinage is specifically an unnatural act of in-

* Pol. V. x. 10 (1310b40); cf. Eth. ix (1160b2).
† Romans iii. 8.

justice. For it is natural for certain natural riches to multiply, like grains of corn, 'which,' as Ovid says, 'when sown, the field with ample interest repays.' * But it is monstrous and unnatural that an unfruitful thing should bear, that a thing specifically sterile, such as money, should bear fruit and multiply of itself. Therefore when profit is made from money, not by laying it out in the purchase of natural wealth, its proper and natural use, but by changing it into itself, as changing one form of it for another, or giving one form for another, such profit is vile and unnatural. It is by this reasoning that Aristotle proves, in the first book of the Politics,† that usury is against nature, because the natural use of money is as an instrument for the exchange of natural wealth, as has frequently been said. Anyone therefore who uses it otherwise, misuses it against the natural institution of money, for he causes money to beget money, which, as Aristotle says, is against nature. And, besides, in these changes by which profit accrues it is necessary to call something which in truth is not a penny, a penny, and which is not a pound, a pound, as has already been said in another connexion. But it is clear that this is no less than to disturb the order of nature and of reason, of which Cassiodorus says:‡

> Pay your shilling, and keep something back if you are strong enough; deliver a pound, and make it less if you can. In all such cases, as the names themselves show, you pay in full, or you are not giving what you say you give. You cannot by any means use the names of whole units and yet make fraudulent deductions. Is not such a violation of nature's secrets, such an attempt to obscure the greatest certainties, plainly a cruel and disgraceful wound to truth itself? Weight and measure are the first things to prove, for all is chaos where there is deceit in the unit of measurement.

Again, it is said in the book of Wisdom § that God ordered all things by measure, weight and number; but in changing of money there is no profit unless fraud is committed in these most certain things, as I have declared before. Therefore he who seeks to profit from such changes of money sins against God and against nature.

CHAPTER XVII That Profit from the Change of Money Is Worse Than Usury

It seems to me that there are three ways in which profit may be made from money, without laying it out for its natural purpose; one is the

* Epp. ex Ponto I. v. 26.
† Pol. I. x. 5 (1258*b*7).
‡ Variae I. 10. 7 and 6.
§ Wisdom xi. 21.

art of the money-changer, banking or exchange, another is usury, a third alteration of the coinage. The first way is contemptible, the second bad and the third worse. Aristotle mentioned the first two,* but not the third, because in his times such wickedness had not yet been invented. That the first is contemptible and disreputable, Aristotle proves by the reasons given in the last chapter, for this is as it were to make money beget money. He also calls exchange 'obolostatic,' what we commonly call *Poitevinage*. It was for that reason that Saint Matthew, the apostle who had been a money-changer, did not return to his former calling after our Lord's resurrection, as Saint Peter, who had been a fisherman, did. And in giving this reason, the Blessed Gregory says:† 'It is one thing to earn a living by fishing, and another to amass money from the profits of receipt of custom. For there are many trades which can scarcely if ever be practised without sin, etc.' For there are certain vulgar crafts which defile the body, such as cleaning the sewers,‡ and others which, like this, defile the soul. As to usury, it is certainly bad, detestable and unjust, and Holy Scripture says so. But it remains to show that gaining money by altering the coinage is even worse than usury. The usurer has lent his money to one who takes it of his own free will, and can then enjoy the use of it and relieve his own necessity with it, and what he repays in excess of the principal is determined by free contract between the parties. But a prince, by unnecessary change in the coinage, plainly takes the money of his subjects against their will, because he forbids the older money to pass current, though it is better, and anyone would prefer it to the bad; and then unnecessarily and without any possible advantage to his subjects, he will give them back worse money. And even if he makes better money than before, it is only with a view to a future debasement, and that he may give them (meanwhile) less of the good money than the corresponding value of the old. In either case he keeps back part for himself. In so far then as he receives more money than he gives, against and beyond the natural use of money, such gain is equivalent to usury; but is worse than usury because it is less voluntary and more against the will of his subjects, incapable of profiting them, and utterly unnecessary. And since the usurer's interest is not so excessive, or so generally injurious to the many, as this impost, levied tyrannically and fraudulently, against the interest and against the will of the whole community, I doubt whether it should not rather be termed robbery with violence or fraudulent extortion.

* Pol. I. x. 4-5 (1258b1-8).
† Homiliae in Evangelia xxiv (col. 1184c).
‡ The French adds 'chimneys.'

Martin Luther

1483–1546

A theological revolutionary, Martin Luther was an economic conservative. On prices and interest, his position is scarcely to be distinguished from that of the Catholic canonist writers. In the passage that follows, Luther deals first with the question of just price and then with the issue of usury. While there is a recognition of the technical difficulties that impede the promulgation of fair prices and a complaint against the Germans for their aversion to regulation, he nevertheless applies a familiar Thomist criterion: ". . . when the price of goods is not fixed either by law or custom, and you must fix it yourself, then indeed no one can give you any other instruction except to lay it upon your conscience to be careful and not overcharge your neighbor, and seek not avaricious gain, but only an honest living." The just merchant lives in the style of other merchants, he does not seek to aggrandize himself.

Luther's treatment of usury plainly assumes a consumption economy rather than a mercantile community. His illustrations echo a countryside in which moneylenders lend on onerous terms actual commodities like wine and grain, or money itself, to their needy neighbors. Of the depravity of the practice, Luther has no doubt. The Gospel forbids it. Natural law forbids it. Finally, it is against Old Law and New Law ". . . which commands, 'Thou shalt love thy neighbor as thyself.'" Luther's condemnation is actually a good deal more sweeping than the more qualified statements of the later Catholic canonists.

The selection is drawn from Luther's essay "On Trading and Usury" in Volume IV of Works of Martin Luther (*Philadelphia: Muhlenberg Press, 1931*), pp. 15-16, 53-5. Reprinted by permission of the publisher.

On Trading and Usury

You ask, then, How dear may I sell? How am I to get at what is fair and right so as not to overreach or overcharge my neighbor? I answer: That is indeed a thing that will never be governed either by writing or speaking, nor has anyone ever undertaken to fix the price of every sort of wares. The reason is that wares are not all alike: one sort comes from a greater distance than another, one sort costs more than another. On this point, therefore, everything is, and must remain, uncertain and no fixed rule can be made, any more than one can set a certain city as the place from which all wares are to be brought or establish a definite cost price for them, since it may happen that the same wares, brought from the same city by the same road, cost vastly more one year than another, because, perhaps, the weather is bad or the road is worse, or something else happens that raises the cost at one time above that at another time. Now it is fair and right that a merchant take as much profit on his wares as will pay the cost of them and repay him for his trouble, his labor, and his risk. Even a farmhand must have food and hire for his labor; who can serve or labor for nothing? The Gospel says, "The laborer is worthy of his hire."

But in order not to leave this question entirely unanswered, the best and safest way would be for the temporal authorities to appoint over this matter wise and honest men who would appraise the cost of all sorts of wares and fix accordingly the outside price at which the merchant would get his due and have an honest living, just as at certain places they fix the price of wine, fish, bread, and the like. But we Germans are so busy with drinking and dancing that we cannot tolerate any such regulation. Since, then, we cannot hope for such a law, the next best thing is to hold our wares at the price which they bring in the common market or which is customary in the neighborhood. In this matter we can accept the proverb: "Do like others and you are no fool." Any profit made in this way, I consider honest and well earned, since there is risk of loss in wares and outlay, and the profits cannot be all too great.

But when the price of goods is not fixed either by law or custom, and you must fix it yourself, then indeed no one can give you any other instructions except to lay it upon your conscience to be careful and not overcharge your neighbor, and seek not avaricious gain, but only an honest living. Some have wished to make it a rule that a man may take a profit of one-half on all wares; some say one-third; others say something else; but none of these things is a safe rule unless it be so decreed, either by the temporal authorities or by common law; what they would determine would be safe. Therefore you must make up your minds to seek in your trading only your honest living, count your costs, trouble, labor and risk on that basis, and then fix, raise, or lower the price of your goods, so that you are repaid for your trouble and labor.

Twentieth. It follows that they are all usurers who lend their neighbor wine, grain, money, or the like, in such a way that he obligates himself to pay charges on it in a year or at a given time; or that he burdens and overloads himself with a promise to give back more than he has borrowed, or something else that is better. And in order that these men may themselves perceive the wrong that they are doing—though the practice has, unfortunately, become common—we set before them three laws. First, This passage in the Gospel commands that we shall lend. Now lending is not lending unless it be done without charge and without advantage to the lender, as has been said. Crafty avarice, to be sure, sometimes paints itself a pretty color and pretends to take the surplus as a present, but that does not help if the present is the cause of the loan; or if the borrower would rather not make the present, provided he could borrow gratis. And the present is especially suspicious, if the borrower makes it to the lender, or the needy to the wealthy; for it is not natural to suppose that the needy would make a present to the wealthy of his own free will; it is necessity that forces him to do so. Second, This is contrary to the natural law,* which the Lord also announces in Luke vi and Matthew vi, "What ye would that men should do to you, that do also to them." Now, beyond all doubt, there is no one who would that men should lend him rye to be repaid with wheat, bad money to be repaid with good, bad wares to be repaid with good wares; indeed, he would much rather that men should lend him good wares to be repaid with bad, or with equally good wares, but without charge. Therefore it is clear that these usurers are acting against nature, are guilty of mortal sin, and seek their neighbor's injury and their own profit, because they would not put up with such treatment from others, and are thus dealing unfairly with their neighbor. Third, It is also against the Old and the New Law, which commands, "Thou shalt love thy neighbor as thyself." But such lenders love themselves alone, seek only their own, or do not love and seek their neighbor with such fidelity as they love and seek themselves.

Twenty-first. Therefore no better or briefer instruction can be

* i.e., Charging for loans.

given about this, and about all dealing with temporal goods, than that everyone who is to have dealings with his neighbor set before him these commandments, "Whatsoever thou wilt that another do to thee, that do thou to him also," and "Thou shalt love thy neighbor as thyself." If, beside this, he were to think what he would have for himself, if he were in his neighbor's place, he would learn for himself and find for himself all that he needs to know. There would be no need for law books or courts or accusation; nay, all the cases would be quickly and simply decided. For everyone's heart and conscience would tell him how he would like to be dealt with, what he would like to have remitted, what given and what forgiven, and from this he must conclude that he ought to do just that for everyone else. But because we leave these commandments out of view, and look only at the business, and its profit or loss, we must have all the countless books, courts, judges, law suits, blood, and all misery, and thus, upon the violation of God's commandments, must follow the destruction of God's kingdom, which is peace and unity, in brotherly love and faithfulness. And yet these wicked men go about, begging at times and fasting, giving alms at times, but in this matter, on which salvation depends, they are quite heedless and carefree, as if this commandment did not concern them at all, though without it they cannot be saved, even if they did all the other works of all the saints.

Twenty-second. Here we meet two objections. The first is that if lending were done in this way, the interest would be lost, that is, the profit which they could make meanwhile with the goods that were lent. The second is the great example. Everywhere in the world it has become the custom to lend for profit, and especially because scholars, priests, clergy, and churches do it, seeing that the improvement of the church's spiritual goods and of the worship of God is sought, and without these there would be very few Christians in the world, and everyone would be reluctant to lend.

Answer. There is nothing in all of that. In the first place, you must lose the interest and the profit if it be taken from you or if you give to someone outright; why, then, will you seek it and keep it in lending? He who decides to give and lend must give up the interest in advance, or it is neither giving nor lending. In the second place, whether it is a good custom or a bad custom, it is not Christian or divine or natural, and no example helps against that fact. For it is written, "Thou shalt not follow the crowd to do evil, but honor God and His commandments above all things." That the clergy and the churches do this is so much the worse. For spiritual goods and churches have neither authority nor freedom to break God's commandments, rob their neighbor, practice usury, and do wrong. Moreover, the service of God is not improved by it, but corrupted. Keeping God's commandments is improving the service of God; even knaves can improve the church property; and even if the whole world had the custom of lending with this kind of a charge, the churches and the clergy should act the other way, and the more spiritual their possessions were, the more Christian should be the manner in which, according to Christ's command, they would lend them, give them, and let them go. He who does otherwise, is doing so, not for the improvement of the churches or of their spiritual goods, but for his own usury-seeking avarice, which decks itself out with such good names. It is no wonder, then, that Christians are few; for here we see who they are that practice really good works, though many blind and deceive themselves with their own self-chosen good works, which God has not commanded them. But if anyone finds that this makes it hard for him to lend to his neighbor, it is a sign of his great unbelief, because he despises the comforting assurance of Christ, who says, "If we lend and give, we are children of the Highest, and our reward is great." He who does not believe this comforting promise and does not make it a guide for his works, is not worthy of it.

John Calvin

1509–1564

Calvin's Institutes of the Christian Religion, *published at Basel, Switzerland in 1536, represented a stage in the institutionalization of the Protestant Reformation. Only five years later the troubled citizens of Geneva gave Calvin the opportunity to turn their city into "the most perfect school of Christ that ever was on earth since the days of the apostles," as John Knox put it. Calvin did his best to rule his domain in the interests of life eternal rather than of life transitory on this sphere. There could be ". . . no medium between these two extremes, either the earth must become vile in our estimation, or it must retain our immoderate love. Wherefore if we have any concern about eternity, we must use our most diligent efforts to extricate ourselves from these fetters." Calvinism was oppressed with notions of God's omnipotent will and His uncertain disposition which predestined some indeed for salvation but many others for eternal damnation.*

In contrast to Lutheranism, Calvinism refused to accept the supremacy of the civil power. And again in opposition to his great predecessor, Calvin was unwilling to condemn the taking of money as interest as itself sinful. He explicitly denied the Aristotelian doctrine of the barrenness of money. In the course of expounding the rights and the wrongs of interest, Calvin makes the key distinction between lending for productive purposes, which is not sinful, and lending to the needy for their immediate consumption, which is sinful. At least until the modern days of consumer credit, capitalism has rested upon the first kind of borrowing rather than the second.

But if Calvin was not willing to exclude even financial activity from the sphere of Christian conduct, neither was he prepared to endorse outright avarice. In the passage that follows, his characteristic atti-

tude appears. The key notions are vocation and stewardship. The man whose circumstances are humble and whose fortune is small may nevertheless serve the Lord in the vocation to which the Lord has called him. For such a man, ". . . it will be no small alleviation of his cares, labours, troubles, and other burdens . . . that in all these things he has God for his guide." Equally, the magistrate need not feel uneasy in his prosperity and influence, for the Lord has also called him to his position. Moreover, the rich man has no warrant to spend his wealth upon his own selfish gratification. The wealth is granted him in trust and he is to regard himself as its steward: ". . . while all these things are given to us by the Divine goodness, and appointed for our benefit, they are, as it were, deposits intrusted to our care, of which we must one day give an account."

It is no wonder that Max Weber in The Protestant Ethic and the Rise of Capitalism *was able to identify powerful psychological mechanisms in Calvinism, which promoted rational acquisition, personal thrift, and capital accumulation.*

This selection is from A Compend of the Christian Religion *by John Calvin, edited by Hugh Thompson Kerr, pp. 106-7. Copyright, 1939, by the Board of Christian Education, Presbyterian Church U.S.A. Used by permission.*

(4) Rules for Christian Living

It must be laid down as a principle, that the use of the gifts of God is not erroneous, when it is directed to the same end for which the Creator himself has created and appointed them for us; since he has created them for our benefit, not for our injury. . . . But shall the Lord have endued flowers with such beauty, to present itself to our eyes, with such sweetness of smell, to impress our sense of smelling; and shall it be unlawful for our eyes to be affected with the beautiful sight, or our olfactory nerves with the agreeable odour? What! has he not made such a distinction of colours as to render some more agreeable than others? Has he not given to gold and silver, to ivory and marble, a beauty which makes them more precious than other metals or stones? In a word, has he not made many things worthy of our estimation, independently of any necessary use? Let us discard, therefore, that inhuman philosophy which, allowing no use of the creatures but what is absolutely necessary, not only malignantly deprives us of the lawful enjoyment of the Divine beneficence, but which cannot be embraced till it has despoiled man of all his senses, and reduced him to a senseless block. But, on the other hand we must, with equal diligence, oppose the licentiousness of the flesh; which, unless it be rigidly restrained, transgresses every bound. . . . Though the liberty of believers in external things cannot be reduced to certain rules, yet it is evidently subject to this law, That they should indulge themselves as little as possible. . . . [Another] rule will be, That persons whose property is small should learn to be patient under their privations, that they may not be tormented with an immoderate desire of riches. . . . The Scripture has also a third rule, . . . that while all these things are given to us by the Divine goodness, and appointed for our benefit, they are, as it were, deposits intrusted to our care, of which we must one day give an account. . . . Lastly, it is to be remarked, that the Lord commands every one of us, in all the actions of life, to regard his vocation. . . . He has appointed to all their particular duties in different spheres of life. . . . Every individual's line of life . . . is, as it were, a post assigned him by the Lord, that he may not wander about in uncertainty all his days. . . . Our life, therefore, will then be best regulated, when it is directed to this mark; since no one will be impelled by his own temerity to attempt more than is compatible with his calling, because he will know that it is unlawful to transgress the bounds assigned him. He that is in obscurity will lead a private life without discontent, so as not to desert the station in which God has placed him. It will also be no small alleviation of his cares, labours, troubles, and other burdens, when a man knows that in all these things he has God for his guide. The magistrate will execute his office with greater pleasure, the father of a family will confine himself to his duty with more satisfaction, and all, in their respective spheres of life, will bear and surmount the inconveniences, cares, disappointments, and anxieties which befall them, when they shall be persuaded that every individual has his burden laid upon him by God. Hence also will arise peculiar consolation, since there will be no employment so mean and sordid (provided we follow our vocation) as not to appear truly respectable, and be deemed highly important in the sight of God. . . .

Max Weber's powerful association of Calvinism with capitalism has had so strong an effect on the Western imagination that even a half century of criticism, revision, and modification has not dislodged its popularity among students and even teachers. Richard Baxter's Chris- tian Directory, *published in 1673, and John Bunyan's* Life and Death of Mr. Badman, *which appeared seven years later, testify to the mix- ture of old and new attitudes in the very citadels of Puritanism. Bun- yan's condemnations of gouging "men of trade, who without all con- science, when they have an advantage, will make a prey of their neighbours"; of covetous "hucksters that buy up the poor man's victual wholesale and sell it to him again for unreasonable gains"; and of "vile wretches called pawnbrokers that lend money and goods to poor people" are entirely in the spirit of the Catholic canonists.*

While Baxter is less extreme than Bunyan and his work displays an evident wish to grapple with the facts of his time, he was far from the advocacy of unbridled accumulation. Nor was he disposed to sep- arate the life of commerce from the life of the soul. Following Calvin, he denied that interest violated the laws of God. Nevertheless, he declared immoral the charging of interest of the needy. Nor does just price vanish in his wrestling with the commercial realities of the age. If public authorities set prices, then businessmen must charge no more than the legal maximum, though they may with propriety charge less. If no public authority determines a price, the business- man is still not free to charge what he can get. Instead Baxter urges him to obey the "judgment of prudent and good men." The ideal in- vestment shared the risks between lender and borrower and returned to the lender no more than a "fair share of the profits, according to the degree in which God has blessed him by whom the money is

71

used." In all his commercial adventures, the good Christian refrains from that species of monetary gain which injures his neighbor. The injunction applies to landlords in their dealings with tenants, lenders in their relations with borrowers, and sellers in their associations with buyers.

It does not exaggerate the case to say that Baxter is closer to St. Thomas Aquinas than he is to the Adam Smith who celebrated the social benefits which might flow from the clash of naked, unhampered egotisms in unregulated markets. No doubt Baxter's Protestant summa lagged behind the actual practice of businessmen. It apparently did not depart from their aspirations and from their consciences. The trickiest of businessmen apparently found nothing ludicrous in Baxter's direction to "understand your neighbours case aright, and meditate on his wants and interest," and "regard the publick good above your own commodity."

This extract from Baxter is taken from Chapters from Richard Baxter's Christian Directory, *selected by Jeannette Tawney* (London, 1925).

General Directions and Particular Cases of Conscience, About Contracts in General, and About Buying and Selling, Borrowing and Lending, Usury, etc., in Particular [Chap. xix]

TIT. 1—GENERAL DIRECTIONS AGAINST INJURIOUS BARGAINING AND CONTRACTS

Besides the last Directions Chap. 18 take these as more nearly pertinent to this case.

DIRECTION 1—*See that your hearts have the two great principles of Justice deeply and habitually innaturalized or radicated in them: viz. The true Love of your neighbour, and the Denyal of yourself: which in one precept are called, The Loving of your neighbour as yourself.* For then you will be free from the Inclination to injuries and fraud, and from the power of those temptations, which carry men to these sins. They will be contrary to your habitual will or inclination; and you will be more studious to *help* your neighbour, than to get from him.

DIRECTION 2—*Yet do not content yourself with these habits, but be sure to call them up to act, when ever you have any bargaining with others, and let a faithful Conscience be to you as a Cryer to proclaim God's Laws, and say to you, Now remember Love and Self-*

denyal, and Do as you would be done by. If *Alexander Severus* so highly valued this saying *Quod tibi fieri non vis, alteri ne feceris,* as to make it his Motto, and write and engrave it on his doors and buildings (having learned it of some Christians or Jews, saith *Lampridius*), What a crime and shame is it for Christ's own professed disciples neither to learn or love it. Put home the questions when you have any bargaining with others, How would I be dealt with myself, if my case were the same with his?

DIRECTION 3—*When the Tempter draweth you to think only of your own commodity and gain, remember how much more you will lose by sin, than your gain can any way amount to.* If *Acan, Gehezi, Ahab, Judas,* etc., had foreseen the end, and the greatness of their loss, it would have curbed their covetous desires. Believe God's Word from the bottom of your heart, that you shall lose things eternal if you sinfully get things temporal, and then you will not make haste to such a bargain to win the world and lose your souls.

DIRECTION 4—*Understand your neighbours case aright, and meditate on his wants and interest.* You think what you want yourself; but you think not whether his wants with whom you deal, may not be as great as yours: Consider what his commodity costs him: or what the toil of the workman's labour is: What house rent he hath to pay, and what a family to maintain? and whether all this can be well done, upon the rates that you desire to trade with him. And do not believe every common report, of his riches, or of the price of his commodity; For same in such cases is frequently false.

DIRECTION 5—*Regard the publick good above your own commodity.* It is not lawful to take up or keep up any oppressing monopoly or Trade; which tends to enrich you by the loss of the Commonwealth or of many.

DIRECTION 6—*Therefore have a special regard to the Laws of the countrey where you live: both as to your Trade itself, and as to the price of what you sell or buy.* For the law is made for the publick benefit, which is to be preferred before any private mans. And when the Law doth directly or indirectly, set rates upon labours or commodities, ordinarily they must be observed; or else you will commit two sins at once Injury and Disobedience.

DIRECTION 7—*Also have special respect to the common estimate, and to the Market-price.* Though it be not alwayes to be our *Rule,* yet ordinarily it must be a considerable part of it, and of great regard.

DIRECTION 8—*Let not imprudent thinking make you seem more covetous than you are.* Some imprudent persons cannot tell how to make their markets without so many words, even about a penny or a trifle, that it maketh others think them covetous, when it is rather want of it. The appearance of evil must be avoided. I have known some that are ready to give a pound to a charitable use at a word, who will yet use so many words for a penny in their bargaining, as maketh them deeply censured and misunderstood. If you see cause to break for a penny or a small matter, do it more handsomely in fewer words, and be gone! And do not tempt the seller to multiply words, because you do so.

DIRECTION 9—*Have no more to do in bargaining with others, especially with censorious persons, than you needs must.* For in much dealing usually there will be much misunderstanding, offence, censure and complaint.

DIRECTION 10—*In doubtful cases, when you are uncertain what is lawful, choose that side which is safest to the peace of your consciences hereafter; though it be against your commodity, and may prove the losing of your right.*

TIT. 3—SPECIAL CASES ABOUT JUSTICE IN BUYING AND SELLING

Question 1: *Am I bound to endeavour that he whom I deal with, may be a gainer by the bargain as well as I?*

Answer: Yes, if you be equally in want; or in the like condition. But if he be very poor, and you be rich, Charity must be so mixed with justice, that you must endeavour that it be more to his commodity than yours (if he be indeed one that you owe Charity to). And if you be poor, and he be rich, you may be willing to be the only gainer yourself, so be it you covet not anothers nor desire that he be wronged: For when he hath power to deal charitably, you may be willing of his charity or kindness.

Question 2: *May I desire, or take more than my labour or goods are worth, if I can get it?*

Answer: 1. Not by deceit, persuading another that they are worth more than they are. 2. Not by extortion working upon men's ignorance, error or necessity (of which more anon). 3. Not of any one that is poorer than yourself, or of anyone that intendeth but an equal bargain. 4. But if you deal with the rich, who in generosity or liberality stick not at a small matter, and are willing another should be a gainer by them, and understand what they do, it is lawful to take as much as they will give you.

Question 3: *May I ask in the market more than my goods are truly worth?*

Answer: In the case last mentioned you may; when you are selling to the Rich who are willing to show their generosity, to make you gainers: But then the honest way is to say, It is worth but so much; but if you will give so much more because I need it, I will take it thankfully. Some think also where the common custome is to ask more than the worth, and people will not buy unless you come down from your first demand, that then you may lawfully ask more, because else there is no trading with such people. My judgement in this case is this. 1. That ordinarily it is better to ask no more at all than a just gain: And that the inconveniences of doing otherwise are greater than any on the other side: For he that heareth you *ask unjustly,* may well think that you would *take unjustly* if you could get it, and consequently that you are *unjust.* 2. But this just gain lyeth not always just in an indivisible quantity, or determinate price. A man that hath a family to maintain by his trade, may lawfully take a proportionable moderate gain: Though if he take less he may get something too. To be alwayes just at a word, is not convenient: For he that may lawfully get two or three shillings or more in the pound of the rich, may see cause to let a poorer person have it for less: But never ask above what its reasonable to take. 3. And if you once peremptorily say, *I will take no less,* then it is not fit to go from your word. 4. And if you do meet with such fools or proud gallants, who will not deal with you unless you ask dear, it is just that, when they have given you more than it is worth, you tell them so, and offer them the overplus again. And for them that expect that you abate much of your asking, it is an inconvenience to be born, which will be ever to your advantage when you are once better known.

Question 4: *How shall the worth of a commodity be judged of?*

Answer: 1. When the Law setteth a rate upon anything (as on bread and drink with us) it must be observed. 2. *If you go to the Market,* the Market-price is much to be observed. 3. If it be in an equal contract, with one that is not in want, you may estimate your goods as they cost you, or are worth to you, though it be above the common price; seeing the buyer is free to take or leave them. 4. But if that which you have to sell, be extraordinary desirable, or worth to some one person, more than to you or another man, you must not make too great an advantage of his convenience or desire; but be glad that you can pleasure him, upon equal, fair and honest terms. 5. If there be a secret worth in your commodity which the Market will take no notice of (as it is usual in a Horse), it is lawful for you to take according to that true worth, if you can get it. But it is a false Rule of them, that think their commodity is worth as much as anyone will give.

Question 5: *Is it lawful to make a thing seem better than it is, by trimming, adorning or setting the best side outward or in sight; or to conceal the faults of what I am to sell?*

Answer: It is lawful to dress, polish, adorn or set out your commodity, to make it seem *as it is indeed*, but not to make it seem *better* than it is; except in some very few unusual cases: As if you deal with some fantastical fool, who will not buy it, nor give you the true worth except it be so set out, and made in some respects to seem better than it is. It is lawful so far to serve their curiosity or humour, as to get the worth of your commodity. But if you do it to get more than the worth by deceiving, it is a sin. And such glossing hath so notable an appearance of deceit, that for that scandal it should be avoided.

2. And as for *concealing* the fault the case is the same: You ought not to deceive your neighbour, but to do as you would be done by: And therefore must not conceal any fault which he desireth, or is concerned to know: Except it be when you deal with one who maketh a far greater matter of that fault than there is cause, and would wrong you in the price if it were known: Yea, and *that exception* will not hold neither, except in a case when you must needs sell, and they must buy it: Because 1. You may not have another man's money against his will, though it be no more than the thing is worth. 2. Because it will be scandalous when the fault is known by him that buyeth it.

Question 6: *What if the fault was concealed from me when I bought it, or if I was deceived or over-reacht by him that sold it me, and gave more than the worth, may I not repair my loss by doing as I was done by?*

Answer: No: no more than you may cut another's purse, because yours was cut: You must do as you would be done by, and not as you *are* done by. What you may do with the same man that deceived you, is a harder question: But doubtless you may not wrong an honest man, because you were wronged by a knave.

Object: *But it is taken for granted in the Markets, that every man will get as much as he can have, and that* Caveat emptor *is the only security; and therefore every man trusteth to his own wit, and not to the sellers honesty, and so resolveth to run the hazard.*

Answer: It is not so among Christians, nor Infidels who profess either truth or common honesty. If you come among a company of

Cut-purses, where the match is made, Look thou to thy purse and I will look to mine, and he that can get most let him take it, then indeed you have no reason to trust another. But there are no Tradesmen or Buyers who will profess that they look not to be trusted, or will say, I will lye and deceive you if I can. Among Thieves and Pirats such total distrust may be allowed. But among sober persons in Civil Societies and Converse, we must in reason and charity expect some truth and honesty, and not presume them to be all lyars and deceivers, that we may seem to have allowance to be such ourselves. Indeed we trust them, not absolutely as Saints, but with a mixture of distrust, as fallible and faulty men: And so as to trust our own circumspection above their words when we know not the persons to be very just. But we have no cause to make a Market a place of meer deceit, where every one saith, Trust not me, and I will not trust thee, but let us all take one another for cheaters and liars, and get what we can. Such censures savour not of Charity, or of Just intentions.

Question 7: *What if I foresee a plenty and cheapness in a time of dearth, which the buyer foreseeth not (as if I know that there are ships coming in with store of that commodity, which will make it cheap) am I bound to tell the buyer of it, and hinder my own gain?*

Answer: There may be some instances in trading with enemies, or with Rich men, that regard not such matters, or with men that are supposed to know it as well as you, in which you are not bound to tell them. But in your ordinary equal trading, when you have reason to think that the buyer knoweth it not, and would not give so dear if he knew it, you are bound to tell him: Because you must love your neighbour as yourself, and do as you would be done by, and not take advantage of his ignorance.

Question 8: *If I foresee a dearth, may I not keep my commodity till then?*

Answer: Yes; unless it be to the hurt of the Common wealth, as if your keeping it in, be the *cause* of the dearth, and your bringing it forth would help to prevent it.

Question 9: *May one use many words in buying and selling?*

Answer: You must use no more than are true, and just, and useful: but there are more words needful with some persons who are talkative and unsatisfied, than with others.

Question 10: *May I buy as cheap as I can get it, or give* less *than the thing is worth?*

Answer: If it be worth more to you than the Market price (through your necessity) you are not bound to give above the market price: If it be worth less to you than the market price, you are not bound *to give* more than it is *worth to you*, as suited to your use: But you must not *desire* nor *seek* to get anothers goods or labour for less than it is worth in both these respects (in common estimate, and to you).

Question 11: *May I take advantage of anothers Necessity to buy for less than the worth, or sell for more? As, e.g., a poor man must needs have money suddenly for his goods, though he sell them but for half the worth: and I have no need of them: Am I bound to give him the worth when I have no need? and when it is a great kindness to him to give him any thing in that straight? So also when I have no desire to sell my Horse, and anothers necessity maketh him willing to give more than he is worth, may I not take it?*

Answer: To the first case: You must distinguish between an act of *Justice* and of *Charity:* and between your *need* of the thing, and the *worth* of it to you. Though you have no *need* of the poor mans goods, yet if you buy them, both Justice and Charity require that you give him as much as they are *worth to you*, though not so much as they are worth in the market: yea, and that you buy them of him in his necessity: For if you give him but what they are *worth to you*, you are no *loser* by it: And you should do another good, when it is not to your hurt or loss. By what they are worth to you, I mean so much as that you be no loser. As if it be meat or drink, though you have no present need, perhaps you will shortly have need, and if you buy not that, you must buy as much of somewhat else. In *strict Justice* you may be *a saver*, but not a *gainer*, by buying of the poor in their necessity. 2. But if you buy a *durable commodity*, for less than it is worth, you should take it but as a *pledge*, and allow the seller liberty to redeem it, if he can, that he may get more after of another. 3. And to the *poor* in such necessity, *Charity* must be exercised as well as *Justice*. Therefore if you are able to lend them money to save them the loss of underselling, you should do it: (I account that man only *able* who hath money which no greater service of God requireth). And if you are not able yourself, you should endeavour to get some others to relieve him, if you can without a greater inconvenience.

And for the second case, it is answered before: You may not take more than it is worth, ever the more for anothers necessity; nor in any other case than you might have done it in, if there had been no such necessity of his.

Question 12: *May I not make advantage of anothers ignorance or error in bargaining?*

Answer: Not to get more than your commodity is worth, nor to get his goods for less than the worth; no nor to get the true worth against *his will,* or with *scandal:* But if it be only to get a true worth of your commodity when he is willing, but would be offended if his ignorance in some point were cured, you may so far make use of his ignorance to a lawful end, as is said before in the case of *concealing faults.*

Question 13: *May I strive to get before another, to get a good bargain which he desireth?*

Answer: Yes, if you do it not out of a greedy mind, nor to the injury of one that is poorer than yourself: You should rather further the supply of your neighbours greater needs: Otherwise speed and industry in your Calling is no fault, nor yet the crossing of a covetous mans desires: You are not bound to let every man have what he would have.

Question 14: *May I buy a thing out of anothers hand, or hire a servant, which another is about, or is treating with? Or may I call a Chapman from another to buy of me?*

Answer: There are some cases in which you may not do it, and some in which you may. You may not do it out of greedy covetousness; nor to the injury of the poor: nor when the other hath gone so far in the bargain that it cannot be honestly broken: For then you injure the third person, and tempt the other to a sin: nor may you do it so as to disturb that due and civil order, which should be among moderate men in trading. And it is a great matter how the thing is accounted of by the custome of the country or market where you bargain: For where it is of ill report, and accounted as unjust, the scandal should make you avoid such a course. But yet in some cases it is *lawful,* and in some a *needful duty.* It is *lawful* when none of the foresaid reasons (or any such other) are against it: It is a *duty* when *Charity* to the poor or oppressed doth require it. As, e.g., a poor man must needs sell his Land, his Horse, his Corn or Goods: A Covetous oppressor offereth him less than it is worth. The poor man must take his offer if he can get no more: The oppressor saith that it is injustice for anyone to take his bargain out of his hand, or offer money till he have done: In this case it may be a *duty,* to offer the poor man the worth of his commodity, and save him from the oppressor. A covetous man offereth a *Servant* or *Labourer* less than their service or labour is worth; and will accuse you, if you interrupt his bargain and would offer his Servant more: In this case it may be your duty to help the servant to a better Master. A Chapman is ready to be cheated by an unconscionable Tradesman, to give much more for a commodity than its worth: Charity may oblige in such case to offer it him cheaper. In a word, if you do it for your own gain, in a greedy manner, it is a sin: But if you do it when it is not scandalous or injurious, or do it in charity for anothers good, it is lawful, and sometime a duty.

Question 15: *May I dispraise anothers commodity, to draw the buyer to my own?*

Answer: This case is sufficiently answered in the former:

1. You may not use any *false* dispraise:
2. Nor a *true one* out of Covetousness, nor in a scandalous manner;
3. But you may help to save another from a Cheater, by opening the deceit in charity to him.

Question 16: *What should I do in doubtful cases, where I am uncertain whether the thing be just or not?*

Answer: Causeless perplexing melancholy scruples, which would stop a man in the course of his duty, are not to be indulged. But in rational doubts, first use your utmost diligence (as much as the nature of the cause requireth) to be resolved: and if yet you doubt, be sure to go the safer way, and to avoid sin rather than loss: and to keep your consciences in peace.

Question 17: *If the buyer lose the commodity between the bargain and the payment (as if he buy your Horse, and he die before payment or presently after) what should the seller do to his relief?*

Answer: If it were by the sellers fault, or by any fault in the Horse which he concealed, he is to make the buyer full satisfaction. If it were casualty only, rigorous Justice will allow him nothing: And therefore, if it be either to a man that is Rich enough to bear it without any great sense of the loss, or in a case where in common custom the buyer always standeth to the loss, mere justice will make him no amends. But if it be where custom maketh some abatement judged a duty, or where the person is so poor as to be pinched by the loss, that common humanity, which all good men use in bargaining, which tempereth Justice with Charity, will teach men to bear their part of the loss, because they must do as they would be done by.

Question 18: *If the thing bought and sold prove afterward of much more worth than was by either party understood (as in buying of amber-chryse, and Jewels, it oft falleth out) is the buyer bound to give the seller more than was bargained for?*

Answer: Yes, if it was the sellers meer ignorance and insufficiency in that business, which caused him so to undersell it: (as if an ignorant Countrey man sell a Jewel or *Amber-chryse*, who knoweth not what it is, a moderate satisfaction should be made him). But if it was the sellers trade, in which he is to be supposed sufficient, and if it be

taken for granted before hand, that both buyer and seller will stand
to the bargain whatever it prove, and that the seller would have
abated nothing if it had proved less worth than the price, then the
buyer may enjoy his gain: Much more if he run any notable hazard
for it, as merchants use to do.

Question 19: *What if the title of the thing sold prove bad, which
was before unknown?*

Answer: If the seller either knew it was bad, or through his notable negligence was ignorant of it, or did not fully acquaint the buyer
with so much of the uncertainty and danger as he knew; or if it was
anyway his fault that the buyer was deceived, and not the buyers
fault, he is bound to make him proportionable satisfaction. As also
in case that by Law or bargain he be bound to warrant the title to
the buyer. But not in case that it be their explicite or implicite agreement that the buyer stand to the hazard, and the seller hath done his
duty to make him know whats doubtful.

Question 20: *What if a change of Powers or Laws do overthrow the
title, almost as soon as it is sold (as it oft falls out about Offices and
Lands)? Who must bear the loss?*

Answer: The case is near the same with that in *Quest.* 17. It is
supposed that the seller should have lost it himself if he had kept it
but a little longer: And that neither of them foresaw the change:
And therefore that the seller hath all his money, rather for his good
hap, than for his Lands or Office (which the buyer hath not). Therefore except it be to a rich man that feeleth not the loss, or one that
expressly undertook to stand to all hazards, foreseeing a possibility of
them, Charity and humanity, will teach the seller to divide the loss.

The same is the case of *London* now consumed by fire: where
thousands of suits are like to rise between the Landlords and the Tenants. Where the providence of God (permitting the burning zeal of
some Papists), hath deprived men of the houses which they had
hired or taken leases of, humanity and charity requireth the Rich to
bear most of the loss, and not to exact their Rents, or Rebuilding
from the poor, whatever the Law saith, which could not be supposed
to foresee such accidents. Love your neighbours as yourselves: Do as
you would be done by; and Oppress not your poor brethren; and
then by these three Rules you will yourselves decide a multitude of
such doubts and difficulties, which the uncharitable only cannot understand.

Question 12: *Is it lawful to lend upon usury, interest or increase?*
Answer: This controversie hath so many full Treatises written on

it, that I cannot expect that so few words as I must lay out upon it should satisfy the studious reader. All the disputes about the *name* of *Usury* I pass by: It being *The receiving of any additional gain as due from money lent* which is commonly meant by the word, and which we mean in the question. For the questions, whether we may bargain for it, or tie the debtor to pay it? whether we may take it only after his gain as partaking in it, or before? whether we must partake also in the loss if the debtor be a loser? with other such like, are but subsequent to the main question, *Whether any gain* (called *Use*) may be taken by the lender as his due for the money lent? My judgement is as followeth.

1. *There is some such gain or Usury lawful and commendable.*

2. *There is some such gain or usury unlawful and a heinous sin.*

I shall first give my reasons of the first proposition.

1. If all *Usury* be forbidden it is either by the Law of Nature, or by some positive law of supernatural revelation. If the latter, it is either by some Law of Moses, or by some Law of Christ: If the former, it is either as against the Rule of Piety to God, or against Justice or Charity to men. That which is neither a violation of the Natural Laws of Piety, Justice or Charity, nor against the supernaturally revealed Laws of Moses or of Christ, is not unlawful. But there is some Usury which is against none of all these. *Ergo* there is some Usury which is not unlawful.

I will first lay you down the instances of such usury, and then prove it. There is a parcel of Land to be sold for a thousand pound, which is worth forty pound *per annum,* and hath Wood on it worth a thousand pound: (Some such things we have known). *John N.* is willing to purchase it. But he hath a poor neighbour, *T.S.* that hath no money, but a great desire of the bargain. *J.N.* loving his neighbour as himself and desiring his wealth, lendeth him the thousand pound upon usury for one year. *T.S.* buyeth the land, and selleth the wood for the same money, and repayeth it in a year, and so hath all the land for almost nothing, as if *J.N.* had purchased the land and freely given it him, after a year or two: The gift had been the same.

Object: *Here you suppose the seller wronged by selling his land almost for nothing.*

Answer: 1. Thats nothing at all to the present case, but a different case by itself: 2. I can put many cases in which such a sale may be made without any wrong to the seller: As when it is done by some Prince, or State, or Noble and liberal person, purposely designing the enriching of the subjects; or after a war, as lately in *Ireland.* So that the question is, whether *J.N.* may not give *T.S.* a thousand or eight hundred pounds worth of land, taking a years rent first out of the land, or a years use for the money, which cometh to the same summ.

Another: A Rich Merchant trading into the *East Indies*, having five thousand pound to lay out upon his commodities in Traffick, when he hath laid out four thousand five hundred pound, lendeth in charity the other five hundred pound to one of his servants to lay out upon a commodity, which when it cometh home will be worth two thousand pound, and offereth him to secure the carriage with his own, requiring only the *Use* of his money at 6 *per cent.* Here the taking of thirty pound Use, is but the free giving him one thousand four hundred and seventy pound, and is all one with deducting so much of the gift.

Another instance: Certain Orphans having nothing left them but so much money as will, by the allowed use of it, find them bread and poor clothing. The guardian cannot lay it out in Lands for them, And if he maintain them upon the stock, it will be quickly spent, and he must answer for it. A rich man that is their neighbour tradeth in Iron-works, (Furnaces and Forges) or Lead works or other such commodities, in which he constantly getteth the double of the stock which he employeth, or at least twenty pound or forty pound in the hundred. The Guardian dare not lend the money to any poor man, lest he break and never be able to pay it: Therefore he lendeth it this rich man. And, if he have it without Usury, the poor Orphans give the rich man freely twenty pound or forty pound a year supposing their stock to be an hundred: If he take usury, the rich man doth but give the poor Orphans some part of his constant gain.

Another instance: In a City or Corporation where there is a rich Trade of Clothing or making Silks, there is a stock of money given by Legacy for the poor, and entrusted into the hands of the richest of the City, to trade with and give the poor the Use of it: And there is another stock left to set up young beginners, who have not a stock to set up themselves, on condition that they give the third part of their gain to the poor, and at seven years end resign the stock. The question is, Whether the poor should be without this use of their money, and let the rich go away with it? or whether they may take it?

Now I prove that such Usury is not forbidden by God. 1. It is not forbidden *us* by the Law of *Moses:* 1. Because *Moses* Law never did forbid it: For, 1. It is expressly forbidden as an act of unmercifulness; and therefore forbidden only to the poor and to brethren, *Exod.* xxii.

25, *Levit*. xxv. 36, 37. Yea, when the *poor* are not named, it is the poor that are meant:* Because in that Countrey they did not keep up stocks for Merchandise or Trading, but lent usually to the needy only: At least the circumstances of the several Texts shew, that it is only *Lending to the needy*, and not lending to drive on any enriching Trade, which is meant where Usury is forbidden. 2. And it is expressly allowed to be used to strangers, *Deut*. xxiii. 19, 20, to whom nothing unjust or uncharitable might be done; only such a *measure* of Charity was not required towards them as unto brethren. And there were more merchants of strangers that traded with them in foreign commodities, than of Jews that fetcht them home: So that the prohibition of Usury is in the Law itself restrained only to their lending to *the poor*. But in the Prophets who do but reprove the sin, it is expressed without that limitation, partly because it supposeth the meaning of the law to be known, which the *Prophets* did but apply: and partly because there was little or no lending used among the Jews, but to the needy as an act of charity.

2. And if it had been forbidden in *Moses* Law only, it would not extend to Christians now, Because the law of *Moses as such*, is not in force. The matter of it is much of the law of Nature indeed; but, as *Mosaical*, it was proper to the Jews and Proselytes, or at least extended not to the Christian Gentiles, as is plain in *II. Cor*. iii. 7, *Gal*. iii. 19, 24, and v. 3. *Eph*. ii. 15, *I. Tim*. i. 7, *Heb*. vii. 12, 16, 19. *Moses* Law as such never bound any other Nations, but the proselytes that joyned themselves to the Jews (nor was all the world obliged so to be proselyted as to take up their laws). Much less do they bind us that are the servants of Christ, so long after the dissolution of their Common-wealth. So much of them as are part of the Law of Nature, or of any positive Law of Christ, or of the Civil Law of any State, are binding as they are such *Natural, Christian* or *Civil Laws*. But not one of them as Mosaical: Though the *Mosaical* Law is of great use to help us to understand the law of nature in many particular instances, in which it is somewhat difficult to us.

3. There is no *Positive* law of *Christ* forbidding all usury: As for *Luke* vi. 32, 25, it is plainly nothing to the case: For he saith not, *Lend, looking for no gain or increase*, but *looking for nothing again*. And the Context sheweth that the meaning must be one of these two: Either q.d., Lend not only to them that will lend to you again when you are in want, but even to the poor, that you can never hope to

---

* *Exod*. xxii. 21. Thou shalt neither vex a stranger nor oppress him. *Exod*. xxiii. 9. Thou shalt not oppress a stranger, etc. So that usury to a stranger was no oppression.

borrow of: Or else, Lend not only to them that are able to pay you, and where your stock is secured, but to the needy where your money is hazarded; and though they will pay you if they are able, yet you have little or no hope that ever they should be able to repay: Lend so, as to be willing to make a gift of it in case the borrower never repay it. And there is no other text that can be pretended against it, in the New Testament.

3. And that the Law of Nature doth not forbid all usury, will appear by examining the several parts of it. The law of nature forbiddeth but three sorts of sins: 1. Those that are against Piety to God: 2. Those that are against *our own welfare*. 3. Those that are against our neighbours good: And that is, 1. Against *Justice:* 2. Against *Charity*. There is none that falleth not under some of these heads.

1. And that *Usury* is not naturally evil as against *Piety* to God,

2. Or as against our *selves*, and our own welfare, I need not prove, because no reason nor reasonable person doth lay any such accusation against it. Though they that think it absolutely unlawful, say that it is consequently against God, as every violation of his Law is. But thats nothing to the case.

3. Therefore there is no doubt but the whole controversie is resolved into this last question, whether all Usury be against Justice or Charity to our neighbour. *Justice* obligeth me to give him *his own:* Charity obligeth me to give him more than his own, in certain cases, as one that love him as myself. That which is not against *Justice*, may be against *Charity:* But that which is against Charity, is not always against Justice strictly taken. And that which is an act of true Charity, is never against Justice: Because he that giveth his neighbour *more* than his own, doth give him *his own* and *more*. There is a *Usury* which is against *Justice* and *Charity*. There is a *Usury* which is against *Charity*, but not against meer *Justice:* And there is a Usury which is against neither *Justice* nor *Charity*. If I prove it *Charitable*, it is superfluous to say more.

All the instances before given are notoriously charitable. That which is for the preservation of the lives and comforts of the poor, and of Orphans, or for the enriching of my neighbour, is an act of Charity. But such is some Usury, past all doubt, as is before declared. Where the contrary is an act of cruelty, the Usury is not against Charity, but for it. For the Rich to deny to the poor and Orphans a part of that gain, which they make by the improvement of their own money, is oppression and cruelty. If it be cruel to let a beggar dye or starve, when we should feed and clothe him of our *own*, much more to let the poor and Orphans starve and perish rather than give them the increase of *their* own, or part of it at least. As for them that say, It may be as well improved otherwise, they are unexperienced men. It is a known falsehood as to the most; though some few may meet with such opportunities. At least it is nothing to them that cannot have other wayes of improving it: who are very many.

Moreover, when it is *not an act of Charity*, yet it may be not against *Charity* in these cases:

1. When the lender is poor and the borrower rich: Yea, it may be a sin to lend it freely: *Prov.* xxii. 16. *He that oppresseth the poor to increase his riches, and he that giveth to the rich, shall surely come to want.* It is a *giving to the rich* to lend freely that money which they improve to the increase of their riches.

2. When the *lender* is not obliged to that act of *Charity*, though the borrower be poorer than himself. Which falleth out in an hundred cases, which may be comprised under this one general: *When the lender is obliged to expend* that *same money in some other greater, better work*. As at the same time while a man that is worth but twenty pound a year, is in debt to a man that hath a thousand pound a year, there may be a hundred or thousand poor people worth *nothing* ready to perish, whom the rich is rather bound to succour, than him that hath but twenty pound a year. And there may be works of piety (as to set up a School, or promote the preaching of the Gospel) which may be as great as either. And the richest that is, cannot do all the good that is to be done, nor relieve all the persons that are in want. Therefore when we must leave much undone, if he would give all his substance, it is (*caeteris paribus*) a sin to give that to a man that can make shift without it, and pass by an hundred in much deeper necessity and distress. So that he who either exerciseth *Charity* in his *Usury*, or doth nothing against *Charity* and *Justice*, certainly sinneth not by that *Usury*. For all the scriptures which speak against Usury, speak against it as a cruel or uncharitable thing.

Object: *But it is sometimes necessary for a law to forbid that which otherwise would be good, when it cannot be done without encouraging others to a greater evil, such as ordinary Usury is: And then that Law must be observed.*

Answer: This is true *in thesi*, that such cases there are: But it is unproved and untrue in this case: For, 1. There is no such Law. 2. There is no such reason or necessity of such a law. For God can as well make laws against unrighteous or uncharitable *increase* or *Usury*, without forbidding that which is *charitable* and *just*, as he can make laws against *unrighteous* or *uncharitable buying* and *selling*, without condemning that which is good and just: Or as he can forbid gluttony, drunkenness, idleness, pride, without forbidding eating, drinking, *apparel* or *riches*. He can easily tell men of whom and in what case to take Use, and when not.

He that would see all other Objections answered, and the case fully handled, hath many Treatises on both sides extant to inform him.

II. That there is a sort of *Usury* which is evil I know of no man that doubteth, and therefore need not stand to prove.

Question: *When is usury sinful?*

Answer: As is before said, When its against either Justice or Charity: 1. When its like cheating bargaining, which under pretence of *consent* and a form of Justice doth deceive, or oppress, and get from another that which is not truly *ours* but *his*. 2. When you lend for increase where charity obligeth you to lend freely: Even as it is a sin to lend expecting your own again, when *Charity* obligeth you to *give* it. 3. When you uncharitably exact that which your brother is disabled utterly to pay, and use cruelty to procure it, (be it the Use, or the principal). 4. When you allow him not such a proportion of the gain as his labour, hazard or poverty doth require; but because the money is yours, will live at ease upon his labours. 5. When in case of his losses you rigorously exact your due, without that abatement, or forgiving debts (whether *Use* or *principal*), which humanity and charity require. In a word, when you are *selfish* and do not as, according to true judgement, you may desire to be done by, if you were in his case.

Question: *But when am I bound to exercise this charity, in not taking use?*

Answer: As I said before, 1. *When ever* you have no more urgent, and necessary, and excellent work, to lay out that money on, which you are so to receive. 2. Yea, though another work may be in itself better, (as to relieve many poorer better men with that money) yet when you cannot take it, without the utter undoing of the debtor, and bringing him into as bad a case, as any single person whom you would relieve, it is the safer side to leave the other unrelieved, (unless it be a person on whom the public good much dependeth) rather than to extort your own from such a one to give another. Because that which you cannot get, without a scandalous appearance of cruelty, is *quod jus in re* not yours to give, till you can better get possession of it. And therefore God will not expect that you should give it to another.

In all this I imply that as you must prefer the lives of others in giving Alms, before your own *conveniences* and *comforts*, and must not say, *I cannot spare it*, when your *necessity* may spare it, though not your *pleasure:* So also in taking *Use* of those that you are bound to shew charity to, the same rule and proportions must be observed in your charity.

Note also, that in all this it appeareth, that the case is but gradually different, between taking the *Use* and taking the *principal.* For when the reason for remitting is the same you are as well bound to remit the principal as the use.

But this difference there is, that many a man of low estate may afford to lend freely to a poorer man for a little time, who cannot afford to give it. And prudence may direct us to choose one man to lend freely to for a time, because of his sudden necessity, when yet another is fitter to give it to.

Question 13: *Is lending a duty? If so, must I lend to all that ask me? or to whom?*

Answer: Lending is a duty, when we have it, and our brothers necessity requireth it, and true prudence telleth us that we have no better way to lay it out, which is inconsistent with that. And therefore rich men ordinarily should both lend and give as prudence shall direct. But there is an imprudent and so a sinful *lending:* As, 1. When you will lend that which is anothers, and you have no power to lend. 2. When you lend that which you must needs require again, while you might easily foresee that the borrower is not like to pay. Lend nothing but what you have either great probability will be repaid, or else which you are willing to give in case the debtor cannot or will not pay; or, at least, when suing for it, will not have scandalous and worse effects than *not lending.* For it is very ordinary when you come to demand it and sue for it, to stir up the hatred of the debtor against you, and to make him your enemy, and to break his charity by your imprudent charity. In such a case, if you are obliged to relieve him, give him so much as you can spare, rather than lend him that which you cannot spare, but must sue for. In such cases, if Charity go not without *Prudence,* nor *prudence* without charity, you may well enough see when to lend, and how much.

Question 14: *Is it lawful to take upon usury in necessity, when the creditor doth unjustly or unmercifully require it?*

Answer: Not in case that the consequence (by encouraging sin or otherwise) be like to do more hurt, than the money will do you good. Else, it is lawful, when it is for your benefit: As it is lawful to take part of your wages for your work, or part of the work of your commodity, when you cannot have the whole: And as it is lawful to purchase your rights of an enemy, or your life of a Thief as is aforesaid. A man may buy his own benefit of an unrighteous man.

Question 15: *Doth not contracting for a certain sum of gain make usury to be in that case unlawful, which might lawfully be taken of one thats free?*

Answer: Yes, in case that *contracting determine an uncertain case without sufficient cause:* As if you agree, that whether the borrower gain or lose, and be poor or rich, I will have so much gain: that is, whether it prove merciful or unmerciful, I will have it. But then in that case, if it so prove unmerciful, it may not be taken *without contracting,* if freely offered. No contract may tie the debtor to that which is against justice or charity: And no contract may *absolutely* require that which *may prove* uncharitable; unless there be a tacit condition, or exception of such a case implied. Otherwise I see no scripture or reason, why a contract altereth the case, and may not be used to secure that increase which is neither unrighteous nor unmerciful: It may be the bond of equity, but not of iniquity. As, in case of a *certain gain by the borrower, a certain use* may be contracted for. And in case of an uncertain gain to the borrower, a conditional contract may be made. Yea, in case of Merchandize, where mens poverty forbiddeth not such bargains, I see not but it is lawful to sell a greater uncertain gain, for a smaller certain gain; and so to make the contracts absolute: (As *Amesius Cas. Consc.* on this question sheweth). As all oppression and unmercifulness must be avoided, and all men must do as they would (judiciously) be done by; So it is a bad thing to corrupt religion, and fill the world with causeless scruples, by making that a sin which is no sin. Divines that live in great Cities and among Merchandize, are usually fitter judges in this case, than those that live more obscurely (without experience) in the Countrey.

Leo XIII's great encyclical Rerum Novarum, *promulgated May 15, 1891, should be taken as a culmination of the nineteenth-century Catholic effort to come to terms with industrialism and its transforming effect upon traditional social relationships. Inevitably what Leo XIII noted as the "vast expansion of intellectual pursuits," the "marvelous discoveries of science," the "changed relations between masters and workmen," the "enormous fortunes of some few individuals, and the utter poverty of the masses," the "increased self-reliance and closer mutual combination of the working classes," and the "prevailing moral degeneracy" offered perplexing problems of interpretation to a Church wedded to the co-operation, rather than the conflict, between classes, and to the unity of human experience in all aspects of life. Thus the encyclical is many things. It is a warning against socialism and a defense of private property: ". . . private ownership is in accordance with the law of nature." Socialism, on the other hand, ". . . must be utterly rejected, since it only injures those whom it would seem meant to benefit, is directly contrary to the natural rights of mankind, and would introduce confusion and disorder into the commonweal." It is a plea for social harmony: "Capital cannot do without Labor, nor Labor without Capital." It is an appeal that harks back to St. Thomas for justice in the laborer's dealings with his employer and his employer's dealings with him. The employer's ". . . great and principal duty is to give every one a fair wage."*

Pope Leo XIII broke new ground in his treatment of the state and of labor unions. His position on the first point appears most sharply in his repetition of Pauline text in another encyclical, Immortale Dei, *"The State is the minister of God for good." Clearly Leo believed that the state's role was as the impartial protector of all classes. Since it was the poor who needed protection most and the rich, well able to tend their own interests, who needed it least, state intervention would most frequently favor the working classes. Although ". . . civil society exists for the common good," it accords ". . . individual interests . . . their due place and degree."*

Leo's endorsement of unions is a good deal more qualified than is often believed. For a union to deserve his endorsement, it must ". . . pay special and chief attention to the duties of religion and morality." It must be honestly run and prudently led. It must have in mind the general welfare as much as the special interests of union members. More than an echo of the medieval guild's merger of economic and moral objectives is to be heard.

Leo's teachings have had their effect on the Catholic parliamentary parties of France, Italy, and Germany even today. Their general sympathy toward welfare legislation and their support of the Catholic trade-union movement are closely consonant with the doctrines of Rerum Novarum.

Rerum Novarum

We have said that the state must not absorb the individual or the family; both should be allowed free and untrammelled action so far as is consistent with the common good and the interests of others. Rulers should, nevertheless, anxiously safeguard the community and all its members: the community, because the conservation thereof is so emphatically the business of the supreme power that the safety of the commonwealth is not only the first law, but it is a government's whole reason of existence; and the members, because both philosophy and the Gospel concur in laying down that the object of the government of the State should be, not the advantage of the ruler, but the benefit of those over whom he is placed. The gift of authority derives from God, and is, as it were, a participation in the highest of all sovereignties; and should be exercised as the power of God is exercised—with a fatherly solicitude which not only guides the whole but reaches also to details.

Whenever the general interest or any particular class suffers, or is threatened with mischief which can in no other way be met or prevented, the public authority must step in to deal with it. Now, it interests the public, as well as the individual, that peace and good order should be maintained; that family life should be carried on in accordance with God's laws and those of nature; that religion should be reverenced and obeyed; that a high standard of morality should prevail, both in public and private life; that the sanctity of justice should be respected, and that no one should injure another with impunity; that the members of the commonwealth should grow up to man's estate strong and robust, and capable, if need be, of guarding and defending their country. If by a strike, or other combination of workmen, there should be imminent danger of disturbance to the public peace; or if circumstances were such as that among the laboring population the ties of family life were relaxed; if religion were found to suffer through the operatives not having time and opportunity afforded them to practise its duties; if in workshops and factories there were danger to morals through the mixing of the sexes or from other harmful occasions of evil; or if employers laid burdens upon their workmen which were unjust, or degraded them with conditions repugnant to their dignity as human beings; finally, if health were endangered by excessive labor, or by work unsuited to sex or age in such cases, there can be no question but that, within certain limits, it would be right to invoke the aid and authority of the law. The limits must be determined by the nature of the occasion which calls for the law's interference—the principle being that the law must not undertake more, nor proceed further, than is required for the remedy of the evil or the removal of the mischief.

Rights must be religiously respected wherever they exist; and it is the duty of the public authority to prevent and to punish injury, and to protect every one in the possession of his own. Still, when there is a question of defending the rights of individuals, the poor and helpless have a claim to especial consideration. The richer class have many ways of shielding themselves, and stand less in need of help from the State; whereas those who are badly off have no resources of their own to fall back upon, and must chiefly depend upon the assistance of the State. And it is for this reason that wage-earners, who are undoubtedly among the weak and necessitous, should be specially cared for and protected by the Government.

Here, however, it is expedient to bring under special notice certain matters of moment. It should ever be borne in mind that the chief thing to be realized is the safeguarding of private property by legal enactment and public policy. Most of all it is essential, amid such a fever of excitement, to keep the multitude within the line of duty; for if all may justly strive to better their condition, neither justice nor the common good allows any individual to seize upon that which belongs to another, or, under the futile and shallow pretext of equality, to lay violent hands on other people's possessions. Most true it is that by far the larger part of the workers prefer to better themselves by honest labor rather than by doing any wrong to others. But there are not a few who are imbued with evil principles and eager for revolutionary change, whose main purpose is to stir up tumult and bring about measures of violence. The authority of the State should intervene to put restraint upon such firebrands, to save the working classes from their seditious arts, and protect lawful owners from spoliation.

When working men have recourse to a strike, it is frequently because the hours of labor are too long, or the work too hard, or because they consider their wages insufficient. The grave inconvenience of this not uncommon occurrence should be obviated by public remedial measures; for such paralyzing of labor not only affects the masters and their work-people alike, but is extremely injurious to trade and to the general interests of the public; moreover, on such occasions, violence and disorder are generally not far distant, and thus it frequently happens that the public peace is imperilled. The laws should forestall and prevent such troubles from arising; they should lend their influence and authority to the removal in good time of the causes which lead to conflicts between employers and employed.

But if owners of property should be made secure, the workingman, in like manner, has property and belongings in respect to which he should be protected; and foremost of all, his soul and mind. Life on earth, however good and desirable in itself, is not the final purpose for which man is created; it is only the way and the means to that attainment of truth and that practice of goodness in which the full life of the soul consists. It is the soul which is made after the image and likeness of God; it is in the soul that the sovereignty resides in virtue whereof man is commanded to rule the creatures below him and to use all the earth and the ocean for his profit and advantage. *Fill the earth and subdue it; and rule over the fishes of the sea, and the fowls of the air, and all living creatures which move upon the earth.* * In this respect all men are equal; there is no difference between rich and poor, master and servant, ruler and ruled, *for the same is Lord over all.*† No man may with impunity outrage that human dignity which God Himself treats *with reverence,* nor stand in the way of that higher life which is the preparation for the eternal life

* Genesis i. 28.
† Rom. x. 12.

of heaven. Nay, more: no man has in this matter power over himself. To consent to any treatment which is calculated to defeat the end and purpose of his being is beyond his right; he cannot give up his soul to servitude; for it is not man's own rights which are here in question, but the rights of God, the most sacred and inviolable of rights.

From this follows the obligation of the cessation from work and labor on Sundays and certain holy days. The rest from labor is not to be understood as mere giving way to idleness; much less must it be an occasion for spending money and for vicious indulgence, as many would have it to be; but it should be rest from labor, hallowed by religion. Rest (combined with religious observances), disposes man to forget for a while the business of his every-day life, to turn his thoughts to things heavenly, and to the worship which he so strictly owes to the Eternal Godhead. It is this, above all, which is the reason and motive of Sunday rest; a rest sanctioned by God's great law of the ancient covenant—*Remember thou keep holy the Sabbath day,** and taught to the world by His own mysterious "rest" after the creation of man: *He rested on the seventh day from all work which He had done.*†

If we turn now to things external and corporeal, the first concern of all is to save the poor workers from the cruelty of greedy speculators, who use human beings as mere instruments of money-making. It is neither just nor human so to grind men down with excessive labor as to stupefy their minds and wear out their bodies. Man's powers, like his general nature, are limited, and beyond these limits he cannot go. His strength is developed and increased by use and exercise, but only on condition of due intermission and proper rest. Daily labor, therefore, should be so regulated as not to be protracted over longer hours than strength admits. How many and how long the intervals of rest should be must depend on the nature of the work, on circumstances of time and place, and on the health and strength of the workmen. Those who work in mines and quarries, and extract coal, stone, and metals from the bowels of the earth, should have shorter hours in proportion as their labor is more severe and trying to health. Then, again, the season of the year should be taken into account; for not infrequently a kind of labor is easy at one time which at another is intolerable or exceedingly difficult. Finally, work which is quite suitable for a strong man cannot reasonably be required from a woman or a child. And, in regard to children, great care should be

* Exod. xx. 8.
† Genesis ii. 2.

taken not to place them in workshops and factories until their bodies and minds are sufficiently developed. For just as very rough weather destroys the buds of spring, so does too early an experience of life's hard toil blight the young promise of a child's faculties, and render any true education impossible. Women, again, are not suited for certain occupations; a woman is by nature fitted for home work, and it is that which is best adapted at once to preserve her modesty and to promote the good bringing up of children and the well-being of the family. As a general principle it may be laid down that a workman ought to have leisure and rest proportionate to the wear and tear of his strength; for waste of strength must be repaired by cessation from hard work.

In all agreements between masters and work-people there is always the condition, expressed or understood, that there should be allowed proper rest for soul and body. To agree in any other sense would be against what is right and just; for it can never be just or right to require on the one side, or to promise on the other, the giving up of those duties which a man owes to his God and to himself.

We now approach a subject of great and urgent importance and one in respect of which, if extremes are to be avoided, right notions are absolutely necessary. Wages, as we are told, are regulated by free consent, and therefore the employer, when he pays what was agreed upon, has done his part and seemingly is not called upon to do anything beyond. The only way, it is said, in which injustice might occur would be if the master refused to pay the whole of the wages, or if the workman should not complete the work undertaken; in such cases the State should intervene, to see that each obtains his due—but not under any other circumstances.

This mode of reasoning is, to a fair-minded man, by no means convincing, for there are important considerations which it leaves out of account altogether. To labor is to exert one's self for the sake of procuring what is necessary for the purposes of life, and chief of all for self-preservation. *In the sweat of thy brow thou shalt eat thy bread.*** Hence a man's labor bears two notes or characters. First of all, it is *personal,* inasmuch as the exertion of individual strength belongs to the individual who puts it forth, employing such strength to procure that personal advantage on account of which it was bestowed. Secondly, man's labor is *necessary;* for without the result of labor a man cannot live; and self-preservation is a law of nature, which it is wrong to disobey. Now, were we to consider labor so far as it is *personal* merely, doubtless it would be within the workman's

* Genesis iii. 19.

right to accept any rate of wages whatsoever; for in the same way as he is free to work or not, so is he free to accept a small remuneration or even none at all. But this is a mere abstract supposition; the labor of the workingman is not only his personal attribute, but it is *necessary;* and this makes all the difference. The preservation of life is the bounden duty of one and all, and to be wanting therein is a crime. It follows that each one has a right to procure what is required in order to live; and the poor can procure it in no other way than through work and wages.

Let it be then taken for granted that workman and employer should, as a rule, make free agreements, and in particular should agree freely as to the wages; nevertheless, there underlies a dictate of natural justice more imperious and ancient than any bargain between man and man, namely, that remuneration ought to be sufficient to support a frugal and well-behaved wage-earner. If through necessity or fear of a worse evil the workman accept harder conditions because an employer or contractor will afford him no better, he is made the victim of force and injustice. In these and similar questions, however —such as, for example, the hours of labor in different trades, the sanitary precautions to be observed in factories and workshops, etc.— in order to supersede undue interference on the part of the State, especially as circumstances, times, and localities differ so widely, it is advisable that recourse be had to societies or boards such as We shall mention presently, or to some other mode of safeguarding the interests of the wage-earners; the State being appealed to, should circumstances require, for its sanction and protection.

If a workman's wages be sufficient to enable him to maintain himself, his wife, and his children in reasonable comfort, he will not find it difficult, if he be a sensible man, to study economy; and he will not fail, by cutting down expenses, to put by some little savings and thus secure a small income. Nature and reason alike would urge him to this. We have seen that this great labor question cannot be solved save by assuming as a principle that private ownership must be held sacred and inviolable. The law, therefore, should favor ownership, and its policy should be to induce as many as possible of the humbler class to become owners.

Many excellent results will follow from this; and first of all, property will certainly become more equitably divided. For the result of civil change and revolution has been to divide society into two widely differing castes. On the one side there is the party which holds power because it holds wealth; which has in its grasp the whole of labor and trade; which manipulates for its own benefit and its own purposes all the sources of supply, and which is even represented in the councils of the State itself. On the other side there is the needy and powerless multitude, broken down and suffering, and ever ready for disturbance. If working-people can be encouraged to look forward to obtaining a share in the land, the consequence will be that the gulf between vast wealth and sheer poverty will be bridged over, and the respective classes will be brought nearer to one another. A further consequence will result in the greater abundance of the fruits of the earth. Men always work harder and more readily when they work on that which belongs to them; nay, they learn to love the very soil that yields, in response to the labor of their hands, not only food to eat but an abundance of good things for themselves and those that are dear to them. That such a spirit of willing labor would add to the produce of the earth and to the wealth of the community is self-evident. And a third advantage would spring from this: men would cling to the country in which they were born; for no one would exchange his country for a foreign land if his own afforded him the means of living a decent and happy life. These three important benefits, however, can be reckoned on only provided that a man's means be not drained and exhausted by excessive taxation. The right to possess private property is derived from nature, not from man; and the State has the right to control its use in the interests of the public good alone, but by no means to absorb it altogether. The State would therefore be unjust and cruel if under the name of taxation it were to deprive the private owner of more than is fitting.

In the last place—employers and workmen may of themselves effect much in the matter we are treating, by means of such associations and organizations as afford opportune aid to those who are in distress, and which draw the two classes more closely together. Among these may be enumerated societies for mutual help; various benevolent foundations established by private persons to provide for the workman, and for his widow or his orphans, in case of sudden calamity, in sickness, and in the event of death; and what are called "patronages," or institutions for the care of boys and girls, for young people, as well as homes for the aged.

The most important of all are workingmen's unions; for these virtually include all the rest. History attests what excellent results were brought about by the artificers' guilds of olden times. They were the means of affording not only many advantages to the workmen, but in no small degree of promoting the advancement of art, as numerous monuments remain to bear witness. Such unions should be suited to the requirements of this our age—an age of wider education, of different habits, and of far more numerous requirements in daily life. It is gratifying to know that there are actually in existence not a few associations of this nature, consisting either of workmen alone, or of workmen and employers together; but it were greatly to be desired that they should become more numerous and more efficient. We have spoken of them more than once; yet it will be well to explain here how notably they are needed, to show that they exist of their own right, and what should be their organization and their mode of action.

The consciousness of his own weakness urges man to call in aid from without. We read in the pages of holy writ: *It is better that two should be together than one; for they have the advantage of their society. If one fall he shall be supported by the other. Woe to him that is alone, for when he falleth he hath none to lift him up.** And further: *A brother that is helped by his brother is like a strong city.*† It is this natural impulse which binds men together in civil society; and it is likewise this which leads them to join together in associations of citizen with citizen, associations which, it is true, cannot be called societies in the full sense of the word, but which, notwithstanding, *are* societies.

These lesser societies and the society which constitutes the State differ in many respects, because their immediate purpose and aim is different. Civil society exists for the common good, and hence is concerned with the interests of all in general, albeit with individual interests also in their due place and degree. It is therefore called *public* society, because by its agency, as St. Thomas of Aquin says, "Men establish relations in common with one another in the setting up of a commonwealth." ‡ But societies which are formed in the bosom of the State are styled *private*, and rightly so, since their immediate purpose is the private advantage of the associates. "Now a private society," says St. Thomas again, "is one which is formed for the purpose of carrying out private objects; as when two or three enter into partnership with the view of trading in common." § Private societies, then, although they exist within the State, and are severally part of the State, cannot nevertheless be absolutely, and as such, prohibited by the State. For to enter into a "society" of this kind is the natural right of man; and the State is bound to protect natural rights, not to destroy them; and if it forbid its citizens to form associations, it con-

* Ecclesiastes iv. 9, 10.
† Prov. xviii. 19.
‡ Contra impugnantes Dei cultum et religionem, ii.
§ Ibid.

tradicts the very principle of its own existence; for both they and it exist in virtue of the like principle, namely, the natural tendency of man to dwell in society.

There are occasions, doubtless, when it is fitting that the law should intervene to prevent associations; as when men join together for purposes which are evidently bad, unlawful, or dangerous to the State. In such cases public authority may justly forbid the formation of associations, and may dissolve them if they already exist. But every precaution should be taken not to violate the rights of individuals and not to impose unreasonable regulations under pretence of public benefit. For laws only bind when they are in accordance with right reason, and hence with the eternal law of God.*

And here we are reminded of the confraternities, societies, and religious orders which have arisen by the Church's authority and the piety of Christian men. The annals of every nation down to our own days bear witness to what they have accomplished for the human race. It is indisputable that on grounds of reason alone such associations, being perfectly blameless in their objects, possess the sanction of the law of nature. In their religious aspect, they claim rightly to be responsible to the Church alone. The rulers of the State accordingly have no rights over them, nor can they claim any share in their control; on the contrary, it is the duty of the State to respect and cherish them, and, if need be, to defend them from attack. It is notorious that a very different course has been followed, more especially in our own times. In many places the State authorities have laid violent hands on these communities, and committed manifold injustice against them; it has placed them under control of the civil law, taken away their rights as corporate bodies, and despoiled them of their property. In such property the Church had her rights, each member of the body had his or her rights, and there were also the rights of those who had founded or endowed these communities for a definite purpose, and furthermore, of those for whose benefit and assistance they had their being. Therefore We cannot refrain from complaining of such spoliation as unjust and fraught with evil results; and with all the more reason do We complain because, at the very time when the law proclaims that association is free to all, We see that Catholic societies, however peaceful and useful, are

---

* "Human law is law only by virtue of its accordance with right reason; and thus it is manifest that it flows from the eternal law. And in so far as it deviates from right reason it is called an unjust law; in such case it is no law at all, but rather a species of violence."—St. Thomas of Aquin, Summa Theologica, 1a 2ae Q. xciii. art. 3.

hampered in every way, whereas the utmost liberty is conceded to individuals whose purposes are at once hurtful to religion and dangerous to the State.

Associations of every kind, and especially those of workingmen, are now far more common than heretofore. As regards many of these there is no need at present to inquire whence they spring, what are their objects, or what the means they employ. There is a good deal of evidence, however, which goes to prove that many of these societies are in the hands of secret leaders, and are managed on principles ill-according with Christianity and the public well-being; and that they do their utmost to get within their grasp the whole field of labor, and force workingmen either to join them or to starve. Under these circumstances Christian workingmen must do one of two things: either join associations in which their religion will be exposed to peril, or form associations among themselves—unite their forces and shake off courageously the yoke of so unrighteous and intolerable an oppression. No one who does not wish to expose man's chief good to extreme risk will for a moment hesitate to say that the second alternative should by all means be adopted.

Those Catholics are worthy of all praise—and they are not a few—who, understanding what the times require, have striven, by various undertakings and endeavors, to better the condition of the working class without any sacrifice of principle being involved. They have taken up the cause of the workingman, and have spared no efforts to better the condition both of families and individuals; to infuse a spirit of equity into the mutual relations of employers and employed; to keep before the eyes of both classes the precepts of duty and the laws of the Gospel—that Gospel which by inculcating self-restraint, keeps men within the bounds of moderation, and tends to establish harmony among the divergent interests, and the various classes which compose the State. It is with such ends in view that we see men of eminence meeting together for discussion, for the promotion of concerted action, and for practical work. Others, again, strive to unite workingmen of various grades into associations, help them with their advice and means, and enable them to obtain fitting and profitable employment. The bishops, on their part, bestow their ready good-will and support; and with their approval and guidance many members of the clergy, both secular and regular, labor assiduously in behalf of the spiritual and mental interests of the members of such associations. And there are not wanting Catholics blessed with affluence, who have, as it were, cast in their lot with the wage-earners, and who have spent large sums in founding and widely spreading benefit and insurance societies, by means of which the workingman may without difficulty acquire, through his labor, not only many present advantages but also the certainty of honorable support in days to come. How greatly such manifold and earnest activity has benefited the community at large is too well known to require Us to dwell upon it. We find therein grounds for most cheering hope in the future, provided always that the associations We have described continue to grow and spread, and are well and wisely administered. Let the State watch over these societies of citizens banded together for the exercise of their rights; but let it not thrust itself into their peculiar concerns and their organization; for things move and live by the spirit inspiring them, and may be killed by the rough grasp of a hand from without.

In order, then, that an association may be carried on with unity of purpose and harmony of action, its organization and government should be firm and wise. All such societies, being free to exist, have the further right to adopt such rules and organizations as may best conduce to the attainment of their respective objects. We do not judge it expedient to enter into minute particulars touching the subject of organization; this must depend on national character, on practice and experience, on the nature and aim of the work to be done, on the scope of the various trades and employments, and on other circumstances of fact and of time—all of which should be carefully considered.

To sum up, then, We may lay it down as a general and lasting law, that workingmen's associations should be so organized and governed as to furnish the best and most suitable means for attaining what is aimed at; that is to say, for helping each individual member to better his condition to the utmost in body, mind, and property. It is clear that they must pay special and chief attention to the duties of religion and morality, and that their internal discipline must be guided very strictly by these weighty considerations; otherwise they would lose wholly their special character, and end by becoming little better than those societies which take no account whatever of religion. What advantage can it be to a workingman to obtain by means of a society all that he requires, and to endanger his soul for lack of spiritual food? *What doth it profit a man if he gain the whole world and suffer the loss of his own soul?* * This, as Our Lord teaches, is the mark or character that distinguishes the Christian from the heathen. *After all these things do the heathens seek. . . . Seek ye first the kingdom of God and His justice, and all these things shall be added*

* Matt. xvi. 26.

*unto you.** Let our associations, then, look first and before all things
to God; let religious instruction have therein the foremost place, each
one being carefully taught what is his duty to God, what he has to
believe, what to hope for, and how he is to work out his salvation;
and let all be warned and strengthened with special care against
wrong principles and false teaching. Let the workingman be urged
and led to the worship of God, to the earnest practice of religion, and,
among other things, to the keeping holy of Sundays and holydays.
Let him learn to reverence and love Holy Church, the common
Mother of us all; and hence to obey the precepts of the Church, and
to frequent the sacraments, since they are the means ordained by
God for obtaining forgiveness of sin and for leading a holy life.

The foundations of the organization being thus laid in religion, We
next proceed to make clear the relations of the members one to another, in order that they may live together in concord and go forward
prosperously and with good results. The offices and charges of the
society should be apportioned for the good of the society itself, and
in such mode that difference in degree or standing should not interfere with unanimity and good-will. Office-bearers should be appointed
with due prudence and discretion, and each one's charge should be
carefully mapped out. Hereby no member will suffer injury. Let the
common funds be administered with strict honesty, in such a way that
a member may receive assistance in proportion to his necessities. The
rights and duties of the employers, as compared with the rights and
duties of the employed, ought to be the subject of careful consideration. Should it happen that either a master or a workman believe himself injured, nothing would be more desirable than that a committee
should be appointed composed of reliable and capable members of
the association, whose duty would be, conformably with the rules of
the association, to settle the dispute. Among the several purposes
of a society one should be to try to arrange for a continuous supply of
work at all times and seasons, as well as to create a fund out of which
the members may be effectually helped in their needs, not only in
cases of accident but also in sickness, old age, and distress.

Such rules and regulations, if willingly obeyed by all, will sufficiently ensure the well-being of the poor; whilst such mutual associations among Catholics are certain to be productive in no small degree
of prosperity to the State. It is not rash to conjecture the future from
the past. Age gives way to age, but the events of one century are
wonderfully like those of another; for they are directed by the provi-

* Matt. vi. 32, 33.

dence of God, who overrules the course of history in accordance with His purposes in creating the race of man. We are told that it was cast as a reproach on the Christians in the early ages of the Church that the greater number among them had to live by begging or by labor. Yet, destitute though they were of wealth and influence, they ended by winning over to their side the favor of the rich and the good-will of the powerful. They showed themselves industrious, hard-working, assiduous, and peaceful, ruled by justice, and, above all, bound together in brotherly love. In presence of such mode of life and such example, prejudice gave way, the tongue of malevolence was silenced, and the lying legends of ancient superstition little by little yielded to Christian truth.

At the time being, the condition of the working classes is the pressing question of the hour; and nothing can be of higher interest to all classes of the State than that it should be rightly and reasonably adjusted. But it will be easy for Christian workingmen to decide it aright if they will form associations, choose wise guides, and follow on the path which with so much advantage to themselves and the commonweal was trodden by their fathers before them. Prejudice, it is true, is mighty, and so is the greed of money; but if the sense of what is just and rightful be not debased through depravity of heart, their fellow-citizens are sure to be won over to a kindly feeling towards men whom they see to be in earnest as regards their work and who prefer so unmistakably right dealing to mere lucre, and the sacredness of duty to every other consideration.

And further great advantage would result from the state of things We are describing; there would exist so much more ground for hope, and likelihood even, of recalling to a sense of their duty those workingmen who have either given up their faith altogether, or whose lives are at variance with its precepts. Such men feel in most cases that they have been fooled by empty promises and deceived by false pretexts. They cannot but perceive that their grasping employers too often treat them with great inhumanity and hardly care for them outside the profit their labor brings; and if they belong to any union, it is probably one in which there exists, instead of charity and love, that intestine strife which ever accompanies poverty when unresigned and unsustained by religion. Broken in spirit and worn down in body, how many of them would gladly free themselves from such galling bondage! But human respect, or the dread of starvation, makes them tremble to take the step. To such as these Catholic associations are of incalculable service, by helping them out of their

difficulties, inviting them to companionship, and receiving the returning wanderers to a haven where they may securely find repose.

We have now laid before you, Venerable Brethren, both who are
the persons and what are the means whereby this most arduous
question must be solved. Every one should put his hand to the work
which falls to his share, and that at once and straightway, lest the
evil which is already so great become through delay absolutely beyond remedy. Those who rule the State should avail them of the laws
and institutions of the country; masters and wealthy owners must be
mindful of their duty; the poor, whose interests are at stake, should
make every lawful and proper effort; and since religion alone, as We
said at the beginning, can avail to destroy the evil at its root, all men
should rest persuaded that the main thing needful is to return to real
Christianity, apart from which all the plans and devices of the wisest
will prove of little avail.

In regard to the Church, her co-operation will never be found
lacking, be the time or the occasion what it may; and she will intervene with all the greater effect in proportion as her liberty of action
is the more unfettered. Let this be carefully taken to heart by those
whose office it is to safeguard the public welfare. Every minister of
holy religion must bring to the struggle the full energy of his mind
and all his power of endurance. Moved by your authority, Venerable
Brethren, and quickened by your example, they should never cease
to urge upon men of every class, upon the high-placed as well as the
lowly, the Gospel doctrines of Christian life; by every means in their
power they must strive to secure the good of the people; and above
all must earnestly cherish in themselves, and try to arouse in others,
charity, the mistress and the queen of virtues. For the happy results
we all long for must be chiefly brought about by the plenteous out-
pouring of charity; of that true Christian charity which is the fulfilling of the whole Gospel law, which is always ready to sacrifice itself
for others' sake, and is man's surest antidote against worldly pride
and immoderate love of self; that charity whose office is described
and whose Godlike features are outlined by the Apostle St. Paul in
these words: *Charity is patient, is kind, . . . seeketh not her own,
. . . suffereth all things, . . . endureth all things.**

* 1 Corr. xiii. 4-7.

The Oxford Conference

1937

The Oxford Conference on Church, Community, and State gathered together some 425 persons, three hundred of them appointed by the principal Protestant denominations in England, the United States, the British Dominions, and continental Europe. Reports were adopted by the Conference on such themes as Church and Community, Church and State, and Church, Community, and State in Relation to Education. What appears below is part of the Report on the Relation of Church, Community, and State to the Economic Order.

In tone this document reflects the economic liberalism that characterized much church opinion during the 1930's. In measured words, the report attacks acquisitiveness, unfair inequalities of opportunity and divisive class distinctions, irresponsible economic power, and the character of employments that make it impossible for men to find a "sense of Christian vocation in their daily life." At the same time, the report takes pains to warn the reader that human problems are personal problems of sin and guilt, not simply external, institutional troubles.

What can the Christian do? Here the report is at its most vague. The Christian members of the community ought to "bear witness to their faith within the existing economic order." They ought also to ". . . test all economic institutions in the light of their understanding of God's will." Almost at once the writers of the report warn against a general expectation of agreement among Christians, especially on issues where "technical factors predominate," or where opinions naturally differ because of disparate "economic, geographical, and historical circumstances." A severe secular critic of the Conference's statement might accuse its writers of yielding to something very like the ethical relativism which the religious routinely condemn. What is certain at any rate is the surrender of jurisdiction at the key moment where the problems become difficult and technical.

The selection is from The Churches Survey Their Task, *The Report of the Oxford Conference on Church, Community, and State (London: George Allen & Unwin, Ltd., 1937), pp. 87-90. Reprinted by permission of George Allen & Unwin, Ltd., and World Council of Churches.*

Summary Statements

1. THE RELEVANCE OF THE CHRISTIAN GOSPEL TO THE ECONOMIC ORDER

The Christian Church approaches the problems of the social and economic order from the standpoint of her faith in the revelation of God in Christ. Through His redemptive work Christ made the whole range of human life subject to that law of love which He perfectly embodied in His own life and death. The charter of Christian practice is therefore given to us in that second commandment which Christ said to be like unto the first, and without obedience to which the first could not be obeyed—namely, "Thou shalt love thy neighbour as thyself." Obedience to this commandment of love in the economic sphere means the pursuit of justice. Christians must therefore do everything in their power to create a more just ordering of economic life, by attempting to secure for all who are their neighbours such opportunities as are necessary for their full development as persons in body, mind, and spirit. The responsibility of the Church is to insist on the true relationship of spiritual and economic goods. Our human wealth consists in fellowship with God and in Him with our brethren. To this fellowship the whole economic order must be made subservient.

2. THE CHIEF POINTS IN THE ECONOMIC SPHERE AT WHICH THE PURPOSE OF GOD IS CHALLENGED

The subordination of God's purpose for human life to the demands of the economic process seems in practice to be a tendency common to all existing kinds of economic organization. In particular we draw attention to certain features of modern life in the so-called capitalist countries of the world.

(1) The ordering of economic life has tended to enhance acquisitiveness and to set up a false standard of economic and social success.

(2) Indefensible inequalities of opportunity in regard to education, leisure, and health continue to prevail; and the existence of economic classes presents an obstacle to human fellowship which cannot be tolerated by the Christian conscience.

(3) Centres of economic power have been formed which are not responsible to any organ of the community and which in practice constitute something in the nature of a tyranny over the lives of masses of men.

(4) The only forms of employment open to many men and women, or the fact that none is open at all, prevent them from finding a sense of Christian vocation in their daily life.

3. HOSTILITY TO CHRISTIANITY OF SOME MOVEMENTS WHICH HAVE ARISEN IN CONSEQUENCE OF THESE EVILS

We are witnessing new movements which have arisen in reaction to these evils but which combine with their struggle for social justice the repudiation of all religious faith. Aware of the reality of sin, the Church knows that no change in the outward ordering of life can of itself eradicate social evil. The Church, therefore, cannot surrender to the utopian expectations of these movements, and their godlessness it must unequivocally reject; but in doing so it must recognize that Christians in their blindness to the challenging evils of the economic order have been partly responsible for the anti-religious character of these movements.

4. THE RESPONSE OF THE CHRISTIAN TO THESE CHALLENGES

Christians have a double duty—both to bear witness to their faith within the existing economic order, and also to test all economic institutions in the light of their understanding of God's will. The forces of evil against which Christians have to contend are found not only in the hearts of men as individuals, but have entered into and infected the structure of society, and there also must be combated.

In spite of agreement on the necessity of effecting changes in the economic order, Christians have no reason to expect that they will always find themselves in agreement on particular issues or belonging to one political party. This is especially true of issues in which technical factors predominate, concerning which honest differences of judgment must be expected. Nor do Christians escape those deeper differences of social conviction which are rooted in differing economic, geographical, and historical circumstances. The very recognition of this fact by all groups within the Church might well mitigate the extremism to which each group is tempted. The Church should be a fellowship in Christ which transcends differences of judgment and divergences of action in relation to the concrete economic situation.

Reinhold Niebuhr

1892–

Reinhold Niebuhr's enormous contribution to the political and theological thought of our time has frequently taken the shape of emphasis upon the complexities and the dilemmas of human action. In the economic sphere, as in others, the individual must compromise between the law of love and the law of self-love. The tragic ambiguity of action, as perceived by Niebuhr, leads him to criticize both the rational certainties of Catholic natural law and the individualistic assurance of many Protestants.

The realism of Niebuhr's approach to economic behavior leads to an absence of specific injunction and detailed guide to the intricate problems a Christian executive faces when he endeavors to balance the rival claims of his customers, his stockholders, his employees, his suppliers, his community, and his family. It has little to say to the lender about the height of the interest he may charge and the terms of the loan he extends. And it offers no help to the union official who must reconcile the claims of his members, the interests of the economy, and the valid personal claims of his own ambitions.

Niebuhr's statement fairly represents the ethical difficulty. The norms of economic behavior are not moral. The economist usually states them as commitments to efficiency, variety, and economic progress. Ethical norms must come from outside economic life. But it is prodigiously difficult to apply these norms to the technical data of actual business life. Even medieval efforts to proscribe usury and regulate prices broke down under the impetus of economic change and economic development. In the end the best that Niebuhr can recommend is increased personal sensitivity to moral conflict. His hope is a circumscribed one: ". . . a genuine Christian contribution to the ideological conflict in democratic society must serve to miti-

gate, rather than aggravate, the severity of the conflict; for it will prevent men from heedlessly seeking their own interests in the name of justice and from recklessly denominating value preferences, other than their own, as evil."

This selection is drawn from "The Christian Faith and the Economic Life of Liberal Society," by Reinhold Niebuhr, from Goals of Economic Life, *edited by A. Dudley Ward, pp. 438-49. Copyright, 1953, by The Federal Council of the Churches of Christ in America. Reprinted by permission of Harper & Brothers. The volume itself is a valuable collection of efforts by specialists in many disciplines to relate economic life and ethical values.*

Ethics and Economics

The question is how the Christian faith enters this debate or makes significant contributions to its solution. Most thoughtful readers will observe that several authors, social scientists of great repute, have considered the ethical problems of our economic life without explicit recourse to uniquely Christian standards of judgment. Yet they are practically unanimous in finding no source for ethical standards in pure economic analyses and in recognizing that ethical norms are nevertheless either implicitly or explicitly involved in the judgments which economists and other social scientists make about our common life. All of these ethical judgments might, however, be reduced to varying interpretations of the concept of "justice." No doubt the Christian heritage of our civilization colors our ideas of justice, even when the civilization has become highly secularized. But no civilization can exist without some notion of justice, for it is not possible to form a real community if its several members do not have the desire to "give each man his due."

Does the Christian faith add anything significant to the concept of justice? The most immediate answer to this question is that it subordinates justice to an even higher standard, that of love. According to Christ, "all the law and the prophets" are summarized in the twofold love commandment, which enjoins both the love of God and the love of the neighbor. However, if it is assumed that the Christian contribution to economic and political life is simply contained in the purity of its ethical ideal of love (an assumption which some modern versions of the Christian faith have sought to inculcate), the relation of Christianity to man's economic and political life would seem to become even more problematic. For the question would then arise whether this ideal has any relevance to the organization of economic or political society. The most ideal social possibility for man may well be so perfect an accord of life with life that each member of a community is ready to sacrifice his interests for the sake of others. But, as David Hume observed, politics (and for that matter economics too) must assume the selfishness of men.

It is certainly significant, as Professor Snygg suggests in his chapter, that the highest religious visions of the good life always culminate in the concept of this perfect accord. The ideal of love is not superimposed upon human history by scriptural, or any other, authority. Human existence, when profoundly analyzed, yields the law of love as the final law of human freedom. Man's unique freedom, in which he rises indeterminately above his determinate existence, requires that his life be fulfilled not within himself but in others. It also requires that this realization of himself in others should not be pursued merely from his own standpoint. That is, he cannot regard others simply as tools and instruments of his self-realization.

Yet that is precisely what he is inclined to do. Any religious faith which merely discovers the law of love but does not also make men aware of the other law, that of self-love, is a sentimental perversion of Christianity. It is a perversion which lacks true inwardness of religious experience. For in such experience men become aware, as St. Paul testified, not only of the final law of life but of another law "which wars against the law that is in my mind."

It is from the standpoint of both of these laws, from the recognition of the validity of the one and the reality of the other, that Christianity must make its contribution to the organization of man's common life, whether in economic or in political terms. From the standpoint of the law of love every scheme and structure of justice will be recognized to be tentative and provisional. Not merely the positive law of particular communities but also the notions of justice, from the standpoint of which positive law is criticized, are touched by interest and passion. They always contain an ideological element, for they tend to justify a given equilibrium of power in a given historical situation.

It was an achievement of Catholic moral theory that it recognized the necessity of standards of justice for the institutional life of mankind below the level of love. But it was a weakness in the theory that love became a "counsel of perfection" and lost its dialectical relation to the law of justice. Justice, meanwhile, was conceived in terms of classic rationalism. It was assumed that human history, like nature, had an inflexible structure to which human actions must conform.

The standards of human conduct and of human association, ostensibly derived from an inflexible "natural law," were, however, conditioned by the peculiar power relations of the feudal-agrarian culture. Such standards could not be applied adequately to the new economic vitalities and interests developed by the rising middle-class civilization.

The consequence of this situation was the open rebellion of middle-class life against traditional standards of justice. They had become instruments of injustice precisely because they covered particular historical social forms with the aura of the absolute. In the relation of religion to culture it is important to distinguish sharply between the absolute and the relative. If the authority of religion is used primarily to give absolute validity to relative values, the consequence is a fanaticism which Professor Knight deprecates as a characteristic fruit of religion. It is characteristic from the standpoint of modern culture to ascribe fanaticism to religion, and not without cause. It is, however, significant that modern culture, which hoped to destroy religious fanaticism by the power of reason, did not anticipate the even more grievous fanaticisms of modern political religions which would express themselves in the name of reason and of science. Modern culture did not, in short, measure the depth of this problem, or rightly gauge the persistence with which men will use standards of justice as instruments of their interest and use religion to obscure, and thus to aggravate, the ideological taint in their reasoning about justice.

A modern Protestant analogue to Catholic conceptions of "natural law" is the tendency of certain types of Protestant pietistic individualism to endow "natural law," as eighteenth-century rationalism conceived it, with religious sanction. Thus the characteristic prejudices of middle-class life, its tendency toward extravagant individualism, its lack of a sense of community or justice, its devotion to the principles of laissez faire, are falsely raised to religious absolutes; and confusion is worse confounded. Recently there has been a strong recrudescence of this type of thought in Protestant circles; and it has been so heavily financed by interested political and economic groups that its ideological corruption is even more evident than was the religious support of traditional "natural law" concepts at the rise of modern commercial society.

Standards of justice may be said to be (1) expressions of the law of love, insofar as the love of the neighbor requires a calculation of competitive claims when there is more than one neighbor and (2) a practical compromise between the law of love and the law of self-love. They are a compromise in the sense that norms of justice seek to arrive at an equitable adjustment of conflicting claims, assuming the selfish inclination of men to take advantage of each other. A Christian contribution to standards of justice in economic and political life must therefore not be found primarily in a precise formulation of the standard. It must be found rather in strengthening both the inclination to seek the neighbor's good and the contrite awareness that we are not inclined to do this. The inclination to seek the neighbor's good must be accompanied by an awareness that every norm of justice is but a very relative approximation of this goal. The awareness that even good men are not consistently inclined to do this will lay bare the ideological taint, the corruption of self-interest, in every historic standard.

Thus a genuine Christian contribution to the ideological conflict in democratic society must serve to mitigate, rather than aggravate, the severity of the conflict; for it will prevent men from heedlessly seeking their own interests in the name of justice and from recklessly denominating value preferences, other than their own, as evil. If Christian piety or any other kind of piety does not yield these fruits of humility and charity, it must be consistently rejected as the "salt that has lost its savor."

Part II | **THE HEROIC STATESMAN**

While it is extravagant to see in this Elizabethan attempt to regulate wages the beginnings of the welfare state, the Statute of Artificers did reflect a concern over the impact of rising prices upon labor and a continuing preoccupation with equity, which is an extension of medieval doctrines of just price. Wages were to be set locally by Justices of the Peace and the objective was to raise them to the level set by the earlier Statute of Laborers, which rising prices had rendered inoperative. The Justices of the Peace very frequently were interested parties. As large employers of labor, they tended to reaffirm wage rates rather than to adjust them according to the fluctuations of prices. The mechanism of annual review is described in this passage:

> . . . the justices of the peace of every shire . . . and the sheriff of that county if he conveniently may, and every mayor, bailiff or other head office within any city . . . shall before the 10th day of June next coming, and afterward yearly at every general sessions first to be holden after Easter . . . calling unto them such discreet and grave persons of the said country or city as they shall think meet, and conferring together respecting the plenty or scarcity of the time and other circumstances necessary to be considered, have authority within the limits of their several commissions to rate and appoint the wages as well of such of the said artificers. . . .

But the Statute endeavored to do much more than set wages. As its detailed provisions suggest, it sought to regulate the relations between master and servant, apprentice and employer, and buyer and seller. It was a major effort to design a national labor policy for the realm of England. As is usual in English public administration, enforcement was never complete and always variable. Nevertheless, it *was a sufficient annoyance as late as 1776 to lead Adam Smith to attack it, and it was not actually repealed until the nineteenth century.*

The spelling and diction of the original statute are retained. The selection is from Tudor Economic Documents, *edited by* R. H Tawney and Eileen Power *(England: Longmans, 1924), pp. 338-49.*

The Statute of Artificers (5 Eliz. c. 4), 1563[*]

An Acte towching dyvers Orders for Artificers Laborers Servantes of Husbandrye and apprentises.

Althoughe there remayne and stande in force presentlie a greate nombre of Actes and Statutes concernynge the reteynynge departinge wages and orders of Apprentices Servantes and Laborers, as well in husbandrye as in diuers other Artes Misteries and occupacions, yet partlye for thimperfeccion and contraritie that is founde and doo appere in sondrie of the saide Lawes, and for the varietie and nombre of them, and chieflie for that the wages and allouances lymytted and rated in many of the said statutes are in dyuerse places to small and not answerable to this tyme, respecting thaduancement of pryses of all thinges belonginge to the saide seruantes and laborers, the saide lawes cannot convenyentlie withoute the greate greyfe and burden of the poore laborer and hired man, be put in good and due execution: and as the saide severall Actes and Statutes were at the tyme of the makinge of them thought to be very good and beneficiall for the common welthe of this Realme, *as dyvers of them yet are,* So yf the substaunce of the manny of the saide lawes as are mete to be contynued shalbe digested and reduced into one sole lawe and statute, And in the same an unyforme ordre prescribed and lymytted concernynge the wages and other ordres for apprentices seruauntes and laborers, their is good hope that it will come to passe that the same lawe, beinge duelie executed, shoulde bannyshe idlenes, avaunce husbandrie, and yelde unto the hyred persone bothe in the tyme of scarcitie and in the tyme of plentie a convenyent proporcion of Wages.

I. *Be it therefore* enacted . . . That as moche of all the estatutes heretofore made, and every braunche of them as touche or concerne the hyringe kepinge departinge woorckinge wages or ordre of ser-

[*] The printed text of this act will be found in Stats. of the Realm, Vol. IV., Pt. I, pp. 414-22. The present text has been copied from the original statute in the House of Lords and differs in spelling from the printed version. Words and sentences in italics are additions made in the bill after engrossment and are therefore amendments made in the later stages of the bill's progress through the Houses.

vantes Workemen Artificers apprentices and laborers, or any of them, and the penalties and forfeytures concernyng the same shalbe from and after the last daye of Septembre nexte ensuynge repealed. . . .

II. And be it further enacted . . . that no manner of persone or persones after the foresaide laste daye of Septembre . . . shall reteyne hyre or take into service, or cause to be reteyned hyred or taken into service, nor any persone shalbee reteyned, or hyred, or taken into service, by any meanes or collour to worcke for anny lesse tyme, or terme, then forr one hoole yere in any of the sciences craftes mysterys or arts of clotheires, wollen clothe wevers, tuckers, fullers, Clothworkers, Sheremen, dyers, hosyers, *Taylours,* shomakers, Tanners, Pewterers, Bakers, Brewers, Glovers, Cutlers, Smythes, Ferroers, *Curryers,* Sadlers, spurryers, Turners, Cappers, Hatmakers or feltemakers, Bowyers, fletchers, arrowhedmakers, Butchers, Cookes, *or* Myllers.

III. . . . That every person being unmarryed, and every *other* person being under thage of thirtie yeres, that after the Feaste of Easter next shall marrye, and havinge bene brought upp in anny of the saide Artes, craftes or sciences, or that hath used or exercysed anny of them by the space of three yeres or more, and not havinge landes, Tenementes, Rentes or Heredyamentes, Copyholde or Freholde, of one estate of inherytaunce, or for terme of anny Lyfe or lyves of the clere value of xl *s.,* nor beinge worth of his owen Goodes the clere value of x poundes, and so allowed by twoo Justices of the peace of the Countie [etc.] . . . nor beinge reteyned with anny person in husbondrie, or in anny of thaforesaide Artes . . . nor llaufullie reteyned in anny other Arte or Science, nor . . . in housholde, or in anny office with anny noble man gentle man or others, accordinge to the lawes of this Realme, nor havinge a convenyent ferme, or other holdinge in tyllage, whereupon he maye employe his Labor, shall, duringe the tyme that he or they shall so be unmarryed, or under the saide Age of xxx^tie yeres, uppon request made by anny person usinge the Arte or mystery, wherein the saide person so required hath beyne exercised as is aforesaide, be reteyned and shall not refuse to serue accordinge to the tenor of this statute, uppon the payne and penaltie hereafter mencioned.

IV. . . . That no person which shall retayne anny servaunte shall putt away his or her said seruaunte and that no person reteyned accordinge to this statute shall departe from his Master, Mistress or Dame before the ende of his or her terme, uppon the payne hereafter mencioned, unles it be for some reasonable and sufficient cause or matter to be allowed before twoo Justices of Peace, or one at the least, within the saide Countie or before the mayor or other chief officer of the citie Burrough or towne corporate, wherin the saide Master [etc.] inhabiteth, to whome anny of the parties greved shall complayne, which saide Justice [etc.] shall haue and take uppon them or hym the hearinge and ordringe of the matter, betwixte the saide Master [etc.] and servaunte accordinge to the equitie of the cause. And that no suche Master [etc.] shall putt awaye anny *suche* servaunte, at thende of his terme, or that anny suche Servaunte shall departe from his Master [etc.] at thend of his terme, withoute one quarter warnynge gyven before thend of his said terme, either by the saide Master [etc.], or servaunte the one to the other, uppon the payne hereafter ensuynge.

V. . . . Every person betwene the age of Twelve yeres and the age of Threescore yeres, not beinge laufullie reteyned, nor apprentice with any fysherman or maryner haunting the Seas, *nor being in Service with any Kyddyer or Carryer of any corne grayne or meale for provision of the citye of London,* nor withe any husbondman in husbondrie, nor in any Citie, Towne Corporate or Market Towne, in any of thartes or Sciences . . . appoynted by this Estatute to haue or take apprentices, nor beinge reteyned by the yere or half the yere at the leaste, for the diggynge seeking, fyndinge, gettinge, meltinge, fynynge, workinge, tryinge, makinge of any Syluer, Tynne, lede, Iron, Coper, Stone, sea coole, stone coole, moore Coole, or Cherk cole, nor beinge occupied in *or aboute* the makinge of any glasse, nor being a gentleman borne, nor beinge a student or scoller *in any* of the universities or in anny scole, nor havinge landes [etc. as above, Section III.] . . . *nor having a ffather or mother than lyvyng, or other Auncestour whose heire apparent he ys, then* having lands [etc.] of the yerely value of x poundes or above, or Goodes or cattelles of the value of xl poundes, nor beinge a necessarie or convenyent officer or servaunt laufullie reteyned as is aforesaid, nor havinge a convenyent ferme, or holdinge wherupon he maye or shall employe his labor, *nor being otherwise lawfully reteyned according to the true meanyng of this Statute,* shall . . . by virtue of this estatute, be compelled to be reteyned to serve in husbandrye by the yere, withe any person that kepeth husbandrie, and will require anny suche person so to serve within the same shire wher he shalbee so requyred.

VI. . . . [Penalty on masters unduly dismissing servants, 40s.; on servants unduly departing or refusing to serve, imprisonment.]

VII. . . . That none of the saide reteyned persons in husbandrye or in eny the artes or sciences above remembred, after the tyme of his reteynor expired, shall departe fourth of one citie towne or parishe to another, nor oute of the . . . Hundred, nor oute of the Countie or Shire where he last served, to serve in any other Citie . . . or Countie, unles he have a testymonyall under the Seale of the saide citie . . . or of the Constable or constables or other head officer and of twoo other honest house holders of the Citie Towne or parishe where he *last* served declaring his lawfull departure . . . , which Sertificatt or Testymonyall shalbe wrytten and delyvered unto the said servaunte and also registred by the Parson Vicar *or* Curate of the Parishe where suche Master [etc.] doth or shall dwell. . . .

VIII. . . . Upon the payne that every suche Servante so departing withoute suche Certificate or Testymonyall shalbe imprysoned untill he procure a testymonyall . . . , the whiche if he cannot doo within the space of xxj dayes next after the first daye of his ymprysonment, then the sayde persone to be whipped and used as a vagabunde . . . ; and that every person reteynyng any suche servaunte withoute showinge suche testymonyall . . . shall forfaite for every suche offence v *li.* And yf any suche person shalbe taken withe any countrefeyte or forged Testymonyall, then to be whipped as a Vacabounde.

IX. . . . That all Artificers and laborers being hyred for wages for the Daye or weeke shall, betwixt the myddest of the monethes of Marche and September, be and continue at there worke at or before v of the clock in the mornyng and contynewe at worke and not Departe untyll betwixt vij and viij of the Cloke at night, except it be in the tyme of breakefast Dynner or Drincking, the which tymes at the most shall not excede above ij howers and a half in the daye, That is to saye at every drynkyng one halfe howre, for his Dynner one hower, and for his Slepe when he is allowed to slepe, the which is from the middest of May to the mydest of August, halfe an houre at the most, and at every Breakefast one halfe hower; and all the saide Artificers and laborers betwene the middest of September and the myddst of Marche, shalbe and contynewe at there worke from the springe of the daye in the mornynge untill the nyght of the same daye, except it be in tyme afore appoynted for breakefast and dynner, upon payne to lose and forfeit one penny for every howers absence, to be deducted . . . oute of his wages that shall so offende.

X. . . . that every artificer and Laborer . . . shall contynewe and not departe from the same worke . . . before the fynyshyng of the said worke, upon payne of ymprysonement by one monethe withoute bayle . . . and the forfeyture of the somme of fyve powndes to the partie from whom he shall so departe. . . .

XI. . . . And for the declaracion and lymytacion what wages serv-

auntes laborers and Artyficers either by the yere or daye or otherwyse shall have and receyve: Bee it enacted . . . that the Justices
of Peace of every shire . . . within the lymytes of their severall
comyssions, *or the more parte of them being then resident within the
same,* and the sherife of that countie if he conveniently may, and
every mayour, bailyf or other hed officer within any citie . . .
wherein is any justice of peace within the lymittes of the said Citie
. . . *shall before the tenthe day of June next commyng, and after-
warde shall yerely* at every general sessions first to *be* holden and
kept after Easter or at some time convenyent within six wekes next
followinge every of the said Feastes of Easter, assembel . . . and
callinge unto them *suche discreate and* grave persons of the said
Countie or of the said Citie or Towne Corporate as they shall thinke
mete, and conferrynge togither respectynge the plentie or scarcity of
the tyme and other circumstaunces, necessaryly to be considered,
shall have authorytie by vertue herof, within the lymytes and Pre-
cinctes of their severall comyssions, to lymyt rate and appoynte the
wage as well of Suche and so many of the said Artificers Handy-
craftesmen . . . or any other laborer, servante or woorkemen whose
wages in tyme past hath bynn by any lawe or statute rated and appoynted, as also the wages of all other laborers . . . which have not
been rated, as they . . . shall thinke mete by their discresions to be
rated . . . by the yere or by the Daye, Weke, Monethe, or otherwyse, with meate and Drincke *or without Meate and Drincke,* and
what Wages every Workman or laborer shall take by the greate for
mowinge, reapinge or thresheinge of corne and grayne, and for mowinge or makinge of heye . . . and for any *other* kynde of reasonable
Laboures or Service: and shall yerely before the xij[th] daye of Iuly
next after the said assessement rate so appointed and made, certifie
the same . . . with the consideracions and causes therof . . . into
the . . . Courte of Chauncerey, wheruppon it shalbe lawfull to
the lorde chauncellor of Englande or Lorde keper . . . upon Declaracion therof to the queenes majestie . . . to cause to be prynted
and sent downe, before the first daye of September next after the
said Certificat, into every County . . . x or xij Proclamacions or
more conteynyng in every of them the severall rates appoynted . . .
with commaundement . . . straightly tobserve the same and to all
Iustices [etc.] . . . to se the same duelie and severely observed
. . . ; uppon receyte wherof the saide Shirefes Iustices etc. shall
cause the same proclamacion to be entred of record . . . and . . .
shall fourthewithe in open Markettes upon the market dayes before
mychhelmas then ensuynge, cause the same proclamacion to be pro-

claymed . . . and to be fixed in some convenient Place . . . ; And if the saide shrifes Iustices [etc.] shall at there saide generall Sessions, or at any tyme after within vj wekes then following . . . thinke it convenyent to reteyne and kepe for the yere then to come the rates of Wages that they certefied the yere before or to chaunge . . . them, . . . they shall before the saide xij^{th} day of Iuly yerely certyfie into the saide Courte of chauncerey theire resoluciones . . . to thintente that proclamacions may accordingly be renewed and sent downe; And if yt shall happen that ther be no nede of any . . . alteracion of the rates . . . then the proclamacions for the yere past shall remayne in force.

XII. . . . *That yf all the said justices . . . doo not . . . assemble . . . and rate the Wages . . . or be negligent . . . then every Justice . . . by some credible person assessed and taxed in the Booke of Subsidie . . . to the clere value of Fyve Poundes at the least, or by such other person as the most part of such Justices shall allow and accept to take suche othe, shall for such Negligence forfeite unto her queenes majestie . . . Tenne Pounds.*

XIII. [Penalty for giving wages higher than the rate, ten days imprisonment and fine of 5 *l.*; for receiving the same, twenty-one days' imprisonment.]

XIV. [Penalty on servants, etc., assaulting masters, etc., one years' imprisonment.]

XV. Prouided . . . that in the tyme of hey or corne harvest, the Iustices of Pease . . . and also the cunstable or other hed officer of every towneshipe, vpon request and for thavoydinge of the losse of any corne grayne or heye, shall and may cause all suche artyficers and persons as be mete to labour . . . to serve by the daye for the mowinge reapinge . . . inning of corne, grayne and hey . . . , and that none of the saide persons shall refuse so to do vpon paine to suffer ymprysonment in the stockes by the space of twoo daies and one nyght . . .

XVI. . . . all persons of the Counties where they haue accustomed to go into other Shires for Harvest worke and havinge at the tyme no Harvest worke sufficient in the same towne nor countie . . . bringinge . . . a testimoniall . . . may repayre . . . unto any other place or countie for the onely nowynge reapinge, [etc.].

XVII. . . . That twoo Iustices of Pease, the Mayor or other Hed Officer of any Citie [etc.] and twoo aldermen, or twoo other discrete burgesses . . . yf there be no aldermen, shall and may by vertue herof appoynt any suche woman as is of thage of xii yeres and vnder thage of xl yeres and vnmaryed and furthe of service . . . to be reteyned or serve by the yere or by the weke or day, for suche wages and in suche reasonable sorte and maner as they shall thinke mete: And if any suche woman shall refuse so to serve, then it shalbe lawfull for the saide Iustices [etc.] to commyt suche woman to warde untill she shalbe bounden to serve as is aforesaide.

XVIII. And for the better advuncement of Husbondry and tillage, and to thintente that suche as are fyt to be made apprentices to Husbondry may be bounden therevnto . . . That every person beinge an housholder and havinge and usinge halfe a ploughe land at the least in tillage, may have and receyve as an apprentice any person above thage of tenne yeres and under thage of xviij yeres to serve in husbandry untill his Age of xxj yeres at the least, or until thage of xxiiij yeres as the parties can agree . . .

XIX. . . . That every person being an Housholder and xxiiij yeres olde at the least, dwelling . . . in any cytie or towne Corporate, and usinge and exercising any arte mysterye or manuell occupacion there, shall and may after the Feast of St John Baptist next comynge . . . reteyn the sonne of any freman not occupying husbandry nor beinge a laborer and inhabyting in the same or in any other citie or towne . . . incorporate, to serve and be bounde as an apprentice after the Custome and Order of the Citie of london for seven yeres at the least, so as the tearme and yeares of such apprentice Do not expire or determyn afore suche apprentice shalbe of thage of xxiiij yeres at the leaste.

XX. Provided . . . that it shall not be lawfull to any person dwellinge in any Citie or Towne Corporate usinge exercysinge any of the mystereis or craftes of a merchante trapheiquinge by trapheke or trade into any partes beyonde the seae, mercer, draper, goldesmith, ironmonger, Inbroderer or clothear that dothe or shall put clothe to makynge and saile, to take any Apprentice or Servaunte to be enstructed or taughte in any of the artes . . . which they . . . exercise, except *such Servaunt or Apprentice be his Son, orels that* the Father or Mother of Suche Apprentice or Servaunte shall have . . . landes, tenementes [etc.] of the clere yerely value of xl *s.* of one estate of inheritance or freeholde at the leaste . . .

XXI. . . . That frome and After the said Feast of St John the baptist nexte, yt shalbe Lawfull to every person beynge an housholder and xxiiij yeres Olde at the least, and not occupienge Husbondry, nor beynge a laborer Dwellinge . . . in any Towne not beynge incorporat, that now is or hereafter shalbe A markytt Towne . . . , and exercysinge any arte mysterye or Manuell Occupacion . . . , to have in lyke maner to Apprentyes the Childe or Children of any other artificer . . . not occupienge husbondrye nor beyinge a laborer, whiche . . . shall Inhabyte . . . in the same or in any other suche markytt Towne within the same shyre, to serve as Apprentice . . . as is aforesaid, to any suche Arte [etc.] as hath bene usually exercysed In any suche markytt Towne where such Apprentice shalbebounde. . . .

XXII. Provided . . . that yt shall not be Lawfull to any person Dwellinge . . . in any suche markytt Towne, exercysinge the feate mystery or arte of a merchant traphecquinge . . . into the parties beyond the seaes, Mercer [etc., as above, Section XX.] to take any Apprentyce or in any wyse to teache or Instructe Any person in thartes . . . last before recyted, after the feast of St John baptist aforesayd, except *such Servaunte or Apprentice shalbe his son or elles* that the father or mother of suche Apprentice shall have landes [etc.] . . . of the clere yerely value of three poundes of one estate of inheritance or freeholde at the least. . . .

XXIII. . . . That frome and after the said feast yt shalbe Lawfull to any person . . . exercysynge tharte . . . of a Smythe whelwright, *plowewright,* mylewright, carpenter, Roughe mayson, playsterer, sawyer, lymeburner, bryckemaker, bryke layer, Tyler, Slater, helyer, Tylemaker, lynnen wever, turner, Cowper, Myllers, Earthen potters, wollenwevers weaving huswyfies or householde clothe only and none other, Clothe Fuller otherwyse called Tucker or walker, *Burner of Ore and Woade ashes,* thatcher or Shingler, wheresoever he or they shall dwell . . . to have . . . the sonne of any person as Apprentyce. . . . Albeyt the father or mother of any suche Apprentyce have not any Landes, Tenementes nor hereditamentes.

XXIV. . . . *That after the first daye of Maye next commyng* yt shall not be lawfull to any person or persons other then suche as nowe do Lawfully use or exercyse any arte mystery or manuall Occupacion to sett up occupye use or exercyse any crafte . . . *nowe used or occupyed within the Realme of England or Wales* excepte he shall have bene brought uppe therin Seven yeres at the least as Apprentyce, in maner and forme abovesaid, nor to sett anye person on worke in suche . . . Occupacion beinge not a workeman at this day, except he shall have bene apprentyce as is aforesaid, orels having servyd as an Apprentyce . . . will becomme a Jorneyman or be hyred by the yere: Apon paine that every person willingly offendinge or doynge the contrary shall forfett . . . for every Default xls. for every moneth.

XXV. Provided . . . that no person . . . exercysinge the arte or mystery of a wollen Clothe wever other than suche as be inhabitinge within the counties of cumberlande, westmerlende, lancaster and wales, weavinge Fryzes Cottons or houswyfes clothe only, makinge and weavinge wollen clothe comonly solde or to be solde by any clotherman or clotheor shall . . . have any Apprentyce or shall . . . instructe any person . . . in the Scyence . . . of weavinge aforesaid in any village towne or Place, (Cities Townes corporate and market Townes only except) etc. . . . unles *suche person bee his Sonne, or els that* the father or mother of such apprentyce or servaunte shall . . . have landes [etc.] to the clere yerely value of three poundes at the leaste of an estate of Inheritance or freehold . . . upon paine of forfeyture of xxs. for every monethe. . . .

XXVI. . . . That all and every person or persons that shall have Three Apprentices in any of the said craftes . . . of a clothemaker, fuller, shereman, weaver, tailor or shomaker, shall reteyne and kepe *one* Jorneyman and for every other Apprentyce above the nomber of the said three Apprentyces one other Jorneyman, upon paine for every defaulte therin tenne poundes.

XXVII. . . . That this act . . . shall not extende to prejudice the companye . . . or worstedmakers . . . of Norwyche. . . .

XXVIII. . . . That yf any person shalbe required by any housholder havinge and usinge halfe a Ploughelande at the least in tillage to be an Apprentyce and to serve in Husbandry as in any other kynde of arte [etc.] before expressed, and shall refusse so to doo, that then upon the Complaynt of suche houskeaper made to one Iustice of peace of the countie wherin the said refusall is or shalbe made, or of such housholder Inhabyting in any Cytty towne corporate or markytt Towne to the mayor and bailiefes or hede officer of the said cytty [etc.] . . . they shall have full poure . . . to sende for the same person so refusing, And yf the said Iustice [etc.] shall thynke the saide person meate . . . to serve as an apprentyce in that arte . . . the said Iustic . . . or hede officer shall have powre . . . to commit him unto Warde, there to remayne untill he be . . . bounden to serve as an apprentise shoulde serve . . . ; And yf any suche Master shall mysuse or evill intreat his apprentyce . . . or thapprentyce do not his deiutie to his Master, Then the said Master or Prentyce, beyinge grevyd . . . shall repaire unto one Iustice of peas [etc.] . . . who shall by his wysdome and dyscreasion take suche order and direction betwene the said Master and his Apprentyce as thequitie of the cause shall require: and yf for wante of good conformitie in the said Master the said Iustice [etc.] or hedd officer cannot compound and Agree the matter betwene hym and his Apprentyce, then the said Iustice [etc.] or Hedd officer shall take bande of the said

Master to Appere at the next sessyons then to bee holden in the said Countrie within the said Cytty [etc.] . . . , and uppon his Apparance and heringe of the matter . . . yf yt be thought mete unto theme to dyscharge the said Apprentyce of his Apprenticehodd, That then the said Iustices or fowere of them at the least, wherof one to be of the quorum, or the said . . . hedd officer, with the consent of thre other of his Bretherne or Men of beste Reputacion within the said Cytty [etc.] shall have powre . . . to pronownce [etc.] that they have dyscharged the said Apprentyce of his apprenticehode; . . . and yf the Defaulte shalbe founde to be in the Apprentyce then the said Iustices etc. or hedd offycer with thassistentes aforesaid, shall cause suche Due correction and Punishment to be mynestred unto hym, as by their wisdome and dyscreacions shalbe thought mete.

XXIX. Provided . . . that no person shall be force [etc.] of this Estatute be bounden to enter into any apprenticeshipe other then suche as be under thage of xxi yeres.

XXX. And to thende that this Estatute maye from tyme to tyme be carefully . . . put in good execusion . . . Be it enacted . . . that the Iustices of peas of every countie Devydinge themeselves into severall lymyttes, and lykewyse every maiar and hed officer of any cytty or towne corporat, shall yerely betwene the beast of S^t michell tharchangell and the nativitee of our lord, and betwene the Feast of the Annuncyacion of our lady and the feaste of the Nativity of St John baptist . . . make a speciall and dyligent inquirie of the Braunches and articles of this Estatut, and of the good executione of the same, and where they shall finde any defaultes to see the same severely corrected and punyshed without favore . . . or dyspleasur.

The Navigation Act of 1651

Adam Smith exempted from his sweeping strictures against mercantilist price fixing, tariffs, bounties, wage regulation, and the like, the English Navigation Acts. His grounds were practical; since defense was to be preferred to opulence, a strong English merchant marine was a necessity. The merchant marine was the nursery of the seamen which England required to wage her naval wars. Adam Smith's position identified one of the major arguments which supported the intricate restrictions that England placed upon entry into her ports, shipment of her goods to other countries, and colonial efforts to develop a rival merchant marine.

But broader mercantilist doctrine simply reinforced this cogent argument for restriction. Viewed from the American angle no doubt, the Navigation Acts unfairly forced our ships to stop in England and transship their cargoes onto British vessels, wherever we had destined the cargoes and whatever the cost and inconvenience of the maneuver. But from the British standpoint, this was quite fair, since the role assigned to the colony was the production of raw materials, not the construction of an independent merchant marine or the manufacture of its own finished goods. Whatever expanded British carrying trade diminished the share of its rivals. On the usual mercantilist premises, the consequence was a happy impact upon the balance of trade and an expanded influx of the precious metals. On this line of argument longer voyages were more profitable than shorter ones, and goods imported from far places were more advantageous to the realm than those which came from nearby sources.

The Navigation Act of 1651 was one of a series of statutes that dated from the reign of Richard II. It in turn was amplified by enactments passed in 1660, 1663, 1672, and 1696. The major objective of the

Act of 1651 was the harassment of Dutch shipping and the destruction of Dutch power. Later laws, shifting in emphasis, devoted more attention to the rising rivalry of the American colonies. Enforcement of all of these laws tended to fluctuate. American rage in the eighteenth century was as likely to follow a determined attempt to enforce existing statutes as the passage of an additional piece of legislation.

The Navigation Act of 1651 is contained in Volume I of Introduction to Contemporary Civilization in the West (*New York: Columbia University Press, 1954*), *pp. 842-5.*

The Navigation Act of 1651

AN ACT FOR INCREASE OF SHIPPING, AND ENCOURAGEMENT OF THE NAVIGATION OF THIS NATION

For the increase of the Shipping and the Encouragement of the Navigation of this Nation, which under the good Providence and Protection of God, is so great a means of the Welfare and Safety of this Commonwealth; Be it Enacted by this present Parliament, and the Authority thereof, That from and after the First day of December, One thousand six hundred fifty and one, and from thence forwards, no Goods or Commodities whatsoever, of the Growth, Production or Manufacture of Asia, Africa or America, or of any part thereof; or of any Islands belonging to them, or any of them, or which are described or laid down in the usual Maps or Cards of those places, as well of the English Plantations as others, shall be Imported or brought into this Commonwealth of England, or into Ireland, or any other Lands, Islands, Plantations or Territories to this Commonwealth belonging, or in their Possession, in any other Ship or Ships, Vessel or Vessels whatsoever, but onely in such as do truly and without fraud belong onely to the People of this Commonwealth, or the Plantations thereof, as the Proprietors or right Owners thereof; and whereof the Master and Mariners are also for the most part of them, of the People of this Commonwealth, under the penalty of the forfeiture and loss of all the Goods that shall be Imported contrary to this Act; as also of the Ship (with all her Tackle, Guns and Apparel) in which the said Goods or Commodities shall be so brought in and Imported; the one moyety to the use of the Commonwealth, and the other moyety to the use and behoof of any person or persons who shall seize the said Goods or Commodities, and shall prosecute the same in any Court of Record within this Commonwealth.

And it is further Enacted by the Authority aforesaid, That no

Goods or Commodities of the Growth, Production or Manufacture of Europe, or of any part thereof, shall after the First day of December, One thousand six hundred fifty and one, be imported or brought into this Commonwealth of England, or into Ireland, or any other Lands, Islands, Plantations or Territories to this Commonwealth belonging, or in their possession, in any Ship or Ships, Vessel or Vessels whatsoever, but in such as do truly and without fraud belong onely to the people of this Commonwealth, as the true Owners and Proprietors thereof, and in no other, except onely such Forein Ships and Vessels as do truly and properly belong to the people of that Countrey or Place, of which the said Goods are the Growth, Production or Manufacture; or to such Ports where the said Goods can onely be, or most usually are first shipped for Transportation; And that under the same penalty of forfeiture and loss expressed in the former Branch of this Act, the said Forfeitures to be recovered and imployed as is therein expressed.

And it is further Enacted by the Authority aforesaid, That no Goods or Commodities that are of Forein Growth, Production or Manufacture, and which are to be brought into this Commonwealth, in Shipping belonging to the People thereof, shall be by them Shipped or brought from any other place or places, Countrey or Countreys, but onely from those of their said Growth, Production or Manufacture; or from those Ports where the said Goods and Commodities can onely, or are, or usually have been first shipped for Transportation; and from none other Places or Countreys, under the same penalty of forfeiture and loss expressed in the first Branch of this Act, the said Forfeitures to be recovered and imployed as is therein expressed.

And it is further Enacted by the Authority aforesaid, That no sort of Codfish, Ling, Herring, Pilchard, or any other kinde of salted Fish, usually fished for and caught by the people of this Nation; nor any Oyl made, or that shall be made of any kinde of Fish whatsoever; nor any Whale-fins, or Whale-bones, shall from henceforth be Imported into this Commonwealth, or into Ireland, or any other Lands, Islands, Plantations, or Territories thereto belonging, or in their possession, but onely such as shall be caught in Vessels that do or shall truly and properly belong to the people of this Nation, as Proprietors and Right Owners thereof: And the said Fish to be cured, and the Oyl aforesaid made by the people of this Commonwealth, under the penalty and loss expressed in the said first Branch of this present Act; the said Forfeit to be recovered and imployed as is there expressed.

And it is further Enacted by the Authority aforesaid, That no sort of Cod, Ling, Herring, Pilchard, or any other kinde of Salted Fish whatsoever, which shall be caught and cured by the people of this Commonwealth, shall be from and after the First day of February, One thousand six hundred fifty three, exported from any place or places belonging to this Commonwealth, in any other Ship or Ships, Vessel or Vessels, save onely in such as do truly and properly appertain to the people of this Commonwealth, as Right Owners; and whereof the Master and Mariners are for the most part of them English, under the penalty and loss expressed in the said first Branch of this present Act; the said Forfeit to be recovered and imployed as is there expressed.

Provided always, That this Act, nor any thing therein contained, extend not, or be meant to restrain the Importation of any of the Commodities of the Straights or Levant Seas, loaden in the Shipping of this Nation as aforesaid, at the usual Ports or places for lading of them theretofore, within the said Straights or Levant Seas, though the said Commodities be not of the very Growth of the said places.

Provided also, That this Act nor any thing therein contained, extend not, nor be meant to restrain the Importing of any East-India Commodities loaden in the Shipping of this Nation, at the usual Port or places for Lading of them heretofore in any part of those Seas, to the Southward and Eastward of Cabo Bona Esperanza, although the said Ports be not the very places of their Growth.

Provided also, That it shall and may be lawful to and for any of the People of this Commonwealth, in Vessels or Ships to them belonging, and whereof the Master and Mariners are of this Nation as aforesaid, to load and bring in from any of the Ports of Spain and Portugal, all sorts of Goods or Commodities that have come from, or any way belonged unto the Plantations or Dominions of either of them respectively.

Be it also further Enacted by the authority aforesaid, That from henceforth it shall not be lawful to any person or persons whatsoever, to load or cause to be loaden and carried in any Bottom or Bottoms, Ship or Ships, Vessel or Vessels whatsoever, whereof any Stranger or Strangers born (unless such as be Denizens or Naturalized) be Owners, part Owners, or Master, any Fish, Victual, Wares, or things of what kinde or nature soever the same shall be from one Port or Creek of this Commonwealth, to another Port or Creek of the same, under penalty to every one that shall offend contrary to the true meaning of this Branch of this present Act, to forfeit all the Goods that shall be so laden or carried, as also the Ship upon which they shall be so laden or carried, the same Forfeit to be recovered and imployed as directed in the first Branch of this present Act.

Lastly, That this Act nor any thing therein contained, extend not to Bullion, nor yet to any Goods taken, or that shall be taken by way of Reprizal by any Ship or Ships, having Commission from this Commonwealth.

Provided, That this Act, or any thing therein contained, shall not extend, nor be construed to extend to any Silk or Silkwares which shall be brought by Land from any parts of Italy, and there bought with the proceed of English Commodities, sold either for Money or in Barter; but that it shall and may be lawful for any of the People of this Commonwealth to ship the same in English Vessels from Ostend, Newport, Roterdam, Middleburgh, Amsterdam, or any Ports thereabouts; the Owners and Proprietors first making Oath by themselves, or other credible Witness, before the Commissioners of the Customs for the time being, or their Deputies, or one of the Barons of the Exchequer, that the Goods aforesaid were so bought for his or their own proper accompt in Italy.

The French Woolens Regulation
of 1669

In their efforts to regulate all aspects of economic life, internal as well as external, mercantilist statesmen did not neglect the question of quality. Their interest was not that of the domestic consumer, but rather that of the sovereign whose power and prosperity depended upon an influx of precious metal. This influx in turn demanded a favorable balance of trade. And this balance could not be achieved unless the goods that were exported to foreigners were both low in price and high in quality.

It was in pursuit of these objectives that Colbert, the greatest of seventeenth-century French mercantilists, clamped enormously detailed controls upon manufactures. Colbert sought nothing less than national uniformity of finished products. In any age the aim was formidable; in the jungle of local interests which was seventeenth-century France it was almost impossible. Nevertheless, Colbert never ceased trying. The meticulousness and detail of his règlements and those of his successors is suggested by the fact that the decrees of the period 1666-1730 filled four quarto volumes and totaled 2,200 pages. Three supplements, nearly as substantial, reinforced them.

The wool règlement, part of which is printed below, comprised fifty-nine articles. The two dyeing règlements contained, respectively, sixty-two and ninety-eight articles, and the largest of the general dyeing instructions achieved the magnificent total of three hundred and seventeen articles. Each one had the force of law and the weight of the King's writ. Supposedly, regulation followed the course of production, from raw material, through each process, to the ultimate finished product. But enforcement was a constant worry. The intendant who was the King's representative in each district was responsible for the obedience of manufacturers and merchants. His agents made periodic, unheralded inspections. When they found cloth at any stage of manufacture that fell below specification, their *authority enabled them to slash it. Such was the penalty for a first offense. Later transgressions led to fines or even imprisonment. But, despite all severities, violations were frequent, agents were too few, and warnings of visits were not unknown.*

The passage is taken from Volume I of Introduction to Contemporary Civilization in the West *(New York: Columbia University Press, 1954), pp. 821-7. It was originally published in its English translation in Charles W. Cole's* Colbert and a Century of French Mercantilism *(New York: Columbia University Press, 1939).*

The French Woolens Regulation of 1669

ORDINANCES AND REGULATIONS ON THE LENGTH, WIDTH, AND QUALITY OF CLOTHS, SERGES, AND OTHER STUFFS OF WOOL AND LINEN

1. All Spanish-style cloths, white, gray, or mixed, shall be made one and one-half ells wide including the selvage, and the aforesaid selvages are not to be more than two inches wide. The piece is to be twenty-one ells long. . . .

28. *Tiretaines* [linen and wool, like linsey-woolsey in England], white and gray, made of wool and linen, shall be three-fourths ell wide and thirty-five to forty ells long, all by the measure (*aulnage*) of Paris. And the warp of all the above-mentioned fabrics shall be of a number of threads sufficient for and suitable to their width, to make them of the fineness, goodness, and strength required for their type and quality.

29. The narrow serges of Ville-de-Roy shall be two-thirds ell wide and twenty-one ells long; and those that are not all wool shall have a blue selvage and the same length and width as the above-mentioned.

30. There shall henceforth be made no fabrics, however low may be their price, by a draper, a serge-maker, or by anyone at all, that are not [at least] one-half ell wide by the measurement of Paris.

31. All master drapers actually making cloth, and serge-makers, are enjoined to make the selvages of the cloths the same length as the material, so that the cloths and serges may be easier to clip and so that they may not be badly joined: and to make these selvages strong enough so as not to tear when the cloths are put to dry.

32. All stuffs of wool and linen of the same name or of the same type and quality as those above-mentioned, and which could not be specified above, shall uniformly have the same length and width as the above-mentioned ones of the same type and quality, throughout

the whole extent of the kingdom. And these cloths and serges and other fabrics shall be of the same uniform strength and quality for the whole length and width of the piece, without any difference. And the weavers and workers shall not make the warp of these fabrics except of the widths before-mentioned, nor employ wool nor linen thread nor other material of a finer quality at one end of the piece than in all the rest of its length and width; all this under penalty of confiscation and twenty *livres* fine for each contravention.

33. To enforce effectively the lengths and widths of these cloths, serges, and other goods of wool and linen herebeforementioned, four months after the publication of these regulations, all the treadles (*lames*) and combs (*rôts*) of the looms for these fabrics shall be changed and made over to the width and size above prescribed for these fabrics; and where any looms are found, after the lapse of that interval, which are not of the above-mentioned widths, they shall be taken apart immediately to be made over to the above width and size, and those to whom they belong shall be condemned to a fine of three *livres* for each loom.

34. The associations and guilds of the crafts of draper and serge-maker of all the cities and towns of the kingdom shall be composed indiscriminately of all masters who have been received in those crafts, or who practice them by virtue of letters patent granted by His Majesty and by the kings, his predecessors, in consequence whereof they shall peacefully continue the practice of these crafts without being disturbed, provided that they cause to be inscribed their names and status of masters, both on the registers of the administrative judges who have jurisdiction over the regulation of manufacturers, and on those of their guild, within one month after the publication of the present statutes and regulations; failing which, this time having passed, they cannot practice their trades as masters without the permission of these civil judges; or without going through their apprenticeship in the manner which shall be mentioned hereafter. And all persons other than the masters of these crafts, without any exceptions, shall not occupy themselves with the making of cloths, serges, or other fabrics, under penalty of confiscation of the cloth and a fine of 150 *livres*.

35. To maintain the masters and guilds of these crafts in the proper unity of good feeling, and to enforce the present statutes and regulations, there shall be named each year by a plurality of votes on the same day on which elections have heretofore been held, and for places where none have been held on such a day as shall be chosen by the officers who have a right to do so, the number of

Wardens or Sworn Guardians of these crafts of draper and serge-maker that is proper for the places where the elections are held; and these wardens will swear before the above-mentioned officers to do well and duly the duties of their office during its term, which shall be not less than one year. And when these wardens go out of office, a new election for other wardens shall be held, but in such a way that there shall always be two old ones, or one at least, to instruct the new ones; and so on successively from year to year, the same order shall always be observed. And the aforesaid wardens and sworn guardians shall be obliged to do the duties of their office, well and duly, and to report faithfully to the administrative judge of manufactures all contraventions of the present statutes and regulations which may be committed, under penalty of losing their office and their position as masters. The masters, journeymen, and apprentices of the aforesaid crafts shall not assemble for the election of the aforesaid wardens nor for any other purpose whatsoever unless they have permission from the officers who have the right to give it, under penalty of a thirty *livres* fine for each of the offenders, and of having their case brought up and carried through under the special procedure used for those involved in seditions. And when the aforesaid wardens and sworn guardians leave office, they shall turn over to their successors all registers and papers concerning the affairs of the aforesaid guild.

36. The measures (*aulneurs*) shall not measure any goods unless they are marked with the mark of the place [of manufacture], and unless on them is the name of the weaver at the top and first end of the piece, worked on the loom and not with a needle, under penalty of fifty *livres* fine the first time, and the second a similar fine and loss of office; should this occur, they shall be replaced by the officers having administration of manufactures.

37. The measurers shall not be brokers (*courtiers*), nor shall the brokers be measurers, agents (*commissionaires*), or factors (*facteurs*), nor shall they buy or cause to be bought any wool or other materials involved in cloth-making or serge-making, for their own account, or for anyone else, to resell them for profit directly or indirectly, under penalty of confiscation of the aforesaid goods and of one hundred *livres* fine, and of loss of their positions. . . .

39. All cloths, serges, and other fabrics shall be seen and inspected, when they come back from the fuller, by the wardens and sworn guardians then in office, and marked by them with the mark of the place where they were made, if they conform to the present regulation. And if they find any defects, they will have them seized and will make their report of the matter to the judge administering manu-

factures, so that he may order the confiscation of them in the manner that they shall think best. And if they are not of the width ordered by these presents, their selvages shall be torn publicly. And to facilitate the aforesaid inspection and marking of the aforesaid goods, there shall be in all the cities, towns, and villages of the kingdom where the aforesaid manufactures are established, a room of the necessary size in the town hall or at the office of the guilds of the aforesaid crafts if it is possible, or at some other very convenient place; to which room the weavers and workmen shall be obliged to bring their goods, there to be inspected and marked, as has been said, on the days and at the hours which shall be set and determined by the judges administering manufactures, and for this purpose the aforesaid wardens and sworn guardians shall be obliged to present themselves there. And if the aforesaid goods are taken to other cities to be sold there, and also all such goods from foreign lands without any exceptions, they shall be taken directly to be unloaded in the markets or other places designated for the inspection of goods and not elsewhere, except those which are taken to fairs, so that they may also be seen and inspected there by the masters and the wardens of the cloth industry of the aforesaid cities and marked by them if they are of the requisite quality. And in the cases where they are not of the requisite quality, or for those manufactured in France where the mark of the place where they were made has not been put upon them, or where the name of the weaver, done on the loom and not by needle, has not been placed upon the top and first end of the pieces of the aforesaid goods, they shall be seized; and on the report and by the proceedings of the aforesaid masters and wardens and sworn guardians, the confiscation of them shall be sought before the judges administering manufactures. And no merchants and weavers shall expose for sale, sell, or buy the aforesaid goods, unless previously they have been marked as has been said; nor shall the wardens and sworn guardians of the places where the aforesaid goods were made, mark them with any mark other than that of the aforesaid places, all under penalty of confiscation of the aforesaid goods and of greater penalties for further offenses. . . .

45. The merchant drapers of the cities and towns of the kingdom who shall buy goods from manufacturing drapers and serge-makers, either in the markets or at the fairs or elsewhere, shall complete and settle their accounts within two or three days after the sale and delivery of the aforesaid goods, at the latest, so that the delay they cause in the matter may not injure the aforesaid drapers and serge-makers, under penalty, in case of delay, of forty *sous* for each day

that the aforesaid drapers and serge-makers are forced to wait, from the day of the protest made by them to the day of the settlement of the account.

46. And the masters, journeymen, and apprentices of the craft of draper and serge-maker in the cities and towns of this kingdom shall be held to follow and conform to the special statutes which have been granted to them and confirmed in the Council of Commerce. And as for the other cities and towns where no special statutes have been granted, the system prescribed by the following articles for masters, journeymen, and apprentices, drapers, and serge-makers shall be punctually observed.

47. No one shall be received as a master who has not served apprenticeship with a master of the aforesaid craft and remained in the service of his master: to wit, for the drapers during the space of two complete and consecutive years, and for the serge-makers during the space of three years, also complete and consecutive, as to which a certificate shall be sworn to before a notary, which certificate shall be registered on the book of the guild. No master shall be allowed to take more than two apprentices, nor shall the aforesaid apprentices absent themselves from the house of their master during the time of their apprenticeship without a cause which is legitimate and which is held to be such by the administrative judge. And in case of contravention, their masters may have them arrested, in virtue of the present regulations, to make them finish their time; or else the masters may summon them to do so and, after having waited for a month, may have their names erased from the register of the guild, and may take others to replace them; and after that the aforesaid apprentices who have gone away shall not be able to count the time which has elapsed during their absence and first apprenticeship, but the aforesaid apprentices may bind themselves again to a new master for the same time as above. The master shall not dismiss his apprentice without a cause which is legitimate and is held to be such by the administrative judge, nor shall he take another, if one absents himself, until the above-mentioned month has expired, under penalty of a fine of thirty *livres*. And if it chances that any master should absent himself from the city in which he has dwelt, and should cease his work, another master shall be provided for the aforesaid apprentice after a month. Nor shall the masters of the aforesaid craft entice or attract to themselves the apprentice or journeyman of another master, nor give him employment directly or indirectly, under penalty of a fine of sixty *livres*.

48. His apprenticeship completed, the candidate who wishes to

become a master shall make his masterpiece, and if judged capable, shall be received as a master, and his letters of reception shall be delivered to him upon the payment of six *livres* for all fees, and without his giving any banquet. And no wardens of the aforesaid craft and no other persons shall receive a gift or present before, during, or after the making of the masterpiece, nor shall the aforesaid candidate give them any, under penalty of suspension from the status of master for a year, and 100 *livres* fine for each offender. For which a writ of execution shall be delivered by the administrative judge, after the summary hearing which he shall be obligated to hold after complaint about the matter or information as to it has been laid before him; and if any dispute shall arise as to the acceptance of the aforesaid masterpiece, it shall be seen and inspected by the administrative judge or another named or appointed by him for this purpose. . . .

52. The master drapers, serge-makers, workmen, fullers, and others shall not draw out, lengthen nor stretch on tenters any piece of goods, either white or dyed, in such a way that it might shrink [later] in length or width, under penalty of a fine of 100 *livres* and confiscation of the goods for the first time, and, in case of a second offense, deprivation of their status as masters.

53. The greases called *flambart* [the grease that rises to the top of the water when pork is boiled] shall not be used for the oiling (*ensimage*) of cloth and serges, but only the whitest hog's lard [the use of grease other than lard was held to interfere with proper dyeing]. And the shearers (*tondeurs*) shall not make use of cards (*cardes*) to lay (*coucher*) the aforesaid cloth and serges, nor shall they keep any of them in their houses; but they shall make use of teasels (*chardons*), under penalty of a fine of twelve *livres* for each offense. . . .

55. The seizure, distraint, and forced sale by legal procedure of mills, looms, tools, and utensils used for any manufacture whatsoever shall not be allowed for any debt, cause, or occasion whatsoever, save for the rent of the houses occupied by the aforesaid weavers and masters, but not for the sums due for the *tailles* nor the *gabelles* [salt tax]. And no officers and sergeants shall make such seizures or sales, under penalty of deprivation of office, a fine of 150 *livres*, and all costs, damages, and interest due to the parties against whom the seizure is made. . . .

57. The aforesaid wardens, actually in office, shall assemble in the room of their guild the first Monday of each month at two o'clock in the afternoon, and more often if need be, to confer on the affairs of the aforesaid guild, to hear the complaints and information as to in-

fractions, which shall be made to them by the masters and apprentices on matters concerning their craft, to be settled in a friendly manner. And in case important matters should arise, having to do with aforesaid guild, which might give rise to a lawsuit, the wardens and sworn guardians actually in office shall collect in their room the greatest number of masters of the aforesaid guild, at least five or six, together with those who have been in office during the two preceding years, before whom they shall lay the matters in question, so that they may be settled by a majority vote. And what shall be thus decided on shall be transcribed into the above-mentioned register of the guild and carried out by all the masters of the aforesaid guild, as if all of them had been present at the meeting.

58. The money from all the fines which shall be levied as a result of these presents, and for infractions of them, shall be paid: to wit, one-half to His Majesty, one-quarter to the wardens actually in office, and the other quarter to the poor of the place where the judgment providing for payment of the aforesaid fines shall have been rendered.

59. And so that it may be known whether the wardens and sworn guardians are fulfilling the duties of their office well and have carefully executed these present regulations, and also so that ways to perfect the aforesaid manufactures and to increase the trade in them may be sought the more, in all the cities and towns of the kingdom where there are or shall be hereafter guilds of master drapers and serge-makers, the officials administering manufactures shall cause to assemble before themselves, in the month of January of each year, the wardens of the crafts of the aforesaid manufactures of wool and linen who are in office, together with those who went out of office in the preceding year, and four other persons from each of the aforementioned guilds, such as they see fit to choose, together with two prominent *bourgeois,* so that the wardens and sworn guardians who are in office may inform the gathering of the existing conditions in the aforesaid manufactures, of their progress, of the steps which they think necessary to perfect them, of the observance or nonobservance which they have noted to be accorded to the present regulation, and of the ways by which it would be proper to improve the observance of it; so that, in regard to all this, the aforementioned gathering may give its advice as to what it shall think most useful and reasonable for the welfare of the public and of the trade in goods, of which a report shall be drawn up by the aforesaid officers administering manufactures, who shall be required to send a copy of it, within a month, to the superintendent of arts and manufactures of France; all this to be done free and without charge.

Thomas Mun

1571–1641

The mercantilist love of treasure is a theme that runs through several centuries of mercantilist rumination. But with the lapse of time the love expressed itself with increasing sophistication. Among others, Edwin Cannan (and Adam Smith) distinguished between an early school of mercantilists, whom they termed "bullionists," and a later school, whose members were obsessed primarily with the maintenance of a proper balance of trade, an excess of exports over imports. The bullionist love of treasure was sufficiently direct and uncomplicated as to make them reluctant to permit gold and silver to leave the country on any pretext whatsoever. The balance-of-trade theorists tended to argue that proper policy allowed the precious metals temporarily to leave the country if the ultimate consequence was a return to the same country of an even larger quantity of gold and silver.

This distinction was cogently made by Thomas Mun, whose England's Treasure by Forraign Trade *was probably written in 1630, though it was not published until the 1660's. Mun severely criticized the bullionist attempt to embargo gold and silver exports. As an East India merchant himself, with a direct interest in the free flow of the metals, he maintained that money, if exported to purchase raw materials, would return to the country in larger amounts after the raw materials had been converted into manufactures and re-exported. Another point of interest in his work is his attempt to draw up a balance of trade.*

Was the mercantilist emphasis upon treasure no more than one of the errors that dot human thought? Did it rest upon some logical premise? The answer to both of these questions might well be affirmative. There is indeed a logical inconsistency in a doctrine that sees ultimate benefit from persuading foreigners to take more of one's own

139

produce than one takes from them, and there is a logical impossibility that prevents all nations simultaneously from succeeding in such a policy. Nevertheless, the mercantilist conception of the world made excellent sense in a Europe almost constantly at war. In the garrison state there is nothing peculiar about the wish to keep one's assets liquid. With gold and silver, soldiers could be hired from other lands, goods could be purchased, and the means to fight a successful war enlarged. The doctrines of free trade demand a world at peace and a cosmopolitan notion of self-interest. Mercantilism is an almost instinctive reflection of danger.

This excerpt is from England's Treasure by Forraign Trade, *by Thomas Mun, in* Early English Tracts on Commerce, *edited by J. R. McCulloch (Cambridge University Press, 1952), pp. 125-6.*

The Means to Enrich This Kingdom, and to Encrease Our Treasure

Although a Kingdom may be enriched by gifts received, or by purchase taken from some other Nations, yet these are things uncertain and of small consideration when they happen. The ordinary means therefore to increase our wealth and treasure is by *Forraign Trade*, wherein wee must ever observe this rule; to sell more to strangers yearly than wee consume of theirs in value. For suppose that when this Kingdom is plentifully served with the Cloth, Lead, Tinn, Iron, Fish and other native commodities, we doe yearly export the overplus to forraign Countreys to the value of twenty two hundred thousand pounds; by which means we are enabled beyond the Seas to buy and bring in forraign wares for our use and Consumptions, to the value of twenty hundred thousand pounds: By this order duly kept in our trading, we may rest assured that the Kingdom shall be enriched yearly two hundred thousand pounds, which must be brought to us in so much Treasure; because that part of our stock which is not returned to us in wares must necessarily be brought home in treasure.

For in this case it cometh to pass in the stock of a Kingdom, as in the estate of a private man; who is supposed to have one thousand pounds yearly revenue and two thousand pounds of ready money in his Chest: If such a man through excess shall spend one thousand five hundred pounds *per annum*, all his ready money will be gone in four years; and in the like time his said money will be doubled if he take a Frugal course to spend but five hundred pounds *per an-*

num, which rule never faileth likewise in the Commonwealth, but in some cases (of no great moment) which I will hereafter declare, when I shall shew by whom and in what manner this ballance of the Kingdoms account ought to be drawn up yearly, or so often as it shall please the State to discover how much we gain or lose by trade with forraign Nations. But first I will say something concerning those ways and means which will encrease our exportations and diminish our importations of wares; which being done, I will then set down some other arguments both affirmative and negative to strengthen that which is here declared, and thereby to show that all the other means which are commonly supposed to enrich the Kingdom with Treasure are altogether insufficient and meer fallacies.

Sir James Steuart

1712–1780

Frequently doctrines receive their completest exposition shortly before they are superseded. Presumably, what Galbraith has called the conventional wisdom is at its most solemn and its least useful just before events finally outrun it. Sir James Steuart's An Inquiry into the Principles of Political Economy was written in 1767, less than a decade before The Wealth of Nations. Its two quarto volumes are a compendium of mercantilist doctrine. Steuart favors low wages and long hours of labor. He is urgent in his advocacy of a favorable balance of trade and an inflow of gold and silver. He favored a larger population because more people would produce more goods to the greater advantage of the export trade. No premonition of diminishing returns from either land or manufacture qualified his certainty.

Steuart is especially interesting as one of the most extreme advocates of a central position for the mercantilist statesman. In fact, the statesman is the true hero of the glum mercantilist universe. Here is Steuart's description of his attributes: "He who fits at the head of this operation, is called the statesman. I suppose him to be constantly awake, attentive to his employment, able and uncorrupted, tender in his love for the society that he governs, impartially just in his indulgence for every class of inhabitants, and disregardful of the interests of individuals, when that regard is inconsistent with the general welfare." A good deal to ask of an imperfect human being!

Nor is this the end of the statesman's distinction from the common run of mortals. Everybody in the community except the statesman is prone to follow his own self-interest. The statesman alone is free of this taint and able to enlist the self-interest of others to accomplish the objectives he disinterestedly favors. In Steuart's words,

. . . *the principle of self-interest will serve as a general key to this inquiry; and it may in one sense, be considered as the ruling principle of my subject, and may therefore be traced through the whole. This is the main spring and only motive which a statesman should make use of, to engage a free people to concur in the plans which he lays down for their government. I beg I may not here be understood to mean, that self-interest should conduct the statesman: by no means. Self-interest when considered with regard to him, is public spirit; and it can only be called self-interest when it is applied to those who are to be governed by it.*

The contrast with Adam Smith is sharp. In The Wealth of Nations the market process harmonizes the clashing purposes of individual agents. The merchant, the manufacturer, the laborer, the landlord, none of them intends the public prosperity and each intends his own. But the impersonal mechanism of exchange forces individual and public interest to coincide. The moral Steuart draws is quite different. The statesman, the single altruistic agent, uses the self-interest of his subjects because he fears that their unbridled selfishness will be harmful, not beneficial, to the community. If Smith's view teaches the natural harmony of interests, Steuart's as clearly implies the natural disharmony of interests. The mercantilist confidence in the disinterestedness of the statesman, contrary to much contemporary evidence, represented the only romantic element in their hardheaded faith.

This passage comes from Volume I of The Works of Sir James Steuart (*London, 1805*), pp. 2-3, 4-5, and 15-16.

The Statesman

The whole oeconomy must be directed by the head, who is both lord and steward of the family. It is however necessary, that these two offices be not confounded with one another. As lord, he establishes the laws of his oeconomy; as steward, he puts them in execution. As lord, he may restrain and give his commands to all within the house as he thinks proper; as steward, he must conduct with gentleness and address, and is bound by his own regulations. The better the oeconomist, the more uniformity is perceived in all his actions, and the less liberties are taken to depart from stated rules. He is not so much master, as that he may break through the laws of his oeconomy, although in every respect he may keep each individual within the house, in the most exact subordination to his commands. Oeconomy and government, even in a private family, present therefore two different ideas, and have also two different objects.

What oeconomy is in a family, political oeconomy is in a state: with these essential differences, however, that in a state there are no servants, all are children: that a family may be formed when and how a man pleases, and he may there establish what plan of oeconomy he thinks fit; but states are found formed, and the oeconomy of these depends upon a thousand circumstances. The *statesman* (this is a general term to signify the legislature and supreme power, according to the form of government) is neither master to establish what oeconomy he pleases, or, in the exercise of his sublime authority, to overturn at will the established laws of it, let him be the most despotic monarch upon earth.*

The great art therefore of political oeconomy is, first to adapt the different operations of it to the spirit, manners, habits, and customs of the people; and afterwards to model these circumstances so as to be able to introduce a set of new and more useful institutions.

The principal object of this science is to secure a certain fund of subsistence for all the inhabitants, to obviate every circumstance which may render it precarious; to provide every thing necessary for supplying the wants of the society, and to employ the inhabitants (supposing them to be freemen) in such a manner as naturally to create reciprocal relations and dependencies between them, so as to make their several interests lead them to supply one another with their reciprocal wants.

It is the business of a statesman to judge of the expediency of different schemes of oeconomy, and by degrees to model the minds of his subjects so as to induce them, from the allurement of private interest, to concur in the execution of his plan.

The speculative person who, removed from the practice, extracts the principles of this science from *observation* and *reflection,* should divest himself, as far as possible, of every prejudice in favour of established opinions, however reasonable, when examined relatively to particular nations: he must do his utmost to become a citizen of the world, comparing customs, examining minutely institutions which appear alike, when in different countries they are found to produce different effects: he should examine the cause of such differences

---

* Although in common language we call ministers of state, and even such as are eminent for their knowledge in state affairs, by the name of *statesmen,* the reader is here advised to attend carefully to the definition given of this word in the text, because the term *statesman* is uniformly taken in the same acceptation through this whole work.

with the utmost diligence and attention. It is from such inquiries that the true principles are discovered.

He who takes up the pen upon this subject, keeping in his eye the customs of his own or any other country, will fall more naturally into a description of one particular system of it, than into an examination of the principles of the science in general; he will applaud such institutions as he finds rightly administered at home; he will condemn those which are administered with abuse; but, without comparing different methods of executing the same plan in different countries, he will not easily distinguish the disadvantages which are essential to the institution, from those which proceed from the abuse. For this reason a land-tax excites the indignation of a Frenchman, an excise that of an Englishman. One who looks into the execution of both, in each country, and in every branch of their management, will discover the real effects of these impositions, and be able to distinguish what proceeds from abuse, from what is essential to the burden.

Nothing is more effectual towards preparing the spirit of a people to receive a good plan of oeconomy, than a proper representation of it. On the other hand, nothing is better calculated to keep the statesman, who is at the head of affairs, in awe.

When principles are well understood, the real consequences of burdensome institutions are clearly seen: when the purposes they are intended for are not obtained, the abuse of the statesman's administration appears palpable. People then will not so much cry out against the imposition, as against the misapplication. It will not be a land-tax of four shillings in the pound, nor an excise upon wines and tobacco, which will excite the murmurs of a nation; it will be the prodigal dissipation and misapplication of the amount of these taxes after they are laid on. But when principles are not known, all inquiry is at an end, the moment a nation can be engaged to submit to the burden. It is the same with regard to many other parts of this science: while people remain blind they are always mistrustful.

In turning and working upon the spirit of a people, nothing is impossible to an able statesman. When a people can be engaged to murder their wives and children, and to burn themselves, rather than submit to a foreign enemy; when they can be brought to give their most precious effects, their ornaments of gold and silver, for the support of a common cause; when women are brought to give their hair to make ropes, and the most decrepit old men to mount the walls of a town for its defence; I think I may say, that by properly conducting and managing the spirit of a people, nothing is impossible to be accomplished. But when I say, nothing is impossible, I must be understood to mean, that nothing essentially necessary for the good of the people is impossible; and this is all that is required in government.

That it requires a particular talent in a statesman to dispose the minds of a people to approve even of the scheme which is the most conducive to their interest and prosperity, appears from this; that we see examples of wise, rich, and powerful nations languishing in inactivity, at a time when every individual is animated with a quite contrary spirit; becoming a prey to their enemies, like the city of Jerusalem, while they are taken up with their domestic animosities, merely because the remedies proposed against these evils contradict the spirit of the times. *

The great art of governing is to divest oneself of prejudices and attachments to particular opinions, particular classes, and above all to particular persons; to consult the spirit of the people, to give way to it in appearance, and in so doing to give it a turn capable of inspiring those sentiments which may induce them to relish the change, which an alteration of circumstances has rendered necessary.

* This was written in the year 1756, about the time the island of Minorca was taken by the French.

Alexander Hamilton

1757–1804

In the economic statecraft that followed the ratification of the Constitution, Hamilton's was the major role. Jefferson may have become President, but it was Hamilton who recognized the needs of the new republic and possessed the force of mind and character to fill these needs. In summary, Hamilton's program is simple to state. Indispensable to it was a strong national government in which resided powers over commerce and currency adequate to hold in check the particularism of local interests. A sound currency and a stable banking system were essential to rapid economic progress, and both of these grand objectives presupposed the sympathetic encouragement of the propertied classes in the community. Hence Hamilton advocated the funding of the national debt, and the establishment of a central bank.

Even more perceptively Hamilton foresaw an American future which centered upon industry rather than agriculture. In his reasoned case for the protection of burgeoning industry—the well-known infant-industry argument—Hamilton strongly influenced Friedrich List's later application of protectionist remedies to German circumstances. Much of Hamilton's case ran in terms of bounties rather than tariffs, which on equity grounds are much more fair, since the entire community, rather than the customers of a particular industry, share the burden of protection. Hamilton believed that the greater prosperity of industry would promote the welfare of other groups as well. He put the case with great skill:

> It is not proper to proceed a step further, and to enumerate the principal circumstances from which it may be inferred that manufacturing establishments not only occasion a positive augmentation of the produce and revenue of the society, but that they contribute

147

*essentially to rendering them greater than they could possibly be
without establishments. These circumstances are:*

1. *The Division of Labor.*
2. *An extension of the use of machinery.*
3. *Additional employment to classes of the community not ordinarily engaged in the business.*
4. *The promoting of emigration from foreign countries.*
5. *The furnishing greater scope for the diversity of talents and
   dispositions, which discriminate men from each other.*
6. *The affording a more ample and various field for enterprise.*
7. *The creating, in some instances, of a new, and securing, in
   all, a more certain and steady demand for the surplus produce
   of the soil.*

Which is to say that, unlike the English classical economists who
implicitly at the least foresaw economic opposition between manufacturer and landowner, Hamilton in the very different American circumstances preached the doctrine of class harmony in the context
of an expanding industrial economy.

While not very many underdeveloped countries today would be
charmed by the fourth of Hamilton's recommendations, many of
their leaders act more like twentieth-century Hamiltonians than
twentieth-century Jeffersonians. If a willingness to use the machine of
the state, encourage industry, and discriminate against agriculture
are the stigmata of the Hamiltonian, then there is scarce a later-day
Jefferson in sight.

Some of Hamilton's measures resemble superficially the preferences
of the mercantilists. The critical distinction of assumption between
Hamilton and the mercantilists is over the expansibility of the economy, and the prospects of economic improvement for all orders of
society.

This passage from the Report on Manufactures is taken from The
Shaping of the American Tradition, *edited by Louis M. Hacker (New
York: Columbia University Press, 1947), pp. 300-1, 303-4.*

Report on the Subject of Manufactures

. . . II. But, without contending for the superior productiveness of
manufacturing industry, it may conduce to a better judgment of the
policy which ought to be pursued respecting its encouragement, to
contemplate the subject under some additional aspects, tending not
only to confirm the idea that this kind of industry has been improperly
represented as unproductive in itself, but to evince, in addition, that

the establishment and diffusion of manufactures have the effect of
rendering the total mass of useful and productive labor, in a community, greater than it would otherwise be. In prosecuting this discussion, it may be necessary briefly to résumé and review some of the
topics which have been already touched.

To affirm that the labor of the manufacturer is unproductive, because he consumes as much of the produce of land as he adds value
to the raw material which he manufactures, is not better founded
than it would be to affirm that the labor of the farmer, which furnishes materials to the manufacturer, is unproductive, because he
consumes an equal value of manufactured articles. Each furnishes a
certain portion of the produce of his labor to the other, and each
destroys a corresponding portion of the produce of the labor of the
other. In the meantime, the maintenance of two citizens, instead of
one, is going on; the State has two members instead of one; and they,
together, consume twice the value of what is produced from the land.

If, instead of a farmer and artificer, there were a farmer only, he
would be under the necessity of devoting a part of his labor to the
fabrication of clothing and other articles, which he would procure of
the artificer, in the case of there being such a person; and of course
he would be able to devote less labor to the cultivation of his farm,
and would draw from it a proportionately less product. The whole
quantity of production, in this state of things, in provisions, raw materials, and manufactures, would certainly not exceed in value the
amount of what would be produced in provisions and raw materials
only, if there were an artificer as well as a farmer.

Again, if there were both an artificer and a farmer, the latter would be left at liberty to pursue exclusively the cultivation of
his farm. A greater quantity of provisions and raw materials would,
of course, be produced, equal, at least, as has been already observed,
to the whole amount of the provisions, raw materials, and manufactures, which would exist on a contrary supposition. The artificer, at
the same time, would be going on in the production of manufactured
commodities, to an amount sufficient, not only to repay the farmer,
in those commodities, for the provisions and materials which were
procured from him, but to furnish the artificer himself with a supply
of similar commodities for his own use. Thus, then, there would be
two quantities or values in existence, instead of one; and the revenue
and consumption would be double, in one case, what it would be in
the other.

If, in place of both of these suppositions, there were supposed to be
two farmers and no artificer, each of whom applied a part of his labor

to the culture of land and another part to the fabrication of manufactures; in this case, the portion of the labor of both, bestowed upon land, would produce the same quantity of provisions and raw materials only, as would be produced by the entire sum of the labor of one, applied in the same manner; and the portion of the labor of both, bestowed upon manufactures, would produce the same quantity of manufactures only, as would be produced by the entire sum of the labor of one, applied in the same manner. Hence, the produce of the labor of the two farmers would not be greater than the produce of the labor of the farmer and artificer; and hence it results, that the labor of the artificer is as positively productive as that of the farmer, and as positively augments the revenue of the society.

The labor of the artificer replaces to the farmer that portion of his labor with which he provides the materials of exchange with the artificer, and which he would otherwise have been compelled to apply to manufactures; and while the artificer thus enables the farmer to enlarge his stock of agricultural industry, a portion of which he purchases for his own use, he also supplies himself with the manufactured articles of which he stands in need. He does still more. Besides this equivalent, which he gives for the portion of agricultural labor consumed by him, and this supply of manufactured commodities for his own consumption, he furnishes still a surplus, which compensates for the use of the capital advanced, either by himself or some other person, for carrying on the business. This is the ordinary profit of the stock employed in the manufactory, and is, in every sense, as effective an addition to the income of the society as the rent of land.

The produce of the labor of the artificer, consequently, may be regarded as composed of three parts: one, by which the provisions for his subsistence and the materials for his work are purchased of the farmer; one, by which he supplies himself with manufactured necessaries; and a third, which constitutes the profit on the stock employed. The two last portions seem to have been overlooked in the system which represents manufacturing industry as barren and unproductive.

In the course of the preceding illustrations, the products of equal quantities of the labor of the farmer and artificer have been treated as if equal to each other. But this is not to be understood as intending to assert any such precise equality. It is merely a manner of expression, adopted for the sake of simplicity and perspicuity. Whether the value of the produce of the labor of the farmer be somewhat more or less than that of the artificer, is not material to the main scope of the argument, which, hitherto, has only aimed at showing that the one, as well as the other, occasions a positive augmentation of the total produce and revenue of the society.

It is now proper to proceed a step further, and to enumerate the principal circumstances from which it may be inferred that manufacturing establishments not only occasion a positive augmentation of the produce and revenue of the society, but that they contribute essentially to rendering them greater than they could possibly be without such establishments. These circumstances are:

1. The division of labor.

2. An extension of the use of machinery.

3. Additional employment to classes of the community not ordinarily engaged in the business.

4. The promoting of emigration from foreign countries.

5. The furnishing greater scope for the diversity of talents and dispositions, which discriminate men from each other.

6. The affording a more ample and various field for enterprise.

7. The creating, in some instances, a new, and securing, in all, a more certain and steady demand for the surplus produce of the soil.

Each of these circumstances has a considerable influence upon the total mass of industrious effort in a community; together, they add to it a degree of energy and effect which is not easily conceived. Some comments upon each of them, in the order in which they have been stated, may serve to explain their importance.

1. *As to the division of labor*

It has justly been observed, that there is scarcely any thing of greater moment in the economy of a nation than the proper division of labor. The separation of occupations causes each to be carried to a much greater perfection than it could possibly acquire if they were blended. This arises principally from three circumstances:

1st. The greater skill and dexterity naturally resulting from a constant and undivided application to a single object. It is evident that these properties must increase in proportion to the separation and simplification of objects, and the steadiness of the attention devoted to each; and must be less in proportion to the complication of objects, and the number among which the attention is distracted.

2d. The economy of time, by avoiding the loss of it, incident to a frequent transition from one operation to another of a different nature. This depends on various circumstances: the transition itself, the orderly disposition of the implements, machines, and materials employed in the operation to be relinquished, the preparatory steps to the commencement of a new one, the interruption of the impulse which the mind of the workman acquires from being engaged in a particular operation, the distractions, hesitations, and reluctances which attend the passage from one kind of business to another.

3d. An extension of the use of machinery. A man occupied on a single object will have it more in his power, and will be more naturally led to exert his imagination, in devising methods to facilitate and abridge labor, than if he were perplexed by a variety of independent and dissimilar operations. Besides this the fabrication of machines, in numerous instances, becoming itself a distinct trade, the artist who follows it has all the advantages which have been enumerated, for improvement in his particular art; and, in both ways, the invention and application of machinery are extended.

And from these causes united, the mere separation of the occupation of the cultivator from that of the artificer, has the effect of augmenting the productive powers of labor, and with them, the total mass of the produce or revenue of a country. In this single view of the subject, therefore, the utility of artificers or manufacturers, towards producing an increase of productive industry, is apparent. . . .

5. *As to the furnishing greater scope for the diversity of talents and dispositions, which discriminate men from each other*

This is a much more powerful means of augmenting the fund of national industry, than may at first sight appear. It is a just observation, that minds of the strongest and most active powers for their proper objects, fall below mediocrity, and labor without effect, if confined to uncongenial pursuits. And it is thence to be inferred, that the results of human exertion may be immensely increased by diversifying its objects. When all the different kinds of industry obtain in a community, each individual can find his proper element, and can call into activity the whole vigor of his nature. And the community is benefited by the services of its respective members, in the manner in which each can serve it with most effect.

If there be any thing in a remark often to be met with, namely, that there is, in the genius of the people of this country, a peculiar aptitude for mechanic improvements, it would operate as a forcible reason for giving opportunities to the exercise of that species of talent, by the propagation of manufactures.

6. *As to the affording a more ample and various field for enterprise*

This also is of greater consequence in the general scale of national exertion than might, perhaps, on a superficial view be supposed, and has effects not altogether dissimilar from those of the circumstance last noticed. To cherish and stimulate the activity of the human mind, by multiplying the objects of enterprise, is not among the least considerable of the expedients by which the wealth of a nation may be promoted. Even things in themselves not positively advantageous sometimes become so, by their tendency to provoke exertion. Every new scene which is opened to the busy nature of man to rouse and exert itself, is the addition of a new energy to the general stock of effort.

The spirit of enterprise, useful and prolific as it is, must necessarily be contracted or expanded, in proportion to the simplicity or variety of the occupations and productions which are to be found in a society. It must be less in a nation of mere cultivators, than in a nation of cultivators and merchants; less in a nation of cultivators and merchants, than in a nation of cultivators, artificers, and merchants.

7. *As to the creating, in some instances, a new, and securing, in all, a more certain and steady demand for the surplus produce of the soil*

This is among the most important of the circumstances which have been indicated. It is a principal means by which the establishment of manufactures contributes to an augmentation of the produce or revenue of a country, and has an immediate and direct relation to the prosperity of agriculture.

It is evident that the exertions of the husbandman will be steady or fluctuating, vigorous or feeble, in proportion to the steadiness or fluctuation, adequateness or inadequateness, of the markets on which he must depend for the vent of the surplus which may be produced by his labor; and that such surplus, in the ordinary course of things, will be greater or less in the same proportion.

For the purpose of this vent, a domestic market is greatly to be preferred to a foreign one; because it is, in the nature of things, far more to be relied upon.

It is a primary object of the policy of nations, to be able to supply themselves with subsistence from their own soils; and manufacturing nations, as far as circumstances permit, endeavor to procure from the same source the raw materials necessary for their own fabrics. This disposition, urged by the spirit of monopoly, is sometimes even carried to an injudicious extreme. It seems not always to be recollected, that nations who have neither mines nor manufactures can only obtain the manufactured articles of which they stand in need, by an exchange of the products of their soils; and that if those who can best furnish them with such articles are unwilling to give a due course to this exchange, they must, of necessity, make every possible effort to manufacture for themselves; the effect of which is, that the manufacturing nations abridge the natural advantages of their situation, through an unwillingness to permit the agricultural countries to enjoy the advantages of theirs, and sacrifice the interests of a mutually beneficial intercourse to the vain project of selling every thing and buying nothing.

But it is also a consequence of the policy which has been noted, that the foreign demand for the products of agricultural countries is, in a great degree, rather casual and occasional, than certain or constant. To what extent injurious interruptions of the demand for some of the staple commodities of the United States may have been experienced from that cause, must be referred to the judgment of those who are engaged in carrying on the commerce of the country; but it may be safely affirmed, that such interruptions are, at times, very inconveniently felt, and that cases not unfrequently occur, in which markets are so confined and restricted as to render the demand very unequal to the supply.

Independently, likewise, of the artificial impediments which are created by the policy in question, there are natural causes tending to render the external demand for the surplus of agricultural nations a precarious reliance. The differences of seasons in the countries which are the consumers, make immense differences in the produce of their own soils, in different years; and consequently in the degrees of their necessity for foreign supply. Plentiful harvests with them, especially if similar ones occur at the same time in the countries which are the furnishers, occasion, of course, a glut in the markets of the latter.

Considering how fast and how much the progress of new settlements in the United States must increase the surplus produce of the soil, and weighing seriously the tendency of the system which prevails among most of the commercial nations of Europe, whatever dependence may be placed on the force of natural circumstances to counteract the effects of an artificial policy, there appear strong reasons to regard the foreign demand for that surplus as too uncertain a reliance, and to desire a substitute for it in an extensive domestic market.

To secure such a market there is no other expedient than to promote manufacturing establishments. Manufacturers, who constitute the most numerous class, after the cultivators of land, are for that reason the principal consumers of the surplus of their labor.

This idea of an extensive domestic market for the surplus produce of the soil, is of the first consequence. It is, of all things, that which most effectually conduces to a flourishing state of agriculture. If the effect of manufactories should be to detach a portion of the hands which would otherwise be engaged in tillage, it might possibly cause a smaller quantity of lands to be under cultivation; but, by their tendency to procure a more certain demand for the surplus produce of the soil, they would, at the same time, cause the lands which were in cultivation to be better improved and more productive. And while by their influence, the condition of each individual farmer would be meliorated, the total mass of agricultural production would probably be increased. For this must evidently depend as much upon the degree of improvement, if not more, than upon the number of acres under culture.

It merits particular observation, that the multiplication of manufactories not only furnishes a market for those articles which have been accustomed to be produced in abundance in a country, but it likewise creates a demand for such as were either unknown or produced in inconsiderable quantities. The bowels as well as the surface of the earth are ransacked for articles which were before neglected. Animals, plants, and minerals acquire a utility and a value which were before unexplored.

The foregoing considerations seem sufficient to establish, as general propositions, that it is the interest of nations to diversify the industrious pursuits of the individuals who compose them; that the establishment of manufactures is calculated not only to increase the general stock of useful and productive labor, but even to improve the state of agriculture in particular—certainly to advance the interests of those who are engaged in it. There are other views that will be hereafter taken of the subject, which it is conceived will serve to confirm these inferences. . . .

A native of Württemberg, Friedrich List was a polemical journalist whose forthrightness won him expulsion from his native state. He traveled extensively in Europe and spent some years in the United States. He was a fervent German nationalist, who burned with shame at the thought of Germany's weakness and disunity. His National System of Political Economy used history as a tool to construct a stronger Germany, and, incidentally, to raze the structure of English classical economics. His book was a not very fair polemic against Adam Smith who was guilty of the sins—in List's eyes—of cosmopolitanism and individualism. Parodying Smith, he remarked: ". . . that may be wisdom in national economy which would be folly in private economy." Smith had neglected the nation; List, on the other hand, ". . . would indicate as the distinguishing characteristic of my system, NATIONALITY."

The book began with a historical survey. List rapidly reviewed the city-states of Renaissance Italy, the Hanseatic League, France, England, Holland, and Germany. Their past had a clear moral to List: the teachings of history associated prosperity and decline with four circumstances. Wherever economic progress had been rapid, as in England, the nation had been strong and unified. History's second lesson was a criticism of individualism. The productive powers of individuals did not depend upon their own initiative and ability. Instead they were the consequence of social conditions and human institutions. Since we were all the products of our society, that society had the right to call upon us to subordinate our own interests to the great good. More than Bentham's arithmetic sum of individuals, the state was an organism that was different from and greater than its parts.

In his third lesson of history, List declared that navigation and trade could flourish only when manufacturing prospered—a doc-

trine implicitly embraced by most of the underdeveloped countries of the twentieth century. For this reason, he had qualified praise for the restrictions that English mercantilists placed upon trade. They did properly stress the interests of the nation and they did foster English manufacturing. Smith was wrong when he attacked the Navigation Acts. These acts so well and truly protected English interests that England finally was able to discard them.

The final lesson of history emphasized that internal freedom was an essential condition of economic advance. With Germany ever in his mind, List wanted to end the intricate restrictions upon the flow of trade and the free movement of economic resources which hampered German economic growth. The Zollverein of the 1830's owes something to List's inspiration.

From his tendentious reading of history, List drew his policy recommendations. No doubt where universal peace reigned, free trade would be a wonderful arrangement. But if the facts of national sovereignty and national rivalry were granted their appropriate importance, it became clear that free trade would simply extend English dominion. England, after all, enjoyed the advantage of a considerable head start in manufacturing. Since only manufacturing fully released the nation's productive powers, the state should encourage manufacturing. It could do so by introducing protective tariffs, which enabled manufacturing to be developed despite the competition of countries that had begun earlier. This argument has come to be known as the infant-industry argument for protective tariffs. It is still accepted by many economists as conceptually valid, although most of the economists would add that there is enormous administrative difficulty first in identifying the proper industries to protect and then in removing the protection when the infant has grown to maturity.

The selection is from National System of Political Economy *(Philadelphia, 1856), pp. 72-82.*

Infant Industries

In the economical development of nations, it is necessary to distinguish the following principal stages: the savage state, the pastoral state, the agricultural state, the agricultural and manufacturing state, and finally, the agricultural, manufacturing, and commercial state.

It is obvious that a nation possessing an extensive territory, enriched with varied resources and a numerous population, uniting agriculture and manufactures with an external and internal trade, is beyond comparison more civilized, politically more developed and more powerful than any merely agricultural country. But manufactures constitute the basis of external and internal trade, of navigation, of an improved agriculture, consequently of civilization and political power; and should any nation succeed in monopolizing all the manufacturing activity of the world, and in checking all other nations in their economical development by reducing them to the mere production of agricultural commodities and raw materials, and other indispensable local productions, it would undoubtedly attain to very wide, if not to universal dominion.

A nation that greatly values its independence and its safety, must make a vigorous effort to elevate itself as fast as possible, from an inferior to a higher state of civilization, uniting and perfecting as quickly as possible, its own agriculture, manufactures, navigation, and commerce.

The transition from the savage to the pastoral, and from the pastoral to the agricultural state, as well as the first progress in agriculture, is very efficiently promoted by free intercourse among manufacturing and commercial nations.

The elevation of an agricultural people to the condition of countries at once agricultural, manufacturing, and commercial, can only be accomplished under the law of free trade, when the various nations engaged at the time in manufacturing industry shall be in the same degree of progress and civilization; when they shall place no obstacle in the way of the economical development of each other, and not impede their respective progress by war or adverse commercial legislation.

But some of them, favored by circumstances, having distanced others in manufactures, commerce, and navigation, and having early perceived that this advanced state was the surest mode of acquiring and keeping political supremacy, have adopted and still persevere in a policy so well adapted to give them the monopoly of manufactures, of industry and of commerce, and to impede the progress of less advanced nations or those in a lower degree of culture. The measures enforced by such nations, taken as a whole, the prohibitions, the duties on imports, the maritime restrictions, premiums upon exports, &c., are called the protective system.

The anterior progress of certain nations, foreign commercial legislation and war have compelled inferior countries to look for special means of effecting their transition from the agricultural to the manufacturing stage of industry, and as far as practicable, by a system of duties, to restrain their trade with more advanced nations aiming at manufacturing monopoly.

The system of import duties is consequently not, as has been said, an invention of speculative minds; it is a natural consequence of the tendency of nations to seek for guarantees of their existence and prosperity, and to establish and increase their weight in the scale of national influence.

Such a tendency is legitimate and reasonable only so far as it renders easy, instead of retarding, the economical development of a nation; and it is not in opposition to the higher objects of society, the universal confederation of the future.

As human association ought to be considered under two points of view, that is to say, the cosmopolitan, embracing all the human race, and the political or merely national, every economy, private or public, ought to be considered under two different aspects, the individual, social and material power, by means of which riches are produced, and the interchangeable value of the products of industry.

There is, consequently, a cosmopolitan economy and a political economy, a theory of interchangeable value, and a theory of productive power. These doctrines are distinct in their essence, and require to be developed separately.

The productive power of nations is not solely dependent on the labor, the saving, the morality, and the intelligence of individuals, or on the possession of natural advantage and material capital; it is dependent also upon institutions and laws, social, political, and civil, but, above all, on the securities of their duration, their independence, and their power as nations. Individuals would be in vain laborious, economical, ingenious, enterprising, intelligent, and moral, without a national unity, without a division of labor and a co-operation of productive power. A nation cannot otherwise attain to a high degree of prosperity and power, nor maintain itself in the permanent possession of its intellectual, social, and material riches.

The principle of the division of labor has been hitherto but imperfectly understood. Industrial production depends much less on the apportioning of the various operations of a manufacture among several individuals, than on the moral and material association of those individuals for a common end.

This principle applies not only to a manufacture or to a rural industry; it extends also to every kind of national industry, agricultural, manufacturing, and commercial.

The division of labor and the combination of productive power take place in a nation when the intellectual power is applied so as to co-operate freely and efficiently with national production, when manufacturing industry and trade are equally and harmoniously developed.

A merely agricultural people in free intercourse with manufacturing and trading nations, will lose a considerable part of their productive power and natural resources, which must remain idle and unemployed. Its intellectual and political culture, and its means of defence, will thus be limited. It can possess neither an important navigation, nor an extensive trade; its prosperity, as far as it results from external commerce, may be interrupted, disturbed, or annihilated by foreign legislation or by war.

On the other hand, manufacturing industry is favorable to science, art, and political progress; it promotes the general welfare, increases population, public revenue, and the power of the country; it enables the latter to extend its influence to all parts of the world, and to found colonies; it sustains fisheries and navies, mercantile and national. By it only, can agriculture rise to any high degree of efficiency and perfection.

Agriculture and manufacturing industry united in the same nation, under the same political power, live in perpetual peace; they are disturbed in their reciprocal action, neither by war, nor by foreign legislation; they ensure to a nation the continued development of its prosperity, civilization, and power.

Agriculture and manufacturing industry are subjected by nature to special conditions.

The countries of the temperate zone are especially fit for the development of manufacturing industry; for the temperate zone is the region of intellectual and physical effort.

If the countries of the torrid zone are little favored in reference to manufactures, they possess, on the other hand, the natural monopoly of many precious commodities which the inhabitants of the temperate climates greatly prize. The exchange of the manufactured products of the one for the commodities of the other, constitutes a division of labor and a co-operation of productive power throughout the chief commercial nations, and mainly constitutes the great international trade of the world.

A country of the torrid zone would make a very fatal mistake, should it try to become a manufacturing country. Having received no invitation to that vocation from nature, it will progress more rapidly in riches and civilization if it continues to exchange its agricultural productions for the manufactured products of the temperate zone.

It is true that tropical countries sink thus into dependence upon those of the temperate zone, but that dependence will not be without compensation, if competition arises among the nations of temperate climes in their manufacturing industry in their trade with the former, and in their exercise of political power. This competition will not only ensure a full supply of manufactures at low prices, but will prevent any one nation from taking advantage by its superiority over the weaker nations of the torrid zone. There would be danger and damage in this dependence only so far as manufactures, important branches of trade, foreign commerce, and maritime power should become the monopoly of a single nation.

Nations of the temperate zone possessing extensive territory enriched with varied resources, have lost one of the richest sources of prosperity, civilization and power, if they do not succeed in realizing a national division of labor and a co-operation of national productive power, as soon as they possess the necessary conditions, economical, intellectual, and social, for accomplishing it.

By economical conditions, we understand an advanced stage of agriculture, which cannot be sensibly stimulated by the export of its products; by moral conditions, a high moral culture among individuals; by social conditions, we mean legal security to citizens for their persons and properties, and the free exercise of their moral and physical faculties; institutions regulating and facilitating trade, and suppressing all restraints upon industry, liberty, intelligence, and morality, as for instance, feudal institutions.

It is of the utmost concern for a nation uniting such advantages, first fully to supply its own wants, its own consumption, with the products of its own manufactures, then to form direct connections progressively with the countries of the torrid zone, transmitting to them, upon its own vessels, its manufactured products, receiving in exchange their commodities.

In comparison with this exchange of the manufactured products of the temperate, for the agricultural productions of the torrid zone, other international trade is of a secondary importance, if we but except the trade in a few special articles; wine, for instance.

The production of raw materials and commodities among the great nations of temperate climes, has no real importance but in regard to internal trade. An uncultivated nation may at the beginning advance its agriculture by the exportation of wheat, wine, flax, hemp, and wool; but no great nation ever arrived at wealth, civilization, and power, by such policy.

It may be stated as a principle, that a nation is richer and more powerful, in proportion as it exports more manufactured products, imports more raw materials, and consumes more tropical commodities.

Productions of the tropics serve to manufacturing countries of temperate climes, not only as raw materials, and alimentary commodities, but also, and especially, as stimulants for agricultural and industrial labor. The nation which consumes the greatest quantity of tropical commodities, will always be that of which the agricultural and manufacturing production is relatively the most considerable, and that which consumes the greatest quantity of its own products.

In the economical development of nations by means of external trade, four periods must be distinguished. In the first, agriculture is encouraged by the importation of manufactured articles, and by the exportation of its own products; in the second, manufactures begin to increase at home, whilst the importation of foreign manufactures to some extent continues; in the third, home manufactures mainly supply domestic consumption and the internal markets; finally, in the fourth, we see the exportation upon a large scale of manufactured products, and the importation of raw materials and agricultural products.

The system of import duties being considered as a mode of assisting the economical development of a nation, by regulating its external trade, must constantly take as a rule the principle of the industrial education of the country.

To encourage agriculture by the aid of protective duties is vicious policy; for agriculture can be encouraged only by promoting manufacturing industry; and the exclusion of raw materials and agricultural products from abroad, has no other result than to impede the rise of national manufactures.

The economical education of a country of inferior intelligence and culture, or one thinly populated, relatively to the extent and the fertility of its territory, is effected most certainly by free trade, with more advanced, richer, and more industrious nations. Every commercial restriction in such a country aiming at the increase of manufactures, is premature, and will prove detrimental, not only to civilization in general, but the progress of the nation in particular. If its intellectual, political, and economical education, under the operation of free trade, has advanced so far, that the importation of foreign manufactures, and the want of markets for its own products has become an obstacle to its ulterior development, then only can protective measures be justified.

A nation without extensive territory and of otherwise limited resources, which does not control the mouths of its rivers, or which has not suitable boundaries, cannot resort to the protective system, or at least cannot employ it with full success. It must be first enlarged by way of conquest or negotiation.

Manufacturing industry is concerned with so many branches of science and art, it implies so much experience, practice, and adaptation, that the industrial training and education of a country can proceed but slowly. All excessive or premature protection is expiated by a diminution of national prosperity.

No commercial policy is more dangerous and reprehensible than a sudden resort to absolute prohibition of foreign products. It may, however, be justified, when a country, separated from others by a long war, finds itself almost in a compulsory state of prohibitions in regard to foreign products, and under the absolute necessity of offering a high premium to the industry which will enable it to supply its own wants.

The return from such a condition must be by gradual transition from the prohibitive to the protective system, and should be effected by means of duties fixed by anticipation, and decreasing gradually. On the other hand, a nation which is to pass from free trade to the protective system should commence with low duties to be afterwards raised by degrees according to a suitable scale.

Duties thus fixed by anticipation must be strictly maintained by the government; it must be careful not to diminish them before the appointed time, and equally careful to raise them if they should prove insufficient.

Duties upon imports so high as absolutely to exclude foreign competition are prejudicial to the country which adopts them; for they suppress all rivalry between domestic and foreign manufacturers, and encourage indolence among the former.

When, under the rule of suitable and progressive duties, the manufactures of a country do not thrive, it is an evidence that the country does not yet possess the conditions requisite to a manufacturing people.

Duties designed to favor an industry should never be put so low as to endanger the existence of the latter from foreign competition. It should be a rule to preserve what exists—to protect national industry in its trunk and in its roots.

Foreign competition should not have more than its share in the annual increase of consumption. Duties should be raised when foreign commodities supply the greatest part or the whole of the increased annual consumption.

A country like England, which is far in advance of all its competitors, cannot better maintain and extend its manufacturing and commercial industry than by a trade as free as possible from all restraints. For such a country, the cosmopolitan and the national principle are one and the same thing.

This explains the favor with which the most enlightened economists of England regard free trade, and the reluctance of the wise and prudent of other countries to adopt this principle in the actual state of the world.

A quarter of a century since, the prohibitive and protective system of England operated to her detriment and to the advantage of her rivals.

Nothing could be more prejudicial to England than her restrictions upon the importation of raw material and food.

Union of customs and commercial treaties are the most efficient means of facilitating national exchanges.

But treaties of commerce are legitimate and durable only when the advantages are reciprocal. They are fatal and illegitimate when they sacrifice one country to another; when one country, to purchase advantage for its agriculture, sacrifices a manufacturing industry already well advanced; such a treaty was that of Methuen, a compact in which one party took the lion's share.

The treaty concluded between England and France in 1786 was one of those leonine treaties. And all the propositions made since by England and France to other countries are of the same nature.

If protective duties enhance for a time the price of domestic manufactures, they secure afterwards lower prices by means of internal competition; for an industry that has reached its full development can safely reduce its prices far below those which were necessary to ensure its growth, and thus save to its consumers the whole expense of transportation and the whole profits of trade, which are consequent upon imports of the same articles from other countries.

The loss occasioned by protective duties consists, after all, only in values; whilst the country thus acquires a power, by which it is enabled to produce a great mass of values. This loss in values must be considered as the price of the industrial training of the country.

Protective duties upon manufactured products do not press heavily upon the agriculture of a country. By the development of manufacturing industry, the wealth, population, consumption of agricultural products, rent, and exchangeable value of real estate are vastly increased, whilst the manufactured products consumed by farmers gradually fall in price. The gain, thus realized, exceeds, in the proportion of ten to one, the loss which agriculturalists incur by the transient rise of manufactured products.

Internal and external trade flourish alike under the protective system; these have no importance but among nations supplying their own wants by their own manufacturing industry, consuming their own agricultural products, and purchasing foreign raw materials and commodities with the surplus of their manufactured articles. Home and foreign trade are both insignificant in the merely agricultural countries of temperate climes, and their external commerce is usually in the hands of the manufacturing and trading nations in communication with them.

A good system of protection does not imply any monopoly in the manufacturers of a country; it only furnishes a guarantee against losses to those who devote their capital, their talents, and their exertions to new branches of industry.

There is no monopoly, because internal competition comes in the place of foreign competition, and every individual has the privilege of taking his share in the advantages offered by the country to its citizens; it is only an advantage to citizens as against foreigners, who enjoy in their own country a similar advantage.

But this protection is useful not only because it awakens the sleeping energies of a country and puts in motion its productive power, but because it attracts the productive power of foreign countries, including capital, both material and moral, and skilful masters as well as skilful men.

On the other hand, the absence of manufacturing industry in a nation long civilized, the productive powers of which cannot be sensibly excited by the export of raw materials and agricultural products, and, by the importation of foreign manufactures, exposes it to numerous and serious inconveniences.

The agriculture of such a country must necessarily suffer; for the surplus population, which, in a great manufacturing development, finds means of living in factories and creates a large demand for agricultural products, thus affording substantial profits to agriculture, will be reduced to the labor of the fields, and thence will follow a subdivision of farms and a small culture, both as prejudicial to the power and the civilization of a country as to its wealth.

An agricultural people consisting chiefly of proprietors of small estates, can neither fill the channels of internal trade with large quantities of commodities, nor furnish a large consumption for manufactured goods; in such a country, every one is limited almost to his own production and his own consumption. In circumstances like these, no complete system of communications can be established, and the immense advantages which they afford are lost to the country.

Hence ensues necessarily, moral and material, individual and political weakness. The danger is aggravated when neighboring nations pursue a different policy: some making progress in every respect, others retrograding; some hoping for a brighter future, the courage and enterprise of their people being aroused; the absence of hope extinguishing by degrees in others all courage, intelligence, and enterprise.

History is not without examples of entire nations having perished, because they knew not and seized not the critical moment for the solution of the great problem of securing their moral, economical, and political independence, by the establishment of manufacturing industry, and the formation of a powerful class of manufacturers and tradesmen.

John Maynard Keynes

1883–1946

Like Keynes's rehabilitation of Malthus as a precursor of his own doctrines of underemployment equilibrium and general glut, his treatment of the mercantilists exemplifies a great theorist's purposeful manipulation of the history of his subject to emphasize both the past and the virtues of his own kind of analysis. Although Keynes wrote fairly extensively in the history of doctrine—his Essays in Biography consist largely of graceful tributes to earlier economists—he was also capable of impatience at the merely antiquarian. It was in this mood that Keynes once wondered why he should concern himself with the wrong ideas of dead men.

But, as the passage below indicates, dead men occasionally had the right ideas, even though they were unclear about their justifications. Reading the mercantilist literature rather selectively (as Eli Heckscher, the great historian of mercantilism charged), Keynes concluded that mercantilist policies designed to promote favorable trade balances and gold inflows were the only practicable devices available to officials who lacked central banking controls, for the maintenance of high levels of employment. Echoing Hume at a distance of nearly two centuries, Keynes believed that the major impact of a favorable balance of trade was an increase in the domestic supply of money, which in turn encouraged trade and lowered internal rates of interest.

Full comprehension of Keynes's position and terminology demands a complete reading of The General Theory of Employment, Interest and Money. *But the skeleton of his theory can be quickly sketched. To begin with, Keynes was convinced that price and wage adjustments were incapable of moving a depressed economy automatically to a position of high employment. Say's Law, if it ever had adequately identified such a tendency, had long been repealed by events. Employment depended on total spending, not on price and wage flexibility. Total spending, in turn, depended upon the behavior of consumers and of investors. Keynes considered that consumers varied their consumption in harmony with variations in their income. As incomes increased, consumption also increased, although by an amount smaller than the rise in income. And, similarly, when incomes declined consumption also declined by a smaller amount. Since consumption itself was a dependent variable, then the independent element in income determination was necessarily investment. Hence the central objective of the Keynesian theory is an explanation of how investment takes place.*

This explanation focused on the relationship between expected rates of profit (Keynes's "marginal efficiency of capital") and actual rates of interest. Businessmen tended to invest as long as the profits they might reasonably anticipate exceeded the rate of interest that they had to pay. How could investment be expanded? If expected rates of profit rose, then more propositions would appeal to investors. But the state of long-term expectations upon which the marginal efficiency of capital largely depends is as much a matter of emotion— "animal spirits"—as it is of reason. Certainly it is difficult for a government to be confident of what will encourage the reluctant investor's optimism. But there was a way of affecting investment which did lie within the power of a concerned government, manipulation of the rate of interest. The logic of Keynes's demonstration implied that lower interest rates encouraged investment much as higher marginal efficiencies of capital stimulated business commitment to new ventures.

In the modern world, central banks can lower interest rates by devices familiar to all readers of newspapers: reserve requirements can be lowered, rediscount rates can be dropped, and, most effective of all, open market operations can increase the supply of loanable funds available to commercial banks and persuade these banks to lower their lending rates. In the mercantilist world, banking and the complex machinery of credit were still comparatively primitive. Yet the mercantilists intuitively perceived the desirability of easy money and low rates of interest. To this intuitive perception, their trade policies gave effect.

Keynes's tendentious history is less important as justice to the mercantilists than as an indication of Keynes's own belief that a larger role for the statesman was indispensable in modern economies. Here the thrust of his exposition suggests that credit policy—lower interest rates—was adequate to move a sluggish economy back to satisfactory levels of employment and production. Elsewhere in The General Theory of Employment, Interest and Money, *he casts doubt on the efficacy of the monetary remedy and contemplates solutions as extreme as the partial nationalization of investment. Much in the contemporary discussions of the British Labour Party accords with this sentiment.*

The passage that follows is from The General Theory of Employment, Interest and Money, *by John Maynard Keynes, pp. 333–40. Reprinted by permission of Harcourt, Brace & World, Inc.*

Notes on Mercantilism, the Usury Laws, Stamped Money and Theories of Under-Consumption

I

For some two hundred years both economic theorists and practical men did not doubt that there is a peculiar advantage to a country in a favourable balance of trade, and grave danger in an unfavourable balance, particularly if it results in an efflux of the precious metals. But for the past one hundred years there has been a remarkable divergence of opinion. The majority of statesmen and practical men in most countries, and nearly half of them even in Great Britain, the home of the opposite view, have remained faithful to the ancient doctrine; whereas almost all economic theorists have held that anxiety concerning such matters is absolutely groundless except on a very short view, since the mechanism of foreign trade is self-adjusting and attempts to interfere with it are not only futile, but greatly impoverish those who practise them because they forfeit the advantages of the international division of labour. It will be convenient, in accordance with tradition, to designate the older opinion as *Mercantilism* and the newer as *Free Trade,* though these terms, since each of them has both a broader and a narrower signification, must be interpreted with reference to the context.

Generally speaking, modern economists have maintained not merely that there is, as a rule, a balance of gain from the international division of labour sufficient to outweigh such advantages as mercantilist practice can fairly claim, but that the mercantilist argument is based, from start to finish, on an intellectual confusion.

Marshall,* for example, although his references to Mercantilism

---

* *Vide* his *Industry and Trade,* Appendix D; *Money, Credit and Commerce,* p. 130; and *Principles of Economics,* Appendix I.

are not altogether unsympathetic, had no regard for their central theory as such and does not even mention those elements of truth in their contentions which I shall examine below.* In the same way, the theoretical concessions which free-trade economists have been ready to make in contemporary controversies, relating, for example, to the encouragement of infant industries or to the improvement of the terms of trade, are not concerned with the real substance of the mercantilist case. During the fiscal controversy of the first quarter of the present century I do not remember that any concession was ever allowed by economists to the claim that Protection might increase domestic employment. It will be fairest, perhaps, to quote, as an example, what I wrote myself. So lately as 1923, as a faithful pupil of the classical school who did not at that time doubt what he had been taught and entertained on this matter no reserves at all, I wrote: "If there is one thing that Protection can *not* do, it is to cure Unemployment. . . . There are some arguments for Protection, based upon its securing possible but improbable advantages, to which there is no simple answer. But the claim to cure Unemployment involves the Protectionist fallacy in its grossest and crudest form." † As for earlier mercantilist theory, no intelligible account was available; and we were brought up to believe that it was little better than nonsense. So absolutely overwhelming and complete has been the domination of the classical school.

II

Let me first state in my own terms what now seems to me to be the element of scientific truth in mercantilist doctrine. We will then compare this with the actual arguments of the mercantilists. It should be understood that the advantages claimed are avowedly national advantages and are unlikely to benefit the world as a whole.

When a country is growing in wealth somewhat rapidly, the further progress of this happy state of affairs is liable to be interrupted, in conditions of *laissez-faire,* by the insufficiency of the inducements

* His view of them is well summed up in a footnote to the first edition of his *Principles,* p. 51: "Much study has been given both in England and Germany to medieval opinions as to the relation of money to national wealth. On the whole they are to be regarded as confused through want of a clear understanding of the functions of money, rather than as wrong in consequence of a deliberate assumption that the increase in the net wealth of a nation can be effected only by an increase of the stores of the precious metals in her."

† *The Nation and the Athenaeum,* November 24, 1923.

to new investment. Given the social and political environment and the national characteristics which determine the propensity to consume, the well-being of a progressive state essentially depends, for the reasons we have already explained, on the sufficiency of such inducements. They may be found either in home investment or in foreign investment (including in the latter the accumulation of the precious metals), which, between them, make up aggregate investment. In conditions in which the quantity of aggregate investment is determined by the profit motive alone, the opportunities for home investment will be governed, in the long run, by the domestic rate of interest; whilst the volume of foreign investment is necessarily determined by the size of the favourable balance of trade. Thus, in a society where there is no question of direct investment under the aegis of public authority, the economic objects, with which it is reasonable for the government to be preoccupied, are the domestic rate of interest and the balance of foreign trade.

Now, if the wage-unit is somewhat stable and not liable to spontaneous changes of significant magnitude (a condition which is almost always satisfied), if the state of liquidity-preference is somewhat stable, taken as an average of its short-period fluctuations, and if banking conventions are also stable, the rate of interest will tend to be governed by the quantity of the precious metals, measured in terms of the wage-unit, available to satisfy the community's desire for liquidity. At the same time, in an age in which substantial foreign loans and the outright ownership of wealth located abroad are scarcely practicable, increases and decreases in the quantity of the precious metals will largely depend on whether the balance of trade is favourable or unfavourable.

Thus, as it happens, a preoccupation on the part of the authorities with a favourable balance of trade served *both* purposes; and was, furthermore, the only available means of promoting them. At a time when the authorities had no direct control over the domestic rate of interest or the other inducements to home investment, measures to increase the favourable balance of trade were the only *direct* means at their disposal for increasing foreign investment; and, at the same time, the effect of a favourable balance of trade on the influx of the precious metals was their only *indirect* means of reducing the domestic rate of interest and so increasing the inducement to home investment.

There are, however, two limitations on the success of this policy which must not be overlooked. If the domestic rate of interest falls so low that the volume of investment is sufficiently stimulated to raise employment to a level which breaks through some of the critical points at which the wage-unit rises, the increase in the domestic level of costs will begin to react unfavourably on the balance of foreign trade, so that the effort to increase the latter will have overreached and defeated itself. Again, if the domestic rate of interest falls so low relatively to rates of interest elsewhere as to stimulate a volume of foreign lending which is disproportionate to the favourable balance, there may ensue an efflux of the precious metals sufficient to reverse the advantages previously obtained. The risk of one or other of these limitations becoming operative is increased in the case of a country which is large and internationally important by the fact that, in conditions where the current output of the precious metals from the mines is on a relatively small scale, an influx of money into one country means an efflux from another; so that the adverse effects of rising costs and falling rates of interest at home may be accentuated (if the mercantilist policy is pushed too far) by falling costs and rising rates of interest abroad.

The economic history of Spain in the latter part of the fifteenth and in the sixteenth centuries provides an example of a country whose foreign trade was destroyed by the effect on the wage-unit of an excessive abundance of the precious metals. Great Britain in the pre-war years of the twentieth century provides an example of a country in which the excessive facilities for foreign lending and the purchase of properties abroad frequently stood in the way of the decline in the domestic rate of interest which was required to ensure full employment at home. The history of India at all times has provided an example of a country impoverished by a preference for liquidity amounting to so strong a passion that even an enormous and chronic influx of the precious metals has been insufficient to bring down the rate of interest to a level which was compatible with the growth of real wealth.

Nevertheless, if we contemplate a society with a somewhat stable wage-unit, with national characteristics which determine the propensity to consume and the preference for liquidity, and with a monetary system which rigidly links the quantity of money to the stock of the precious metals, it will be essential for the maintenance of prosperity that the authorities should pay close attention to the state of the balance of trade. For a favourable balance, provided it is not too large, will prove extremely stimulating; whilst an unfavourable balance may soon produce a state of persistent depression.

It does not follow from this that the maximum degree of restriction of imports will promote the maximum favourable balance of trade.

The earlier mercantilists laid great emphasis on this and were often to be found opposing trade restrictions because on a long view they were liable to operate adversely to a favourable balance. It is, indeed, arguable that in the special circumstances of mid-nineteenth-century Great Britain an almost complete freedom of trade was the policy most conducive to the development of a favourable balance. Contemporary experience of trade restrictions in post-war Europe offers manifold examples of ill-conceived impediments on freedom which, designed to improve the favourable balance, had in fact a contrary tendency.

For this and other reasons the reader must not reach a premature conclusion as to the *practical* policy to which our argument leads up. There are strong presumptions of a general character against trade restrictions unless they can be justified on special grounds. The advantages of the international division of labour are real and substantial, even though the classical school greatly overstressed them. The fact that the advantage which our own country gains from a favourable balance is liable to involve an equal disadvantage to some other country (a point to which the mercantilists were fully alive) means not only that great moderation is necessary, so that a country secures for itself no larger a share of the stock of the precious metals than is fair and reasonable, but also that an immoderate policy may lead to a senseless international competition for a favourable balance which injures all alike.* And finally, a policy of trade restrictions is a treacherous instrument even for the attainment of its ostensible object, since private interest, administrative incompetence and the intrinsic difficulty of the task may divert it into producing results directly opposite to those intended.

Thus, the weight of my criticism is directed against the inadequacy of the *theoretical* foundations of the *laissez-faire* doctrine upon which I was brought up and which for many years I taught—against the notion that the rate of interest and the volume of investment are self-adjusting at the optimum level, so that preoccupation with the balance of trade is a waste of time. For we, the faculty of economists, prove to have been guilty of presumptuous error in treating as a puerile obsession what for centuries has been a prime object of practical statecraft.

Under the influence of this faulty theory the City of London gradually devised the most dangerous technique for the maintenance of

* The remedy of an elastic wage-unit, so that a depression is met by a reduction of wages, is liable, for the same reason, to be a means of benefiting ourselves at the expense of our neighbours.

equilibrium which can possibly be imagined, namely, the technique of bank rate coupled with a rigid parity of the foreign exchanges. For this meant that the objective of maintaining a domestic rate of interest consistent with full employment was wholly ruled out. Since, in practice, it is impossible to neglect the balance of payments, a means of controlling it was evolved which, instead of protecting the domestic rate of interest, sacrificed it to the operation of blind forces. Recently, practical bankers in London have learnt much, and one can almost hope that in Great Britain the technique of bank rate will never be used again to protect the foreign balance in conditions in which it is likely to cause unemployment at home.

Regarded as the theory of the individual firm and of the distribution of the product resulting from the employment of a given quantity of resources, the classical theory has made a contribution to economic thinking which cannot be impugned. It is impossible to think clearly on the subject without this theory as a part of one's apparatus of thought. I must not be supposed to question this in calling attention to their neglect of what was valuable in their predecessors. Nevertheless, as a contribution to statecraft, which is concerned with the economic system as whole and with securing the optimum employment of the system's entire resources, the methods of the early pioneers of economic thinking in the sixteenth and seventeenth centuries may have attained to fragments of practical wisdom which the unrealistic abstractions of Ricardo first forgot and then obliterated. There was wisdom in their intense preoccupation with keeping down the rate of interest by means of usury laws (to which we will return later in this chapter), by maintaining the domestic stock of money and by discouraging rises in the wage-unit; and in their readiness in the last resort to restore the stock of money by devaluation, if it had become plainly deficient through an unavoidable foreign drain, a rise in the wage-unit,* or any other cause.

* Experience since the age of Solon at least, and probably, if we had the statistics, for many centuries before that, indicates what a knowledge of human nature would lead us to expect, namely, that there is a steady tendency for the wage-unit to rise over long periods of time and that it can be reduced only amidst the decay and dissolution of economic society. Thus, apart altogether from progress and increasing population, a gradually increasing stock of money has proved imperative.

Gunnar Myrdal

1898–

The Swedish economist and international civil servant Gunnar Myrdal
is one of the great living social scientists of our time. His massive
study a generation ago in An American Dilemma of Negro-White relations in the United States presciently identified the tensions between
American libertarian ideals and American discriminatory practices.
There is little doubt that his remarkable study was one of the elements that accelerated the Supreme Court's desegregation decision in
Brown v. Board of Education.

As an economist Gunnar Myrdal has had a varied career. This has
spanned original contributions to the line of analysis which culminated
in Keynes's General Theory of Employment, Interest and Money;
close criticism of the English classical economists in his 1931 volume
The Political Element in the History of Economic Ideas; and, in recent years, concentration on the conditions of economic progress in
the underdeveloped countries of the world. In Rich Lands and Poor
Lands and An International Economy, Myrdal took a much more
pessimistic view of the economic prospects of the poorer nations
than is usually held by economists. This view was based upon an
analysis that stressed an actual tendency of income differentials to
widen rather than narrow between the advanced and the backward
nations, noted the shortage of entrepreneurial and organizational talent in these countries, gave due weight to the population problem,
and added as a final handicap the slight degree of social integration
which was characteristic of the poorer countries. To Myrdal the
great advantage of the mature democracies of the Western world
is the relatively high degree of identification people in different
classes and in different geographical regions nevertheless feel with
each other. It is this integration, this element of social cohesion,

175

which has made possible welfare advances and high rates of taxation. Before the underdeveloped countries can fully succeed, they need to approach Western levels of integration. But, argues Myrdal, before international prosperity becomes a reality it will be necessary for the degree of integration which already exists in the rich countries to be reproduced in the relations among countries. One of the discouraging elements in the world scene which Myrdal stresses is the very tendency of internal integration to be accompanied by external indifference to other countries.

How can the underdeveloped countries make the most of their opportunities and resources? Myrdal's answer departs very far indeed from the classical prescriptions. Because both talent and capital are scant, central planning is inevitable and desirable. Because the world is far from integrated, tariff protection and subsidy to the important industries are policies that underdeveloped countries must in their own interest pursue. The underdeveloped countries should not swallow the economics of the richer countries without criticism. In fact, Myrdal recommends to these lands the development of their own economists and their own economic doctrines. Even with central planning and novel economic doctrines, the task of development is seen by Myrdal as very great. Stagnation and vested exploitation are deeply rooted in these countries and a massive governmental initiative is required to get development started.

It is an open question whether these countries are capable of developing the enlightened and charismatic leaders who alone can do the job. If Myrdal is right, development will not otherwise take place.

The selection is from An International Economy, *by Gunnar Myrdal, pp. 200-5. Copyright © 1956 by Harper & Brothers.*

Planning

It is interesting to note the unanimity with which central economic planning as a policy is pressed upon the underdeveloped countries. "It has been a minor irony of the postwar experience of the United States," Professor W. W. Rostow observes, "that its agents, both in Europe and in underdeveloped countries, have found themselves urging an increased role for government planning in the economies of the areas where the American interest was engaged. This was the consequence of no conspiracy among New Dealers or Socialists who found their way into American foreign operations. This was a realistic response to the nature of the societies where a sustained rate of economic development was sought in the American interest."

Professor Norman S. Buchanan makes this assessment of the situation: "The nineteenth-century sequence will probably not be repeated. The state rather than the drive of private enterprise in pursuit of profits will determine the major features of industrial development in the [now] low income areas. Domestic savings and investment, labor training and mobility, imports and exports, foreign borrowing and home finance will be guided by the visible hand of the state in the quest for higher incomes through industrialization." Professor John H. Williams again and again repeats his belief that "the kind of development program now needed for a better balanced world requires planning, whether or not we like that word, because it would not be at all certain otherwise how the parts might fit together"; he is then thinking of the problem of international relations but would, of course, find still more important reasons for internal planning in the underdeveloped countries.

Even Professor Jacob Viner—though somewhat grudgingly, for reasons which I partly share—finds himself among the planners, having to admit that "what the proper division is between government initiative and private enterprise must depend largely on the extent to which the general public is able and disposed to exercise the needed initiative, enterprise, and skill. In some countries the masses of the people are probably too poor, too ignorant, and too bound by old patterns of behavior to do much for themselves; and, if there is to be progress, it must be initiated and, for a time at least, largely conducted from above."

All special advisers to underdeveloped countries who have taken the time and trouble to acquaint themselves with the problems, no matter who they are—teams of experts from the International Bank or other international agencies, including the Colombo Plan; officials of the American Point Four Program; private foundations and consultant firms; independent social scientists; journalists or visiting politicians—all recommend central planning as a first condition for progress. Implicitly they all assume a different approach to the social and economic problems of the underdeveloped countries today than that which historically was applied in the advanced countries. They all assume a very much greater role for the state.

Most of the advisers from the advanced countries who are now urging the underdeveloped ones toward central planning of their social and economic reforms are not doctrinaires, sold on planning as a panacea, but on the contrary usually more at home among the critics of central planning. Yet, faced with the peculiar problems of the underdeveloped countries they nearly all become zealous planners.

If governments of underdeveloped countries have gone far in central planning and in preparing for large-scale state interventions, it is rarely because of the earnest advice of the experts from the advanced countries. As I pointed out in Chapter XI, the very definition of economic development as an attempt to raise living standards for the broad masses of people—which is common in all underdeveloped countries and generally accepted in the entire discussion of the problem—and the further concept of this attempt as a political drive, strongly associated emotionally with the cravings after economic and political independence, identify economic development as the pursuit of a government plan or program.

Behind this general trend of thinking is also the appreciation of the desperate situation of most of these countries and the need for speedy reforms. I have just shown this in regard to the population problem where, if grave and imminent dangers are to be avoided, natural forces cannot be left to work themselves out and a policy is therefore urgently required. More generally, there are compelling reasons to achieve a much more rapid economic development than could be hoped for without central planning and government initiative. There is also a comprehension of the opportunities for using the more powerful technical knowledge now available and which will not be exploited fully if development is left to take an undetermined route. There are many other reasons for central planning and large-scale state intervention in underdeveloped countries which, however, are all included under these general formulas.

Thus, to exploit effectively modern technical possibilities, investment and production projects will nowadays often have to be larger in scope than private initiative in these countries can handle. For the same reason, initial investments will have to be directed more to the sphere of external economies, in the provision of power, means of transport, etc., and to various social purposes, from schooling to housing. Technological development has changed the basic conditions for industrialization during the last hundred years.

If rapid development is desired in a low-income, stagnating peasant economy, geared to self-sufficiency—unlike a progressive industrial one—so much more attention needs also to be given in the initial stages to balancing the growth of different industries, so that the increased supply of various goods meets an effective demand. Leaving economic development to natural forces means in most cases continued stagnation or unnecessarily slow development. A progressive economy can take better care of itself because it has momentum; a stagnant economy must first be given momentum.

In most of these countries the social chasms and the inequalities of distribution have considerably hampered the growth of the commercial middle class, which in the advanced countries played such an important role in economic progress. As Rostow points out, "it is easy to forget that, before the industrial revolution came to Western Europe and the United States, it was preceded by several centuries of commercial and early industrial development, which had formed a class of private entrepreneurs prepared morally, intellectually and technically to exploit the potentialities of the innovations that came forward. The middle class, in a sense, was the most important of the economic innovations of modern times; and it is not susceptible of rapid diffusion throughout the underdeveloped regions of the contemporary world."

It is, further, highly characteristic of all the underdeveloped countries that their business classes are bent upon earning quick profits not by promoting long-term real investment and production but by buying and selling, moneylending, and other easier ways of making money, which also often escape taxation. Profits tend to be invested in land, or else hoarded or transferred abroad, when they are not dissipated in a costly display of wealth and social status. There is a low propensity to save and to invest productively in new enterprises.

In these countries there is everywhere a relative lack of the entrepreneurial spirit. As Staley points out: "Private enterprise fails to function effectively in most underdeveloped countries, not so much because it is repressed or interfered with as because it does not yet exist in the modern sense in which Americans automatically think of it." The problem is not merely to release it but to cultivate it. The real task is one of "institution-building."

If there is to be economic development, the state will almost inevitably have to take the initiative. The Secretariat of the Economic Commission for Asia and the Far East, when discussing this problem, concluded that "the experience of the last few years suggests that only in Japan and Hong-Kong is private business fully capable of developing the economy by its own resources and on its own initiative."

The Problem of Administration

This urge to central planning and the necessity for the state to be the initiator and promoter of business projects—at least in the beginning, until the social and economic conditions have been created for private business on a larger scale—confronts all the underdeveloped countries with a major problem: that of efficiency and incorruptibility in government and administration. This is another thing about which there is *consensus sapientium*.

It is a quite common complaint in the reports on the development problems of underdeveloped countries, which now abound in the publications and archives of international agencies, that one of the important obstacles to development is the state of public administration: it is ineffective, untrained, incompetent, and often corrupt. In all programs for international technical assistance improvement of public administration plays a prominent role.

But here, too, the underdeveloped countries are faced with a much more difficult problem than that once solved in the now advanced countries. In the countries of the northwestern corner of Europe, which have gone furthest in cleansing and rationalizing politics and administration and have often succeeded in making public enterprises models of efficiently organized business, there was, to begin with, an age-old tradition of legalism. Since heathen times these cultures have shown a fanaticism in explicitly regulating the relations among individuals and between individuals and the community in terms of honesty and fairness and equality under the law.

The inefficiency and corruption that nevertheless did creep into the politics and administration of these countries were finally cleaned out at a time, a little more than a hundred years ago, when the state had still few economic functions. The strong state—in the sense of being incorrupt and efficient—was in these countries the accomplishment of economic liberalism, and the job was so well done that the state could later gradually enlarge the scope of its activities by taking on more and more functions without becoming corrupt and inefficient. The paradoxical truth is that it was economic liberalism that perfected the main instrument for central economic planning and public interventions in the modern welfare state.

Underdeveloped countries have to attempt to create an efficient and honest political and administrative machinery without much in the way of legal traditions. And time does not allow them a purgatory era of economic liberalism; *they have to reform their politics and their administration at the same time as the state is increasingly compelled to handle vast public funds and run business on a large scale.* From this point of view, too, one of the most valuable heritages the British Empire has left to its former colonies is the tradition of the British civil service.

As "it takes good administration to improve bad administration," here is another vicious circle that creates deadlocks and obstructions, if it is not broken by vigorous and successful action.

Development requires good administration, yet good administration is itself a result of economic development. It is not, of course, a necessary result, for some highly developed countries have very bad administrations. The difference is that once development has been achieved, bad administration can be afforded as a luxury, while where administration is poor from the beginning, economic development is made more difficult if the government becomes its main agency, whether by choice or because of the absence of innovating entrepreneurs.

The United States is, of course, the main example of a developed country which has not attained the highest standards of administration. If the Americans are far ahead of us all in business and production, this is entirely due to their productive efficiency on the farms, in the factories, and in the stores. Their politics and public administration, at all times and under all parties, have suffered, and still suffer, from serious shortcomings. In administration there is waste of effort, overcentralization, lack of uncomplicated delegation of authority, etc., which are related to insecurity of tenure and of social status and many lingering traditions from primitive democracy and the spoils system, as well as many other peculiar traits that have developed fixed patterns. Economic liberalism never carried out its purges in politics and administration in the United States.

It is an interesting sociological problem why the nation which has so successfully rationalized its private economic life and accomplished the highest level of labor saving in production and distribution, has tolerated so much waste and inefficiency in administration and politics. What has to be done is usually done, though mostly in a very cumbersome and expensive way. Even a good administrative unit in the United States spends several times the manpower on a specific task that a Swede or Dutchman would employ.

The United States can, of course, afford a more cumbersome and therefore relatively expensive administration; the underdeveloped countries cannot. American administration can also to a large extent stay out of economic life as its business is efficiently organized. As a matter of fact the relative inefficiency of public administration in the United States is in that country an important and rational motive for the state to stay out of business as far as possible—as indeed it also was in Adam Smith's Britain. The underdeveloped countries, on the contrary, are dependent on the administration to perform a great number of functions that in the United States can be left—and had better be left—to private initiative.

Not unconnected with its less efficient administration, the United States has, however, the large and often valuable scientific literature, the great university institutions, and the legions of experts on administration. Nearer home we have, incidentally, a similar division of practice and theory: some European countries, for instance, are distinguished by a highly efficient and inexpensive system of tax collection, while others have the professors of public finance and fiscal administration.

I have often reflected on the consequences of the fact that the underdeveloped countries get so much of their advice on administrative reform from American experts. There are clear advantages in this: an American expert has experience and training in how to fight various shortcomings in administration which a British or Scandinavian expert may lack. On the other hand, an expert from the rich and exuberant United States may by his upbringing be less disturbed by the wasteful habit of having too many officials on a job, which is a common vice in all underdeveloped countries. Because of the great scarcity of trained personnel and the larger scope of administrative responsibility, it is much less tolerable there than in the United States.

Part III | **THE AGE OF LAISSEZ-FAIRE**

A. THEORY

Sir Dudley North
1641–1691

A leading student of seventeenth-century economic thought, Professor Jacob Viner, judged North one of the first free traders. Of North, Ricardo wrote in a letter to McCulloch: "I had no idea that anyone entertained such correct opinions, as are expressed in this publication, at so early a period." Ricardo might even have identified a hint of his own fondness for strong cases in North's third-person description of his own method: ". . . he reduceth things to their Extreams, wherein all discriminations are most gross and sensible, and then shows them; and not in the state of ordinary concerns, whereof the terms are scarcely distinguishable."

Professing himself an admirer of Descartes, North wrote anonymously, explaining that ". . . the Publick is an acute as well as merciless Beast, which neither oversees a failing, nor forgives it." There was no doubt of the sharpness of North's analysis. A merchant himself, he said of other merchants, ". . . whenever Men consult for the Publick Good, as for the advancement of Trade, wherein all are concerned, they usually esteem the immediate Interest of their own to be the common Measure of Good and Evil. And there are many, who to gain a little in their own Trades, care not how much others suffer; and each man strives that all others may be forc'd in their dealings to act subserviently for his Profit, but under the cover of the Publick."

Like other mercantilists, North believed in the strength of self-interest, but his notion of the effects of the motive diverged widely from seventeenth-century opinion. The following comment takes no noble view of trading motives, but it does concede what was to be at the center of classical economics, that unregulated trade benefited the community: "The main spur to Trade, or rather to Industry and Ingenuity, is the exorbitant Appetites of Men, which they will take *pains to gratify, and so be disposed to work, when nothing else will incline them to it; for did Men content themselves with bare Necessaries, we should have a poor World." North affirmed the harmony of economic interests, saw the whole world as a trading area, and condemned regulation that forced men into trades against their inclination.*

North's other opinions were consonant with this laissez-faire standard. Laws should not regulate trade. The state should not interfere with the free flow of money. Indeed the supply of money conformed to the needs of trade and even the outward flow of money in the service of trade enriched the nation. North disposed of centuries of canonist disputation about the legality of interest in a sentence: "I will not say any thing to the Theological Arguments against Interest of Moneys; but their 3 per Cent is no more lawful, than 4, or 12." High interest rates attracted funds from their hiding places, to the benefit of the community. Low rates promoted hoarding. Best, like the "wise Hollanders," to let borrowers and lenders make their own terms.

What has already been said suggests how far in advance of his time North was. A century before The Wealth of Nations *here was a man who favored almost completely free trade, distrusted government, believed in a natural harmony of interest, conceived that trade among the nations might benefit all of them, sketched the doctrine of free specie flows, and preferred peace to war. Through Dudley North, the rationalism of the eighteenth century, not the dogmatism of the mercantilists, spoke with a clear voice. No doubt, he was wise to write anonymously.*

This brief selection is from the Preface to Discourses on Trade, *by Dudley North, from* Early English Tracts on Commerce, *edited by J. R. McCulloch. Cambridge University Press.*

Preface

Now it may appear strange to hear it said,

That the whole World as to Trade, is but as one Nation or People, and therein Nations are as Persons.

That the loss of a Trade with one Nation, is not that only, separately considered, but so much of the Trade of the World rescinded and lost, for all is combined together.

That there can be no Trade unprofitable to the Publick; for if any prove so, men leave it off; and wherever the Traders thrive, the Pub-lick, of which they are a part, thrives also.

That to force Men to deal in any prescrib'd manner, may profit such as happen to serve them; but the Publick gains not, because it is taking from one Subject, to give to another.

That no Laws can set Prices in Trade, the Rates of which, must and will make themselves: But when such Laws do happen to lay any hold, it is so much Impediment to Trade, and therefore prejudicial.

That Money is a Merchandize, whereof there may be a glut, as well as a scarcity, and that even to an Inconvenience.

That a People cannot want Money to serve the ordinary dealing, and more than enough they will not have.

That no Man shall be the richer for the making much Money, nor have any part of it, but as he buys it for an equivalent price.

That the free Coynage is a perpetual Motion found out, whereby to Melt and Coyn without ceasing, and so to feed Goldsmiths and Coyners at the Publick Charge.

That debasing the Coyn is defrauding one another, and to the Pub-lick there is no sort of Advantage from it; for that admits no Char-acter, or Value, but Intrinsick.

That the sinking Money by Allay or Weight is all one.

That Exchange and ready Money, are the same, nothing but Car-riage and re-carriage being saved.

That Money Exported in Trade is an increase to the Wealth of the Nation; but spent in War, and Payments abroad, is so much Impov-erishment.

In short, That all favour to one Trade or Interest against another, is an Abuse, and cuts so much of Profit from the Publick. With many other like Paradoxes, no less strange to most men, than true in them-selves; but in my Opinion, clearly flowing from the Principles, and Dis-courses that follow, which you may freely peruse and censure, for now I have done.

There were few subjects which David Hume did not see more clearly than his contemporaries. Economics was no exception. Writing at the tag end of the mercantilist era, preceding Smith whose friend he was, David Hume in his Political Discourses concisely foreshadowed later doctrines. In contrast to the mercantilists who insisted on the natural opposition between sovereign and subject, Hume considered the interests of both parties parallel: ". . . according to the most natural course of things, industry and arts and trade encrease the power of the sovereign as well as the happiness of the subjects; and that policy is violent, which aggrandizes the public by the poverty of the individual." At a time when sober men of affairs thought that the state was richer when the bulk of its citizens were poorer, Hume warned against ". . . a too great disproportion among the citizens. . . . Every person, if possible, ought to enjoy the fruits of his labour, in a full possession of all the necessaries, and many of the conveniences of life. No one can doubt, but such an equality is most suitable to human nature and diminishes much less from the happiness of the rich than it adds to that of the poor." A natural cosmopolitan, Hume praised free trade in characteristically felicitous language: "Nature, by giving a diversity of geniuses, climates, and soils, to different nations, has secured their mutual intercourse and commerce, as long as they all remain industrious and civilized." And could the magnanimity of an Englishman extend further than Hume's inclusion of France: "I should therefore venture to acknowledge, that, not only as a man, but as a British subject, I pray for the flourishing commerce of GER-MANY, SPAIN, ITALY, and even FRANCE itself. I am at least certain that GREAT BRITAIN and all those nations, would flourish more, did their *sovereigns and ministers adopt such enlarged and benevolent senti-ments towards each other." Even France!*

While Hume was free of the usual mercantilist fixations on gold and silver, he did see an advantage in a favorable balance of trade and a consequent influx of precious metals. His explanation foreshad-owed a characteristic Keynesian doctrine of two centuries later. When gold and silver entered the realm, a temporary gap between prices and costs resulted. Since prices rose first, profits increased. And higher profits stimulated industry and output. This, however, was the only advantage of an inflow of the precious metals. Hume explicitly de-nied, in general, that shortage of money injured a country internally.

If Hume had written a treatise instead of a few nearly casual essays, he, rather than Smith, might have won title to the founding of the science of political economy. The present extract is from David Hume's Writings on Economics, *edited by Eugene Rotwein. Thomas Nelson and Sons Ltd.*

The Merchant

Every thing useful to the life of man arises from the ground; but few things arise in that condition which is requisite to render them use-ful. There must, therefore, beside the peasant and the proprietors of land, be another rank of men, who receiving from the former the rude materials, work them into their proper form, and retain part for their own use and subsistence. In the infancy of society, these contracts be-tween the artisans and the peasants, and between one species of ar-tisans and another are commonly entered into immediately by the persons themselves, who, being neighbours, are easily acquainted with each other's necessities, and can lend their mutual assistance to supply them. But when men's industry encreases, and their views en-large, it is found, that the most remote parts of the state can assist each other as well as the more contiguous, and that this intercourse of good offices may be carried on to the greatest extent and intricacy. Hence the origin of *merchants*, one of the most useful races of men, who serve as agents between those parts of the state, that are wholly unacquainted, and are ignorant of each other's necessities. Here are in a city fifty workmen in silk and linen, and a thousand customers; and these two ranks of men, so necessary to each other, can never rightly meet, till one man erects a shop, to which all the workmen and all the customers repair. In this province, grass rises in abun-dance: The inhabitants abound in cheese, and butter, and cattle; but want bread and corn, which, in a neighbouring province, are in too great abundance for the use of the inhabitants. One man discovers this. He brings corn from the one province and returns with cattle; and supplying the wants of both, he is, so far, a common benefactor. As the people encrease in numbers and industry, the difficulty of their intercourse encreases: The business of the agency or merchandize becomes more intricate; and divides, subdivides, compounds, and mixes to a greater variety. In all these transactions, it is necessary, and reasonable, that a considerable part of the commodities and labour should belong to the merchant, to whom, in a great measure, they are owing. And these commodities he will sometimes preserve in kind, or more commonly convert into money, which is their common representation. If gold and silver have encreased in the state together with the industry, it will require a great quantity of these metals to represent a great quantity of commodities and labour. If industry alone has encreased, the prices of every thing must sink, and a small quantity of specie will serve as a representation.

There is no craving or demand of the human mind more constant and insatiable than that for exercise and employment; and this desire seems the foundation of most of our passions and pursuits. Deprive a man of all business and serious occupation, he runs restless from one amusement to another; and the weight and oppression, which he feels from idleness, is so great, that he forgets the ruin which must follow him from his immoderate expences. Give him a more harmless way of employing his mind or body, he is satisfied, and feels no longer that insatiable thirst after pleasure. But if the employment you give him be lucrative, especially if the profit be attached to every particular exertion of industry, he has gain so often in his eye, that he acquires, by degrees, a passion for it, and knows no such pleasure as that of seeing the daily encrease of his fortune. And this is the reason why trade encreases frugality, and why, among merchants, there is the same overplus of misers above prodigals, as, among the possessors of land, there is the contrary.

Commerce encreases industry, by conveying it readily from one member of the state to another, and allowing none of it to perish or become useless. It encreases frugality, by giving occupation to men, and employing them in the arts of gain, which soon engage their affection, and remove all relish for pleasure and expence. It is an infallible consequence of all industrious professions, to beget frugality, and make the love of gain prevail over the love of pleasure. Among lawyers and physicians who have any practice, there are many more who live within their income, than who exceed it, or even live up to it. But lawyers and physicians beget no industry; and it is even at the expence of others they acquire their riches; so that they are sure to diminish the possessions of some of their fellow-citizens, as fast as they encrease their own. Merchants, on the contrary, beget industry, by serving as canals to convey it through every corner of the state: And at the same time, by their frugality, they acquire great power over that industry, and collect a large property in the labour and commodities, which they are the chief instruments in producing. There is no other profession, therefore, except merchandize, which can make the monied interest considerable, or in other words, can encrease industry, and, by also encreasing frugality, give a great command of that industry to particular members of the society. Without commerce, the state must consist chiefly of landed gentry, whose prodigality and expence make a continual demand for borrowing; and of peasants, who have no sums to supply that demand. The money never gathers into large stocks or sums, which can be lent at interest. It is dispersed into numberless hands, who either squander it in idle show and magnificence, or employ it in the purchase of the common necessaries of life. Commerce alone assembles it into considerable sums; and this effect it has merely from the industry which it begets, and the frugality which it inspires, independent of that particular quantity of precious metal which may circulate in the state.

Thus an encrease of commerce, by a necessary consequence, raises a great number of lenders, and by that means produces lowness of interest. We must now consider how far this encrease of commerce diminishes the profits arising from that profession, and gives rise to the *third* circumstance requisite to produce lowness of interest.

Adam Smith

1723-1790

One's estimate of Adam Smith is likely to pivot on history. Viewed from the perspective of the twentieth century, Smith seems a conservative advocate of small government and unrestrained laissez-faire. His attachment to natural liberty, his confidence that an "invisible hand" would guide clashing egotisms toward a socially beneficial result, and his fervent attack upon mercantilist interventions into economic affairs all contribute to the image of a thinker who exalted individual energy over collective welfare. In the twentieth century, it is difficult to avoid thought of the excesses and hardships of the factory system, of the disruptions and disorganizations of the unplanned movement from countryside to city, and of the unmet needs for community action.

An eighteenth-century perspective alters the vision. Smith wrote not in the context of the factory system but in that of the small handicraft worker. His famous example of division of labor completely omits machinery. All the gains are derived from the increased dexterity, ingenuity, and economy of time which divisions of labor bring in their train. The role that government played in his England was not designed to promote social welfare. Its principal effect, indeed, appeared to be a limitation of the capacity of apprentices to become independent workmen, rural laborers to move to the cities, businessmen to invest their capital in the most profitable places, and merchants to import and export as they listed. Hence a huge portion of The Wealth of Nations *devotes itself to the destruction of the mercantilist restraints: navigation acts, treaties of commerce, tariffs, bounties, and drawbacks—the last the refunds on duties paid extended to merchants who processed and exported raw materials from other countries. The demolition is systematic, ruthless, and not quite fair, after the manner of almost all polemics.*

The demolition was definitely not designed to advance the interests of any rising capitalist class. Smith's own sympathies, on the contrary, were with the laborer and the rural worker. His suspicions usually fell on the business classes. Consider his remarks on trade gatherings: "People of the same trade seldom meet together, even for merriment and diversion, but the conversation ends in a conspiracy against the public, or in some contrivance to raise prices." Almost a text for the electrical equipment industry of the twentieth century! The agricultural classes do better: "Country gentleman and farmers are, to their great honor, of all people, the least subject to the wretched spirit of monopoly." For the consumer, Smith had one of the first good words in the record of economics: "Consumption is the sole end and purpose of all production; and the interest of the producer ought to be attended to, only so far as it may be necessary for promoting that of the consumer."

Enough has been said to suggest that Smith's purpose was less the erection of a tight new system of economic reasoning than it was the destruction of a bad system of economic regulation and the substitution of the natural order of liberty. For that reason our selection from Smith is an example of his criticism of mercantilism rather than a piece of theoretical analysis. It is, however, true that Smith was also the father of economic analysis. Sir Alexander Gray's conclusion that ". . . it is again a tribute to the greatness of Smith that all schools of thought may trace to him their origin or inspiration," fairly states the case. For in Smith are to be found most of the theories, in embryo, which defined the classical school: the wages-fund doctrine, a hint of Malthusian population theory, the labor theory of value, several theories of rent including one which later found favor, the subsistence theory of wages, and the mutual-benefit doctrine of international trade.

The greatness of Smith did not reside in his analytical capacities. Schumpeter no doubt was correct when he said that "The Wealth of Nations *does not contain a single analytic idea, principle, or method that was entirely new in 1776." What Smith produced was a treatise of massive rhetorical impact which destroyed a system of ideas, allied itself naturally to the interests of a new order of vigorous men, and stimulated the development of a whole school of economic thought.*

The selection comes from The Wealth of Nations, *edited by Edwin Cannan (New York: Modern Library, 1937).*

Of Restraints upon the Importation from Foreign Countries of Such Goods as Can Be Produced at Home

By restraining, either by high duties, or by absolute prohibitions, the importation of such goods from foreign countries as can be produced at home, the monopoly of the home market is more or less secured to the domestic industry employed in producing them. Thus the prohibition of importing either live cattle or salt provisions from foreign countries secures to the graziers of Great Britain the monopoly of the home market for butcher's meat. The high duties upon the importation of corn, which in times of moderate plenty amount to a prohibition, give a like advantage to the growers of that commodity. The prohibition of the importation of foreign woollens is equally favourable to the woollen manufacturers. The silk manufacture, though altogether employed upon foreign materials, has lately obtained the same advantage. The linen manufacture has not yet obtained it, but is making great strides towards it. Many other sorts of manufacturers have, in the same manner, obtained in Great Britain, either altogether, or very nearly a monopoly against their countrymen. The variety of goods of which the importation into Great Britain is prohibited, either absolutely, or under certain circumstances, greatly exceeds what can easily be suspected by those who are not well acquainted with the laws of the customs.

That this monopoly of the home-market frequently gives great encouragement to that particular species of industry which enjoys it, and frequently turns towards that employment a greater share of both the labour and stock of the society than would otherwise have gone to it, cannot be doubted. But whether it tends either to increase the general industry of the society, or to give it the most advantageous direction, is not, perhaps, altogether so evident.

The general industry of the society never can exceed what the capital of the society can employ. As the number of workmen that can be kept in employment by any particular person must bear a certain proportion to his capital, so the number of those that can be continually employed by all the members of a great society, must bear a certain proportion to the whole capital of that society, and never can exceed that proportion. No regulation of commerce can increase the quantity of industry in any society beyond what its capital can maintain. It can only divert a part of it into a direction into which it might not otherwise have gone; and it is by no means certain that this artificial direction is likely to be more advantageous to the society than that into which it would have gone of its own accord.

Every individual is continually exerting himself to find out the most advantageous employment for whatever capital he can command. It is his own advantage, indeed, and not that of the society, which he has in view. But the study of his own advantage naturally, or rather necessarily leads him to prefer that employment which is most advantageous to the society.

First, every individual endeavours to employ his capital as near home as he can, and consequently as much as he can in the support of domestic industry; provided always that he can thereby obtain the ordinary, or not a great deal less than the ordinary profits of stock.

Thus, upon equal or nearly equal profits, every wholesale merchant naturally prefers the home-trade to the foreign trade of consumption, and the foreign trade of consumption to the carrying trade. In the home-trade his capital is never so long out of his sight as it frequently is in the foreign trade of consumption. He can know better the character and situation of the persons whom he trusts, and if he should happen to be deceived, he knows better the laws of the country from which he must seek redress. In the carrying trade, the capital of the merchant is, as it were, divided between two foreign countries, and no part of it is ever necessarily brought home, or placed under his own immediate view and command. The capital which an Amsterdam merchant employs in carrying corn from Konnigsberg to Lisbon, and fruit and wine from Lisbon to Konnigsberg, must generally be the one-half of it at Konnigsberg and the other half at Lisbon. No part of it need ever come to Amsterdam. The natural residence of such a merchant should either be at Konnigsberg or Lisbon, and it can only be some very particular circumstances which can make him prefer the residence of Amsterdam. The uneasiness, however, which he feels at being separated so far from his capital, generally determines him to bring part both of the Konnigsberg goods which he destines for the market of Lisbon, and of the Lisbon goods which he destines for that of Konnigsberg, to Amsterdam: and though this necessarily subjects him to a double charge of loading and unloading, as well as to the payment of some duties and customs, yet for the sake of having some part of his capital always under his own view and command, he willingly submits to this extraordinary charge; and it is in this manner that every country which has any considerable share of the carrying trade, becomes always the emporium, or general market, for the goods of all the different countries whose trade it carries on. The merchant, in order to save a second loading and unloading, endeavours always to sell in the home-market as much of the goods of all those different countries as he can, and thus, so far as he can, to convert his carrying trade into a foreign trade of consumption. A merchant, in the same manner, who is engaged in the foreign trade of consumption, when he collects goods for foreign markets, will always be glad, upon equal or nearly equal profits, to sell as great a part of them at home as he can. He saves himself the risk and trouble of exportation, when, so far as he can, he thus converts his foreign trade of consumption into a home-trade. Home is in this manner the center, if I may say so, round which the capitals of the inhabitants of every country are continually circulating, and towards which they are always tending, though by particular causes they may sometimes be driven off and repelled from it towards more distant employments. But a capital employed in the home-trade, it has already been shown, necessarily puts into motion a greater quantity of domestic industry, and gives revenue and employment to a greater number of the inhabitants of the country, than an equal capital employed in the foreign trade of consumption: and one employed in the foreign trade of consumption has the same advantage over an equal capital employed in the carrying trade. Upon equal, or only nearly equal profits, therefore, every individual naturally inclines to employ his capital in the manner in which it is likely to afford the greatest support to domestic industry, and to give revenue and employment to the greatest number of people of his own country.

Secondly, every individual who employs his capital in the support of domestic industry, necessarily endeavours so to direct that industry, that its produce may be of the greatest possible value.

The produce of industry is what it adds to the subject or materials upon which it is employed. In proportion as the value of this produce is great or small, so will likewise be the profits of the employer. But it is only for the sake of profit that any man employs a capital in the support of industry; and he will always, therefore, endeavour to employ it in the support of that industry of which the produce is likely to be of the greatest value, or to exchange for the greatest quantity either of money or of other goods.

But the annual revenue of every society is always precisely equal to the exchangeable value of the whole annual produce of its industry, or rather is precisely the same thing with that exchangeable value. As every individual, therefore, endeavours as much as he can both to employ his capital in the support of domestic industry, and so to direct that industry that its produce may be of the greatest value; every individual necessarily labours to render the annual revenue of the society as great as he can. He generally, indeed, neither intends to promote the public interest, nor knows how much he is promoting it. By preferring the support of domestic to that of foreign industry, he intends only his own security; and by directing that industry in such a manner as its produce may be of the greatest value, he intends only his own gain, and he is in this, as in many other cases, led by an invisible hand to promote an end which was no part of his intention. Nor is it always the worse for the society that it was no part of it. By pursuing his own interest he frequently promotes that of the society more effectually than when he really intends to promote it. I have never known much good done by those who affected to trade for the public good. It is an affectation, indeed, not very common among merchants, and very few words need be employed in dissuading them from it.

What is the species of domestic industry which his capital can employ, and of which the produce is likely to be of the greatest value, every individual, it is evident, can, in his local situation, judge much better than any statesman or lawgiver can do for him. The statesman, who should attempt to direct private people in what manner they ought to employ their capitals, would not only load himself with a most unnecessary attention, but assume an authority which could safely be trusted, not only to no single person, but to no council or senate whatever, and which would nowhere be so dangerous as in the hands of a man who had folly and presumption enough to fancy himself fit to exercise it.

To give the monopoly of the home-market to the produce of domestic industry, in any particular art or manufacture, is in some measure to direct private people in what manner they ought to employ their capitals, and must, in almost all cases, be either a useless or a hurtful regulation. If the produce of domestic can be brought there as cheap as that of foreign industry, the regulation is evidently useless. If it cannot, it must generally be hurtful. It is the maxim of every prudent master of a family, never to attempt to make at home what it will cost him more to make than to buy. The taylor does not attempt to make his own shoes, but buys them of the shoemaker. The shoemaker does not attempt to make his own clothes, but employs a taylor. The farmer attempts to make neither the one nor the other, but employs those different artificers. All of them find it for their interest to employ their whole industry in a way in which they have some advantage over their neighbours, and to purchase with a part of its produce, or what is the same thing, with the price of a part of it, whatever else they have occasion for.

What is prudence in the conduct of every private family, can scarce be folly in that of a great kingdom. If a foreign country can supply us with a commodity cheaper than we ourselves can make it, better buy it of them with some part of the produce of our own industry, employed in a way in which we have some advantage. The general industry of the country, being always in proportion to the capital which employs it, will not thereby be diminished, no more than that of the above-mentioned artificers; but only left to find out the way in which it can be employed with the greatest advantage. It is certainly not employed to the greatest advantage, when it is thus directed towards an object which it can buy cheaper than it can make. The value of its annual produce is certainly more or less diminished, when it is thus turned away from producing commodities evidently of more value than the commodity which it is directed to produce. According to the supposition, that commodity could be purchased from foreign countries cheaper than it can be made at home. It could, therefore, have been purchased with a part only of the commodities, or, what is the same thing, with a part only of the price of the commodities, which the industry employed by an equal capital would have produced at home, had it been left to follow its natural course. The industry of the country, therefore, is thus turned away from a more, to a less advantageous employment, and the exchangeable value of its annual produce, instead of being increased, according to the intention of the lawgiver, must necessarily be diminished by every such regulation.

By means of such regulations, indeed, a particular manufacture may sometimes be acquired sooner than it could have been otherwise, and after a certain time may be made at home as cheap or cheaper than in the foreign country. But though the industry of the society may be thus carried with advantage into a particular channel sooner than it could have been otherwise, it will by no means follow that the sum total, either of its industry, or of its revenue, can ever be augmented by any such regulation. The industry of the society can augment only in proportion as its capital augments, and its capital can augment only in proportion to what can be gradually saved out of its revenue. But the immediate effect of every such regulation is to diminish its revenue, and what diminishes its revenue is certainly not very likely to augment its capital faster than it would have augmented of its own accord, had both capital and industry been left to find out their natural employments.

Though for want of such regulations the society should never acquire the proposed manufacture, it would not, upon that account, necessarily be the poorer in any one period of its duration. In every period of its duration its whole capital and industry might still have been employed, though upon different objects, in the manner that was most advantageous at the time. In every period its revenue might have been the greatest which its capital could afford, and both capital and revenue might have been augmented with the greatest possible rapidity.

Jeremy Bentham

1748–1832

In conformity with the wishes of his father, Jeremy Bentham began his career as a student of law. But even at Lincoln's Inn and Oxford (where he studied at the feet of Blackstone himself), his interests led him to a study of the bolder students of human affairs, including such names of dubious reputation among the respectable as Montesquieu, Hume, Priestley, Hartley, Beccaria, and Helvétius. Although Bentham was admitted to the bar in 1769, he thought less and less of practicing and more and more of benefiting the world.

As a man who aspired to becoming the Newton of the moral universe, Bentham concentrated upon the written word by which he hoped to reform English institutions and, above all, English law. His first published work appeared anonymously in 1776. Entitled A Fragment on Government, it was a most vigorous assault upon his former teacher and that teacher's major work, Blackstone's Commentaries. In 1789 he published his Introduction to the Principles of Morals and Legislation, the source of the passage that is here reprinted. Although this production was much superior to the somewhat similar effort of Archdeacon Paley in 1785, it aroused no comment. But if at home Bentham was a prophet without honor, abroad he attracted the faithful Dumont who translated much of Bentham into French.

In England he began to achieve fame only in 1808 when he met James Mill, the father of John Stuart Mill. The meeting was historic. When it occurred, Bentham was a man of sixty, known in England mostly as the inventor of a new model prison, the Panopticon, which was constructed on circular principles so that a single warder could observe each cell and prisoners could be protected from evil association. James Mill, a young man of thirty-five, was a Scot, come to London to make his way by his wits. At the time he was supporting himself by hack journalism, superintending the education of children

*destined to attain the noble number of nine, and trying to make his
reputation by writing* A History of British India. *The two were
made for each other. Bentham gave Mill a doctrine and Mill gave
Bentham a school. Mill was a born intellectual entrepreneur, a vigorous and convincing conversationalist, and a forceful and logical writer.
In all of these capacities, he was energetic beyond the limits of ordinary men. The Philosophical Radicals, the militant intellectual reformers who were involved in most of the good causes of the first
half of the nineteenth century, owed allegiance to Bentham and the
great doctrine of utility, but they owed their existence as a group to
the organizing talents of James Mill.*

*As a technical economist, Bentham "owed everything"—the words
were his—to Adam Smith. His single contribution to economic discussion that is still remembered was the* Defence of Usury *(1787),
and this work simply corrected a bad piece of reasoning by Adam
Smith. Bentham argued that Smith was wrong to support the general
principle of natural liberty while simultaneously defending public
regulation of interest rates. Why, Bentham wondered, should interest
rates be regulated any more than any other price? If natural liberty
invalidated price regulation in general, then it invalidated regulation
in all particular cases. While this should have sufficed to establish his
point, Bentham, never a writer who stinted argument, added five
further defects of the usury laws of which the most prominent was
the difficulty a most useful class of men—projectors or promoters—
encountered in borrowing.*

*Although Bentham was no more than a minor economist, he was a
major influence upon major economists. David Ricardo was his friend
and John Stuart Mill even as a mature thinker rated him as one of
the two seminal minds of his century. The conception of human
psychology which is implicit in classical economics is Benthamite.
Men calculate pleasures and pains, they learn by association, they
are motivated by egotism, and they are passive rather than active
participants in their environment.*

*The first part of the selections that follow states Bentham's funda-
mental principle of utility. The second portion here reprinted is a
practical application of his principles to one of the areas where his
contribution to English thought was most substantial, criminal law.
The application is a typical endeavor to ascertain a reasonable theory
of punishment. A rational system of penalties to Bentham inflicted
just enough pain on the criminal as to dissuade him from further
crime. The criminal should be helped by an appropriate penal system
to value the pain of punishment as greater than the pleasure of crime's*

proceeds. Any punishment more severe than would be necessary to achieve this objective added to the sum of social pain and was, therefore, on utilitarian grounds ill-judged.

The selections come from Principles of Morals and Legislation, 1789 (Hafner edition), pp. 1-7, 29-32, and 178-88.

CHAPTER I Of the Principle of Utility

I. Nature has placed mankind under the governance of two sovereign masters, *pain* and *pleasure*. It is for them alone to point out what we ought to do, as well as to determine what we shall do. On the one hand the standard of right and wrong, on the other the chain of causes and effects, are fastened to their throne. They govern us in all we do, in all we say, in all we think: every effort we can make to throw off our subjection, will serve but to demonstrate and confirm it. In words a man may pretend to abjure their empire: but in reality he will remain subject to it all the while. The principle of utility° recognises this subjection, and assumes it for the foundation of that system, the object of which is to rear the fabric of felicity by the hand of reason and of law. Systems which attempt to question it, deal in sounds instead of sense, in caprice instead of reason, in darkness instead of light.

But enough of metaphor and declamation: it is not by such means that moral science is to be improved.

II. The principle of utility is the foundation of the present work: it will be proper therefore at the outset to give an explicit and deter-

---

° Note by the Author, July 1822.

To this denomination has of late been added, or substituted, the *greatest happiness* or *greatest felicity* principle: this for shortness, instead of saying at length *that principle* which states the greatest happiness of all those whose interest is in question, as being the right and proper, and only right and proper universally desirable, end of human action: of human action in every situation, and in particular in that of a functionary or set of functionaries exercising the powers of Government. The word *utility* does not so clearly point to the ideas of *pleasure* and *pain* as the words *happiness* and *felicity* do: nor does it lead us to the consideration of the *number*, of the interests affected; to the *number*, as being the circumstance, which contributes, in the largest proportion, to the formation of the standard here in question; the *standard of right and wrong*, by which alone the propriety of human conduct, in every situation, can with propriety be tried. This want of a sufficiently manifest connexion between the ideas of *happiness* and *pleasure* on the one hand, and the idea of *utility* on the other, I have every now and then found operating, and with but too much efficiency, as a bar to the acceptance, that might otherwise have been given, to this principle.

minate account of what is meant by it. By the principle* of utility is meant that principle which approves or disapproves of every action whatsoever, according to the tendency which it appears to have to augment or diminish the happiness of the party whose interest is in question: or, what is the same thing in other words, to promote or to oppose that happiness. I say of every action whatsoever; and therefore not only of every action of a private individual, but of every measure of government.

III. By utility is meant that property in any object, whereby it tends to produce benefit, advantage, pleasure, good, or happiness, (all this in the present case comes to the same thing) or (what comes again to the same thing) to prevent the happening of mischief, pain, evil, or unhappiness to the party whose interest is considered: if that party be the community in general, then the happiness of the community: if a particular individual, then the happiness of that individual.

IV. The interest of the community is one of the most general expressions that can occur in the phraseology of morals: no wonder that the meaning of it is often lost. When it has a meaning, it is this. The community is a fictitious *body*, composed of the individual persons who are considered as constituting as it were its *members*. The interest of the community then is, what?—the sum of the interests of the several members who compose it.

V. It is in vain to talk of the interest of the community, without understanding what is the interest of the individual.† A thing is said to promote the interest, or to be *for* the interest, of an individual, when it tends to add to the sum total of his pleasures: or, what comes to the same thing, to diminish the sum total of his pains.

VI. An action then may be said to be conformable to the principle of utility, or, for shortness sake, to utility, (meaning with respect

* The word principle is derived from the Latin *principium:* which seems to be compounded of the two words *primus,* first, or chief, and *cipium,* a termination which seems to be derived from *capio,* to take, as in *mancipium, municipium;* to which are analogous, *auceps, forceps,* and others. It is a term of very vague and very extensive signification: it is applied to any thing which is conceived to serve as a foundation or beginning to any series of operations: in some cases, of physical operations; but of mental operations in the present case.

The principle here in question may be taken for an act of the mind; a sentiment; a sentiment of approbation; a sentiment which, when applied to an action, approves of its utility, as that quality of it by which the measure of approbation or disapprobation bestowed upon it ought to be governed.

† Interest is one of those words, which not having any superior *genus,* cannot in the ordinary way be defined.

to the community at large) when the tendency it has to augment the happiness of the community is greater than any it has to diminish it.

VII. A measure of government (which is but a particular kind of action, performed by a particular person or persons) may be said to be conformable to or dictated by the principle of utility, when in like manner the tendency which it has to augment the happiness of the community is greater than any which it has to diminish it.

VIII. When an action, or in particular a measure of government, is supposed by a man to be conformable to the principle of utility, it may be convenient, for the purposes of discourse, to imagine a kind of law or dictate, called a law or dictate of utility: and to speak of the action in question, as being conformable to such law or dictate.

IX. A man may be said to be a partizan of the principle of utility, when the approbation or disapprobation he annexes to any action, or to any measure, is determined by and proportioned to the tendency which he conceives it to have to augment or to diminish the happiness of the community: or in other words, to its conformity or unconformity to the laws or dictates of utility.

X. Of an action that is conformable to the principle of utility one may always say either that it is one that ought to be done, or at least that it is not one that ought not to be done. One may say also, that it is right it should be done; at least that it is not wrong it should be done: that it is a right action; at least that it is not a wrong action. When thus interpreted, the words *ought*, and *right* and *wrong*, and others of that stamp, have a meaning: when otherwise, they have none.

XI. Has the rectitude of this principle been ever formally contested? It should seem that it had, by those who have not known what they have been meaning. Is it susceptible of any direct proof? it should seem not: for that which is used to prove every thing else, cannot itself be proved: a chain of proofs must have their commencement somewhere. To give such proof is as impossible as it is needless.

XII. Not that there is or ever has been that human creature breathing, however stupid or perverse, who has not on many, perhaps on most occasions of his life, deferred to it. By the natural constitution of the human frame, on most occasions of their lives men in general embrace this principle, without thinking of it: if not for the ordering of their own actions, yet for the trying of their own actions, as well as those of other men. There have been, at the same time, not many, perhaps, even of the most intelligent, who have been disposed to embrace it purely and without reserve. There are even few who have not taken some occasion or other to quarrel with it, either on account of their not understanding always how to apply it, or on account of some prejudice or other which they were afraid to examine into, or could not bear to part with. For such is the stuff that man is made of: in principle and in practice, in a right track and in a wrong one, the rarest of all human qualities is consistency.

XIII. When a man attempts to combat the principle of utility, it is with reasons drawn, without his being aware of it, from that very principle itself.* His arguments, if they prove any thing, prove not

---

* 'The principle of utility (I have heard it said), is a dangerous principle: it is dangerous on certain occasions to consult it.' This is as much as to say, what? that it is not consonant to utility, to consult utility: in short, that it is *not* consulting it, to consult it.

Addition by the Author, July 1822.

Not long after the publication of the Fragment on Government, anno 1776, in which, in the character of an all-comprehensive and all-commanding principle, the principle of *utility* was brought to view, one person by whom observation to the above effect was made was *Alexander Wedderburn,* at that time Attorney or Solicitor General, afterwards successively Chief Justice of the Common Pleas, and Chancellor of England, under the successive titles of Lord Loughborough and Earl of Rosslyn. It was made—not indeed in my hearing, but in the hearing of a person by whom it was almost immediately communicated to me. So far from being self-contradictory, it was a shrewd and perfectly true one. By that distinguished functionary, the state of the Government was thoroughly understood: by the obscure individual, at that time not so much as supposed to be so: his disquisitions had not been as yet applied, with any thing like a comprehensive view, to the field of Constitutional Law, nor therefore to those features of the English Government, by which the greatest happiness of the ruling *one* with or without that of a favoured few, are now so plainly seen to be the only ends to which the course of it has at any time been directed. The *principle of utility* was an appellative, at that time employed—employed by me, as it had been by others, to designate that which, in a more perspicuous and instructive manner, may, as above, be designated by the name of the *greatest happiness principle.* 'This principle (said Wedderburn) is a dangerous one.' Saying so, he said that which, to a certain extent, is strictly true: a principle, which lays down, as the only *right* and justifiable end of Government, the greatest happiness of the greatest number—how can it be denied to be a dangerous one? dangerous it unquestionably is, to every government which has for its *actual* end or object, the greatest happiness of a certain *one,* with or without the addition of some comparatively small number of others, whom it is matter of pleasure or accommodation to him to admit, each of them, to a share in the concern, on the footing of so many junior partners. *Dangerous* it therefore really was, to the interest—the sinister interest—of all those functionaries, himself included, whose interest it was, to maximize delay, vexation, and expense, in judicial and other modes of procedure, for the sake of the profit, extractible out of the expense. In a Government which had for its end in view the greatest happiness of the greatest number, Alexander Wedderburn might have been Attorney General and then Chancellor: but he would not have been Attorney General with £15,000

that the principle is *wrong*, but that, according to the applications he supposes to be made of it, it is *misapplied*. Is it possible for a man to move the earth? Yes; but he must find out another earth to stand upon.

XIV. To disprove the propriety of it by arguments is impossible; but, from the causes that have been mentioned, or from some confused or partial view of it, a man may happen to be disposed not to relish it. Where this is the case, if he thinks the settling of his opinions on such a subject worth the trouble, let him take the following steps, and at length, perhaps, he may come to reconcile himself to it.

1. Let him settle with himself, whether he would wish to discard this principle altogether; if so, let him consider what it is that all his reasonings (in matters of politics especially) can amount to?

2. If he would, let him settle with himself, whether he would judge and act without any principle, or whether there is any other he would judge and act by?

3. If there be, let him examine and satisfy himself whether the principle he thinks he has found is really any separate intelligible principle; or whether it be not a mere principle in words, a kind of phrase, which at bottom expresses neither more nor less than the mere averment of his own unfounded sentiments; that is, what in another person he might be apt to call caprice?

4. If he is inclined to think that his own approbation or disapprobation, annexed to the idea of an act, without any regard to its consequences, is a sufficient foundation for him to judge and act upon, let him ask himself whether his sentiment is to be a standard of right and wrong, with respect to every other man, or whether every man's sentiment has the same privilege of being a standard to itself?

5. In the first case, let him ask himself whether his principle is not despotical, and hostile to all the rest of human race?

6. In the second case, whether it is not anarchial, and whether at this rate there are not as many different standards of right and wrong as there are men? and whether even to the same man, the same thing, which is right to-day, may not (without the least change in its nature) be wrong to-morrow? and whether the same thing is not right and wrong in the same place at the same time? and in either case, whether all argument is not at an end? and whether, when two men have said, 'I like this,' and 'I don't like it,' they can (upon such a principle) have any thing more to say?

7. If he should have said to himself, No: for that the sentiment

---

a year, nor Chancellor, with a peerage with a veto upon all justice, with £25,000 a year, and with 500 sinecures at his disposal, under the name of Ecclesiastical Benefices, besides *et caeteras*.

which he proposes as a standard must be grounded on reflection, let him say on what particulars the reflection is to turn? if on particulars having relation to the utility of the act, then let him say whether this is not deserting his own principle, and borrowing assistance from that very one in opposition to which he sets it up: or if not on those particulars, on what other particulars?

8. If he should be for compounding the matter, and adopting his own principle in part, and the principle of utility in part, let him say how far will he adopt it?

9. When he has settled with himself where he will stop, then let him ask himself how he justifies to himself the adopting it so far? and why he will not adopt it any farther?

10. Admitting any other principle than the principle of utility to be a right principle, a principle that it is right for a man to pursue; admitting (what is not true) that the word *right* can have a meaning without reference to utility, let him say whether there is any such thing as a *motive* that a man can have to pursue the dictates of it: if there is, let him say what that motive is, and how it is to be distinguished from those which enforce the dictates of utility: if not, then lastly let him say what it is this other principle can be good for?

CHAPTER IV Value of a Lot of Pleasure or Pain, How to Be Measured

I. Pleasures then, and the avoidance of pains, are the *ends* which the legislator has in view: it behoves him therefore to understand their *value*. Pleasures and pains are the *instruments* he has to work with: it behoves him therefore to understand their force, which is again, in other words, their value.

II. To a person considered *by himself*, the value of a pleasure or pain considered *by itself*, will be greater or less, according to the four following circumstances;°

° These circumstances have since been denominated *elements* or *dimensions* of *value* in a pleasure or a pain.

Not long after the publication of the first edition, the following memoriter verses were framed, in the view of lodging more effectually, in the memory, these points, on which the whole fabric of morals and legislation may be seen to rest.

> Intense, long, certain, speedy, fruitful, pure—
> Such marks in *pleasures* and in *pains* endure.
> Such pleasures seek if *private* be thy end:
> If it be *public*, wide let them extend.
> Such *pains* avoid, whichever be thy view:
> If pains *must* come, let them *extend* to few.

1. Its *intensity*.
2. Its *duration*.
3. Its *certainty* or *uncertainty*.
4. Its *propinquity* or *remoteness*.

III. These are the circumstances which are to be considered in estimating a pleasure or a pain considered each of them by itself. But when the value of any pleasure or pain is considered for the purpose of estimating the tendency of any *act* by which it is produced, there are two other circumstances to be taken into the account; these are,

5. Its *fecundity*, or the chance it has of being followed by sensations of the *same* kind: that is, pleasures, if it be a pleasure: pains, if it be a pain.

6. Its *purity*, or the chance it has of *not* being followed by sensations of the *opposite* kind: that is, pains, if it be a pleasure: pleasures, if it be a pain.

These two last, however, are in strictness scarcely to be deemed properties of the pleasure or the pain itself; they are not, therefore, in strictness to be taken into the account of the value of that pleasure or that pain. They are in strictness to be deemed properties only of the act, or other event, by which such pleasure or pain has been produced; and accordingly are only to be taken into the account of the tendency of such act or such event.

IV. To a *number* of persons, with reference to each of whom the value of a pleasure or a pain is considered, it will be greater or less, according to seven circumstances: to wit, the six preceding ones; *viz.*

1. Its *intensity*.
2. Its *duration*.
3. Its *certainty* or *uncertainty*.
4. Its *propinquity* or *remoteness*.
5. Its *fecundity*.
6. Its *purity*.

And one other; to wit:

7. Its *extent;* that is, the number of persons to whom it *extends;* or (in other words) who are affected by it.

V. To take an exact account then of the general tendency of any act, by which the interests of a community are affected, proceed as follows. Begin with any one person of those whose interests seem most immediately to be affected by it: and take an account,

1. Of the value of each distinguishable *pleasure* which appears to be produced by it in the *first* instance.

2. Of the value of each pain which appears to be produced by it in the *first* instance.

3. Of the value of each pleasure which appears to be produced by it *after* the first. This constitutes the *fecundity* of the first *pleasure* and the *impurity* of the first *pain*.

4. Of the value of each *pain* which appears to be produced by it after the first. This constitutes the *fecundity* of the first *pain*, and the *impurity* of the first pleasure.

5. Sum up all the values of all the *pleasures* on the one side, and those of all the pains on the other. The balance, if it be on the side of pleasure, will give the *good* tendency of the act upon the whole, with respect to the interests of that *individual* person; if on the side of pain, the *bad* tendency of it upon the whole.

6. Take an account of the *number* of persons whose interests appear to be concerned; and repeat the above process with respect to each. *Sum up* the numbers expressive of the degrees of *good* tendency, which the act has, with respect to each individual, in regard to whom the tendency of it is *good* upon the whole: do this again with respect to each individual, in regard to whom the tendency of it is *good* upon the whole: do this again with respect to each individual, in regard to whom the tendency of it is *bad* upon the whole. Take the *balance;* which, if on the side of *pleasure,* will give the general *good tendency* of the act, with respect to the total number or community of individuals concerned; if on the side of pain, the general *evil tendency,* with respect to the same community.

VI. It is not to be expected that this process should be strictly pursued previously to every moral judgment, or to every legislative or judicial operation. It may, however, be always kept in view: and as near as the process actually pursued on these occasions approaches to it, so near will such process approach to the character of an exact one.

VII. The same process is alike applicable to pleasure and pain, in whatever shape they appear: and by whatever denomination they are distinguished: to pleasure, whether it be called *good* (which is properly the cause or instrument of pleasure) or *profit* (which is distant pleasure, or the cause or instrument of distant pleasure,) or *convenience,* or *advantage, benefit, emolument, happiness,* and so forth: to pain, whether it be called *evil,* (which corresponds to *good*) or *mischief,* or *inconvenience,* or *disadvantage,* or *loss,* or *unhappiness,* and so forth.

VIII. Nor is this a novel and unwarranted, any more than it is a useless theory. In all this there is nothing but what the practice of mankind, wheresoever they have a clear view of their own interest, is perfectly conformable to. An article of property, an estate in land, for instance, is valuable, on what account? On account of the pleasures of all kinds which it enables a man to produce, and what comes to the same thing the pains of all kinds which it enables him to avert. But the value of such an article of property is universally understood to rise or fall according to the length or shortness of the time which a man has in it: the certainty or uncertainty of its coming into possession: and the nearness or remoteness of the time at which, if at all, it is to come into possession. As to the *intensity* of the pleasures which a man may derive from it, this is never thought of, because it depends upon the use which each particular person may come to make of it; which cannot be estimated till the particular pleasures he may come to derive from it, or the particular pains he may come to exclude by means of it, are brought to view. For the same reason, neither does he think of the *fecundity* or *purity* of those pleasures.

Thus much for pleasure and pain, happiness and unhappiness, in *general*. We come now to consider the several particular kinds of pain and pleasure.

CHAPTER XIV   Of the Proportion Between Punishments and Offences

I. We have seen that the general object of all laws is to prevent mischief; that is to say, when it is worth while; but that, where there are no other means of doing this than punishment, there are four cases in which it is *not* worth while.

II. When it *is* worth while, there are four subordinate designs or objects, which, in the course of his endeavours to compass, as far as may be, that one general object, a legislator, whose views are governed by the principle of utility, comes naturally to propose to himself.

III. 1. His first, most extensive, and most eligible object, is to prevent, in as far as it is possible, and worth while, all sorts of offences whatsoever: * in other words, so to manage, that no offence whatso-

IV. 2. But if a man must needs commit an offence of some kind or other, the next object is to induce him to commit an offence *less* mischievous, *rather* than one *more* mischievous: in other words, to choose always the *least* mischievous, of two offences that will either of them suit his purpose.

* By *offences* I mean, at present, acts which appear to him to have a tendency to produce mischief.
ever may be committed.

V. 3. When a man has resolved upon a particular offence, the next object is to dispose him to do *no more* mischief than is *necessary* to his purpose: in other words, to do as little mischief as is consistent with the benefit he has in view.

VI. 4. The last object is, whatever the mischief be, which it is proposed to prevent, to prevent it at as *cheap* a rate as possible.

VII. Subservient to these four objects, or purposes, must be the rules or canons by which the proportion of punishments* to offences is to be governed.

VIII. Rule 1. The first object, it has been seen, is to prevent, in as far as it is worth while, all sorts of offences; therefore,

The value of the punishment must not be less in any case than what is sufficient to outweigh that of the profit† of the offence.‡

If it be, the offence (unless some other considerations, independent of the punishment, should intervene and operate efficaciously in the character of tutelary motives) will be sure to be committed notwithstanding:§ the whole lot of punishment will be thrown away: it will be altogether *inefficacious.*

---

* The same rules (it is to be observed) may be applied, with little variation, to rewards as well as punishment: in short, to motives in general, which, according as they are of the pleasurable or painful kind, are of the nature of *reward* or *punishment:* and, according as the act they are applied to produce is of the positive or negative kind, are styled impelling or restraining.

† By the profit of an offence, is to be understood, not merely the pecuniary profit, but the pleasure or advantage, of whatever kind it be, which a man reaps, or expects to reap, from the gratification of the desire which prompted him to engage in the offence.

It is the profit (that is, the expectation of the profit) of the offence that constitutes the *impelling* motive, or, where there are several, the sum of the impelling motives, by which a man is prompted to engage in the offence. It is the punishment, that is, the expectation of the punishment, that constitutes the *restraining* motive, which, either by itself, or in conjunction with others, is to act upon him in a *contrary* direction, so as to induce him to abstain from engaging in the offence. Accidental circumstances apart, the strength of the temptation is as the force of the seducing, that is, of the impelling motive or motives. To say then, as authors of great merit and great name have said, that the punishment ought not to increase with the strength of the temptation, is as much as to say in mechanics, that the moving force or *momentum* of the *power* need not increase in proportion to the momentum of the *burthen.*

‡ Beccaria, dei diletti, §6. id. trad. par. Morellet, §23.

§ It is a well-known adage, though it is to be hoped not a true one, that every man has his price. It is commonly meant of a man's virtue. This saying, though in a very different sense, was strictly verified by some of the Anglo-Saxon laws: by which a fixed price was set, not upon a man's virtue indeed, but upon his life: that of the sovereign himself among the rest. For 200 shillings you might have killed a peasant: for six times as

IX. The above rule has been often objected to, on account of its seeming harshness: but this can only have happened for want of its being properly understood. The strength of the temptation, *caeteris paribus*, is as the profit of the offence: the quantum of the punishment must rise with the profit of the offence: *caeteris paribus*, it must therefore rise with the strength of the temptation. This there is no disputing. True it is, that the stronger the temptation, the less conclusive is the indication which the act of delinquency affords of the depravity of the offender's disposition. So far then as the absence of any aggravation, arising from extraordinary depravity of disposition, may operate, or at the utmost, so far as the presence of a ground of extenuation, resulting from the innocence or beneficence of the offender's disposition, can operate, the strength of the temptation may operate in abatement of the demand for punishment. But it can never operate so far as to indicate the propriety of making the punishment ineffectual, which it is sure to be when brought below the level of the apparent profit of the offence.

The partial benevolence which should prevail for the reduction of it below this level, would counteract as well those purposes which such a motive would actually have in view, as those more extensive purposes which benevolence ought to have in view: it would be cruelty not only to the public, but to the very persons in whose behalf it pleads: in its effects, I mean, however opposite in its intention. Cruelty to the public, that is cruelty to the innocent, by suffering them, for want of an adequate protection, to lie exposed to the mischief of the offence: cruelty even to the offender himself, by punishing him to no purpose, and without the chance of compassing that

---

much, a nobleman: for six-and-thirty times as much you might have killed the king.[1] A king in those days was worth exactly 7.200 shillings.

[1] Wilkins' Leg. Anglo-Sax. p. 71, 72. See Hume, Vol. I, App. I. p. 219.
If then the heir to the throne, for example, grew weary of waiting for it, he had a secure and legal way of gratifying his impatience: he had but to kill the king with one hand, and pay himself with the other, and all was right. An earl Godwin, or a duke Streon, could have bought the lives of a whole dynasty. It is plain, that if ever a king in those days died in his bed, he must have had something else, besides this law, to thank for it. This being the production of a remote and barbarous age, the absurdity of it is presently recognised: but, upon examination, it would be found, that the freshest laws of the most civilised nations are continually falling into the same error.[2] This, in short, is the case wheresoever the punishment is fixed while the profit of delinquency is indefinite: or, to speak more precisely, where the punishment is limited to such a mark, that the profit of delinquency may reach beyond it.

[2] See in particular the *English Statute laws* throughout, *Bonaparte's* Penal code, and the recently enacted or not enacted *Spanish* Penal Code. —Note by the Author, July 1822.

beneficial end, by which alone the introduction of the evil of punishment is to be justified.

X. Rule 2. But whether a given offence shall be prevented in a given degree by a given quantity of punishment, is never any thing better than a chance; for the purchasing of which, whatever punishment is employed, is so much expended in advance. However, for the sake of giving it the better chance of outweighing the profit of the offence,

The greater the mischief of the offence, the greater is the expense, which it may be worth while to be at, in the way of punishment. *

XI. Rule 3. The next object is, to induce a man to choose always the least mischievous of two offences; therefore

Where two offences come in competition, the punishment for the greater offence must be sufficient to induce a man to prefer the less.†

XII. Rule 4. When a man has resolved upon a particular offence, the next object is, to induce him to do no more mischief than what is necessary for his purpose: therefore

The punishment should be adjusted in such manner to each particular offence, that for every part of the mischief there may be a motive to restrain the offender from giving birth to it.‡

XIII. Rule 5. The last object is, whatever mischief is guarded against, to guard against it at as cheap a rate as possible: therefore

The punishment ought in no case to be more than what is necessary to bring it into conformity with the rules here given.

XIV. Rule 6. It is further to be observed, that owing to the differ-

* For example, if it can ever be worth while to be at the expense of so horrible a punishment as that of burning alive, it will be more so in the view of preventing such a crime as that of murder or incendiarism, than in the view of preventing the uttering of a piece of bad money.

† Espr. des Loix, L. vi. c. 16.

‡ If any one have any doubt of this, let him conceive the offence to be divided into as many separate offences as there are distinguishable parcels of mischief that result from it. Let it consist, for example, in a man's giving you ten blows, or stealing from you ten shillings. If then, for giving you ten blows, he is punished no more than for giving you five, the giving you five of these ten blows is an offence for which there is no punishment at all: which being understood, as often as a man gives you five blows, he will be sure to give you five more, since he may have the pleasure of giving you these five for nothing. In like manner, if for stealing from you ten shillings, he is punished no more than for stealing five, the stealing of the remaining five of those ten shillings is an offence for which there is no punishment at all. This rule is violated in almost every page of every body of laws I have ever seen.

The profit, it is to be observed, though frequently, is not constantly, proportioned to the mischief: for example, where a thief, along with the things he covets, steals others which are of no use to him. This may happen through wantonness, indolence, precipitation, &c. &c.

ent manners and degrees in which persons under different circumstances are affected by the same exciting cause, a punishment which is the same in name will not always either really produce, or even so much as appear to others to produce, in two different persons the same degree of pain: therefore

That the quantity actually inflicted on each individual offender may correspond to the quantity intended for similar offenders in general, the several circumstances influencing sensibility ought always to be taken into account.

XV. Of the above rules of proportion, the four first, we may perceive, serve to mark out the limits on the side of diminution; the limits *below* which a punishment ought not to be *diminished:* the fifth, the limits on the side of increase; the limits *above* which it ought not to be *increased.* The five first are calculated to serve as guides to the legislator: the sixth is calculated, in some measure, indeed, for the same purpose; but principally for guiding the judge in his endeavours to conform, on both sides, to the intentions of the legislator.

XVI. Let us look back a little. The first rule, in order to render it more conveniently applicable to practice, may need perhaps to be a little more particularly unfolded. It is to be observed, then, that for the sake of accuracy, it was necessary, instead of the word *quantity* to make use of the less perspicuous term *value.* For the word *quantity* will not properly include the circumstances either of certainty or proximity: circumstances which, in estimating the value of a lot of pain or pleasure, must always be taken into the account. Now, on the one hand, a lot of punishment is a lot of pain; on the other hand, the profit of an offence is a lot of pleasure, or what is equivalent to it. But the profit of the offence *is* commonly more *certain* than the punishment, or, what comes to the same thing, *appears* so at least to the offender. It is at any rate commonly more *immediate.* It follows, therefore, that, in order to maintain its superiority over the profit of the offence, the punishment must have its value made up in some other way, in proportion to that whereby it falls short in the two points of *certainty* and *proximity.* Now there is no other way in which it can receive any addition to its *value,* but by receiving an addition in point of *magnitude.* Wherever then the value of the punishment falls short, either in point of *certainty,* or of *proximity,* of that of the profit of the offence, it must receive a proportionable addition in point of *magnitude.**

---

* It is for this reason, for example, that simple compensation is never looked upon as sufficient punishment for theft or robbery.

XVII. Yet farther. To make sure of giving the value of the punishment the superiority over that of the offence, it may be necessary, in some cases, to take into the account the profit not only of the *individual* offence to which the punishment is to be annexed, but also of such *other* offences of the *same sort* as offender is likely to have already committed without detection. This random mode of calculation, severe as it is, it will be impossible to avoid having recourse to, in certain cases: in such, to wit, in which the profit is pecuniary, the chance of detection very small, and the obnoxious act of such a nature as indicates a habit: for example, in the case of frauds against the coin. If it be *not* recurred to, the practice of committing the offence will be sure to be, upon the balance of the account, a gainful practice. That being the case, the legislator will be absolutely sure of *not* being able to suppress it, and the whole punishment that is bestowed upon it will be thrown away. In a word (to keep to the same expressions we set out with) that whole quantity of punishment will be *inefficacious*.

XVIII. Rule 7. These things being considered, the three following rules may be laid down by way of supplement and explanation to Rule 1.

To enable the value of the punishment to outweigh that of the profit of the offence, it must be increased, in point of magnitude, in proportion as it falls short in point of certainty.

XIX. Rule 8. *Punishment must be further increased in point of magnitude, in proportion as it falls short in point of proximity.*

XX. Rule 9. *Where the act is conclusively indicative of a habit, such an increase must be given to the punishment as may enable it to outweigh the profit not only of the individual offence, but of such other like offences as are likely to have been committed with impunity by the same offender.*

XXI. There may be a few other circumstances or considerations which may influence, in some small degree, the demand for punishment: but as the propriety of these is either not so demonstrable, or not so constant, or the application of them not so determinate, as that of the foregoing, it may be doubted whether they be worth putting on a level with the others.

XXII. Rule 10. *When a punishment, which in point of quality is particularly well calculated to answer its intention, cannot exist in less than a certain quantity, it may sometimes be of use, for the sake of employing it, to stretch a little beyond that quantity which, on other accounts, would be strictly necessary.*

XXIII. Rule 11. *In particular, this may sometimes be the case, where the punishment proposed is of such a nature as to be particularly well calculated to answer the purpose of a moral lesson.**

XXIV. Rule 12. The tendency of the above considerations is to dictate an augmentation in the punishment: the following rule operates in the way of diminution. There are certain cases (it has been seen) in which, by the influence of accidental circumstances, punishment may be rendered unprofitable in the whole: in the same cases it may chance to be rendered unprofitable as to a part only. Accordingly,

In adjusting the quantum of punishment, the circumstances, by which all punishment may be rendered unprofitable, ought to be attended to.

XXV. Rule 13. It is to be observed, that the more various and minute any set of provisions are, the greater the chance is that any given article in them will not be borne in mind: without which, no benefit can ensue from it. Distinctions, which are more complex than what the conceptions of those whose conduct it is designed to influence can take in, will even be worse than useless. The whole system will present a confused appearance: and thus the effect, not only of the proportions established by the articles in question, but of whatever is connected with them, will be destroyed. To draw a precise line of direction in such case seems impossible. However, by way of memento, it may be of some use to subjoin the following rule.

Among provisions designed to perfect the proportion between punishments and offences, if any occur, which, by their own particular good effects, would not make up for the harm they would do by adding to the intricacy of the Code, they should be omitted.†

---

* A punishment may be said to be calculated to answer the purpose of a moral lesson, when, by reason of the ignominy it stamps upon the offence, it is calculated to inspire the public with sentiments of aversion towards those pernicious habits and dispositions with which the offence appears to be connected; and thereby to inculcate the opposite beneficial habits and dispositions.

It is this, for example, if any thing, that must justify the application of so severe a punishment as the infamy of a public exhibition, hereinafter proposed, for him who lifts up his hand against a woman, or against his father.

It is partly on this principle, I suppose, that military legislators have justified to themselves the inflicting death on the soldier who lifts up his hand against his superior officer.

† Notwithstanding this rule, my fear is, that in the ensuing model, I may be thought to have carried my endeavours at proportionality too far. Hitherto scarce any attention has been paid to it. Montesquieu seems to have been almost the first who has had the least idea of any such thing. In such a matter, therefore, excess seemed more eligible than defect. The difficulty is to invent: that done, if any thing seems superfluous, it is easy to retrench.

XXVI. It may be remembered, that the political sanction, being that to which the sort of punishment belongs, which in this chapter is all along in view, is but one of four sanctions, which may all of them contribute their share towards producing the same effects. It may be expected, therefore, that in adjusting the quantity of political punishment, allowance should be made for the assistance it may meet with from those other controlling powers. True it is, that from each of these several sources a very powerful assistance may sometimes be derived. But the case is, that (setting aside the moral sanction, in the case where the force of it is expressly adopted into and modified by the political) the force of those other powers is never determinate enough to be depended upon. It can never be reduced, like political punishment, into exact lots, nor meted out in number, quantity, and value. The legislator is therefore obliged to provide the full complement of punishment, as if he were sure of not receiving any assistance whatever from any of those quarters. If he does, so much the better: but lest he should not, it is necessary he should, at all events, make that provision which depends upon himself.

XXVII. It may be of use, in this place, to recapitulate the several circumstances, which, in establishing the proportion betwixt punishments and offences, are to be attended to. These seem to be as follows:

I. *On the part of the offence:*
  1. The profit of the offence;
  2. The mischief of the offence;
  3. The profit and mischief of other greater or lesser offences, of different sorts, which the offender may have to choose out of;
  4. The profit and mischief of other offences, of the same sort, which the same offender may probably have been guilty of already.

II. *On the part of the punishment:*
  5. The magnitude of the punishment: composed of its intensity and duration;
  6. The deficiency of the punishment in point of certainty;
  7. The deficiency of the punishment in point of proximity;
  8. The quality of the punishment;
  9. The accidental advantage in point of quality of a punishment, not strictly needed in point of quantity;
  10. The use of a punishment of a particular quality, in the character of a moral lesson.

III. *On the part of the offender:*
  11. The responsibility of the class of persons in a way to offend;
  12. The sensibility of each particular offender;
  13. The particular merits or useful qualities of any particular of-

fender, in case of a punishment which might deprive the community of the benefit of them;

14. The multitude of offenders on any particular occasion.

IV. *On the part of the public,* at any particular conjuncture:

   15. The inclinations of the people, for or against any quantity or mode of punishment;

   16. The inclinations of foreign powers.

V. *On the part of the law:* that is, of the public for a continuance:

   17. The necessity of making small sacrifices, in point of proportionality, for the sake of simplicity.

XXVIII. There are some, perhaps, who, at first sight, may look upon the nicety employed in the adjustment of such rules, as so much labour lost: for gross ignorance, they will say, never troubles itself about laws, and passion does not calculate. But the evil of ignorance admits of cure: and as to the proposition that passion does not calculate, this, like most of these very general and oracular propositions, is not true. When matters of such importance as pain and pleasure are at stake, and these in the highest degree (the only matters, in short, that can be of importance) who is there that does not calculate? Men calculate, some with less exactness, indeed, some with more: but all men calculate. I would not say, that even a madman does not calculate.° Passion calculates, more or less, in every man: in different men, according to the warmth or coolness of their dispositions: according to the firmness or irritability of their minds: according to the nature of the motives by which they are acted upon. Happily, of all passions, that is the most given to calculation, from the excesses of which, by reason of its strength, constancy, and universality, society has most to apprehend: I mean that which corresponds to the motive of pecuniary interest: so that these niceties, if such they are to be called, have the best chance of being efficacious, where efficacy is of the most importance.

° There are few madmen but what are observed to be afraid of the strait waistcoat.

Thomas Robert Malthus

1766–1834

Malthus came to the writing of his First Essay on Population *as the consequence of an argument with his father. The parent, Daniel Malthus, was an eccentric country squire, who was an ardent believer in the perfectibility of mankind and whose hopes survived even the entertainment at his country estate, the Rookery, of the terrible-tempered Jean-Jacques Rousseau. His son, down from Oxford where he had won honors in mathematics and read widely in philosophy, was an equally convinced pessimist. The two argued so long that the father recommended to the son that he write it all down. Nothing loath, Thomas Robert Malthus promptly dashed off in 1798 the* First Essay.

It was decidedly a young man's production, full of dashing rhetoric and sweeping prophecy of disaster. Malthus conceived it as a response to such utopians as Godwin and Condorcet and as a demonstration that men could never achieve improvement so long as they remained poor, and they could never cease to be poor unless they restricted their numbers. Since the sexual instinct was powerful and the land was grudging, genuine hope of population limitation was small. If men postponed marriage, they were all too prone to vice. If they married, they were all too prone to overpopulation. Thus hot passion led to surplus souls and cold reason led to sin.

Malthus's Second Essay on Population *(1803) was a much less sweeping statement. He offered a little more hope for moral restraint—late marriage unaccompanied by vice. He was a little less certain that the horrors of the positive check—famine, disease, and the like—would inevitably afflict mankind. Nevertheless, to the end he remained a cheerful pessimist. One of the limited hopes that amended his pessimism was amendment of the poor laws, the subject of the following passage. Malthus's reasoning on his own premises was simple. In their present condition, the poor laws encouraged the poor* to marry early and to procreate large numbers of children. Their action intensified the pressure of population on the food supplies and injured the more prudent as well as themselves. Appropriate amendment, or even repeal, of the poor laws would make the poor think more carefully before they hastened into imprudent marriage. Although such action wore the aspect of cruelty, Malthus was convinced that it was the only true benevolence to the poor that was genuinely possible.

As a doctrine, Malthus's position on the poor laws had an obvious attraction to the payers of rates. His opinions may be said to have triumphed when the New Poor Law Act of 1834 was passed by Parliament.

This passage comes from the First Essay (reprinted by the University of Michigan Press, 1959), pp. 29-34.

Poor-Laws

The poor-laws of England tend to depress the general condition of the poor in these two ways. Their first obvious tendency is to increase population without increasing the food for its support. A poor man may marry with little or no prospect of being able to support a family in independence. They may be said therefore in some measure to create the poor which they maintain, and as the provisions of the country must, in consequence of the increased population, be distributed to every man in smaller proportions, it is evident that the labour of those who are not supported by parish assistance will purchase a smaller quantity of provisions than before and consequently more of them must be driven to ask for support.

Secondly, the quantity of provisions consumed in workhouses upon a part of the society that cannot in general be considered as the most valuable part diminishes the shares that would otherwise belong to more industrious and more worthy members, and thus in the same manner forces more to become dependent. If the poor in the workhouses were to live better than they now do, this new distribution of the money of the society would tend more conspicuously to depress the condition of those out of the workhouses by occasioning a rise in the price of provisions.

Fortunately for England, a spirit of independence still remains among the peasantry. The poor-laws are strongly calculated to eradicate this spirit. They have succeeded in part, but had they succeeded as completely as might have been expected their pernicious tendency would not have been so long concealed.

Hard as it may appear in individual instances, dependent poverty ought to be held disgraceful. Such a stimulus seems to be absolutely necessary to promote the happiness of the great mass of mankind, and every general attempt to weaken this stimulus, however benevolent its apparent intention, will always defeat its own purpose. If men are induced to marry from a prospect of parish provision, with little or no chance of maintaining their families in independence, they are not only unjustly tempted to bring unhappiness and dependence upon themselves and children, but they are tempted, without knowing it, to injure all in the same class with themselves. A labourer who marries without being able to support a family may in some respects be considered as an enemy to all his fellow-labourers.

I feel no doubt whatever that the parish laws of England have contributed to raise the price of provisions and to lower the real price of labour. They have therefore contributed to impoverish that class of people whose only possession is their labour. It is also difficult to suppose that they have not powerfully contributed to generate that carelessness and want of frugality observable among the poor, so contrary to the disposition frequently to be remarked among petty tradesmen and small farmers. The labouring poor, to use a vulgar expression, seem always to live from hand to mouth. Their present wants employ their whole attention, and they seldom think of the future. Even when they have an opportunity of saving they seldom exercise it, but all that is beyond their present necessities goes, generally speaking, to the ale-house. The poor-laws of England may therefore be said to diminish both the power and the will to save among the common people, and thus to weaken one of the strongest incentives to sobriety and industry, and consequently to happiness.

It is a general complaint among master manufacturers that high wages ruin all their workmen, but it is difficult to conceive that these men would not save a part of their high wages for the future support of their families, instead of spending it in drunkenness and dissipation, if they did not rely on parish assistance for support in case of accidents. And that the poor employed in manufactures consider this assistance as a reason why they may spend all the wages they earn and enjoy themselves while they can appears to be evident from the number of families that, upon the failure of any great manufactory, immediately fall upon the parish, when perhaps the wages earned in this manufactory while it flourished were sufficiently above the price of common country labour to have allowed them to save enough for their support till they could find some other channel for their industry.

A man who might not be deterred from going to the ale-house from the consideration that on his death, or sickness, he should leave his wife and family upon the parish might yet hesitate in thus dissipating his earnings if he were assured that, in either of these cases, his family must starve or be left to the support of casual bounty. In China, where the real as well as nominal price of labour is very low, sons are yet obliged by law to support their aged and helpless parents. Whether such a law would be advisable in this country I will not pretend to determine. But it seems at any rate highly improper, by positive institutions, which render dependent poverty so general, to weaken that disgrace, which for the best and most humane reasons ought to attach to it.

The mass of happiness among the common people cannot but be diminished, when one of the strongest checks to idleness and dissipation is thus removed, and when men are thus allured to marry with little or no prospect of being able to maintain a family in independence. Every obstacle in the way of marriage must undoubtedly be considered as a species of unhappiness. But as from the laws of our nature some check to population must exist, it is better that it should be checked from a foresight of the difficulties attending a family and the fear of dependent poverty than that it should be encouraged, only to be repressed afterwards by want and sickness.

It should be remembered always that there is an essential difference between food and those wrought commodities, the raw materials of which are in great plenty. A demand for these last will not fail to create them in as great a quantity as they are wanted. The demand for food has by no means the same creative power. In a country where all the fertile spots have been seized, high offers are necessary to encourage the farmer to lay his dressing on land from which he cannot expect a profitable return for some years. And before the prospect of advantage is sufficiently great to encourage this sort of agricultural enterprize, and while the new produce is rising, great distresses may be suffered from the want of it. The demand for an increased quantity of subsistence is, with few exceptions, constant every where, yet we see how slowly it is answered in all those countries that have been long occupied.

The poor-laws of England were undoubtedly instituted for the most benevolent purpose, but there is great reason to think that they have not succeeded in their intention. They certainly mitigate some cases of very severe distress which might otherwise occur, yet the state of the poor who are supported by parishes, considered in all its circumstances, is very far from being free from misery. But one of the principal objections to them is that for this assistance which some of the poor receive, in itself almost a doubtful blessing, the whole class of the common people of England is subjected to a set of grating, inconvenient, and tyrannical laws, totally inconsistent with the genuine spirit of the constitution. The whole business of settlements, even in its present amended state, is utterly contradictory to all ideas of freedom. The parish persecution of men whose families are likely to become chargeable, and of poor women who are near lying-in, is a most disgraceful and disgusting tyranny. And the obstructions continually occasioned in the market of labour by these laws, have a constant tendency to add to the difficulties of those who are struggling to support themselves without assistance.

These evils attendant on the poor-laws are in some degree irremediable. If assistance be to be distributed to a certain class of people, a power must be given somewhere of discriminating the proper objects and of managing the concerns of the institutions that are necessary, but any great interference with the affairs of other people, is a species of tyranny, and in the common course of things the exercise of this power may be expected to become grating to those who are driven to ask for support. The tyranny of Justices, Churchwardens, and Overseers, is a common complaint among the poor, but the fault does not lie so much in these persons, who probably before they were in power, were not worse than other people, but in the nature of all such institutions.

The evil is perhaps gone too far to be remedied, but I feel little doubt in my own mind that if the poor-laws had never existed, though there might have been a few more instances of very severe distress, yet that the aggregate mass of happiness among the common people would have been much greater than it is at present.

Mr. Pitt's Poor-bill has the appearance of being framed with benevolent intentions, and the clamour raised against it was in many respects ill directed, and unreasonable. But it must be confessed that it possesses in a high degree the great and radical defect of all systems of the kind, that of tending to increase population without increasing the means for its support, and thus to depress the condition of those that are not supported by parishes, and, consequently, to create more poor.

To remove the wants of the lower classes of society is indeed an arduous task. The truth is that the pressure of distress on this part of a community is an evil so deeply seated that no human ingenuity can reach it. Were I to propose a palliative, and palliatives are all that the nature of the case will admit, it should be, in the first place, the total abolition of all the present parish-laws. This would at any rate give liberty and freedom of action to the peasantry of England, which they can hardly be said to possess at present. They would then be able to settle without interruption, wherever there was a prospect of a greater plenty of work and a higher price for labour. The market of labour would then be free, and those obstacles removed, which as things are now, often for a considerable time prevent the price from rising according to the demand.

Secondly, Premiums might be given for turning up fresh land, and all possible encouragements held out to agriculture above manufactures, and to tillage above grazing. Every endeavour should be used to weaken and destroy all those institutions relating to corporations, apprenticeships, &c, which cause the labours of agriculture to be worse paid than the labours of trade and manufactures. For a country can never produce its proper quantity of food while these distinctions remain in favour of artizans. Such encouragements to agriculture would tend to furnish the market with an increasing quantity of healthy work, and at the same time, by augmenting the produce of the country, would raise the comparative price of labour and ameliorate the condition of the labourer. Being now in better circumstances, and seeing no prospect of parish assistance, he would be more able, as well as more inclined, to enter into associations for providing against the sickness of himself or family.

Lastly, for cases of extreme distress, county workhouses might be established, supported by rates upon the whole kingdom, and free for persons of all counties, and indeed of all nations. The fare should be hard, and those that were able obliged to work. It would be desireable that they should not be considered as comfortable asylums in all difficulties, but merely as places where severe distress might find some alleviation. A part of these houses might be separated, or others built for a most beneficial purpose, which has not been unfrequently taken notice of, that of providing a place where any person, whether native or foreigner, might do a day's work at all times and receive the market price for it. Many cases would undoubtedly be left for the exertion of individual benevolence.

A plan of this kind, the preliminary of which should be an abolition of all the present parish laws, seems to be the best calculated to increase the mass of happiness among the common people of England. To prevent the recurrence of misery, is, alas! beyond the power of man. In the vain endeavour to attain what in the nature of things is impossible, we now sacrifice not only possible but certain benefits. We tell the common people that if they will submit to a code of tyrannical regulations, they shall never be in want. They do submit to these regulations. They perform their part of the contract, but we do not, nay cannot, perform ours, and thus the poor sacrifice the valuable blessing of liberty and receive nothing that can be called an equivalent in return.

Notwithstanding then, the institution of the poor-laws in England, I think it will be allowed that considering the state of the lower classes altogether, both in the towns and in the country, the distresses which they suffer from the want of proper and sufficient food, from hard labour and unwholesome habitations, must operate as a constant check to incipient population.

Harriet Martineau

1803–1876

To most Americans Harriet Martineau is probably dimly recalled only as one of that interminable stream of English visitors who came to sneer at the crudities of American society and to make their fortunes by putting the sneers into print. Indeed Harriet Martineau's Society in America and Retrospect of Western Travel met the usual reception of such travelers' books: in England Miss Martineau won wide praise including Dickens's judgment that the first-named of these volumes was the best book written on America; in the United States, she encountered almost universal indignation.

In fact, Miss Martineau was one of the leading journalists of her age and it was in pursuit of this profession that she came to touch upon political economy. Her chosen form was the story with a moral. Her Illustrations of Political Economy were written because she believed that the great doctrines of political economy deserved larger audiences and wider influence. Each tale consisted basically of a large quantity of exposition strung upon a slight strand of story. Weal and Woe in Garveloch, which enunciated Malthusian doctrines, traced the decline of a community that failed to apply preventive checks to population. Messrs Vanderput and Snoek, the source of the present selection, sweetened a solemn exposition of the principles of international exchange with a little romance. The didacticism of style and the dogmatism of doctrine which characterize these stories make them unattractive to modern eyes, but they were an enormous success in the 1820's and the 1830's. Malthus affirmed that Miss Martineau had offered the best simple exposition of his doctrine that was available. And Lord Brougham, the redoubtable champion of the Society for the Diffusion of Useful Knowledge, remarked, with some exasperation, that a deaf girl in Norwich was doing more good than any man in the country.

There is little question that the Illustrations of Political Economy fixed in a great many English minds a conception of political economy as composed of a number of indisputable generalizations, each of them capable of clear exposition, and unqualified application to the social and economic problems of a great many countries. While much study went into Miss Martineau's productions and her exposition frequently attained precision and almost always approached accuracy, the qualifications and the hesitancies that complicated the thought of Ricardo, Malthus, and Smith inevitably vanished. Such is the inescapable effect of popularization.

"Wise Men at Supper" is typical of Miss Martineau's method. The task before her is the explanation of the principles of foreign exchange, and the identification of such key terms as parity of exchange, bills of exchange, and promissory notes. The technique rests heavily upon the conversation and the introductory exposition. It is difficult to believe that such conversations ever took place, but no harder than to believe in the dialogue typical of television commercials. Just in case anyone missed the point of the tale, each volume concluded with a summary of the principles that the volume was designed to illustrate. The summary appended to Messrs Vanderput and Snoek covered two pages of fine type. As a curiosity, it is worth quotation:

> Nations exchange commodities, as individuals do, for mutual accommodation; each imparting of its superfluity to obtain that in which it is deficient.
>
> The importing is therefore only a means of obtaining. Exportation is the means of obtaining importation—the end for which the traffic is instituted.
>
> The importation of money into a country where money is deficient is desirable on the same principle which renders undesirable the supply of any deficient commodity.
>
> The importation of money into a country where money is not deficient is no more desirable than it is to create any excess of any other commodity.
>
> That money is the commodity most generally bought and sold is no reason for its being a more desirable article of importation than commodities which are as much wanted in the country which imports it.
>
> That money is the commodity most generally bought and sold is a reason for its being the commodity fixed up for measuring the relative amounts of other articles of national interchange.

Money bearing different denominations in the different trading countries, a computation of the relative values of these denominations was made in the infancy of commerce, and the result expressed in terms which are retained through all changes in the value of these denominations.

The term by which in each country the original equal proportion was expressed is adopted as the fixed point of measurement called the par of exchange; and any variation in the relative amount of the total money debts of trading nations is called a variation from par.

This variation is of two kinds, nominal and real.

The nominal variation from par is caused by alteration in the value of the currency of any country, which of course destroys the relative proportion of its denominations to the denominations of the currency of other countries. But it does not affect the amount of commodities exchanged.

After further explanation of the relation between representative and real money, Miss Martineau concluded triumphantly:

A self-balancing power being thus inherent in the entire system of commercial exchange, all apprehensions about the results of its unimpeded operation are absurd.

The passage below comes from Messrs Vanderput and Snoek, *No. XVI of the* Illustrations of Political Economy (*London, 1833*), *pp. 56-67.*

CHAPTER IV   Wise Men at Supper

In such a country as Holland was at the time of our story, the prime subject of interest to persons engaged in commerce was the state of the Exchange. By this, the merchants not only found their own affairs determined, but were furnished with an indication of the general condition of trade at home and abroad. As by the Exchange, the debts of individuals residing at a distance from their creditors are cancelled without the transmission of money, the state of the Exchange marks out clearly in which country there has been the greatest amount of purchase, and in which of sale. It affords no indication of the positive amount of purchase and sale, because when this is nearly balanced between different countries, the exchange nearly preserves its level; or, to use technical language, is nearly at par. But the relative amount is infallibly shown by the exchange of any country being above or below par; and this circumstance serves to guide individuals in the conduct of their transactions.

Instead of discharging debts to foreigners in the manner taken for granted by Christian—viz., by transmitting money to a foreign land, as they would to the grocer's or the wine-merchant's in the next street, exporters and importers were early obliged, by an absurd enactment against the exportation of money, to devise some expedient for paying each other without using gold and silver. The most obvious way was to set against one another the values of things bought and sold, so that the balance was all that remained to be discharged. When it did not happen that the same firm at home had bought of the same firm abroad to whom it had sold, it was only necessary to find another firm at home which had bought in the same market abroad, and to exchange acknowledgments of debt, up to the amount at which the respective debts balanced one another; and these acknowledgments of debt served as money, in the same way as the promissory notes of bankers. In 1190, (which is the earliest recorded date of the practice of exchanging debts,) if an English merchant sold 100*l*. worth of cider into Holland, and his Dutch connexion had sold to another London merchant 90*l*. worth of fat cattle, the readiest way of paying the greater part of the debt was for the Dutchman to refer his cider-selling correspondent to his neighbour, the importer of cattle, for 90*l*.: 10*l*. would still remain due; and as the Dutchman was prohibited from sending it in gold and silver, he would look about for some neighbour who had 10*l*. owing to him from England, and would say, "I will pay you 10*l*., if you will desire your debtor to pay the same sum to my correspondent on the other side the water." By this simple mutual accommodation, the expense and risk of sending large sums of money are avoided; the postage, and the stamp charged by government upon such transactions, are the only cost incurred; and the whole process of buying and selling is simplified to all parties.

The convenience of this method being found great, it was improved as commerce increased, till a market was established where merchants might meet and make their exchanges without loss of time, instead of having to run after one another in search of what each wanted. The next thing was to institute a class of persons whose express business should be to manage these transactions. These persons, the bill-brokers, can tell how nearly the debts of different countries balance each other; and it is they who first purchase, and then provide merchants with these acknowledgments of debt, which circulate instead of money. These disposable acknowledgments, called bills of exchange, bear a very small proportion to the bargains between any two trading countries; because, where there is considerable intercourse, the sales of one party generally nearly balance those of the other. The nearness of their approach to a balance determines the price of those bills which remain to be sold, or which are desired to be bought. When bills are scarce, and merchants have difficulty in procuring these ready means of discharging their debts, they are anxious to pay a price for them, in order to be spared the inconvenience of transmitting money. A competition ensues, and it becomes generally known that the country where the bills are scarce has bought more than it has sold; that it owes more money than it has to receive; that (to use the technical term) the exchange is unfavourable to that country. The reverse is known to be the case when there is a superabundance of bills in the market; so that the merchants of a great trading country anxiously watch the exchange-market, not only to get their own debts settled, but to learn the general condition of commerce.

In order to the immediate detection of an alteration in the course of exchange, it was desirable to have a certain fixed point of calculation to which all variations might be referred. This fixed point was called the par of the exchange, and denoted, when it was first instituted, a perfect equality of exchange, both of goods and money, between the trading parties. The exchange between Holland and Great Britain was at par when the two countries sent exactly the same amount of wealth to each other. Supposing ten guilders to go to a pound, the exchange would be at par when the Dutch exported to England one thousand guilders' worth of commodities, and imported from England one hundred pounds' worth of commodities. So that, so long as ten guilders go to a pound, and Holland and England exchange the same quantity of goods, the exchange will not vary, really or seemingly, from the fixed point of calculation. It is only the one country exporting more goods than the other which can really make the amount of value due greater from one than the other: but, because ten guilders have not always gone to a pound, more money has sometimes appeared to be due from one than the other, even while the quantity of goods exchanged has been precisely the same, as computed in anything but the altered money. When eleven guilders go to the pound, while the par of exchange is still called ten, more money will appear to be due from Holland to England for the same quantity of goods as before; and consequently, while the actual state of trade will be exactly the same as before, it will be declared on 'Change that the exchange has turned against Holland; i.e., that Holland owes more money to England than she has to receive. However, merchants whose interest it is to watch the course of exchange, easily distinguish the real from the nominal variation, and learn to make use of the fixed point of calculation with due allowance for the difference caused by the alterations in the value of money. They can ascertain what they want to know of the general state of commerce, in the midst of what would be, to an inexperienced person, a deception; and a merchant who has, by any rare accident, been prevented from going on 'Change, only wants to know the nominal variation from par, and to compare it with his knowledge of the respective currencies of the two countries, to satisfy himself as to which ought to push its exports, and which its imports.

The first question asked by one Dutch merchant of another, in Heins's time, usually related to the exchange. It was that which his old friend Jakob greeted him with this evening, as, punctual to the appointed moment, he entered the apartment where Francesca and supper were waiting to honour and be honoured by him. Heins saw at a glance that better entertainment was provided for him than his wealthy parents had ever thought fit to indulge him with. It had been their method to surround themselves with whatever was essential to comfort, and whatever served as a good investment for their money; but, in all articles of mere consumption, they had been frugal in a way which Slyk and his daughter seemed little disposed to imitate. While the Snoeks' cellars were full of choice French wines and brandies, they drank beer only. While preparing the richest butter and cheese which their fat meadows could produce, their servants and children must be content with an inferior kind, imported salt. Not thus was Jakob's table furnished by his fair daughter. On the present occasion, it looked very tempting. Placed between the windows, so that the eaters might enjoy the amusement of observing the passers by, without the table itself being seen from without, one source of entertainment, always acceptable to a Dutchman, was secure. There was no lack of odoriferous foreign fruits, of flasks whose aspect was not to be mistaken, or of more substantial delicacies from the native pastures and decoys. This array was reflected from each corner of the apartment by mirrors, so placed as to exhibit every object within ken, from the train of passengers on the bridge at the bottom of the street, and the slow-moving barge advancing in an opposite direction, to the beau-pots filled with tulips which stood on the floor in corresponding angles of the apartment. What made the aspect of the place the most dazzling to Heins was, that there were four Francescas, each differing from the other according to the direction in which the gazer looked. Here, the profile of the pretty face and the jewelled arm were most conspicuous; there, the closely fitting jacket, and the knot of hair fastened behind with a silver pin. Now, the bright eyes looked out from between the two ringlets which curled exactly to the same turn on the foreheads of all Dutchwomen; and again, the yellow slipper was seen to rest on the chauffe-pied, whose constant use must infallibly spoil the form of the most beautiful foot that ever trod the quays of Amsterdam. At the further end of this radiant apartment leaned old Jakob, prepared with questions about how matters looked on 'Change: in the middle sat Francesca, deeming it no affront that such affairs were considered of the first importance, even in her presence; and between them stood Heins, commercial *con amore* one moment, and awkwardly gallant the next, till the familiarity of the evening meal enabled him to make his attentions to the father and the daughter more compatible than it had at first appeared possible to render them.

"They may talk of our commerce having declined," said Slyk, "but there is no nation like the Dutch, after all. Our refugee divines preach to more purpose to us than they did in France, about the wisdom of Solomon in his traffic with Hiram, king of Tyre, and all the riches that he gained thereby. We are a people obedient to the Divine word, Mr. Heins; and it pleases Heaven to prosper our industry, in spite of seeming obstacles. Even Solomon's wisdom was not taxed to procure cedar and shittim wood in the face of king Hiram's prohibitions; but we have done as much in getting the exchange with England turned in our favour, notwithstanding her late jealous enactments."

Francesca was of opinion that Holland was now under a special divine blessing for having received and cherished the Huguenots who had been driven from France. Heins thought that this opinion was countenanced by the fact that a considerable part of the prosperity of the States was derived from the industry of these very refugees. On the other hand, England was also open to the Huguenots, and it was against England that the exchange had turned.

This was a difficulty easily answered, Jakob said. England was punished for her jealousy; for her unneighbourly conduct towards the States. Was it not Heins's belief that a vast importation of brandies, velvets, and jewellery from Dutch vessels had been going on in England of late?

"Certainly," replied Heins. "While we can gain no more than two, or, at most, three per cent. on our capital at home, we must invest it abroad, even at some risk; and this has been done in England to such an extent that the government there must be a little surprised at the present course of the exchange. Visscher has put but a small per centage in his pocket today, I rather think; for there is such an abundance of bills on England in the market, and so few are present to buy, that the business has been very languid."

"There will soon be an end of that," replied Slyk. "A flood of this kind of money is presently absorbed. It is not like our hard gold, or our bank money, which rests at the disposal of one nation instead of two."

Heins suggested that bank money was like a ball sent up by a solitary player, which might return or be lost according to the skill or awkwardness with which it was thrown; whereas exchange money was a shuttlecock played between two nations, which was sure to visit each in turn, as long as both were interested in keeping up the game. This flight of fancy, so much more French than Dutch, enhanced Francesca's admiration of the accomplishments of the young merchant. She was not aware, however, that bills of exchange could be exactly called money. She knew that they might, in one sense, be so considered, as they discharged debts; but debts might also be discharged by barter, where no money was present. Heins explained that bills of exchange form an actual currency, temporary in its nature, like bank paper, but possessing all the requisites of a medium of exchange.

"I have been using one as money this very day," he continued. "You must know—(I do not hesitate to speak openly before friends) —I have been trying my fortune, while others did, in a venture to England. I am not in the habit of exporting, as you know; but I shipped a snug package of velvets, which certain great folks are at this moment wearing, perhaps in the king of England's own presence. I was paid in a bill drawn on a timber merchant here, payable at usance—you know what that means?"

Familiar as the term was, the young lady did not know what it meant. Heins explained that bills are paid either at sight, or at a certain specified time after date, or at the period which is pointed out by the custom or law of the place on which the bill is drawn; which period is called the usance of the place. At Amsterdam this was one month after date. Heins went on,

"I was, at the same time, desirous of purchasing some powder and ball, which I had a fine opportunity of disposing of. I therefore offered this bill—not to the owner of the powder, (who would leave Amsterdam before the bill became due, and would have charged me whatever it might cost him to have it changed for a different kind of money,)—but to my friend Visscher, the bill-broker, who sold me a bill on Copenhagen, which suited my powder-merchant's convenience, and put a profit into Visscher's pocket, and saved me the necessity of calling any money out of the Bank. So you see this bill was real money in my hands, is so now in Visscher's, and may be again in a hundred other hands before the month is up."

Slyk thought commerce would slacken grievously if bills did not serve as a circulating medium, as well as being the means of liquidating debts. If people were obliged to depend on their individual stock of money for the prosecution of all their undertakings, they would be stopped short at the outset of many a fine speculation: whereas by having access to the credit-bank (viz., the exchange market), and thus being able to exchange their credit for cash, at a small sacrifice, facilities were afforded, and an equalization of demand was established which was highly favourable to an extensive and beneficial employment of capital. This was the advantage of bills bearing date, instead of being, in all instances, payable at sight. When payable at sight, they were not of course money; and every protraction of date was equivalent to an increase in the quantity of money; as the bill passed through more hands, the longer it had a separate existence from the cash it represented.

"I suppose, then," said Francesca, "that your new undertaking is to be carried on by the help of this kind of money. But perhaps bills of exchange do not circulate so far inland."

"I have nothing to do but to exchange them for inland bills, or for cash," observed her father. "Snoek, you say that foreign bills superabound on 'Change. What say you to some of the spare capital which is afloat being lent to me for a grand and beneficial design which I have in hand some way up the country?"

"I have little or no money to spare just at this time," replied Heins: "for the present state of the exchange, you see, is just that which makes it desirable for us to import to the utmost. I must invest in British produce as much as I can gather together while bills on Britain are cheap. But there must be many exporters who are slackening their business till the exchange turns. They will be ready enough to let you have money at little or nothing above the common rate of interest. What is your object?"

James Mill

1773–1836

*It is history's judgment on the masterful James Mill that he is mainly
remembered as the father of John Stuart Mill. The judgment is unfair to a very considerable figure. James Mill was the author of a
standard history of British India, a journalist of parts, a founder of the
organ of the Benthamites, the* Westminster Review, *and the leading
organizational spirit among Bentham's followers. How that group impressed John Stuart Mill appears in his comment on the ". . . air of
strong conviction with which they wrote, when scarcely any one else
seemed to have an equally strong faith in as definite a creed; the
boldness with which they tilted against the very front of both existing
political parties; their uncompromising profession of opposition to
many of the generally received opinions and the suspicion they lay
under of holding others still more heterodox than they professed."*

*One of this group was David Ricardo, the great English economist
of the first quarter of the nineteenth century. In economics James Mill
considered that his task was that of popularizing the abstruse doctrines that Ricardo had advanced in his* Principles of Political Economy and Taxation *(1817). Mill had provided the subheadings and
index to that work. Now, in 1821, his* Elements of Political Economy
*offered earnest readers a popularization of Ricardo. The following
selection from this work deals entirely with a central doctrine of
Ricardo and a principal prop of classical economics in general, the
theory of differential rent. In combination with the Malthusian principle of population, the doctrine tended to produce some decidedly
gloomy conclusions. If, as Ricardo and Mill argued, worse and worse
land tended to be brought into cultivation as the demand for food
caused by a rising population increased, then the price of grain would
rise, to the height of the cost of production on the worst land put into*

235

use. Landlords on the better land would collect higher and higher rents. Wages would fall to subsistence. Since they could fall no lower without actually reducing the population, the burden of additional increases in rent had to fall upon profits. Hence, the prospect favored the inactive class, the landlords, and penalized the active classes, workers and capitalists.

In the long run the only remedy possible was education of the population to an appreciation of the necessity of late marriages and small families. In the short run, repeal of the Corn Laws, lower food prices, and a rising standard of living might give workers something to preserve and induce them to limit population. The slender prospect that Ricardo offered was a generation of economic advance which might result from such adventitious circumstances and then a population sufficiently prudent to learn the lesson of permanent prosperity.

The selection is from Elements of Political Economy (*London, 1821*), *pp. 29-39.*

Rent

Land is of different degrees of fertility. There is a species of land, the elevated or stony parts, for example, of high mountains, loose sand, and certain marshes, which may be said to produce nothing. Between this and the most productive sort, there are lands of all the intermediate degrees of fertility.

Again; lands, of the highest fertility, do not yield the whole of what they are capable of yielding, with the same facility. A piece of land, for example, may be capable of yielding annually ten quarters of corn, or twice ten, or three times ten. It yields, however, the first ten, with a certain quantity of labour, the second ten, not without a greater, the third ten, not without a greater still, and so on; every additional ten requiring to its production a greater cost than the ten which preceded it. This is well known to be the law, according to which, by a greater expenditure of capital, a greater produce is obtained, from the same portion of land.

Till the whole of the best land is brought under cultivation, and till it has received the application of a certain quantity of capital, all the capital employed upon the land is employed with an equal return. At a certain point, however, no additional capital can be employed upon the same land, without a diminution of return. In any country, therefore, after a certain quantity of corn has been raised, no greater quantity can be raised, but at a greater cost. If such additional quantity is raised, the capital, employed upon the land, may be distinguished into two portions; one, producing a higher; another, a lower return.

When capital producing a lower return is applied to the land, it is applied in one of two ways. It is either applied to new land of the second degree of fertility, then for the first time brought under cultivation; or it is applied to land of the first degree of fertility, which has already received all the capital which can be applied without a diminution of return.

Whether capital shall be applied to land of the second degree of fertility, or in a second dose to the land of the first degree of fertility, will depend, in each instance, upon the nature and qualities of the two soils. If the same capital which will produce only eight quarters, when applied in a second dose to the best land, will produce nine quarters, when applied to land of the second degree of fertility, it will be applied to that land, and *vice versâ*.

The land of the different degrees of fertility; first, or highest sort; second, or next highest, and so on, may, for facility of reference, be denominated, No. 1, No. 2, No. 3, &c. In like manner, the different doses of capital, which may be applied to the same land, one after another, with less and less effect, may be denominated 1st dose, 2d dose, 3d dose, and so on.

So long as land produces nothing, it is not worth appropriating. So long as a part only of the best land is required for cultivation, all that is uncultivated yields nothing; that is, nothing which has any value. It naturally, therefore, remains unappropriated; and any man may have it, who undertakes to render it productive.

During this time, land, speaking correctly, yields no rent. There is a difference, no doubt, between the land which has been cultivated, and the land which is yet uncleared for cultivation. Rather than clear the fresh land, a man will pay an equivalent, annual, or otherwise, for the cost of clearing: and it is evident that he will pay no more. This, therefore, is not a payment for the power of the soil, but simply for the capital bestowed upon the soil. It is not rent; it is interest.

The time, however, arrives, as population, and the demand for food increase, when it is necessary either to have recourse to land of the second quality, or to apply a second dose of capital, less productively, upon land of the first quality.

If a man cultivates land of the second quality, upon which a certain quantity of capital will produce only eight quarters of corn, while the same quantity of capital upon land of the first quality will produce ten quarters; it will make no difference to him, whether he pay two quarters for leave to cultivate the first sort, or cultivate the second without any payment. He will therefore be content to pay two quarters for leave to cultivate the first sort; and that payment constitutes rent.

Let us suppose, again, that instead of cultivating land of the second quality, it is more advisable to apply a second dose of capital to land of the first quality; and that, while the first dose produces ten quarters, the second, of equal amount, will produce only eight quarters; it is equally implied in this, as in the former case, that it is impossible to employ any more capital with so great an effect as the ten supposed quarters, and that there are persons who are willing to apply it with so little a return as eight. But if there are persons who are willing to apply their capital on the land with so little a return as eight quarters, the owners of the land may make a bargain, by which they will obtain all that is produced above eight. The effect upon rent is thus the same in both cases.

It follows that rent increases in proportion as the productive power of the capital, successively bestowed upon the land, decreases. If population has arrived at another stage, when, all the land of second quality being cultivated, it is necessary to have recourse to land of third quality, yielding, instead of eight quarters, only six, it is evident, from the same process of reasoning, that the land of second quality will now yield rent, namely, two quarters; and that land of first quality will yield an augmented rent, namely, two quarters more. The case will be exactly the same, if, instead of having recourse to land of less fertility, a second and a third dose of capital, with the same diminution of produce, are bestowed upon land of the first quality.

We may thus obtain a general expression for rent. In applying capital, either to lands of various degrees of fertility, or, in successive doses, to the same land, some portions of the capital so employed are attended with a greater produce, some with a less. That which yields the least, yields all that is necessary for re-imbursing and rewarding the capitalist. The capitalist will receive no more than this remuneration for any portion of the capital which he employs, because the competition of others will prevent him. All that is yielded above this remuneration, the landlord will be able to appropriate. Rent, therefore, is the difference between the return made to the more productive portions, and that which is made to the least productive portion, of capital, employed upon the land.

Taking, for illustration, the three cases, of ten quarters, eight quarters, and six quarters, we perceive, that rent is the difference between six quarters and eight quarters for the portion of capital which yields only eight quarters; the difference between six quarters and ten quarters for the portion of capital which yields ten quarters; and if three doses of capital, one yielding ten, another eight, and another six quarters, are applied to the same portion of land, its rent will be four quarters for dose No. 2, and two quarters for dose No. 2, making together six quarters for the whole.

If these conclusions are well supported, the doctrine of rent is simple, and the consequences, as we shall see hereafter, are exceedingly important. There is but one objection, which it seems possible to make to them. It may be said, that, after land is appropriated, there is no portion of it which does not pay rent, no owner being disposed to give the use of it for nothing. This objection has, indeed, been raised; and it has been urged, that some rent is paid even for the most barren of the Scottish mountains.

If an objection is taken, it affects the conclusion, either to a material, or to an immaterial extent. Where the matter alleged in objection, even if admitted, would still leave the conclusion substantially, and to all practical purposes, true, the objection must be owing to one or two defects in the mind of the objector; either a confusion of ideas, which prevents him from seeing to how small a degree the matter which he alleges affects the doctrine which he denies; or a disposition to evade the admission of the doctrine, even though nothing solid can be found with which to oppose it.

That the matter alleged in this objection, even if allowed, would leave the conclusion, to all practical purposes, just where it was, can hardly fail to be acknowledged, as soon as the circumstances are disclosed. It cannot be so much as pretended that the rent paid for the barren mountains of Scotland is any thing but a trifle; an evanescent quantity, when we speak of any moderate extent. If it were 5l. for a thousand acres, that is, about one penny per acre, it would bear so small a proportion to the cost of cultivation, which could not be less than several pounds per acre, that it would little affect the truth of the conclusion we have endeavoured to establish.

Let us suppose, for the sake of the argument, that the worst species of land under cultivation pays one penny per acre: rent, in that case, would be the difference between the produce resulting from different portions of capital, as explained above, with the correction required on account of the penny per acre paid as rent for the worst species of land under cultivation. Assuredly, if right in every other respect, we shall not be far wrong in our conclusions, by leaving this penny out of the question. A very slight advantage, in simplifying our language on the subject, would justify this omission.

But it is not true, that our conclusions stand in need of any such correction, even for metaphysical exactness. There is land, such as the sands of Arabia, which yields nothing. Land is found at all the intermediate stages from this to the highest fertility. Some land, though not absolutely incapable of yielding any thing for the accommodation of man, could not be made to yield what would maintain the labourers required for its cultivation. This land can never be cultivated. There is land, the annual produce of which would just maintain the labour necessary for its cultivation, and no more. This land is just capable of being cultivated, but obviously incapable of paying rent. The objection, therefore, is not only practically immaterial, it is metaphysically unsound.

It may be safely affirmed, that there is no country, of any considerable extent, in which there is not land incapable of yielding rent: that is, incapable of yielding to human labour more than would be necessary for the maintenance of that labour. That such, at least, is the case in this country, seems very unlikely to be disputed. There are parts of its mountains where nothing less hardy than heath, others where nothing but moss, can vegetate. When it is asserted that every part of the mountains of Scotland pays rent, the state of the facts is misunderstood. It is only true that there is no tenant of any portion of any man's estate in the highlands of Scotland, who does not pay rent. The reason is, because even in the mountains of Scotland there are spots in the valleys, the produce of which is considerable. It does not follow, though hundreds of acres of mountain are added to these valleys, that therefore every part of the mountain yields rent; it is certain that many parts neither do nor can.

Even where the land is not absolutely barren, and where there is still something for the more hardy of the useful animals to pick up, it is not to be allowed that rent is the necessary consequence. It ought to be remembered, that these cattle are capital, and that the land must afford enough not only to make the return for that capital, but to pay for the tendance of the cattle, of which, in such situations, especially in winter, not a little is required. Unless the land yields all this, and something more, it cannot yield any rent.

In the greater part of this island, there is hardly a farm, of any considerable extent, which does not contain land, some of more, some of less fertility, varying from a high or moderate degree of fertility, down to land which yields not enough to afford any rent. Of course I do not request admission to this affirmation upon my authority; I rest it upon an appeal to the experience of those men who are best acquainted with the circumstances. If the state of the facts corresponds with the affirmation, it follows demonstratively, that the last portion of the land which is placed under cultivation yields no rent. In such farms as those we have now described, the tenant has bargained for a certain sum to the landlord. That, of course, was calculated upon the produce of the land which yielded not only the proper return for the capital with which it was cultivated, but something more. As the motive of the tenant to cultivate is wholly constituted by the proper return to his capital, if there is any portion of the barren land, included in his farm, which will just yield the profit of stock, and no more; though it will not afford any thing for rent, it affords to him the adequate motive for cultivation. It can hardly be denied that, in the insensible degrees by which land declines from greater to less fertility, there will, in all considerable farms, be generally found a portion with this particular degree and no more.

The conclusion, however, may be established, by the clearest evidence, without regard to the question, whether all land pays or does not pay rent. On land which pays the highest rent, we have seen that capital, applied in successive doses, is not attended with equal results. The first dose yields more, possibly much more, than the return for the capital. The second also may yield more, and so on. The rent, if accurately calculated, will be equal to all that is rendered by those several doses, over and above the profits of stock. The cultivator, of course, applies all those several doses of capital on which he has agreed to pay rent. But immediately after them comes another dose, which though it yields nothing for rent, may fully yield the ordinary profits of stock. It is for the profits of stock, and them alone, that the farmer cultivates. As long, therefore, as capital applied to his farm will yield the ordinary profits of stock, he will apply capital, if he has it. I therefore conclude, with assurance, that in the natural state of things, in every agricultural country, one portion of the capital employed upon the land pays no rent; that rent, therefore, consists wholly, of that produce which is yielded by the more productive portions of capital, over and above a quantity equal to that which constitutes the return to the least productive portion, and which must be received, to afford his requisite profits, by the farmer.

David Ricardo

1772–1823

The Wealth of Nations *appeared in that miraculous year 1776. Smith attracted a host of admirers and commentators, Bentham provided a psychology for the economic man, and Malthus erected that very pillar of the classical system, the doctrine of population. Nevertheless, it was not until 1817 and the publication of David Ricardo's* Principles of Political Economy and Taxation *that a new treatise captured the minds of all who loved political economy. It exaggerates little to say that Ricardo's system was dominant in England until the 1870's. The major elements of the system included an attachment to freely competitive markets which echoed Smith's in intensity and surpassed it in precision, an unqualified acceptance of the Malthusian population doctrine, an original theory of rent which identified the tendency of rent to increase as a share of the national income, the theory of comparative advantage in international trade which demonstrated that even efficient nations would benefit from trade with inefficient nations, and a closely reasoned theory of value.*

The selection that follows contains Ricardo's exposition of the sources and meaning of value. A fair sample of the abstract method that Ricardo favored, this passage tends to demonstrate that, qualifications and exceptions apart, commodities in actual markets tend to exchange for each other at prices that reflect the relative quantities of labor needed to produce them. Although George Stigler has in recent years argued that the qualifications to Ricardo's theory of value should deny its title as a labor theory, Ricardo in much of the chapter appears to validate the claims of labor in psychological terms. Since labor is painful and since men strongly resemble each other, the true cost of production is a pain cost which can be approximated by measuring the number of hours of labor embodied in a commodity. Marx was later to infer what Ricardo did not from the labor theory, that since the source of value was labor the whole product of labor appropriately belonged to the worker. Rent, interest, and profit accordingly could only be the consequence of exploitation.

It may be of interest to say something about Ricardo himself. Ricardo's formal education ended when he was fourteen. After making a considerable fortune on the stock exchange, he retired from business and occupied himself with the study of political economy and, later, with membership in the House of Commons. He apparently came to political economy by accident. Happening upon The Wealth of Nations *while vacationing at Bath, he read it with fascination. In form, his own* Principles *are a commentary upon Smith. Ricardo was deeply diffident about his own literary powers, a diffidence that many readers have had occasion to endorse. What drove him to the writing of a book was James Mill. The quality of that worthy's urging is suggested in this excerpt from a letter of James Mill's to Ricardo:*

> *Why do you cry, "Oh that I were able to write a book!" when there is no obstacle to your writing, but this want of confidence in your powers. You want some practice in the art of laying down your thoughts in the way most easy of comprehension to those who have little knowledge, and little attention; and this is to be got infallibly by a little practice. As I am accustomed to wield the authority of a schoolmaster, I, therefore, in the genuine exercise of this honourable capacity, lay upon you my commands, to begin to the first of the three heads of your proposed work, rent, profits, wages—viz. rent without an hour's delay. If you entrust the inspection of it to me, depend upon it I shall compell you to make it all right, before you have done with it.*

Few escaped James Mill without gratifying his wishes. Ricardo was no exception.

The selection comes from The Works and Correspondence of David Ricardo, *edited by Piero Sraffa, Vol. I, Ch. I., pp. 11-19 and 133-6. Reprinted by permission of Cambridge University Press.*

CHAPTER I   On Value

SECTION I. THE VALUE OF A COMMODITY, OR THE
QUANTITY OF ANY OTHER COMMODITY FOR WHICH IT
WILL EXCHANGE, DEPENDS ON THE RELATIVE QUANTITY
OF LABOUR WHICH IS NECESSARY FOR ITS PRODUCTION,
AND NOT ON THE GREATER OR LESS COMPENSATION
WHICH IS PAID FOR THAT LABOUR*

It has been observed by Adam Smith, that "the word Value has two different meanings, and sometimes expresses the utility of some particular object, and sometimes the power of purchasing other goods which the possession of that object conveys. The one may be called *value in use;* the other *value in exchange.* The things," he continues, "which have the greatest value in use, have frequently little or no value in exchange; and, on the contrary, those which have the greatest value in exchange, have little or no value in use." † Water and air are abundantly useful; they are indeed indispensable to existence, yet, under ordinary circumstances, nothing can be obtained in exchange for them. Gold, on the contrary, though of little use compared with air or water, will exchange for a great quantity of other goods.

Utility then is not the measure of exchangeable value, although it is absolutely essential to it. If a commodity were in no way useful—in other words, if it could in no way contribute to our gratification—it would be destitute of exchangeable value, however scarce it might be, or whatever quantity of labour might be necessary to procure it.

Possessing utility, commodities derive their exchangeable value from two sources: from their scarcity, and from the quantity of labour required to obtain them.

There are some commodities, the value of which is determined by their scarcity alone. No labour can increase the quantity of such goods, and therefore their value cannot be lowered by an increased supply. Some rare statues and pictures, scarce books and coins, wines of a peculiar quality, which can be made only from grapes grown on a particular soil, of which there is a very limited quantity, are all of this description. Their value is wholly independent of the quantity of

---

* Ed. 1 does not divide this chapter into sections; ed. 2 divides it into five sections and ed. 3 into seven. Section 1 bears the same heading in ed. 2 and in ed. 3.

† *Wealth of Nations,* Bk. 1, ch. iv; Cannan's ed., vol. 1, p. 30. The passage continues by contrasting water with diamonds.

labour originally necessary to produce them, and varies with the vary-ing wealth and inclinations of those who are desirous to possess them.

These commodities, however, form a very small part of the mass of commodities daily exchanged in the market. By far the greatest part of those goods which are the objects of desire, are procured by labour; and they may be multiplied, not in one country alone, but in many, almost without any assignable limit, if we are disposed to be-stow the labour necessary to obtain them.

In speaking then of commodities, of their exchangeable value, and of the laws which regulate their relative prices, we mean always such commodities only as can be increased in quantity by the exertion of human industry, and on the production of which competition op-erates without restraint.

In the early stages of society, the exchangeable value of these com-modities, or the rule which determines how much of one shall be given in exchange for another, depends almost exclusively* on the comparative quantity of labour expended on each.

"The real price of every thing," says Adam Smith, "what every thing really costs to the man who wants to acquire it, is the toil and trouble of acquiring it. What every thing is really worth to the man who has acquired it, and who wants to dispose of it, or exchange it for something else, is the toil and trouble which it can save to himself, and which it can impose upon other people." "Labour was the first price—the original purchase—money that was paid for all things." Again, "in that early and rude state of society, which precedes both the accumulation of stock and the appropriation of land, the propor-tion between the quantities of labour necessary for acquiring differ-ent objects seems to be the only circumstance which can afford any rule for exchanging them for one another. If among a nation of hunt-ers, for example, it usually cost twice the labour to kill a beaver which it does to kill a deer, one beaver should naturally exchange for, or be worth two deer. It is natural that what is usually the produce of two days', or two hours' labour, should be worth double of what is usu-ally the produce of one day's, or one hour's labour."

That this is really the foundation of the exchangeable value of all things, excepting those which cannot be increased by human industry, is a doctrine of the utmost importance in political economy; for from no source do so many errors, and so much difference of opinion in that science proceed, as from the vague ideas which are attached to the word value.

If the quantity of labour realized in commodities, regulate their

* Eds. 1-2 read 'depends solely.'

exchangeable value, every increase of the quantity of labour must augment the value of that commodity on which it is exercised, as every diminution must lower it.

Adam Smith, who so accurately defined the original source of exchangeable value, and who was bound in consistency to maintain, that all things became more or less valuable in proportion as more or less labour was bestowed on their production, has himself erected another standard measure of value, and speaks of things being more or less valuable, in proportion as they will exchange for more or less of this standard measure. Sometimes he speaks of corn, at other times of labour, as a standard measure; not the quantity of labour bestowed on the production of any object, but the quantity which it can command in the market: as if these were two equivalent expressions, and as if because a man's labour had become doubly efficient, and he could therefore produce twice the quantity of a commodity, he would necessarily receive twice the former quantity in exchange for it.

If this indeed were true, if the reward of the labourer were always in proportion to what he produced, the quantity of labour bestowed on a commodity, and the quantity of labour which that commodity would purchase, would be equal, and either might accurately measure the variations of other things: but they are not equal; the first is under many circumstances an invariable standard, indicating correctly the variations of other things; the latter is subject to as many fluctuations as the commodities compared with it. Adam Smith, after most ably showing the insufficiency of a variable medium, such as gold and silver, for the purpose of determining the varying value of other things, has himself, by fixing on corn or labour, chosen a medium no less variable.

Gold and silver are no doubt subject to fluctuations, from the discovery of new and more abundant mines; but such discoveries are rare, and their effects, though powerful, are limited to periods of comparatively short duration. They are subject also to fluctuation, from improvements in the skill and machinery with which the mines may be worked; as in consequence of such improvements, a greater quantity may be obtained with the same labour. They are further subject to fluctuation from the decreasing produce of the mines, after they have yielded a supply to the world, for a succession of ages. But from which of these sources of fluctuation is corn exempted? Does not that also vary, on one hand, from improvements in agriculture, from improved machinery and implements used in husbandry, as well as from the discovery of new tracts of fertile land, which in other countries may be taken into cultivation, and which will affect the value of corn in every market where importation is free? Is it not on the other hand subject to be enhanced in value from prohibitions of importation, from increasing population and wealth, and the greater difficulty of obtaining the increased supplies, on account of the additional quantity of labour which the cultivation of inferior lands requires? Is not the value of labour equally variable; being not only affected, as all other things are, by the proportion between the supply and demand, which uniformly varies with every change in the condition of the community, but also by the varying price of food and other necessaries, on which the wages of labour are expended?

In the same country double the quantity of labour may be required to produce a given quantity of food and necessaries at one time, that may be necessary at another, and a distant time; yet the labourer's reward may possibly be very little diminished. If the labourer's wages at the former period, were a certain quantity of food and necessaries, he probably could not have subsisted if that quantity had been reduced. Food and necessaries in this case will have risen 100 per cent. if estimated by the *quantity* of labour necessary to their production, while they will scarcely have increased in value, if measured by the quantity of labour for which they will *exchange*.

The same remark may be made respecting two or more countries. In America and Poland, on the land last taken into cultivation, a year's labour of any given number of men, will produce much more corn than on land similarly circumstanced in England.* Now, supposing all other necessaries to be equally cheap in those three countries, would it not be a great mistake to conclude, that the quantity of corn awarded to the labourer, would in each country be in proportion to the facility of production?

If the shoes and clothing of the labourer, could, by improvements in machinery, be produced by one fourth of the labour now necessary to their production, they would probably fall 75 per cent.; but so far is it from being true, that the labourer would thereby be enabled permanently to consume four coats, or four pair of shoes, instead of one, that it is probable† his wages would in no long time be adjusted by the effects of competition, and the stimulus to population, to the new value of the necessaries on which they were expended. If these improvements extended to all the objects of the labourer's consumption, we should find him probably at the end of a very few years, in possession of only a small, if any, addition to his enjoyments, although

---

* In ed. 1 this sentence reads 'In America and Poland, a year's labour will produce much more corn than in England.'

† Eds. 1-2 do not contain 'it is probable.'

the exchangeable value of those commodities, compared with any other commodity, in the manufacture of which no such improvement were made, had sustained a very considerable reduction; and though they were the produce of a very considerably diminished quantity of labour.

It cannot then be correct, to say with Adam Smith, "that as labour may sometimes *purchase* a greater, and sometimes a smaller quantity of goods, it is their value which varies, not that of the labour which purchases them;" and therefore, "that labour *alone never varying in its own value,* is alone the ultimate and real standard by which the value of all commodities can at all times and places be estimated and compared;" *—but it is correct to say, as Adam Smith had previously said, "that the proportion between the quantities of labour necessary for acquiring different objects seems to be the only circumstance which can afford any rule for exchanging them for one another;" or in other words, that it is the comparative quantity of commodities which labour will produce, that determines their present or past relative value, and not the comparative quantities of commodities, which are given to the labourer in exchange for his labour.†

Two commodities vary in relative value, and we wish to know in which the variation has really taken place. If we compare the present value of one, with shoes, stockings, hats, iron, sugar, and all other commodities, we find that it will exchange for precisely the same quantity of all these things as before. If we compare the other with the same commodities, we find it has varied with respect to them all: we may then with great probability infer that the variation has been

* Bk. 1, ch. v; vol. 1, p. 35. The quotations contain some minor inaccuracies and the italics, as in most other cases, are Ricardo's.

† In place of the four paragraphs that follow in the text, and which conclude the section, eds. 1-2 read: 'If any one commodity could be found, which now and at all times required precisely the same quantity of labour to produce it, that commodity would be of an unvarying value, and would be eminently useful as a standard by which the variations of other things might be measured. Of such a commodity we have no knowledge, and consequently are unable to fix on any standard of value. It is, however, of considerable use towards attaining a correct theory, to ascertain what the essential qualities of a standard are, that we may know the causes of the variation in the relative value of commodities, and that we may be enabled to calculate the degree in which they are likely to operate.' See however a similar passage retained in ed. 3, below, p. 275; and cp. Section VI, p. 43 ff., which is inserted in ed. 3.

In eds. 1-2 the paragraph given in this footnote is followed directly by the paragraph which in ed. 3 opens Section II (p. 20); in ed. 1 the two paragraphs are separated by a printer's rule (the only trace of subdivision of this chapter in ed. 1); in ed. 2 the rule is dropped.

in this commodity, and not in the commodities with which we have compared it. If on examining still more particularly into all the circumstances connected with the production of these various commodities, we find that precisely the same quantity of labour and capital are necessary to the production of the shoes, stockings, hats, iron, sugar, &c.; but that the same quantity as before is not necessary to produce the single commodity whose relative value is altered, probability is changed into certainty, and we are sure that the variation is in the single commodity: we then discover also the cause of its variation.

If I found that an ounce of gold would exchange for a less quantity of all the commodities above enumerated, and many others; and if, moreover, I found that by the discovery of a new and more fertile mine, or by the employment of machinery to great advantage, a given quantity of gold could be obtained with a less quantity of labour, I should be justified in saying that the cause of the alteration in the value of gold relatively to other commodities, was the greater facility of its production, or the smaller quantity of labour necessary to obtain it. In like manner, if labour fell very considerably in value, relatively to all other things, and if I found that its fall was in consequence of an abundant supply, encouraged by the great facility with which corn, and the other necessaries of the labourer, were produced, it would, I apprehend, be correct for me to say that corn and necessaries had fallen in value in consequence of less quantity of labour being necessary to produce them, and that this facility of providing for the support of the labourer had been followed by a fall in the value of labour. No, say Adam Smith and Mr. Malthus, in the case of the gold you were correct in calling its variation a fall of its value, because corn and labour had not then varied; and as gold would command a less quantity of them, as well as of all other things, than before, it was correct to say that all things had remained stationary, and that gold only had varied; but when corn and labour fall, things which we have selected to be our standard measure of value, notwithstanding all the variations to which we acknowledge they are subject, it would be highly improper to say so; the correct language will be to say, that corn and labour have remained stationary, and all other things have risen in value.

Comparative Advantage

Under a system of perfectly free commerce, each country naturally devotes its capital and labour to such employments as are most beneficial to each. This pursuit of individual advantage is admirably connected with the universal good of the whole. By stimulating industry, by rewarding ingenuity, and by using most efficaciously the peculiar powers bestowed by nature, it distributes labour most effectively and most economically: while, by increasing the general mass of productions, it diffuses general benefit, and binds together by one common tie of interest and intercourse, the universal society of nations throughout the civilized world. It is this principle which determines that wine shall be made in France and Portugal, that corn shall be grown in America and Poland, and that hardware and other goods shall be manufactured in England.

In one and the same country, profits are, generally speaking, always on the same level; or differ only as the employment of capital may be more or less secure and agreeable. It is not so between different countries. If the profits of capital employed in Yorkshire, should exceed those of capital employed in London, capital would speedily move from London to Yorkshire, and an equality of profits would be effected; but if in consequence of the diminished rate of production in the lands of England, from the increase of capital and population, wages should rise, and profits fall, it would not follow that capital and population would necessarily move from England to Holland, or Spain, or Russia, where profits might be higher.

If Portugal had no commercial connexion with other countries, instead of employing a great part of her capital and industry in the production of wines, with which she purchases for her own use the cloth and hardware of other countries, she would be obliged to devote a part of that capital to the manufacture of those commodities, which she would thus obtain probably inferior in quality as well as quantity.

The quantity of wine which she shall give in exchange for the cloth of England, is not determined by the respective quantities of labour devoted to the production of each, as it would be, if both commodities were manufactured in England, or both in Portugal.

England may be so circumstanced, that to produce the cloth may require the labour of 100 men for one year; and if she attempted to make the wine, it might require the labour of 120 men for the same time. England would therefore find it her interest to import wine, and to purchase it by the exportation of cloth.

To produce the wine in Portugal, might require only the labour of 80 men for one year, and to produce the cloth in the same country, might require the labour of 90 men for the same time. It would therefore be advantageous for her to export wine in exchange for cloth. This exchange might even take place, notwithstanding that the commodity imported by Portugal could be produced there with less labour than in England. Though she could make the cloth with the labour of 90 men, she would import it from a country where it required the labour of 100 men to produce it, because it would be advantageous to her rather to employ her capital in the production of wine, for which she would obtain more cloth from England, than she could produce by diverting a portion of her capital from the cultivation of vines to the manufacture of cloth.

Thus England would give the produce of the labour of 100 men, for the produce of the labour of 80. Such an exchange could not take place between the individuals of the same country. The labour of 100 Englishmen cannot be given for that of 80 Englishmen, but the produce of the labour of 100 Englishmen may be given for the produce of the labour of 80 Portuguese, 60 Russians, or 120 East Indians. The difference in this respect, between a single country and many, is easily accounted for, by considering the difficulty with which capital moves from one country to another, to seek a more profitable employment, and the activity with which it invariably passes from one province to another in the same country.*

* It will appear then, that a country possessing very considerable advantages in machinery and skill, and which may therefore be enabled to manufacture commodities with much less labour than her neighbours, may, in return for such commodities, import a portion of the corn required for its consumption, even if its land were more fertile, and corn could be grown with less labour than in the country from which it was imported. Two men can both make shoes and hats, and one is superior to the other in both employments; but in making hats, he can only exceed his competitor by one-fifth or 20 per cent., and in making shoes he can excel him by one-third or 33 per cent.; will it not be for the interest of both, that the superior man should employ himself exclusively in making shoes, and the inferior man in making hats?

John Stuart Mill

1806–1873

John Stuart Mill was the heir of his father, James Mill, and the elder
Mill was keeper of the pure Benthamite doctrine, the very essence of
Philosophic Radicalism. What effect a Benthamite education had on
John Stuart Mill appears in Mill's comment on his reaction to
Bentham's three-volume Treatise on Legislation, which he read when
he was sixteen:

> When I laid down the last volume of the Traité, I had become a
> different being. The "principle of utility" understood as Bentham
> understood it, and applied in the manner in which he applied it
> through these three volumes, fell exactly into its place as the key-
> stone which held together the detached and fragmentary component
> parts of my knowledge and beliefs. It gave unity to my conceptions
> of things. I now had opinions; a creed, a doctrine, a religion; the
> inculcation and diffusion of which could be made the principal out-
> ward purpose of a life. And I had a grand conception laid before me
> of changes to be effected in the condition of mankind through that
> doctrine.

Although Mill in later life modified his devout belief in Bentham and
even ranked Coleridge as an equally strong influence, he never surrendered the bulk of the Benthamite doctrine. Prominent in that doctrine was a confidence in the efficacy of laissez-faire as the guiding
principle of government and the major stimulus to individual self-
development. His major criticism of the utopian socialists of his day
was of their wish to eliminate competition and substitute state action.
In Mill's opinion government was inefficient, tyrannical, and ineffective in realizing the wishes of the governed. Hence, ". . . laisser-
faire . . . should be the general practice; every departure from it,
unless required by some great good, is a certain evil."

A good case, but it left Mill uncomfortable. There were so many
objectives of value that seemed so unlikely of achievement without

*state intervention. The passage that follows suggests the manner in
which Mill sought the rationale for state action. Since children were
too young to judge for themselves, the state might compel their education. Where the community required government action to give
effect to the wishes of most of its members, as in the case of the Factory Act to which only a few employers objected, another exception
was appropriate. The state had to intervene to supervise individuals
who acted for others, such as the trustees of charities and foundations.
Again, there was warrant for state action when the effects of an action
extended over several generations, as in the case of colonization.*

*Mill's dilemma was the dilemma of a man with a good heart
burdened with a restrictive economic theory. It testifies both to his
goodness of heart and his sharpness of intellect that he was able simultaneously to give effect to the impulses of his heart and retain his
theory.*

This selection comes from Principles of Political Economy, *edited
by W. J. Ashley (London: Longmans, Green, 1909), pp. 953-4,
959-65, and 966-70.*

Exceptions to Laissez-Faire

§8. Now, the proposition that the consumer is a competent judge
of the commodity, can be admitted only with numerous abatements
and exceptions. He is generally the best judge (though even this is
not true universally) of the material objects produced for his use.
These are destined to supply some physical want, or gratify some
taste or inclination, respecting which wants or inclinations there is
no appeal from the person who feels them; or they are the means
and appliances of some occupation, for the use of the persons engaged in it, who may be presumed to be judges of the things required
in their own habitual employment. But there are other things, of
the worth of which the demand of the market is by no means a test;
things of which the utility does not consist in ministering to inclinations, nor in serving the daily uses of life, and the want of which is
least felt where the need is greatest. This is peculiarly true of those
things which are chiefly useful as tending to raise the character of
human beings. The uncultivated cannot be competent judges of cultivation. Those who most need to be made wiser and better, usually
desire it least, and, if they desired it, would be incapable of finding
the way to it by their own lights. It will continually happen, on the
voluntary system, that, the end not being desired, the means will
not be provided at all, or that, the persons requiring improvement

having an imperfect or altogether erroneous conception of what they want, the supply called forth by the demand of the market will be anything but what is really required. Now any well-intentioned and tolerably civilized government may think, without presumption, that it does or ought to possess a degree of cultivation above the average of the community which it rules, and that it should therefore be capable of offering better education and better instruction to the people, than the greater number of them would spontaneously demand. Education, therefore, is one of those things which it is admissible in principle that a government should provide for the people. The case is one to which the reasons of the non-interference principle do not necessarily or universally extend.*

§10. A second exception to the doctrine that individuals are the best judges of their own interest, is when an individual attempts to decide irrevocably now what will be best for his interest at some future and distant time. The presumption in favour of individual judg-

---

* In opposition to these opinions, a writer, with whom on many points I agree, but whose hostility to government intervention seems to me too indiscriminate and unqualified, M. Dunoyer, observes, that instruction, however good in itself, can only be useful to the public in so far as they are willing to receive it, and that the best proof that the instruction is suitable to their wants is its success as a pecuniary enterprise. This argument seems no more conclusive respecting instruction for the mind, than it would be respecting medicine for the body. No medicine will do the patient any good if he cannot be induced to take it; but we are not bound to admit as a corollary from this, that the patient will select the right medicine without assistance. Is it not probable that a recommendation, from any quarter which he respects, may induce him to accept a better medicine than he would spontaneously have chosen? This is, in respect to education, the very point in debate. Without doubt, instruction which is so far in advance of the people that they cannot be induced to avail themselves of it, is to them of no more worth than if it did not exist. But between what they spontaneously choose, and what they will refuse to accept when offered, there is a breadth of interval proportioned to their deference for the recommender. Besides, a thing of which the public are bad judges may require to be shown to them and pressed on their attention for a long time, and to prove its advantages by long experience, before they learn to appreciate it, yet they may learn at last; which they might never have done, if the thing had not been thus obtruded upon them in act, but only recommended in theory. Now, a pecuniary speculation cannot wait years, or perhaps generations for success; it must succeed rapidly, or not at all. Another consideration which M. Dunoyer seems to have overlooked, is, that institutions and modes of tuition which never could be made sufficiently popular to repay, with a profit, the expenses incurred on them, may be invaluable to the many by giving the highest quality of education to the few, and keeping up the perpetual succession of superior minds, by whom knowledge is advanced, and the community urged forward in civilization.

ment is only legitimate, where the judgment is grounded on actual, and especially on present, personal experience; not where it is formed antecedently to experience, and not suffered to be reversed even after experience has condemned it. When persons have bound themselves by a contract, not simply to do some one thing, but to continue doing something for ever or for a prolonged period, without any power of revoking the engagement, the presumption which their perseverance in that course of conduct would otherwise raise in favour of its being advantageous to them, does not exist; and any such presumption which can be grounded on their having voluntarily entered into the contract, perhaps at an early age, and without any real knowledge of what they undertook, is commonly next to null. The practical maxim of leaving contracts free is not applicable without great limitations in case of engagements in perpetuity; and the law should be extremely jealous of such engagements; should refuse its sanction to them, when the obligations they impose are such as the contracting party cannot be a competent judge of; if it ever does sanction them, it should take every possible security for their being contracted with foresight and deliberation; and in compensation for not permitting the parties themselves to revoke their engagement, should grant them a release from it, on a sufficient case being made out before an impartial authority. These considerations are eminently applicable to marriage, the most important of all cases of engagement for life.*

§11. The third exception which I shall notice, to the doctrine that government cannot manage the affairs of individuals as well as the individuals themselves, has reference to the great class of cases in which the individuals can only manage the concern by delegated agency, and in which the so-called private management is, in point of fact, hardly better entitled to be called management by the persons interested than administration by a public officer. Whatever, if left to spontaneous agency, can only be done by joint-stock associations, will often be as well, and sometimes better done, as far as the actual work is concerned, by the state. Government management is, indeed, proverbially jobbing, careless, and ineffective, but so likewise has generally been joint-stock management. The directors of a joint-stock company, it is true, are always shareholders; but also the members of a government are invariably taxpayers; and in the case of directors, no more than in that of governments, is their proportional share of the benefits of good management equal to the interest they may possibly have in mis-management, even without reckoning the

* This last sentence added in 3rd ed. (1852).

interest of their ease. It may be objected, that the shareholders, in their collective character, exercise a certain control over the directors, and have almost always full power to remove them from office. Practically, however, the difficulty of exercising this power is found to be so great, that it is hardly ever exercised except in cases of such flagrantly unskilful, or, at least, unsuccessful management, as would generally produce the ejection from office of managers appointed by the government. Against the very ineffectual security afforded by meetings of shareholders, and by their individual inspection and inquiries, may be placed the greater publicity and more active discussion and comment, to be expected in free countries with regard to affairs in which the general government takes part. The defects, therefore, of government management do not seem to be necessarily much greater, if necessarily greater at all, than those of management by joint-stock.

The true reasons in favour of leaving to voluntary associations all such things as they are competent to perform would exist in equal strength if it were certain that the work itself would be as well or better done by public officers. These reasons have been already pointed out: the mischief of overloading the chief functionaries of government with demands on their attention, and diverting them from duties which they alone can discharge, to objects which can be sufficiently well attained without them; the danger of unnecessarily swelling the direct power and indirect influence of government, and multiplying occasions of collision between its agents and private citizens; and the inexpediency of concentrating in a dominant bureaucracy all the skill and experience in the management of large interests, and all the power of organized action, existing in the community; a practice which keeps the citizens in a relation to the government like that of children to their guardians, and is a main cause of the inferior capacity for political life which has hitherto characterized the over-governed countries of the Continent, whether with or without the forms of representative government.*

* A parallel case may be found in the distaste for politics, and absence of public spirit, by which women, as a class, are characterized in the present state of society, and which is often felt and complained of by political reformers, without, in general, making them willing to recognise, or desirous to remove, its cause. It obviously arises from their being taught, both by institutions and by the whole of their education, to regard themselves as entirely apart from politics. Wherever they have been politicians, they have shown as great interest in the subject, and as great aptitude for it, according to the spirit of their time, as the men with whom they were cotemporaries: in that period of history (for example) in which Isabella of Castile and Elizabeth of England were, not rare exceptions, but merely brilliant

But although, for these reasons, most things which are likely to be even tolerably done by voluntary associations should, generally speaking, be left to them; it does not follow that the manner in which those associations perform their work should be entirely uncontrolled by the government. There are many cases in which the agency, of whatever nature, by which a service is performed, is certain, from the nature of the case, to be virtually single; in which a practical monopoly, with all the power it confers of taxing the community, cannot be prevented from existing. I have already more than once adverted to the case of the gas and water companies, among which, though perfect freedom is allowed to competition, none really takes place, and practically they are found to be even more irresponsible, and unapproachable by individual complaints, than the government. There are the expenses without the advantages of plurality of agency; and the charge made for services which cannot be dispensed with, is, in substance, quite as much compulsory taxation as if imposed by law; there are few householders who make any distinction between their "water-rate" and their other local taxes. In the case of these particular services, the reasons preponderate in favour of their being performed, like the paving and cleansing of the streets, not certainly by the general government of the state, but by the municipal authorities of the town, and the expense defrayed, as even now it in fact is, by a local rate. But in the many analogous cases which it is best to resign to voluntary agency, the community needs some other security for the fit performance of the service than the interest of the managers; and it is the part of government, either to subject the business to reasonable conditions for the general advantage, or to retain such power over it that the profits of the monopoly may at least be obtained for the public. This applies to the case of a road, a canal, or a railway. These are always, in a great degree, practical monopolies; and a government which concedes such monopoly unreservedly to a private company does much the same thing as if it allowed an individual or an association to levy any tax they chose, for their own benefit, on all the malt produced in the country, or on all the cotton imported into it. To make the concession for a limited time is generally justifiable, on the principle which justifies patents for inventions: but the state should either reserve to itself a reversionary property in such public works, or should retain, and freely exercise, the right of fixing a maximum of fares and charges, and, from time to time, varying that maximum. It is perhaps necessary to remark, that the state may be the proprietor

examples of a spirit and capacity very largely diffused among women of high station and cultivation in Europe.

of canals or railways without itself working them; and that they will almost always be better worked by means of a company renting the railway or canal for a limited period from the state.

§12. To a fourth case of exception I must request particular attention, it being one to which, as it appears to me, the attention of political economists has not yet been sufficiently drawn. There are matters in which the interference of law is required, not to overrule the judgment of individuals respecting their own interest, but to give effect to that judgment: they being unable to give effect to it except by concert, which concert again cannot be effectual unless it receives validity and sanction from the law. For illustration, and without prejudging the particular point, I may advert to the question of diminishing the hours of labour. Let us suppose, what is at least supposable, whether it be the fact or not—that a general reduction of the hours of factory labour, say from ten to nine,* would be for the advantage of the workpeople: that they would receive as high wages, or nearly as high, for nine hours' labour as they receive for ten. If this would be the result, and if the operatives generally are convinced that it would, the limitation, some may say, will be adopted spontaneously. I answer, that it will not be adopted unless the body of operatives bind themselves to one another to abide by it. A workman who refused to work more than nine hours while there were others who worked ten, would either not be employed at all, or if employed, must submit to lose one-tenth of his wages. However convinced, therefore, he may be that it is the interest of the class to work short time, it is contrary to his own interest to set the example, unless he is well assured that all or most others will follow it. But suppose a general agreement of the whole class: might not this be effectual without the sanction of law? Not unless enforced by opinion with a rigour practically equal to that of law. For however beneficial the observance of the regulation might be to the class collectively, the immediate interest of every individual would lie in violating it: and the more numerous those who adhered to the rule, the more would individuals gain by departing from it. If nearly all restricted themselves to nine hours, those who chose to work for ten would gain all the advantages of the restriction, together with the profit of infringing it; they would get ten hours' wages for nine hours' work, and an hour's wages besides. I grant that if a large majority adhered to the nine hours, there would

* The original "twelve to ten" (1848) was changed to the present text, and the consequent alterations made in the rest of the paragraph, in the 5th ed. (1862).

be no harm done: the benefit would be, in the main, secured to the class, while those individuals who preferred to work harder and earn more, would have an opportunity of doing so. This certainly would be the state of things to be wished for; and assuming that a reduction of hours without any diminution of wages could take place without expelling the commodity from some of its markets—which is in every particular instance a question of fact, not of principle—the manner in which it would be most desirable that this effect should be brought about, would be by a quiet change in the general custom of the trade; short hours becoming, by spontaneous choice, the general practice, but those who chose to deviate from it having the fullest liberty to do so. Probably, however, so many would prefer the ten hours' work on the improved terms, that the limitation could not be maintained as a general practice: what some did from choice, others would soon be obliged to do from necessity, and those who had chosen long hours for the sake of increased wages, would be forced in the end to work long hours for no greater wages than before. Assuming then that it really would be the interest of each to work only nine hours if he could be assured that all others would do the same, there might be no means of their attaining this object but by converting their supposed mutual agreement into an engagement under penalty, by consenting to have it enforced by law. I am not expressing any opinion in favour of such an enactment, which has never in this country been demanded, and which I certainly should not, in present circumstances, recommend:* but it serves to exemplify the manner in which classes of persons may need the assistance of law, to give effect to their deliberate collective opinion of their own interest, by affording to every individual a guarantee that his competitors will pursue the same course, without which he cannot safely adopt it himself.

§13. Fifthly; the argument against the government interference, grounded on the maxim that individuals are the best judges of their own interest, cannot apply to the very large class of cases, in which those acts of individuals with which the government claims to interfere, are not done by those individuals for their own interest, but for the interest of other people. This includes, among other things, the

---

* "Which has never . . . recommend" was added in the 5th ed. (1862). A Nine Hours Movement made its appearance in the 70's. The hours of labour for women, young persons and children in textile factories were reduced to 56½ per week by the Act of 1874, and to 55½ by the Act of 1901. A Miners' Eight Hours Act was passed in 1908.

important and much agitated subject of public charity. Though individuals should, in general, be left to do for themselves whatever it can reasonably be expected that they should be capable of doing, yet when they are at any rate not to be left to themselves, but to be helped by other people, the question arises whether it is better that they should receive this help exclusively from individuals, and therefore uncertainly and casually, or by systematic arrangements, in which society acts through its organ, the state.

This brings us to the subject of Poor Laws; a subject which would be of very minor importance if the habits of all classes of the people were temperate and prudent, and the diffusion of property satisfactory; but of the greatest moment in a state of things so much the reverse of this, in both points, as that which the British Islands present.

Apart from any metaphysical considerations respecting the foundation of morals or of the social union, it will be admitted to be right that human beings should help one another; and the more so, in proportion to the urgency of the need: and none needs help so urgently as one who is starving. The claim to help, therefore, created by destitution, is one of the strongest which can exist; and there is *primâ facie* the amplest reason for making the relief of so extreme an exigency as certain to those who require it as by any arrangements of society it can be made.

On the other hand, in all cases of helping, there are two sets of consequences to be considered; the consequences of the assistance itself, and the consequences of relying on the assistance. The former are generally beneficial, but the latter, for the most part, injurious; so much so, in many cases, as greatly to outweigh the value of the benefit. And this is never more likely to happen than in the very cases where the need of help is the most intense. There are few things for which it is more mischievous that people should rely on the habitual aid of others, than for the means of subsistence, and unhappily there is no lesson which they more easily learn. The problem to be solved is therefore one of peculiar nicety as well as importance; how to give the greatest amount of needful help, with the smallest encouragement to undue reliance on it.

Energy and self-dependence are, however, liable to be impaired by the absence of help, as well as by its excess. It is even more fatal to exertion to have no hope of succeeding by it, than to be assured of succeeding without it. When the condition of any one is so disastrous that his energies are paralyzed by discouragement, assistance is a tonic, not a sedative: it braces instead of deadening the active faculties: always provided that the assistance is not such as to dispense with self-help, by substituting itself for the person's own labour, skill, and prudence, but is limited to affording him a better hope of attaining success by those legitimate means. This accordingly is a test to which all plans of philanthropy and benevolence should be brought, and whether conducted on the voluntary or on the government principle.

§14. Another class of cases which fall within the same general principle as the case of public charity, are those in which the acts done by individuals, though intended solely for their own benefit, involve consequences extending indefinitely beyond them, to interests of the nation or of posterity, for which society in its collective capacity is alone able, and alone bound, to provide. One of these cases is that of Colonization. If it is desirable, as no one will deny it to be, that the planting of colonies should be conducted, not with an exclusive view to the private interests of the first founders, but with a deliberate regard to the permanent welfare of the nations afterwards to arise from these small beginnings; such regard can only be secured by placing the enterprise, from its commencement, under regulations constructed with the foresight and enlarged views of philosophical legislators; and the government alone has power either to frame such regulations, or to enforce their observance.

The question of government intervention in the work of Colonization involves the future and permanent interests of civilization itself, and far outstretches the comparatively narrow limits of purely economical considerations. But even with a view to those considerations alone, the removal of population from the overcrowded to the unoccupied parts of the earth's surface is one of those works of eminent social usefulness, which most require, and which at the same time best repay, the intervention of government.

§15. The same principle which points out colonization, and the relief of the indigent, as cases to which the principal objection to government interference does not apply, extends also to a variety of cases, in which important public services are to be performed, while yet there is no individual specially interested in performing them, nor would any adequate remuneration naturally or spontaneously attend their performance. Take for instance a voyage of geographical or scientific exploration. The information sought may be of great public value, yet no individual would derive any benefit from it which would repay the expense of fitting out the expedition; and there is no mode of intercepting the benefit on its way to those who profit by it, in order to levy a toll for the remuneration of its authors. Such voyages are, or might be, undertaken by private subscription; but this is a rare and precarious resource. Instances are more frequent in which the expense has been borne by public companies or philanthropic associations; but in general such enterprises have been conducted at the expense of government, which is thus enabled to entrust them to the persons in its judgment best qualified for the task. Again, it is a proper office of government to build and maintain lighthouses, establish buoys, &c., for the security of navigation: for since it is impossible that the ships at sea which are benefited by a lighthouse should be made to pay a toll on the occasion of its use, no one would build lighthouses from motives of personal interest, unless indemnified and rewarded from a compulsory levy made by the state. There are many scientific researches, of great value to a nation and to mankind, requiring assiduous devotion of time and labour, and not unfrequently great expense, by persons who can obtain a high price for their services in other ways. If the government had no power to grant indemnity for expense, and remuneration for time and labour thus employed, such researches could only be undertaken by the very few persons who, with an independent fortune, unite technical knowledge, laborious habits, and either great public spirit, or an ardent desire of scientific celebrity.

Connected with this subject is the question of providing by means of endowments or salaries, for the maintenance of what has been called a learned class. The cultivation of speculative knowledge, though one of the most useful of all employments, is a service rendered to a community collectively, not individually, and one consequently for which it, *primâ facie*, reasonable that the community collectively should pay; since it gives no claim on any individual for a pecuniary remuneration; and unless a provision is made for such services from some public fund, there is not only no encouragement to them, but there is as much discouragement as is implied in the impossibility of gaining a living by such pursuits, and the necessity consequently imposed on most of those who would be capable of them to employ the greatest part of their time in gaining a subsistence. The evil, however, is greater in appearance than in reality. The greatest things, it has been said, have generally been done by those who had the least time at their disposal; and the occupation of some hours every day in a routine employment, has often been found compatible with the most brilliant achievements in literature and philosophy. Yet there are investigations and experiments which require not only a long but a continuous devotion of time and attention: there are also occupations which so engross and fatigue the mental faculties, as to be inconsistent with any vigorous employment of them upon other subjects, even in intervals of leisure. It is highly desirable, therefore, that there should be a mode of insuring to the public the services of scientific discoverers, and perhaps of some other classes of savants, by affording them the means of support consistently with devoting a sufficient portion of time to their peculiar pursuits. The fellowships of the Universities are an institution excellently adapted for such a purpose; but are hardly ever applied to it, being bestowed, at the best, as a reward for past proficiency, in committing to memory what has been done by others, and not as the salary of future labours in the advancement of knowledge. In some countries, Academies of science, antiquities, history, &c., have been formed with emoluments annexed. The most effectual plan, and at the same time least liable to abuse, seems to be that of conferring Professorships, with duties of instruction attached to them. The occupation of teaching a branch of knowledge, at least in its higher departments, is a help rather than an impediment to the systematic cultivation of the subject itself. The duties of a professorship almost always leave much time for original researches; and the greatest advances which have been made in the various sciences, both moral and physical, have originated with those who were public teachers of them; from Plato and Aristotle to the great names of the Scotch, French, and German Universities. I do not mention the English, because until very lately their professorships have been, as is well known, little more than nominal. In the case, too, of a lecturer in a great institution of education, the public at large has the means of judging, if not the quality of the teaching, at least the talents and industry of the teacher; and it is more difficult to misemploy the power of appointment to such an office, than to job in pensions and salaries to persons not so directly before the public eye.

It may be said generally, that anything which it is desirable should be done for the general interests of mankind or of future generations, or for the present interests of those members of the community who require external aid, but which is not of a nature to remunerate individuals or associations for undertaking it, is in itself a suitable thing to be undertaken by government: though, before making the work their own, governments ought always to consider if there be any rational probability of its being done on what is called the voluntary principle, and if so, whether it is likely to be done in a better or more effectual manner by government agency, than by the zeal and liberality of individuals.

Friedrich A. Hayek

1899–

Professor Hayek is a distinguished neoclassical economist whose theoretical work, after the Austrian tradition, has won wide respect in
such diverse fields as economic analysis, money and banking, and
business cycles. He is also a noted historian of economic thought
whose illuminating edition of Thornton's Enquiry into the Nature and
Effects of the Paper Credit of Great Britain and whose collection of
the poignant letters that passed between Harriet Taylor and John
Stuart Mill have enriched the literature.

He is known to a wider public as a sturdy opponent of central
planning, socialism, and the welfare state. His The Road to Serfdom,
from which the following extract is taken, won him a very large audience and the ambiguous distinction of summarization in The Reader's
Digest. Written in 1944, this volume reflects its author's deep detes-
tation of totalitarianism and his fears that a careless democratic state
can move imperceptibly, restriction by restriction, control by control,
down the abyss whose bottom is totalitarianism. The quotation from
David Hume that is on Hayek's title page fairly represents his mood:
"It is seldom that liberty of any kind is lost all at once."

Hayek relies upon competition and the rule of law to preserve freedom. Competition is not only the most efficient of economic arrangements, it is also the only economic arrangement that is truly sympathetic to personal liberty. The proper concern of a democratic state,
therefore, is the creation of the proper legal framework within which
competition will work most effectively. Hayek takes pains to distinguish his position from that of sheer laissez-faire, and, indeed, a state
that acted on Hayek's advice would find itself breaking up large
corporations, curtailing the privileges of unions, and removing the
protections of farmers. It would be a highly active government in-

264

deed. Hayek does not oppose all welfare legislation, but only those measures which impair competition.

Probably John Stuart Mill is closest to the spirit in which Hayek writes. Many of Hayek's careful distinctions will remind readers of the earlier selection from Mill in which Mill examines the category of permissible exceptions to the general rule of state noninterference in economic life. In England, economists like Sir Dennis Robertson and Lord Robbins share to some extent Hayek's position. In this country, the distinguished group of economists at the University of Chicago—Frank Knight, George Stigler, and Milton Friedman—share major Hayekian attitudes.

The Road to Serfdom *evoked several sharp responses. Possibly the sharpest was Herman Finer's* Road to Reaction. *The most balanced criticism of Hayek's thesis is to be found in Barbara Wootton's* Freedom Under Planning, *which endeavors to demonstrate that democratic liberties and central economic planning are entirely compatible.*

The excerpt below is from The Road to Serfdom, *by Friedrich Hayek, pp. 34-42. Reprinted by permission of The University of Chicago Press. 1944.*

Planning

The difficulties caused by the ambiguities of the common political terms are not yet over if we agree to use the term "collectivism" so as to include all types of "planned economy," whatever the end of planning. The meaning of this term becomes somewhat more definite if we make it clear that we mean that sort of planning which is necessary to realize any given distributive ideals. But, as the idea of central economic planning owes its appeal largely to this very vagueness of its meaning, it is essential that we should agree on its precise sense before we discuss its consequences.

"Planning" owes its popularity largely to the fact that everybody desires, of course, that we should handle our common problems as rationally as possible and that, in so doing, we should use as much foresight as we can command. In this sense everybody who is not a complete fatalist is a planner, every political act is (or ought to be) an act of planning, and there can be differences only between good and bad, between wise and foresighted and foolish and shortsighted planning. An economist, whose whole task is the study of how men actually do and how they might plan their affairs, is the last person who could object to planning in this general sense. But it is not in this sense that our enthusiasts for a planned society now employ this term, nor merely in this sense that we must plan if we want the distribution of income or wealth to conform to some particular standard. According to the modern planners, and for their purposes, it is not sufficient to design the most rational permanent framework within which the various activities would be conducted by different persons according to their individual plans. This liberal plan, according to them, is no plan—and it is, indeed, not a plan designed to satisfy particular views about who should have what. What our planners demand is a central direction of all economic activity according to a single plan, laying down how the resources of society should be "consciously directed" to serve particular ends in a definite way.

The dispute between the modern planners and their opponents is, therefore, *not* a dispute on whether we ought to choose intelligently between the various possible organizations of society; it is not a dispute on whether we ought to employ foresight and systematic thinking in planning our common affairs. It is a dispute about what is the best way of so doing. The question is whether for this purpose it is better that the holder of coercive power should confine himself in general to creating conditions under which the knowledge and initiative of individuals are given the best scope so that *they* can plan most successfully; or whether a rational utilization of our resources requires *central* direction and organization of all our activities according to some consciously constructed "blueprint." The socialists of all parties have appropriated the term "planning" for planning of the latter type, and it is now generally accepted in this sense. But though this is meant to suggest that this is the only rational way of handling our affairs, it does not, of course, prove this. It remains the point on which the planners and the liberals disagree.

It is important not to confuse opposition against this kind of planning with a dogmatic laissez-faire attitude. The liberal argument is in favor of making the best possible use of the forces of competition as a means for co-ordinating human efforts, not an argument for leaving things just as they are. It is based on the conviction that, where effective competition can be created, it is a better way of guiding individual efforts than any other. It does not deny, but even emphasizes, that, in order that competition should work beneficially, a carefully thought-out legal framework is required and that neither the existing nor the past legal rules are free from grave defects. Nor does it deny that, where it is impossible to create the conditions necessary to make competition effective, we must resort to other methods of guiding economic activity. Economic liberalism is opposed, however, to competition's being supplanted by inferior methods of coordinating individual efforts. And it regards competition as superior not only because it is in most circumstances the most efficient method known but even more because it is the only method by which our activities can be adjusted to each other without coercive or arbitrary intervention of authority. Indeed, one of the main arguments in favor of competition is that it dispenses with the need for "conscious social control" and that it gives the individuals a chance to decide whether the prospects of a particular occupation are sufficient to compensate for the disadvantages and risks connected with it.

The successful use of competition as the principle of social organization precludes certain types of coercive interference with economic life, but it admits of others which sometimes may very considerably assist its work and even requires certain kinds of government action. But there is good reason why the negative requirements, the points where coercion must not be used, have been particularly stressed. It is necessary in the first instance that the parties in the market should be free to sell and buy at any price at which they can find a partner to the transaction and that anybody should be free to produce, sell, and buy anything that may be produced or sold at all. And it is essential that the entry into the different trades should be open to all on equal terms and that the law should not tolerate any attempts by individuals or groups to restrict this entry by open or concealed force. Any attempt to control prices or quantities of particular commodities deprives competition of its power of bringing about an effective co-ordination of individual efforts, because price changes then cease to register all the relevant changes in circumstances and no longer provide a reliable guide for the individual's actions.

This is not necessarily true, however, of measures merely restricting the allowed methods of production, so long as these restrictions affect all potential producers equally and are not used as an indirect way of controlling prices and quantities. Though all such controls of the methods of production impose extra costs (i.e., make it necessary to use more resources to produce a given output), they may be well worth while. To prohibit the use of certain poisonous substances or to require special precautions in their use, to limit working hours or to require certain sanitary arrangements, is fully compatible with the preservation of competition. The only question here is whether in the particular instance the advantages gained are greater than the social costs which they impose. Nor is the preservation of competition incompatible with an extensive system of social services—so long as the organization of these services is not designed in such a way as to make competition ineffective over wide fields.

It is regrettable, though not difficult to explain, that in the past much less attention has been given to the positive requirements of a successful working of the competitive system than to these negative points. The functioning of a competition not only requires adequate organization of certain institutions like money, markets, and channels of information—some of which can never be adequately provided by private enterprise—but it depends, above all, on the existence of an appropriate legal system, a legal system designed both to preserve competition and to make it operate as beneficially as possible. It is by no means sufficient that the law should recognize the principle of private property and freedom of contract; much depends on the precise definition of the right of property as applied to different things. The systematic study of the forms of legal institutions which will make the competitive system work efficiently has been sadly neglected; and strong arguments can be advanced that serious shortcomings here, particularly with regard to the law of corporations and of patents, not only have made competition work much less effectively than it might have done but have even led to the destruction of competition in many spheres.

There are, finally, undoubted fields where no legal arrangements can create the main conditions on which the usefulness of the system of competition and private property depends: namely, that the owner benefits from all the useful services rendered by his property and suffers for all the damages caused to others by its use. Where, for example, it is impracticable to make the enjoyment of certain services dependent on the payment of a price, competition will not produce the services; and the price system becomes similarly ineffective when the damage caused to others by certain uses of property cannot be effectively charged to the owner of that property. In all these instances there is a divergence between the items which enter into private calculation and those which affect social welfare; and, whenever this divergence becomes important, some method other than competition may have to be found to supply the services in question. Thus neither the provision of signposts on the roads nor, in most circumstances, that of the roads themselves can be paid for by every individual user. Nor can certain harmful effects of deforestation, of some methods of farming, or of the smoke and noise of factories be confined to the owner of the property in question or to those who are willing to submit to the damage for an agreed compensation. In such instances we must find some substitute for the regulation by the price mechanism. But the fact that we have to resort to the substitution of direct regulation by authority where the conditions for the proper working of competition cannot be created does not prove that we should suppress competition where it can be made to function.

To create conditions in which competition will be as effective as possible, to supplement it where it cannot be made effective, to provide the services which, in the words of Adam Smith, "though they may be in the highest degree advantageous to a great society, are, however, of such a nature, that the profit could never repay the expense to any individual or small number of individuals"—these tasks provide, indeed, a wide and unquestioned field for state activity. In no system that could be rationally defended would the state just do nothing. An effective competitive system needs an intelligently designed and continuously adjusted legal framework as much as any other. Even the most essential prerequisite of its proper functioning, the prevention of fraud and deception (including exploitation of ignorance), provides a great and by no means yet fully accomplished object of legislative activity.

The task of creating a suitable framework for the beneficial working of competition had, however, not yet been carried very far when states everywhere turned from it to that of supplanting competition by a different and irreconcilable principle. The question was no longer one of making competition work and of supplementing it but of displacing it altogether. It is important to be quite clear about this: the modern movement for planning is a movement against competition as such, a new flag under which all the old enemies of competition have rallied. And although all sorts of interests are now trying to re-establish under this flag privileges which the liberal era swept away, it is socialist propaganda for planning which has restored to respectability among liberal-minded people opposition to competition and which has effectively lulled the healthy suspicion which any attempt to smother competition used to arouse.* What in effect unites

* Of late, it is true, some academic socialists, under the spur of criticism and animated by the same fear of the extinction of freedom in a centrally planned society, have devised a new kind of "competitive socialism" which they hope will avoid the difficulties and dangers of central planning and combine the abolition of private property with the full retention of individual freedom. Although some discussion of this new kind of socialism has taken place in learned journals, it is hardly likely to recommend itself to practical politicians. If it ever did, it would not be difficult to show (as the author has attempted elsewhere—see *Economica*, 1940) that these plans

the socialists of the Left and the Right is this common hostility to competition and their common desire to replace it by a directed economy. Though the terms "capitalism" and "socialism" are still generally used to describe the past and the future forms of society, they conceal rather than elucidate the nature of the transition through which we are passing.

Yet, though all the changes we are observing tend in the direction of a comprehensive central direction of economic activity, the universal struggle against competition promises to produce in the first instance something in many respects even worse, a state of affairs which can satisfy neither planners nor liberals: a sort of syndicalist or "corporative" organization of industry, in which competition is more or less suppressed but planning is left in the hands of the independent monopolies of the separate industries. This is the inevitable first result of a situation in which the people are united in their hostility to competition but agree on little else. By destroying competition in industry after industry, this policy puts the consumer at the mercy of the joint monopolist action of capitalists and workers in the best organized industries. Yet, although this is a state of affairs which in wide fields has already existed for some time, and although much of the muddled (and most of the interested) agitation for planning aims at it, it is not a state which is likely to persist or can be rationally justified. Such independent planning by industrial monopolies would, in fact, produce effects opposite to those at which the argument for planning aims. Once this stage is reached, the only alternative to a return to competition is the control of the monopolies by the state—a control which, if it is to be made effective, must become progressively more complete and more detailed. It is this stage we are rapidly approaching. When, shortly before the war, a weekly magazine pointed out that there were many signs that British leaders, at least, were growing accustomed to thinking in terms of national development by controlled monopolies, this was probably a true estimate of the position as it then existed. Since then this process has been greatly accelerated by the war, and its grave defects and dangers will become increasingly obvious as time goes on.

The idea of complete centralization of the direction of economic

---

rest on a delusion and suffer from an inherent contradiction. It is impossible to assume control over all the productive resources without also deciding for whom and by whom they are to be used. Although under this so-called "competitive socialism" the planning by the central authority would take somewhat more roundabout forms, its effects would not be fundamentally different, and the element of competition would be little more than a sham.

activity still appalls most people, not only because of the stupendous difficulty of the task, but even more because of the horror inspired by the idea of everything being directed from a single center. If we are, nevertheless, rapidly moving toward such a state, this is largely because most people still believe that it must be possible to find some middle way between "atomistic" competition and central direction. Nothing, indeed, seems at first more plausible, or is more likely to appeal to reasonable people, than the idea that our goal must be neither the extreme decentralization of free competition nor the complete centralization of a single plan but some judicious mixture of the two methods. Yet mere common sense proves a treacherous guide in this field. Although competition can bear some admixture of regulation, it cannot be combined with planning to any extent we like without ceasing to operate as an effective guide to production. Nor is "planning" a medicine which, taken in small doses, can produce the effects for which one might hope from its thoroughgoing application. Both competition and central direction become poor and inefficient tools if they are incomplete; they are alternative principles used to solve the same problem, and a mixture of the two means that neither will really work and that the result will be worse than if either system had been consistently relied upon. Or, to express it differently, planning and competition can be combined only by planning for competition but not by planning against competition.

B. APPLICATIONS

Richard Cobden

1804–1865

In the short space of eight years—1838 to 1846—the Anti-Corn
Law League organized by Richard Cobden and John Bright accomplished the object of their agitation, the repeal of the Corn
Laws. With whirlwind energy, Cobden and Bright spoke all over
England, stimulated the production of scores of pamphlets, and incessantly memorialized Parliament. The center of their support was
Manchester and the movement was essentially a middle-class, urban
phenomenon. The political economists, whose theories seemed certainly to imply repeal of tariff barriers, were by and large cool or indifferent to the agitation. Working-class leaders suspected that the
principal effect of repeal would be cheaper bread, quickly followed
by lower wages. In their view, the only gainers were likely to be
their employers whose profits would expand. Country gentlemen and
their representatives naturally fought to retain a protection which
they considered essential to the preservation of their own prosperity.

That Cobden and Bright won their point was partly a tribute to
their own organizational talents. But it was also an indication
of the greater power and influence of the manufacturing classes in a
reformed House of Commons which was more susceptible to pres-
sures from the new manufacturing centers. The repeal of the Corn
Laws was a nineteenth-century milestone in English history, for it
signalized the complete victory of free trade and the decision of English leaders to cast their destinies with industry and trade rather than
agriculture.

Cobden's own case against agricultural protection was partly moral
and partly economic. On the first ground, he saw no reason why the
nation should favor agriculture over industry. Why should ". . . the
rest of us have a superstitious reverence for the owners of those slug-

gish acres?" The mystique of the soil dies hard. To a degree it persists even in the United States where urban dwellers submit to taxation designed to finance preferential treatment of farmers, partly apparently because they suffer from an atavistic assumption of agricultural superiority. Economically, Cobden denied that wages would fall if the Corn Laws were eliminated. Rather the standard of life would rise for the working classes. There is little doubt that Cobden's argument was honestly intended. Nor is there much doubt that, on the whole, events bore him out. Wages did not fall when food costs dropped.

Cobden's attachment to free trade was part of an even nobler ideal. He was convinced that free trade promoted international amity, mutual economic benefit, and a peaceful world. Seldom has so much been made to rest upon a single economic change of national habit. Cobden's speech is included in The Liberal Tradition: From Fox to Keynes, *edited by Maurice Bullock and Alan Shock (New York: New York University Press, 1957), pp. 48-51.*

Richard Cobden: Speech in London, 8 February 1844

I am a manufacturer of clothing, and I do not know why, in this climate, and in the artificial state of society in which we live, the making of clothes should not be as honourable—because it is pretty near as useful—a pursuit as the manufacture of food. Well, did you ever hear any debates in the House to fix the price of my commodities in the market? Suppose we had a majority of cotton-printers (which happens to be my manufacture) in the House. . . . Let us suppose that you were reading the newspaper some fine morning, and saw an account of a majority of the House having been engaged the night before in fixing the price at which yard-wide prints should be sold: 'Yard-wide prints, of such a quality, 10d. a yard; of such a quality, 9d.; of such a quality, 8d.; of such a quality, 7d.,' and so on. Why, you would rub your eyes with astonishment! . . . Now, did it ever occur to you that there is no earthly difference between a body of men, manufacturers of corn, sitting down in the House, and passing a law enacting that wheat shall be so much, barley so much, beans so much, and oats so much?

Why, then, do you look at this monopoly of corn with such complacency? Simply because you and I and the rest of us have a superstitious reverence for the owners of those sluggish acres, and have a very small respect for ourselves and our own vocation. I say the Corn-law monopolists, who arrogate to themselves power in the House of Commons, are practising an injustice on every other species of capitalists. Take the iron trade, for example—a prodigious interest in this country. Iron of certain qualities has gone down in price, during the last five of six years, from £15 10s. to £5 10s. per ton. Men have seen their fortunes—ay, I have known them—dwindle away from £300,-000 till now they could not sit down and write their wills for £100,-000. Well, did any man ever hear in the House of Commons an attempt made to raise a cry about these grievances there, or to lodge a complaint against the Government or the country because they could not keep up the price of iron? Has any man come forward there proposing that by some law pig-iron should be so much, and bar-iron of such a price, and other kinds of iron in proportion? No; neither has this been the case with any other interest in the country. But how is it with corn? The very first night I was present in the House this session, I saw the Prime Minister get up, having a paper before him, and he was careful to tell us what the price of corn had been for the last fifty years, and what it was now. He is employed for little else but as a kind of corn-steward, to see how the prices may be kept up for his masters. . . .

Our opponents tell us that our object in bringing about the repeal of the Corn-laws is, by reducing the price of corn, to lower the rate of their wages. I can only answer upon this point for the manufacturing districts; but, as far as they are concerned, I state it most emphatically as a truth, that, for the last twenty years, whenever corn has been cheap wages have been high in Lancashire; and, on the other hand, when bread has been dear wages have been greatly reduced. . . .

Now, let me be fully understood as to what Free Traders really do want. We do not want cheap corn merely in order that we may have low money prices. What we desire is plenty of corn, and we are utterly careless what its price is, provided we obtain it at the natural price. All we ask is this, that corn shall follow the same law which the monopolists in food admit that labour must follow; that 'it shall find its natural level in the markets of the world.' . . .

To pay for that corn, more manufactures would be required from this country; this would lead to an increased demand for labour in the manufacturing districts, which would necessarily be attended with a rise of wages, in order that the goods might be made for the purpose of exchanging for the corn brought from abroad. . . . I observe there are narrow-minded men in the agricultural districts, tell-ing us, 'Oh, if you allow Free Trade, and bring in a quarter of corn from abroad, it is quite clear that you will sell one quarter less in England.' . . . What! I would ask, if you set more people to work at better wages—if you can clear your streets of those spectres which are now haunting your thoroughfares begging their daily bread—if you can depopulate your workhouses and clear off the two millions of paupers which now exist in the land, and put them to work at productive industry—do you not think that they would consume some of the wheat as well as you; and may not they be, as we are now, consumers of wheaten bread by millions, instead of existing on their present miserable dietary? . . .

With free trade in corn, so far from throwing land out of use or injuring the cultivation of the poorer soils, free trade in corn is the very way to increase the production at home, and stimulate the cultivation of the poorer soils by compelling the application of more capital and labour to them. We do not contemplate deriving one quarter less corn from the soil of this country; we do not anticipate having one pound less of butter or cheese, or one head less of cattle or sheep: we expect to have a great increase in production and consumption at home; but all we contend for is this, that when we, the people here, have purchased all that can be raised at home, we shall be allowed to go 3,000 miles—to Poland, Russia or America—for more; and that there shall be no let or hindrance put in the way of our getting this additional quantity.

Nassau Senior

1790–1864

Even among economists, Senior is likely to be remembered for the least of his contributions. Marx's savage attack upon Senior's last-hour principle is recalled vaguely as pointing to Senior's reluctance to shorten the working day. Again, students of the theory of income distribution may think of Senior only as the inventor of the doctrine of abstinence. This principle completed the justification of wage income with a similar justification of interest. Ricardo had argued that labor was painful and wages were the means of overcoming the natural reluctance of the laborer to suffer the displeasure of work. Senior maintained that saving—the postponement of present consumption—implied similar pains and demanded a similar payment. Hence interest like wages was based upon a psychic cost—abstinence from present consumption.

Actually Senior performed a valuable role both as a systemizer of economic thought and as a close student of social legislation. In the first capacity, he made a valiant effort to reduce economics to a science. In his An Outline of the Science of Political Economy (1836), he identified four basic principles of his subject: the hedonistic principle, the Principle of Population, the Law of Increasing Returns in Industry, and the Law of Diminishing Returns in Agriculture. Schumpeter has even argued in his History of Economic Analysis that Senior created a complete alternative system to the Ricardian analysis.

Senior and McCulloch are frequently judged to be the most extreme members of the laissez-faire school. This judgment oversimplifies Senior's position. He could scarcely have devoted so much of his life to poor laws, factory acts, the condition of the hand-loom weavers, and the unhappy state of Ireland without feeling that the relation between government and private activity was more complex than a *simple adherence to the police-functions theory of state action would imply. In fact, what Senior was trying to do was very much like what Mill struggled with a bit later. He was eager to reconcile his suspicion of the state, his fear that an interfering government might diminish individual incentives and liberties, with a wish to promote human welfare. Naturally, his struggle to reconcile the two objectives led to differing compromises, according to the issue. In the case of Ireland, Senior advocated public works and public expenditures in aid of emigration. While he opposed restricting the working day to ten hours as injurious to the industrialist, he at the same time advocated housing improvement at the expense of the landlord. In the sad case of the hand-loom weavers, he considered that the competition of mechanical devices had doomed these handicraft workers and that the state would perform no kindness if it intervened to prolong their misery.*

The passage that is reprinted here is a characteristic effort to identify the areas in which state intervention into working conditions is justifiable and those where such intervention is not justifiable. It is interesting to compare Senior's treatment of women workers with Mill's handling of the same topic.

The passage is contained in Senior's Industrial Efficiency and Social Economy, *edited by S. Leon Levy (New York: Henry Holt, 1928), II, 301-3, 305-11.*

Government Regulation of Home and Factory Conditions

1. INTRODUCTION: LAISSEZ FAIRE AND GOVERNMENTAL INTERVENTION. 2. SANITATION AND HOUSING LEGISLATION. 3. LIMITATION OF HOURS OF LABOR FOR ADULTS AND CHILDREN. 4. MERITS AND DEFECTS OF RESTRICTIONS AGAINST FEMALE LABOR.

1. Introduction: Laissez Faire and Governmental Intervention. [In view of the outstanding results of misdirected government control, as indicated in the last chapter, the question is at once raised], what is the proper limit to the functions and to the agency of government? Is it true that governments ought to confine themselves to affording protection against force and fraud, and that, these two things apart, people should be free agents, left to take care of themselves, and while they practice no violence or deception to the injury of others,

entitled to do as they like, without being molested or restricted by judges and legislators?

The strong argument for restricting the functions of government to the mere duty of affording to its subjects protection against foreigners by war or by negotiation, and against one another by the administration of civil and criminal justice, is that this is the field in which the interference of government is not only obviously the most useful, but also obviously the least dangerous. A government may manage ill the foreign affairs of a nation; but we may be sure that it will manage them better than would be done by the people themselves. It may be partial in its administration of justice; but it will be more impartial than each man would be if he were to be judge in his own case. But as soon as it exceeds this narrow limit, as soon as it tries to make men not merely safe but happy, as soon as it tries to impose on them the belief and the conduct which it thinks most conducive to their welfare; when it endeavors to force them to get rich, and if it fail in that tries to protect them from the evils of poverty—these are attempts so liable to fail, indeed to do worse than merely to fail, so liable to produce results precisely the reverse of those intended by the legislator, so liable to aggravate the evils which he proposes to remedy, and to introduce others which could not have arisen without his rash intervention, that many political thinkers have affirmed that they ought never to be made. But this objection, in its largest and most peremptory sense, cannot be supported. I am even inclined to disapprove of [the] use of the word "optional" as applied to the functions of government. Like the words "boon" or "concession," it seems to imply that there may be useful measures which the government of a country may at its discretion adopt or reject.

The only rational foundation of government, the only foundation of a right to govern and of a correlative duty to obey, is expediency—the general benefit of the community. It is the duty of a government to do whatever is conducive to the welfare of the governed. The only limit to this duty is its power. And as the supreme government of an independent state is necessarily absolute, the only limit to its power is physical or moral inability. And whatever it is its duty to do it must necessarily have a right to do.

The opinion which I am controverting appears to have been produced by the fact that the expediency of the exercise of some of the powers of government is more obvious than that of the exercise of some others. It is obviously expedient that a government should protect the persons and the property of its subjects. But if it can also be shown to be expedient that a government should perform any other functions, it must also be its duty and its right to perform them. The expediency may be more difficult of proof, and until that proof has been given, the duty and the right do not arise. But as soon as the proof has been given they are perfect. It is true that in such matters a government may make mistakes. It may believe its interference to be useful when it is really mischievous. There is no government which does not make such mistakes; and the more it interferes the more liable it must be to them. On the other hand, its refusal or neglect to interfere may also be founded on error. It may be passively wrong as well as actively wrong. The advance of political knowledge* must diminish both these errors; but it appears to me that the most fatal of all errors would be the general admission of the proposition that a government has no right to interfere for any purpose except for that of affording protection, for such an admission would prevent our profiting by experience, and even from acquiring it.

[It must be observed, however, that] the greatest objection to the extension of government interference, [is] its tendency to keep the people in leading strings, and to deprive them of the power to manage their own common affairs, by depriving them of the practice without which the arts of administration cannot be acquired. When I have been examining the high organization of many parts of the Continent, where an enlightened central authority educates the people, provides their roads and public buildings, directs their industry, keeps them to their hereditary trades and to their hereditary abodes,

---

* It is often said against the extension of government control that public officials are apt to be less efficient and more corrupt than those employed by private concerns. With reference to this objection, Senior makes the following statement:

"In proportion as men owe to their merit their selection for public office and advancement, and in proportion as a higher standard of morality teaches them that to defraud the public of their time or of their attention, is as dishonest, and therefore as dishonorable, as to plunder it of mere money—will the zeal, activity, and intelligence with which men serve the state approach the intelligence, activity, and zeal with which they serve themselves. No one who compares the state of public service now, and at the beginning of the century, can doubt that we are making great advances in this direction. Where do we see men act in their own concerns with more zeal or more diligence, with more disregard of ease, or comfort, or health, than the officers employed by the government in the relief of Ireland in 1846 and 1847?"

Further, this objection is not applicable to industries where "the magnitude of the concern makes individual agency impracticable, as is the case of railways and gas-works. Here the management must necessarily be by delegates; and a government officer is likely to exhibit as much diligence and as much intelligence as a director, and perhaps greater purity."

and their hereditary sects—thinks for them, in short, in all public and in almost all private matters, I am sometimes disagreeably struck by the contrast of the rude local administration of England, with its narrow-minded prejudices, its jobbing and its negligence. But to this centralization is to be ascribed the childishness and sluggishness of most Continental populations in quiet times; and the madness which seems to seize them if the central power once drops the reins. From unreflecting obedience and torpor, they pass at once to equally unreflecting rebellion, civil war, and foreign war.

[In a former chapter I remarked that it is in the power of the government of a country materially to alter the degree in which wealth is desirable by diminishing either the positive advantages of wealth or the positive disadvantages of poverty. The first mode has already been duly considered. The remainder of this treatise will be devoted to a consideration of] some of the cases in which governments have interfered for the purpose of palliating some of the evils of poverty. They must not be confounded with those in which governments have interfered to prevent poverty, by imposing restrictions for instance on marriage, by the equal division of inheritances or by preventing artifices from quitting their trades; nor again with the measures which they have adopted for the purpose of producing wealth, such as sumptuary laws, laws enforcing apprenticeships or attempts to secure a favorable balance of trade. I confine myself to the cases in which governments, without attempting to prevent the existence of poverty have tried to diminish its evils.

3. Limitation of Hours of Labor for Adults and Children. Another means which governments have sometimes employed to diminish the evils of poverty has been to limit the days or the hours of labor. I do not reckon among these attempts what may at first sight appear to be the most important limitation, the institution of a seventh day of rest. It is true that almost all Christian governments give their aid to the ecclesiastical regulation which prohibits certain acts of work on Sundays;* but they do this on religious not on political grounds.

* One of the exceptions to the principle of noninterference, Senior observes, is that in which "the interference of the law is required, not to overrule the judgment of individuals respecting their own interest, but to give effect to that judgment; they being unable to give effect to it except by concert, which concert again cannot be effectual unless it receives validity and sanction from the law. The observance of Sunday as a day of rest is an instance. There is probably no institution so beneficial to the laboring classes; and they are aware of it. But without the assistance of law they would probably be unable to enforce it. In the few businesses in which

Without doubt it is a most useful institution—one of the institutions to which we owe the superiority of modern over ancient civilization, and it is an institution which though eminently beneficial to the rich is still more beneficial to the poor; but I do not believe that if the divine command to the Israelites had not set the example, a mere expectation of its utility* would ever have occasioned it to be adopted. I am not sure that our conviction of its utility would lead us to continue it, if we could abandon it without feeling that we committed a breach of religious duty. The French when they ceased to be Christian gave up Sunday, and even now observe it very imperfectly. The legislation to which I now allude is that which limits the periods of labor simply on the ground that such a limitation is beneficial to the laborer. The most remarkable instances of this legislation are the Factory Acts of which two have passed—one in 1833, [the 3 and 4 William IV, cap. 103], and another in 1844, [the 7 Victoria, cap. 13], and a third has gone through the House of Commons and is now in the Lords, [the 10 Victoria, cap. 29].

The first forbade the employment of children under thirteen years of age in mills and factories for more than eight hours a day, and the employment of persons between the ages of thirteen and eighteen—technically called young persons—at night, or for more than 69 hours a week, or 11-1/2 a day. The second act restricted the employment of children to six hours a day and put all women of whatever age on the footing of young persons—that is to say, forbade them to

---

Sunday trading is allowed, every shop is open. Though it would be beneficial to the whole body of druggists that every druggist's shop should be shut on Sunday, it is the immediate interest of every individual that his own shop should be open. And the result is that none are closed."

* This view concerning the origin and prospects of the Sabbath the modern reader cannot entirely accept. The institution of a seventh day of rest originated with the Israelites as a reaction to their bitter experience in Egypt where they were forced to undergo unremitting toil. Once freed from Egyptian bondage, these ancient pioneers instituted a number of important reforms—the Sabbath undoubtedly the greatest of all. Just as European bigotry and intolerance ultimately gave rise to the American conception of religious liberty, so the prevalence of slavery and the harshness of the taskmasters gradually taught mankind the value of conscientious rest.

It is, of course, very true that the mass of the people, who cannot easily extricate themselves from long-rooted habits, must usually be guided by the inexplicable, "Thou shalt" or "Thou shalt not!" Yet, in the long run, whatever is found to be conducive to the welfare of society is adopted, and whatever outgrows its original usefulness is discarded. More than two-thirds of the Biblical precepts—such as those relating to purity and impurity, sacrifices, tithes, usury (interest), Jubilee, Sabbatical year, slavery, and witchcraft—are now all obsolete. On the other hand, the modern movement for longer vacations and shorter periods of labor seems to be an extension of the institution that affords one day of rest in seven.

work at night, or for more than 11-1/2 hours a day. The third, which is still pending* proposes to enact that after the 1st of May 1848, no person under the age of eighteen and no female of any age, shall be employed in a factory† for more than ten hours in any one day or more than 58 hours in any one week.

Two objections have been made to the principle of this legislation. One is an objection to which I have already alluded, namely, the

* This section was written in 1847.
† The term "factory," under these Acts, applied only to buildings where cotton, wool, hair, silk, flax, hemp, jute, or tow were manufactured. Printworks, for instance, were excepted from these Acts, because the influential manufacturers strongly objected to such legislation.
"The factory system of education," Senior was informed in 1837 by Mr. Thompson, the owner of extensive printworks at Clitheroe, "is wholly inapplicable to calico printing. The child is actually a part of a machine, like a linchpin: just as when the pin is out, the wheel comes off, so a teer boy absent stops his master. The calico printers are, in fact, much more obnoxious to reproach than the spinners, for they now employ children at a much earlier age, work them harder, and work them longer. An ordinary day's work in a print ground is 10 hours of actual labor; but at the busy season, in spring and autumn, or during the shipping months, the hours of actual labor are extended to 12 or 14, and sometimes (with a relay) through the night. If the law interfered to prevent this, it would not be a question of profit to the manufacturer, but of employment for the people. Time is an element in the calculations of a manufacture, dependent on season, taste, and fashion. That which one month fetches a high profit, in the next is sold for none at all, and, in the following, at a heavy loss. The calico printer cannot work to a stock as a spinner or weaver, whose production being the same from year to year, is salable some time or other. The consequence is, that the printer is often idle for weeks, and often again has double the work he can perform in the ordinary hours of labor. It is the same in all countries—France, Switzerland, Germany, and the north of Europe. It is irremediable: and the law that imposed restrictions on the hours of labor in calico printing would destroy the trade, and involve masters and laborers in common ruin." (Senior's *Letters on the Factory Acts*, p. 43.)
Largely as a consequence of the Report of the Children's Employment Commission of 1843, there was enacted the 8 and 9 Victoria, cap. 28 (June, 1845), which prohibited the employment in printworks of children under the age of eight, and prevented children under thirteen and also females from working late at night, *i.e.*, after 10 in the evening. No other protection, however, was afforded against overwork.
It is with reference to this legislation that Senior remarked in 1860, as follows: "As represented by Mr. Thompson, one of the most intelligent and liberal of their body, [the printers] believed in 1837 that any interference whatever with the hours of labor would be fatal to a trade in which idleness for weeks is succeeded by a pressure of business twice as great as that which can be performed in the ordinary hours—long, almost beyond example, as those of printworks are. Yet since that time infants under eight years old have been excluded from printworks, and children under thirteen and women are excluded from night work—restrictions which, according

supposed principle that the right of a government to control the conduct of its subjects is limited to that portion of their conduct which directly affects third persons. So far as they do not directly injure others they ought, it is said, to be their own masters, masters of their time as well as of their strength, and no more liable to be called to account for working too long than for working too hard.

> The property (says Adam Smith) which every man has in his own labor as it is the original foundation of all other property, so it is the most sacred and inviolable. The patrimony of a poor man lies in the strength and dexterity of his hands; and to hinder him from employing this strength and dexterity in what manner he thinks proper without injury to his neighbor, is a plain violation of this most sacred property. It is a manifest encroachment upon the just liberty both of the workman and those who employ him. As it hinders him from working as he thinks proper, so it hinders the others from employing him as they think proper.

This objection I have already answered. I have already proved, I think satisfactorily, that it is the duty, and therefore the right, of a government to take any measures, however they may interfere with the will of individuals, which are conducive to the general welfare of the community.

The other objection concedes the right of a government to interfere to prevent conduct which may be only indirectly mischievous to third persons. It admits, for instance, that emigrants may be forbidden to embark without providing themselves with necessaries for the voyage. Since by doing so the improvident might exhaust the stores of the provident. It admits that persons may be forbidden to inhabit certain dwellings, their residence in which might occasion contagious disease. But it refuses to a government the power of judging whether it can beneficially interfere to protect the laborer against himself. It affirms that a government which thinks that it knows his interests better than he knows them himself will generally be mistaken; that the few cases in which it will judge correctly will be more than compensated by the many in which it will judge erroneously; and that it is better, therefore, to prescribe noninterference* as a universal rule than to allow exceptions, which in the majority of cases will be mischievous.

---

to Mr. Thompson, were to involve masters and laborers in common ruin. Yet calico printing is more prosperous than it ever was. Block printing, too, which is supposed to render necessary the oppression of the little teerers, is rapidly giving way to machine printing."

  * Writing in 1841 on "the tyranny of combinations," the author stated the

To children this reasoning is obviously inapplicable. They cannot judge for themselves; and if they could, they are not free agents. Nor can it be said that their interests may be safely trusted to their parents. When the child earns wages which the parent spends, the immediate interest of the parent and the permanent interest of the child are in many respects opposed. And whole folios of evidence show that in the uneducated classes indolence and intemperance will generally render the father, and sometimes even the mother, ready to sacrifice the education and the health of her child, if that sacrifice will give the parent some exemption from labor or some additional indulgence in stimulants. With exceptions so few as to be immaterial, all the ill-treatment and overworking of children discovered in the factory inquiries was ill-treatment and overworking by their own parents.

It is difficult perhaps to limit precisely the duration of childhood. It appears to me however that among the laboring classes, who must struggle early with the realities of life, it ends, so far at least as the absence of free agency is concerned, at 16. That is the age at which the parent ceases to be legally bound to maintain the child, and at which therefore it receives its own wages, and often manages its own expenditure. So far, therefore, as respects males between the ages of 16 and 18 the argument in question applies.

4. Merits and Defects of Restrictions against Female Labor. As

following principles of legislation, which may be of interest in this connection:

"I believe that the property of the working man in his strength and skill is as real, and ought to be as much respected by the law, as any other property which the law recognizes.

"I believe that the right of the working man to employ that property in the way which he considers most for his interest, so far as he does not interfere with the exercise of a like free will on the part of another, is a right as sacred as any right for the protection of which laws are maintained.

"I believe, therefore, that it is the duty of the state to protect that property and that right, and that it may be guilty of a breach of duty by acts of commission or of omission. By acts of omission, if it does not protect the laborer from injury on the part of those who assume to dictate to him what he shall do and what he shall not do; by acts of commission, if it assume itself to dictate to him, and to force him to pursue or to abandon a given proceeding, not on the ground that he is interfering with the free will of another, but because his conduct may be detrimental to himself, or to his master, or to the general wealth of society.

"I believe, in short, that in this, as in almost every other matter, the duty of the government is simply to keep the peace, to protect all its subjects from the violence and fraud and malice of one another, and, having done so, to leave them to pursue what they believe to be their interests in the way which they deem advisable."

respects females the legislature seems to deny that at any age whatever they are to be trusted with the management of themselves. It considers them, as some Asiatic legislators have considered them, as in a state of permanent blindness or permanent subservience: either as unable, whatever be their age, to know whether night work or long hours are good for them or not, or as unable to act on their knowledge. I believe this view of the female character to be a mistaken one, especially in the manufacturing population. I believe them to have as clear a perception of their own interest and as much determination and as much power to follow it, as belong to their brothers or to their fathers. I utterly disapprove, therefore, of the principle of the act of 1844 and of the present bill, so far as they place adult women on the footing of children. And I am inclined to agree in the doctrine that, so far as respects persons, whether male or female, above the age of 16 the interference of the legislator to force them to manage their own affairs in the way they do not think most conducive to their welfare, is an interference so likely to be mischievous that it is better to forbear it altogether. It must be recollected that as the supreme authority is necessarily unrestrained, as there is no arbiter between it and its subjects, there is no medium between its interference with their conduct as affecting themselves wherever it thinks fit, and its abstaining from such interference altogether. The government itself must be the judge as to the truth of the premises which it assumes, and as to the correctness of the conclusions which it draws from them. There is no authority to which they can appeal against its errors as to facts or as to inferences.

A third objection to the legislation which I have described is founded not on its general principles but on the facts of the particular case. The question logically stated stands thus. The supporters of the Factory bill now in the House of Lords rest on the following syllogism:

The legislature ought to interfere whenever it believes its interference to be useful.

Its interference to shorten the hours of adult labor in factories is useful.

Therefore it ought so to interfere.

The first two objections deny the major. The third denies the minor. It admits that if the evils of poverty would be diminished by a legal limitation of the hours of labor such a limitation ought to be enforced. But it denies that such will be the result of the bill. It maintains that increase of leisure will be dearly purchased by diminution of wages. That if no female of any age and no male under 18 is allowed to work in a factory for more than 10 hours a day, 10 hours a day will be the utmost time for which the machinery can be kept at work. That the English capitalist using his machinery for only 10 hours a day will be undersold by the German or the American who employs his for 12, 13, 14 and even 15. That the factories which work for the foreign market must be closed, and with them the means of clothing, feeding, and supporting many hundreds of thousands of workpeople. That this will occasion a general fall of wages and a general diminution of comfort, among those who adhere to their present occupation, and will drive the remainder into other employments, more laborious, more irksome and above all, more unhealthy than the comparatively light labor which is exerted in the warm and airy halls of a well-regulated factory. Employments which, not being carried on, like those of a factory, in public, are unsusceptible of control on the part of the legislator, except through a system of inspection and intrusion which the Englishman is not yet ready to submit to.

Into this discussion I shall not at present enter. I have given this brief outline of the factory question merely as a specimen of the attempts made by governments to palliate that portion of the evils of poverty which arise from overwork and of the dangers incident to such attempts.

This sort of legislation is at present in its infancy. It dates from the Reform Act which pushed into the House of Commons a large party depending on the favor of the uneducated classes, and bound to flatter their prejudices, and has as yet been but slightly imitated abroad. The last instance of it I shall mention is the 5 and 6 Victoria, cap. 99, passed in 1842, which forbids females to work in collieries. I class it with the Factory Acts, though its object is somewhat different. The legislator prohibits the presence of women in collieries believing that it leads to immorality and makes them bad wives and mothers. It attempts to improve the condition of the colliers by improving the female portion of the collier population. I believe that this proposition is not open to the third objection which has been made to the Factory Acts. I do not think that the minor premises can be denied. It does appear from the evidence collected by the Commissioners of Mines and Collieries that if there be any work for which females are peculiarly unfit it is this; that their bodies are injured by its severity, and their minds by association with men whom the heat of the mine often forces to go without clothes. And it appears by the report of Mr. Tremenhere, the Commissioner appointed to inquire into the operation of the Act, that it has worked on the whole remarkably well. The colliers themselves, who at first resisted it, would now regret its repeal.

But it was immediately followed by cases of great individual suffering. The legislators for the poor, and I fear that this accusation affects peculiarly those who assume the title of humane, seem to care little for individuals. The act, passed on the ——— day of ———, 1842, enacted that after the ——— day of ——— following no female should work in a colliery. About ——— weeks were given to thousands of women and girls, many of whom had grown up in the business, and none knew any other trade to find for themselves some means of subsistence.

The evidence embodied in Mr. Tremenhere's first report contains some of the results. Mr. Adamson, the minister of Newton in Midlothian, estimates at 119 the unmarried women in his parish whom the Act suddenly deprived of their trade.

> Some of these (adds Mr. Tremenhere) have been reduced from a position in which they could feed and clothe themselves in comfort and decency to the necessity of resorting to the most humiliating employments, such as collecting dung on the roads. Two daughters aged 49 and 40 respectively of a father aged 75 being left to shift for themselves have had recourse to making and vending clamstone. In this occupation, when the weather admits of their going abroad they make on an average 3d. a day, and to do this they sometimes have to walk as far as Haddington, a distance of 14 miles. I had opportunities of seeing many whom the act had thrown into privation. They were anxious to tell their simple tale of distress consequent on their enforced idleness, and to testify their anxiety to get their work. Their scanty dress and general aspect of depression sufficiently showed it.
>
> When the Act passed (says Mr. Baird of Lanarkshire) we had seventy females down the pits. Between 20 and 30 were supporting aged parents, or themselves, having none to help them; and some girls, orphans, were supporting their younger sisters. We have great difficulty in preventing them from going into our pits which have stairs. Rather than not work they rise and go down before daylight, and in consequence of the people all commiserating them no one will give a hint of what is going on.

If any of the higher classes, any of those who can force the public to hear their case, had been thus sacrificed to the public good, they would have demanded compensation and would have received it. I ought perhaps to include among the evils of poverty the carelessness with which the individual interests of the poor are dealt with by the legislature, and particularly, as I have before remarked, by those who profess peculiar humanity.

$$\mathcal{C}harles\ \mathcal{D}ickens$$

1812–1870

We owe Dickens's description of life in the workhouse to his own brief residence in such an institution as a child. While allowances must be made for the demands of fiction, Dickens's account does identify several actual aspects of the New Poor Law of 1834. This law represented a triumph of the Malthusians who had argued that generous "outdoor" relief afforded the poor in their habitations simply subsidized marriage on the dole and multiplied the next generation's supply of paupers. In his Essay on Population, *Malthus had actually suggested that relief be withheld, after a certain date, from the married poor. The Poor Law Act of 1834 went less far, but it did deliberately set out to make the workhouse an unpleasant place, a "house of terror," designed to discourage all but the most desperate of the poor from applying for admission. It did in principle, though not entirely in practice, deny relief to individuals who remained outside of the workhouse.*

Once inside the workhouse, the pauper was fed a miserable diet, the sexes were separated, and the inmates were put to unpleasant penal labor like picking oakum. As Dickens put it, the regulations ". . . undertook to divorce poor married people." In fairness to the poor-law administration of the period, it should be said that the Poor Law Commissioners made reiterated efforts to achieve at least minimum standards in the workhouses, and there was no time at which relief was confined entirely to workhouse residents. David Roberts has even maintained in The Origins of the Welfare State *that the varied commissions of the mid-Victorian era, including the Poor Law Commissioners, actually set the stage for the evolution, later in the century, of a true welfare state.*

This selection is from Oliver Twist (*Novel Library edition*), *pp. 13-16.*

The Workhouse

The members of this board were very sage, deep, philosophical men; and when they came to turn their attention to the workhouse, they found out at once, what ordinary folks would never have discovered —the poor people liked it! It was a regular place of public entertainment for the poorer classes; a tavern where there was nothing to pay; a public breakfast, dinner, tea, and supper all the year round; a brick and mortar elysium, where it was all play and no work. 'Oho!' said the board, looking very knowing; 'we are the fellows to set this to rights; we'll stop it all, in no time.' So, they established the rule, that all poor people should have the alternative (for they would compel nobody, not they), of being starved by a gradual process in the house, or by a quick one out of it. With this view, they contracted with the water-works to lay on an unlimited supply of water; and with a corn-factor to supply periodically small quantities of oatmeal; and issued three meals of thin gruel a day, with an onion twice a week, and half a roll on Sundays. They made a great many other wise and humane regulations, having reference to the ladies, which it is not necessary to repeat; kindly undertook to divorce poor married people, in consequence of the great expense of a suit in Doctors' Commons; and, instead of compelling a man to support his family, as they had theretofore done, took his family away from him, and made him a bachelor! There is no saying how many applicants for relief, under these last two heads, might have started up in all classes of society, if it had not been coupled with the workhouse; but the board were long-headed men, and had provided for this difficulty. The relief was inseparable from the workhouse and the gruel; and that frightened people.

For the first six months after Oliver Twist was removed, the system was in full operation. It was rather expensive at first, in consequence of the increase in the undertaker's bill, and the necessity of taking in the clothes of all the paupers, which fluttered loosely on their wasted, shrunken forms, after a week or two's gruel. But the number of workhouse inmates got thin as well as the paupers; and the board were in ecstasies.

The room in which the boys were fed, was a large stone hall, with a copper at one end: out of which the master, dressed in an apron for the purpose, and assisted by one or two women, ladled the gruel at meal-times. Of this festive composition each boy had one porringer, and no more—except on occasions of great public rejoicing, when he had two ounces and a quarter of bread besides. The bowls never wanted washing. The boys polished them with their spoons till they shone again; and when they had performed this operation (which never took very long, the spoon being nearly as large as the bowls), they would sit staring at the copper, with such eager eyes, as if they could have devoured the very bricks of which it was composed; employing themselves, meanwhile, in sucking their fingers most assiduously, with the view of catching up any stray splashes of gruel that might have been cast thereon. Boys have generally excellent appetites. Oliver Twist and his companions suffered the tortures of slow starvation for three months: at last they got so voracious and wild with hunger, that one boy, who was tall for his age, and hadn't been used to that sort of thing (for his father had kept a small cook-shop), hinted darkly to his companions, that unless he had another basin of gruel *per diem*, he was afraid he might some night happen to eat the boy who slept next him, who happened to be a weakly youth of tender age. He had a wild, hungry eye; and they implicitly believed him. A council was held; lots were cast who should walk up to the master after supper that evening, and ask for more; and it fell to Oliver Twist.

The evening arrived; the boys took their places. The master, in his cook's uniform, stationed himself at the copper; his pauper assistants ranged themselves behind him; the gruel was served out; and a long grace was said over the short commons. The gruel disappeared; the boys whispered each other, and winked at Oliver; while his next neighbours nudged him. Child as he was, he was desperate with hunger, and reckless with misery. He rose from the table; and advancing to the master, basin and spoon in hand, said: somewhat alarmed at his own temerity:

'Please, sir, I want some more.'

The master was a fat, healthy man; but he turned very pale. He gazed in stupefied astonishment on the small rebel for some seconds, and then clung for support to the copper. The assistants were paralysed with wonder; the boys with fear.

'What!' said the master at length, in a faint voice.

'Please, sir,' replied Oliver, 'I want some more.'

The master aimed a blow at Oliver's head with the ladle; pinioned him in his arms; and shrieked aloud for the beadle.

The board were sitting in solemn conclave, when Mr. Bumble

rushed into the room in great excitement, and addressing the gentleman in the high chair, said,

'Mr. Limbkins, I beg your pardon, sir! Oliver Twist has asked for more!'

There was a general start. Horror was depicted on every countenance.

'For *more!*' said Mr. Limbkins. 'Compose yourself, Bumble, and answer me distinctly. Do I understand that he asked for more, after he had eaten the supper allotted by the dietary?'

'He did, sir,' replied Bumble.

'That boy will be hung,' said the gentleman in the white waistcoat. 'I know that boy will be hung.'

Nobody controverted the prophetic gentleman's opinion. An animated discussion took place. Oliver was ordered into instant confinement; and a bill was next morning pasted on the outside of the gate, offering a reward of five pounds to anybody who would take Oliver Twist off the hands of the parish. In other words, five pounds and Oliver Twist were offered to any man or woman who wanted an apprentice to any trade, business, or calling.

'I never was more convinced of anything in my life,' said the gentleman in the white waistcoat, as he knocked at the gate and read the bill next morning: 'I never was more convinced of anything in my life, than I am that that boy will come to be hung.'

John Strachey

1901–

As a young man John Strachey belonged to the British Communist Party and produced, in that phase of his political life, the widely read The Coming Struggle for Power, which predicted the rather rapid bankruptcy of capitalism. Leaving the Communist Party, Strachey held office during the Labour Party governments which followed the Second World War. In Contemporary Capitalism and The End of Empire, he has written two volumes of a series which is intended to result in a considered evaluation of the present economic scene.

Strachey's present intellectual position is highly interesting as much for what he is endeavoring to achieve as for its present implications. To a considerable extent, Strachey remains attached to Marxist economic doctrine. He believes that Marx did correctly describe the tendencies in capitalism toward maldistribution of income and repetitive business crises. But he departs from Marxism at a critical point, the role of the state. The orthodox Marxist conception of the state emphasizes its class character. In a capitalist community the state must be the instrument of the ruling capitalist class, and the range of policies that such a state can pursue is necessarily limited by its commitment to the welfare of a single group. Strachey, on the other hand, is convinced that the present strength of capitalism and the redistribution toward greater income equality which has proved possible in the United States and Great Britain are evidence of the responsiveness of democratic governments to the interests of workers. The thrust of his teaching is in the direction of even more self-conscious use of the parliamentary state to promote the interests of the masses.

Other influences upon Strachey are Galbraith and Myrdal. Galbraith's critique of American habits of consumption in The Affluent

Society *has had considerable impact upon left-wing labor opinion in general. Myrdal's grim picture of the widening gap between standards of life in Western, developed countries and standards of life in much of the remainder of the world has influenced Strachey's views on international policy, very much as his attachment to Keynesian concepts of fiscal policy has made him hopeful about the prospects of high employment in the countries of Western Europe and North America.*

As a descendant of a famous family of British proconsuls, Strachey is unusually well qualified to tell the story of British imperialism in the eighteenth and nineteenth centuries. An American can only envy the ability of a Strachey to dip casually into family papers which cast unexpected lights upon events of the colonial past. The present selection exemplifies one of the more horrible effects of unrestrained laissez-faire. It is taken from The End of Empire, *by John Strachey.* © Copyright, 1959, *by John Strachey. Reprinted by permission of Random House, Inc.*

Famine in Bengal

The immediate economic consequences for Bengal of its conquest by the British, which was thus completed, must now be noted. These are perhaps best illustrated in the change which almost at once occurred in the trading practices of the East India Company. Ever since its foundation 150 years earlier, the Company had found that it had had to trade with India by sending out means of payment, which it called "the investment," with which not only to purchase but also to finance the production of cottons and silks by the Indian weavers. For, as Orme explains, the Indian weavers were too destitute to produce unless they were financed by some factor or merchant during the period of production. This "investment" had always consisted, for the most part, of the precious metals, for there were few European goods for which there was a market in India. It was this export of gold and silver in its annual "investment" which had made the Company vulnerable to the mercantilist criticism that it was draining Britain of its reserve of precious metals for the sake of importing luxuries. The charge was probably ill-founded, for the Company re-sold a considerable part of its Indian-produced goods all over Europe, and at a very high rate of profit. So that it is by no means clear that Britain came out of the transaction, even before the conquest, with what we should now call an adverse balance of payments. But, in any case, soon after the conquest of Bengal the charge became wholly ill-founded, and for the following reason.

The Company ceased (or at least attempted to cease) to send out "an investment" at all.* In other words, Bengal as a whole got nothing at all in exchange for its goods. Of course the individual weavers, working in their huts at their handlooms on cottons or silks for the Company, had still to be paid, or else they would have starved before they could complete their tasks. But the money to pay them, instead of being sent out from Britain, was now raised by taxation in Bengal. In a word, Bengal as a whole was made to pay for its own exports to Britain. When (a few years after Clive's conquest) the Company had itself assumed the "Dewanee," *i.e.*, the direct management of the province (though still for a few years longer nominally on behalf of a functionless "Nawob") all political obstacles to this extreme form of exploitation were removed.†

Logically the value of the whole shipments from India, minus only the cost of their transport and sale, should have become pure profit to the Company. And in principle they did. Nevertheless it is an ironic fact that it was just in this period that the Company, in effect, went bankrupt! But this was only because it was so pillaged by its own agents, by the British government, and in general by everyone who could possibly get their feet into the trough, that it could not meet its obligations. The flow of almost unrequited wealth from Bengal to Britain went on uninterruptedly; it was merely diverted to private pockets and away from the pockets of the stockholders of the Company. The line between the trader and the simple robber, which had disappeared altogether in the case of the Spanish conquistadors, had worn thin.

But, it may be asked, did not Bengal at least receive some recompense by way of good government and law and order for the tribute that it thus paid to its conquerors? No doubt it did, and in the fullness

---

* *Rise and Fulfilment of British Rule in India,* Thompson and Garrett (Macmillan, 1934), p. 99.

† It is true that the servants of the Company went on talking about "the investment" long after this. But now they appear to have meant the working capital of the Company, whether raised, as whenever possible it was, by taxation in India (or borrowed from individuals in the Company's own employment), and not a sum sent out from Britain. On the other hand, as we shall notice in the next chapter, the complete abolition of any actual payment by Britain for the goods she bought in India was an ideal towards which the Company ardently aspired rather than something which they completely and securely achieved. Even at the end of the eighteenth century some money or goods had often to be sent to India as a means of payment, but to a much lower value than the goods received from India.

of time regular government and law and order were to be of value. But for some 15 years after the conquest the fact that Bengal was now protected from being ravaged by its neighbours was of no advantage to the unhappy province. For it was now ravaged far more systematically by its new rulers. No Mahratta raid ever devastated a countryside with the thoroughness with which both the Company and, above all, the Company's servants in their individual capacities, sucked dry the plain of Bengal. In fact in their blind rage for enrichment they took more from the Bengali peasants than those peasants could furnish and live. And the peasants duly died.

It was not principally the exaction of the goods exported to Britain on the Company's account as an unrequited tribute, that caused this frightful result. The natural riches of the province could probably have supported that. It was the fact that the Company's servants, civilian and military alike, with one accord turned to their personal enrichment, not mainly by an overseas trade with Europe, but by engaging in the internal trade of the province. They did so by arbitrarily declaring that the original firman of the Great Mogul (see the previous chapter), which had given the Company extra-territorial rights and exemption from taxes for its export and import trade, which was bad enough, applied to internal trade as well.* This was completely ruinous. Since the taxes and internal custom dues had to be high, in order to enable the Nawob's government to pay its tribute to the Company, any Briton, or in practice his Indian agent to whom he sold his *dustuck*, or *laisser passer*, could undersell and ruin all native competitors. For he traded without paying any taxes or dues. Soon the British and their agents had achieved a virtual monopoly of the trade of the province: but by then it was a dying province. Only 12 years after the conquest in 1769 Mr. Becher, the Company's agent at Murishidabad, was reporting: "I well remember this country when trade was free and the flourishing state it was then in; with concern I now see its present ruinous condition." Still earlier Hastings, then a young servant of the Company, on a visit up-country reported that the approach of his party of British was regarded by the inhabitants rather like that of tigers. "Most of the petty towns and sarais

---

* Orme relates how 40 years earlier when Surman and Stephenson, during "the embassy of complaint," stretched their demands to cover exemptions from taxation for the internal as well as the overseas trade, the Mogul exclaimed oraculary, "The Sea"! Orme writes that this undoubtedly meant that the firman of exemption was to apply only to the overseas trade. But of course by the seventeen-sixties such questions had become a matter of brute force; no one really cared what had been written into the original concession.

(markets) were deserted on our approach, and the shops shut up from the apprehensions of the same treatment from us," *i.e.*, of the same treatment as they were receiving from the other British or their agents.

True there was nothing new in devastation and famine, either in Bengal or in India generally. Civil disorders, the exactions of native princes, or of previous conquerors, had always periodically thrust the peasantry over the edge of subsistence. But there seems no doubt that there was something particularly thorough and systematic about the early British-made famines, particularly that of 1770.* The truth is that law and order, if it is someone else's law and order, may be a still more terrible calamity to the ruled even than anarchy and civil strife. It is precisely when all resistance, all possibility of any alternative or rival authority, has disappeared that an alien authority can extract the whole, and, if it is foolish, temporarily even more than the whole, of the surplus of men's produce above subsistence. Nor is it anything but the bitterest irony for the governed if such alien authority does its work in the most correct, orderly and, as in this case, legalistic, way imaginable.†

. . . Moreover another curse had descended upon the late-nineteenth-century British administrators; the curse of the doctrinaire. *Laisser faire* in general and free trade in particular had become the secular religion of the British middle class. The application of its dogmas to India had frightful consequences. Mr. Philip Woodruff in the second volume of his well-known work, *The Men Who Ruled India,* entitled *The Guardians* (a work specially, and worthily, devoted to celebrating the achievements of the I.C.S.), describes what happened in the matter of famine relief. In 1866 the crops failed in the province of Orissa. The members of the Board of Revenue who advised the Lieutenant-Governor, Sir Cecil Beadon, were—

". . . held by the most rigid rules of the direct political economy." They rejected "almost with horror" the idea of importing grain.

* And this fact was realised by some contemporary opinion in Britain. Horace Walpole wrote: "We have outdone the Spaniards in Peru. They were at least butchers on a religious principle, however diabolical their zeal. We have murdered, deposed, plundered, usurped—nay what think you of the famine in Bengal, in which three millions perished, being caused by a monopoly of the provisions by the servants of the East India Company?"

† Almost the most terrible thing which the British did was to import and impose the whole system and apparatus of British eighteenth-century Law, complete with barristers, judges, High Courts, etc. Such a system proved of course utterly unsuitable, and indeed incomprehensible, in Bengal.

They would not even allow the authorities in Orissa to take the grain from a ship which ran ashore on their coast in March. It was bound for Calcutta and to Calcutta the grain must go. In fact, it rotted in the holds while plans were made to move it.

At Haileybury, everyone had learnt that political economy was a matter of laws, that money and goods would move by themselves in ways beneficial to mankind. The less any government interfered with natural movements, the better. If there was real scarcity in Orissa, prices would rise, grain-dealers from elsewhere would be attracted and would hurry grain to where it was needed. If the government tried to anticipate this process, they would cause waste and incur loss. . . . By the time relief came a quarter of the population were dead.

It is true that as a result of the famines of 1866, 1868 and 1874, this insane doctrine was revised and a "Famine Code" which suspended the "laws" of political economy was drawn up in 1880 by Sir Richard Strachey. But allowing men to starve to death lest feeding them interfere with doctrine was only the most extreme example of something which will concern us throughout this narrative. For if, after 1880, it was possible to interfere with "economic laws" when actual famine had broken out, this was by no means the case at any other time. On the contrary, *laisser faire* in its most rigid interpretation remained the creed of the men who conducted the economic policy of the government of India to the very end of the British period.

Part IV | **THE**
ECONOMICS
OF
UTOPIA

In Plato's discussions of justice and the ideal state in the Republic are to be found his important economic ideas. Just as his doctrine of the state is founded upon the division of labor, so also is his conception of economic activity. Division of labor emerged from the natural differences among human beings, from the "... diversities of nature among us which are adapted to different occupations." Plato's ideal state was big enough to allow appropriate scope for each man's natural talent. This scope, rather than maximum output, was the appropriate goal of the state. The ideal state was small, for if it were large and eager to become larger still, the reason for its size was a degenerate taste for luxury which compelled a more complex division of labor but notably failed to improve the quality of human existence.

Most of us today would consider Plato's state an anti-utopia rather than a utopia, for in it caste is dominant and democracy does not exist. The three major occupations of the citizens are those of the ruler, the soldier, and the worker. In truly beautiful language, Plato described the selection of each class:

> Citizens . . . you are brothers, yet God has framed you differently. Some of you have the power of command, and in the composition of these he has mingled gold, wherefore also they have the greatest honour; others he has made of silver, to be auxiliaries; others again who are to be husbandmen and craftsmen he has composed of brass and iron; and the species will generally be preserved in the children. But as all are of the same original stock, a golden parent will sometimes have a silver son, or a silver parent a golden son.

Plato's derogation of economic activity and economic goals was exemplified in his description of the ideal property arrangements for each class. Only the lowest, farmers and artisans, were allowed to work for

301

profit and accumulate property. Rulers and auxiliaries should have neither homes nor property of their own. Only were this true could they be expected to pursue truth and justice, free of base economic goals.

Plato sought to minimize class conflict by the assignment of appropriate goals. The pursuit of money by the base would not arouse the envy of wise rulers any more than the prudent exercise of power by the latter would antagonize artisans and farmers. "Any city, however small, is in fact divided into two, one the city of the poor, the other of the rich; these are at war with one another." The argument against democracy was partly a judgment on the limitations of most men's talents and partly a generalization of division of labor. Ruling was a full-time job. It was disastrous to entrust government to men who spent the bulk of their time in commerce or agriculture. The ideal state selected its rulers from the men of gold, carefully trained them, and thoroughly tested them before surrendering its fate to their hands.

The selection is from The Dialogues of Plato, *Jowett translation* (*New York: Random House,* 1920), *I,* 679-80, 682-3.

The Parable of the Metals

True, I replied, but there is more coming; I have only told you half. Citizens, we shall say to them in our tale, you are brothers, yet God has framed you differently. Some of you have the power of command, and in the composition of these he has mingled gold, wherefore also they have the greatest honour; others he has made of silver, to be auxiliaries; others again who are to be husbandmen and craftsmen he has composed of brass and iron; and the species will generally be preserved in the children. But as all are of the same original stock, a golden parent will sometimes have a silver son, or a silver parent a golden son. And God proclaims as a first principle to the rulers, and above all else, that there is nothing which they should so anxiously guard, or of which they are to be such good guardians, as of the purity of the race. They should observe what elements mingle in their offspring; for if the son of a golden or silver parent has an admixture of brass and iron, then nature orders a transposition of ranks, and the eye of the ruler must not be pitiful towards the child because he has to descend in the scale and become a husbandman or artisan, just as there may be sons of artisans who having an admixture of gold or silver in them are raised to honour, and become guardians or auxiliaries.

For an oracle says that when a man of brass or iron guards the State, it will be destroyed. Such is the tale; is there any possibility of making our citizens believe in it?

If we proceed along the old path, my belief, I said, is that we shall find the answer. And our answer will be that, even as they are, our guardians may very likely be the happiest of men; but that our aim in founding the State was not the disproportionate happiness of any one class, but the greatest happiness of the whole; we thought that in a State which is ordered with a view to the good of the whole we should be most likely to find justice, and in the ill-ordered State injustice: and, having found them, we might then decide which of the two is the happier. At present, I take it, we are fashioning the happy State, not piecemeal, or with a view of making a few happy citizens, but as a whole; and by-and-by we will proceed to view the opposite kind of State. Suppose that we were painting a statue, and some one came up to us and said, Why do you not put the most beautiful colours on the most beautiful parts of the body—the eyes ought to be purple, but you have made them black—to him we might fairly answer, Sir, you would not surely have us beautify the eyes to such a degree that they are no longer eyes; consider rather whether, by giving this and the other features their due proportion, we make the whole beautiful. And so I say to you, do not compel us to assign to the guardians a sort of happiness which will make them anything but guardians; for we too can clothe our husbandmen in royal apparel, and set crowns of gold on their heads, and bid them till the ground as much as they like, and no more. Our potters also might be allowed to repose on couches, and feast by the fireside, passing round the wine-cup, while their wheel is conveniently at hand, and working at pottery only as much as they like; in this way we might make every class happy—and then, as you imagine, the whole State would be happy. But do not put this idea into our heads; for, if we listen to you, the husbandman will be no longer a husbandman, the potter will cease to be a potter, and no one will have the character of any distinct class in the State. Now this is not of much consequence where the corruption of society, and pretension to be what you are not, is confined to cobblers; but when the guardians of the laws and of the government are only seemingly and not real guardians, then see how they turn the State upside down; and on the other hand they alone have the power of giving order and happiness to the State. We mean our guardians to be true saviours and not the destroyers of the State, whereas our opponent is thinking of peasants at a festival, who are enjoying a life of revelry, not of citizens who are doing their duty to the State. But, if so, we mean different things, and he is speaking of something which is not a State. And therefore we must consider whether in appointing our guardians we would look to their greatest happiness individually, or whether this principle of happiness does not rather reside in the State as a whole. But if the latter be the truth, then the guardians and auxiliaries, and all others equally with them, must be compelled or induced to do their own work in the best way. And thus the whole State will grow up in a noble order, and the several classes will receive the proportion of happiness which nature assigns to them.

William Godwin

1756–1836

Godwin is one of the founders of that school of English socialism which rests its case on the nobility of human nature, the unlimited potentialities of human life, and the essential evil of human institutions, particularly of human governments. His Enquiry Concerning the Principles of Political Justice, and Its Influence on General Virtue and Happiness, *which appeared in 1793, was the rage of the hour. Even now, its central argument has at least the charms of nostalgia. That argument rested upon three, to Godwin, self-evident propositions. The first: "Man is perfectible, or in other words susceptible of perpetual improvement." The second: ". . . truth is omnipotent." And the third: ". . . what is born into the world is an unfinished sketch, without character or decisive features impressed upon it."*

Of course none of this was original. There were good eighteenth-century antecedents for the optimism. The doctrine that children were empty receptacles at birth could be traced back to John Locke and the Essay on Human Understanding. *And early and late rationalists have cherished and exaggerated the power of truth. What distinguished Godwin was the extravagance with which he pursued his argument. For him, the sources of all human troubles were bad government and poor institutions. Education, that sovereign remedy, could solve all difficulties. The human reasons could easily triumph over sexual instinct, with the result that the length of human life could expand and man might approach immortality. Godwin did not preach violent revolution. Appealing to men's understandings, he was convinced that men had only to hear the truth to perceive that simplicity of life, equal distribution of income, and anarchism in place of government, would assure a future overflowing with unprecedented happiness. "Truth is omnipotent."*

305

*When that constitutional pessimist, Thomas Robert Malthus, came
to contemplate the arguments of Godwin's Political Justice, he
dashed Godwin's hope for mankind to the ground by identifying the
sources of human poverty and the reasons for human unhappiness not
in the human institutions which Godwin blamed, but in the sexual
instincts of man which multiplied population, inflicted shortage, and
enlisted the horrors of the positive check to population in the shape
of disease, war, and famine. In fact, one of Malthus's "basic postulata"
affirmed the immutability of sexual passion. Once granted, this immutability shattered all of Godwin's schemes for human equality. In
fact, of all systems of social organization, equality was likely to be the
most disastrous, for it was the most likely to encourage early marriage,
many births, and the most rapid approach to overpopulation.*

*The passage that follows fairly represents Godwin's rhetorical style
of exposition. It is also a characteristic attack upon property in which
Godwin argues as much from the disastrous effect of wealth on the
wealthy as he does from the injustice inflicted upon the poor. Running through the passage is the implicit thought that even the wealthy
can be brought to see the error of their ways and the certainty of
greater happiness for themselves in human equality. The theme of
property and its inequities ran through Godwin's novel* Caleb
Williams, *which has recently been reprinted.*

Genuine System of Property Delineated

The subject of property is the keystone that completes the fabric of
political justice. According as our ideas respecting it are crude or correct, they will enlighten us as to the consequences of a *simple form of
society without government,* and remove the prejudices that attach
us to complexity. There is nothing that more powerfully tends to distort our *judgment* and *opinions* than erroneous notions concerning
the goods of fortune. Finally, the period that shall put an end to the
system of *coercion* and *punishment* is intimately connected with the
circumstance of property's being placed upon an equitable basis.

Various abuses of the most incontrovertible nature have insinu-
ated themselves into the administration of property. Each of these

abuses might usefully be made the subject of a separate investigation. We might enquire into the vexations of this sort that are produced by the dreams of national greatness or magistratical vanity. This would lead us to a just estimate of the different kinds of taxation, landed or mercantile, having the necessaries or the luxuries of life for their subject of operation. We might examine into the abuses which have adhered to the commercial system; monopolies, charters, patents, protecting duties, prohibitions and bounties. We might remark upon the consequences that flow from the feudal system and the system of ranks; seignorial duties, fines, conveyances, entails, estates freehold, copyhold and manorial, vassalage and primogeniture. We might consider the rights of the church, first fruits and tithes; and we might enquire into the propriety of the regulation by which a man, after having possessed as sovereign a considerable property during his life, is permitted to dispose of it at his pleasure at the period which the laws of nature seem to have fixed as the termination of his authority. All these enquiries would tend to show the incalculable importance of this subject. But excluding them all from the present enquiry, it shall be the business of what remains of this work to consider, not any particular abuses which have incidentally risen out of the administration of property, but those general principles by which it has in almost all cases been directed, and which, if erroneous, must not only be regarded as the source of the abuses above enumerated, but of others of innumerable kinds, too multifarious and subtle to enter into so brief a catalogue.

What is the criterion that must determine whether this or that substance capable of contributing to the benefit of a human being ought to be considered as your property or mine? To this question there can be but one answer—Justice. Let us then recur to the principles of justice.

To whom does any article of property, suppose a loaf of bread, justly belong? To him who most wants it, or to whom the possession of it will be most beneficial. Here are six men famished with hunger, and the loaf is, absolutely considered, capable of satisfying the cravings of them all. Who is it that has a reasonable claim to benefit by the qualities with which this loaf is endowed? They are all brothers perhaps, and the law of primogeniture bestows it exclusively on the eldest. But does justice confirm this award? The laws of different countries dispose of property in a thousand different ways; but there can be but one way which is most conformable to reason.

It would have been easy to put a case much stronger than that which has just been stated. I have an hundred loaves in my possession, and in the next street there is a poor man expiring with hunger to whom one of these loaves would be the means of preserving his life. If I withhold this loaf from him, am I not unjust? If I impart it, am I not complying with what justice demands? To whom does the loaf justly belong?

I suppose myself in other respects to be in easy circumstances, and that I do not want this bread as an object of barter or sale, to procure me any of the other necessaries of a human being. Our animal wants have long since been defined, and are stated to consist of food, clothing and shelter. If justice have any meaning, nothing can be more iniquitous than for one man to possess superfluities, while there is a human being in existence that is not adequately supplied with these.

Justice does not stop here. Every man is entitled, so far as the general stock will suffice, not only to the means of being, but of well-being. It is unjust if one man labour to the destruction of his health or his life that another man may abound in luxuries. It is unjust if one man be deprived of leisure to cultivate his rational powers while another man contributes not a single effort to add to the common stock. The faculties of one man are like the faculties of another man. Justice directs that each man, unless perhaps he be employed more beneficially to the public, should contribute to the cultivation of the common harvest, of which each man consumes a share. This reciprocity indeed, as was observed when that subject was the matter of separate consideration, is of the very essence of justice. How the latter branch of it, the necessary labour, is to be secured while each man is admitted to claim his share of the produce we shall presently have occasion to enquire.

This subject will be placed in a still more striking light if we reflect for a moment on the nature of luxuries. The wealth of any state may intelligibly enough be considered as the aggregate of all the incomes which are annually consumed within that state without destroying the materials of an equal consumption in the ensuing year. Considering this income as being, what in almost all cases it will be found to be, the produce of the industry of the inhabitants, it will follow that in civilized countries the peasant often does not consume more than the twentieth part of the produce of his labour, while his rich neighbour consumes perhaps the produce of the labour of twenty peasants. The benefit that arises to this favoured mortal ought surely to be very extraordinary.

But nothing is more evident than that the condition of this man is the reverse of beneficial. The man of an hundred pounds per annum, if he understand his own happiness, is a thousand times more favourably circumstanced. What shall the rich man do with his enormous wealth? Shall he eat of innumerable dishes of the most expensive viands, or pour down hogsheads of the most highly flavoured wines? A frugal diet will contribute infinitely more to health, to a clear understanding, to cheerful spirits, and even to the gratification of the appetites. Almost every other expense is an expense of ostentation. No man but the most sordid epicure would long continue to maintain even a plentiful table if he had no spectators, visitors or servants to behold his establishment. For whom are our sumptuous palaces and costly furniture, our equipages, and even our very clothes? The nobleman who should for the first time let his imagination loose to conceive the style in which he would live if he had nobody to observe, and no eye to please but his own, would no doubt be surprised to find that vanity had been the first mover in all his actions.

The object of this vanity is to procure the admiration and applause of beholders. We need not here enter into the intrinsic value of applause. Taking it for granted that it is as estimable an acquisition as any man can suppose it, how contemptible is the source of applause to which the rich man has recourse? "Applaud me because my ancestor has left me a great estate." What merit is there in that? The first effect then of riches is to deprive their possessor of the genuine powers of understanding and render him incapable of discerning absolute truth. They lead him to fix his affections on objects not accommodated to the wants and the structure of the human mind, and of consequence entail upon him disappointment and unhappiness. The greatest of all personal advantages are independence of mind, which makes us feel that our satisfactions are not at the mercy either of men or of fortune, and activity of mind, the cheerfulness that arises from industry perpetually employed about objects of which our judgment acknowledges the intrinsic value.

In this case we have compared the happiness of the man of extreme opulence with that of the man of one hundred pounds per annum. But the latter side of this alternative was assumed merely in compliance with existing prejudices. Even in the present state of human society we perceive that a man who should be perpetually earning the necessary competence by a very moderate industry, and with his pursuits uncrossed by the peevishness or caprice of his neighbours, would not be less happy than if he were born to that competence. In the state of society we are here contemplating, where, as will presently appear, the requisite industry will be of the lightest kind, it will be the reverse of a misfortune to any man to find himself necessarily stimulated to a gentle activity, and in consequence to feel that no reverse of fortune could deprive him of the means of subsistence and contentment.

But it has been alleged that we find among different men very different degrees of labour and industry, and that it is not just they should receive an equal reward. It cannot indeed be denied that the attainments of men in virtue and usefulness ought by no means to be confounded. How far the present system of property contributes to their being equitably treated it is very easy to determine. The present system of property confers on one man immense wealth in consideration of the accident of his birth. He that from beggary ascends to opulence is usually known not to have effected this transition by methods very creditable to his honesty or his usefulness. The most industrious and active member of society is frequently with great difficulty able to keep his family from starving.

But, to pass over these iniquitous effects of the unequal distribution of property, let us consider the nature of the reward which is thus proposed to industry. If you be industrious, you shall have an hundred times more food than you can eat and an hundred times more clothes than you can wear. Where is the justice of this? If I be the greatest benefactor the human species ever knew, is that a reason for bestowing on me what I do not want, especially when there are thousands to whom my superfluity would be of the greatest advantage? With this superfluity I can purchase nothing but gaudy ostentation and envy, nothing but the pitiful pleasure of returning to the poor under the name of generosity that to which reason gives them an irresistible claim, nothing but prejudice, error and vice.

The doctrine of the injustice of accumulated property has been the foundation of all religious morality. The object of this morality has been to excite men by individual virtue to repair this injustice. The most energetic teachers of religion have been irresistibly led to assert the precise truth upon this interesting subject. They have taught the rich that they hold their wealth only as a trust, that they are strictly accountable for every atom of their expenditure, that they are merely administrators and by no means proprietors in chief.* The defect of this system is that they rather excite us to palliate our injustice than to forsake it.

No truth can be more simple than that which they inculcate. There is no action of any human being, and certainly no action that respects the disposition of property, that is not capable of better and worse, and concerning which reason and morality do not prescribe a specific conduct. He that sets out with acknowledging that other men are of

* See Swift's Sermon on Mutual Subjection, quoted Book II, Chap. II.

the same nature as himself, and is capable of perceiving the precise place he would hold in the eye of an impartial spectator, must be fully sensible that the money he employs in procuring an object of trifling or no advantage to himself, and which might have been employed in purchasing substantial and indispensable benefit to another, is unjustly employed. He that looks at his property with the eye of truth will find that every shilling of it has received its destination from the dictates of justice. He will at the same time however be exposed to considerable pain in consequence of his own ignorance as to the precise disposition that justice and public utility require.

Does any man doubt of the truth of these assertions? Does any man doubt that when I employ a sum of money small or great in the purchase of an absolute luxury for myself, I am guilty of vice? It is high time that this subject should be adequately understood. It is high time that we should lay aside the very names of justice and virtue, or that we should acknowledge that they do not authorise us to accumulate luxuries upon ourselves while we see others in want of the indispensable means of improvement and happiness.

But while religion inculcated on mankind the impartial nature of justice, its teachers have been too apt to treat the practice of justice, not as a debt, which it ought to be considered, but as an affair of spontaneous generosity and bounty. They have called upon the rich to be clement and merciful to the poor. The consequence of this has been that the rich, when they bestowed the most slender pittance of their enormous wealth in acts of charity, as they were called, took merit to themselves for what they gave, instead of considering themselves as delinquents for what they withheld.

Religion is in reality in all its parts an accommodation to the prejudices and weaknesses of mankind. Its authors communicated to the world as much truth as they calculated that the world would be willing to receive. But it is time that we should lay aside the instruction intended only for children in understanding,* and contemplate the nature and principles of things. If religion had spoken out and told us it was just that all men should receive the supply of their wants, we should presently have been led to suspect that a gratuitous distribution to be made by the rich was a very indirect and ineffectual way of arriving at this object. The experience of all ages has taught us that this system is productive only of a very precarious supply. The principal object which it seems to propose is to place this supply in the disposal of a few, enabling them to make a show of generosity with what is not truly their own, and to purchase the gratitude of the poor

* I Cor. III. 1, 2.

by the payment of a debt. It is a system of clemency and charity instead of a system of justice. It fills the rich with unreasonable pride by the spurious denominations with which it decorates their acts, and the poor with servility by leading them to regard the slender comforts they obtain, not as their incontrovertible due, but as the good pleasure and the grace of their opulent neighbours.

Benefits Arising from the Genuine System of Property

Having seen the justice of an equal distribution of property, let us next consider the benefits with which it would be attended. And here with grief it must be confessed that, however great and extensive are the evils that are produced by monarchies and courts, by the imposture of priests and the iniquity of criminal laws, all these are imbecile and impotent compared with the evils that arise out of the established system of property.

Its first effect is that which we have already mentioned, a sense of dependence. It is true that courts are mean-spirited, intriguing and servile, and that this disposition is transferred by contagion from them to all ranks of society. But property brings home a servile and truckling spirit by no circuitous method to every house in the nation. Observe the pauper fawning with abject vileness upon his rich benefactor, and speechless with sensations of gratitude for having received that which he ought to have claimed with an erect mien and with a consciousness that his claim was irresistible. Observe the servants that follow in a rich man's train, watchful of his looks, anticipating his commands, not daring to reply to his insolence, all their time and their efforts under the direction of his caprice. Observe the tradesman, how he studies the passions of his customers, not to correct, but to pamper them, the vileness of his flattery and the systematical constancy with which he exaggerates the merit of his commodities. Observe the practices of a popular election, where the great mass are purchased by obsequiousness, by intemperance and bribery, or driven by unmanly threats of poverty and persecution. Indeed "the age of chivalry is" not "gone"!* The feudal spirit still survives, that reduced the great mass of mankind to the rank of slaves and cattle for the service of a few.

We have heard much of visionary and theoretical improvements. It would indeed be visionary and theoretical to expect virtue from mankind while they are thus subjected to hourly corruption and bred

* Burke's *Reflections*.

from father to son to sell their independence and their conscience for the vile rewards that oppression has to bestow. No man can be either useful to others or happy to himself who is a stranger to the grace of firmness and who is not habituated to prefer the dictates of his own sense of rectitude to all the tyranny of command and allurements of temptation. Here again, as upon a former occasion, religion comes in to illustrate our thesis. Religion was the generous ebullition of men who let their imagination loose on the grandest subjects and wandered without restraint in the unbounded field of enquiry. It is not to be wondered at therefore if they brought home imperfect ideas of the sublimest views that intellect can furnish. In this instance religion teaches that the true perfection of man is to divest himself of the influence of passions; that he must have no artificial wants, no sensuality, and no fear. But to divest the human species under the present system of the influence of passions is an extravagant speculation. The enquirer after truth and the benefactor of mankind will be desirous of removing from them those external impressions by which their evil propensities are cherished. The true object that should be kept in view is to extirpate all ideas of condescension and superiority, to oblige every man to feel that the kindness he exerts is what he is bound to perform, and the assistance he asks what he has a right to claim.

A second evil that arises out of the established system of property is the perpetual spectacle of injustice it exhibits. This consists partly in luxury and partly in caprice. There is nothing more pernicious to the human mind than luxury. Mind, being in its own nature essentially active, necessarily fixes on some object public or personal, and in the latter case on the attainment of some excellence, or something which shall command the esteem and deference of others. No propensity,* absolutely considered, can be more valuable than this. But the established system of property directs it into the channel of the acquisition of wealth. The ostentation of the rich perpetually goads the spectator to the desire of opulence. Wealth, by the sentiments of servility and dependence it produces, makes the rich man stand forward as the only object of general esteem and deference. In vain are sobriety, integrity and industry, in vain the sublimest powers of mind and the most ardent benevolence if their possessor be narrowed in his circumstances. To acquire wealth and to display it is therefore the universal passion. The whole structure of human society is made a system of the narrowest selfishness. If self-love and benevolence were apparently reconciled as to their object, a man

* Second and third editions: "Few propensities," etc.

might set out with the desire of eminence and yet every day become more generous and philanthropical in his views. But the passion we are here describing is accustomed to be gratified at every step by inhumanly trampling upon the interest of others. Wealth is acquired by overreaching our neighbours and is spent in insulting them.

The spectacle of injustice which the established system of property exhibits consists partly in caprice. If you would cherish in any man the love of rectitude, you must take care that its principles be impressed on him not only by words, but actions. It sometimes happens during the period of education that maxims of integrity and consistency are repeatedly enforced, and that the preceptor gives no quarter to the base suggestions of selfishness and cunning. But how is the lesson that has been read to the pupil confounded and reversed when he enters upon the scene of the world? If he ask, "Why is this man honoured?" the ready answer is "Because he is rich." If he enquire farther, "Why is he rich?" the answer in most cases is "From the accident of birth, or from a minute and sordid attention to the cares of gain." The system of accumulated property is the offspring of civil policy; and civil policy, as we are taught to believe, is the production of accumulated wisdom. Thus the wisdom of legislators and senates has been employed to secure a distribution of property the most profligate and unprincipled, that bids defiance to the maxims of justice and the nature of man. Humanity weeps over the distresses of the peasantry of all civilised nations; and when she turns from this spectacle to behold the luxury of their lords, gross, imperious and prodigal, her sensations certainly are not less acute. This spectacle is the school in which mankind have been educated. They have been accustomed to the sight of injustice, oppression and iniquity till their feelings are made callous and their understandings incapable of apprehending the nature of true virtue.

In beginning to point out the evils of accumulated property we compared the extent of those evils with the correspondent evils of monarchies and courts. No circumstances under the latter have excited a more pointed disapprobation than pensions and pecuniary corruption, by means of which hundreds of individuals are rewarded, not for serving, but betraying the public, and the hard earnings of industry are employed to fatten the servile adherents of despotism. But the rent roll of the lands of England is a much more formidable pension list than that which is supposed to be employed in the purchase of ministerial majorities. All riches, and especially all hereditary riches, are to be considered as the salary of a sinecure office, where the labourer and the manufacturer perform the duties, and the principal spends the income in luxury and idleness.* Hereditary wealth is in reality a premium paid to idleness, an immense annuity expended to retain mankind in brutality and ignorance. The poor are kept in ignorance by the want of leisure. The rich are furnished indeed with the means of cultivation and literature, but they are paid for being dissipated and indolent. The most powerful means that malignity could have invented are employed to prevent them from improving their talents and becoming useful to the public.

This leads us to observe, thirdly, that the established system of property is the true levelling system with respect to the human species, by as much as the cultivation of intellect and truth is more valuable and more characteristic of man than the gratifications of vanity or appetite. Accumulated property treads the powers of thought in the dust, extinguishes the sparks of genius, and reduces the great mass of mankind to be immersed in sordid cares; beside depriving the rich, as we have already said, of the most salubrious and effectual motives to activity. If superfluity were banished, the necessity for the greater part of the manual industry of mankind would be superseded; and the rest, being amicably shared among all the active and vigorous members of the community, would be

---

* This idea is to be found in Ogilvie's Essay on the Right of Property in Land . . . , Part I, Sec. iii, par. 38, 39. The reasonings of this author have sometimes considerable merit, though he has by no means gone to the source of the evil.

It might be amusing to some readers to recollect the authorities, if the citation of authorities were a proper mode of reasoning, by which the system of accumulated property is openly attacked. The best known is Plato in his treatise of a Republic. His steps have been followed by Sir Thomas More in his *Utopia*. Specimens of very powerful reasoning on the same side may be found in *Gulliver's Travels*, particularly Part IV, Chap. VI. Mably, in his book *De la Législation*, has displayed at large the advantages of equality, and then quits the subject in despair from an opinion of the incorrigibleness of human depravity. Wallace, the contemporary and antagonist of Hume, in a treatise entitled *Various Prospects of Mankind, Nature and Providence*, is copious in his eulogium of the same system, and deserts it only from fear of the earth becoming too populous. . . . The great practical authorities are Crete, Sparta, Peru and Paraguay. It would be easy to swell this list if we added examples where an approach only to these principles was attempted, and authors who have incidentally confirmed a doctrine so interesting and clear as never to have been wholly eradicated from any human understanding.

It would be trifling to object that the systems of Plato and others are full of imperfections. This indeed rather strengthens their authority, since the evidence of the truth they maintained was so great as still to preserve its hold on their understandings, though they knew not how to remove the difficulties that attended it.

burthensome to none. Every man would have a frugal yet whole-some diet; every man would go forth to that moderate exercise of his corporal functions that would give hilarity to the spirits; none would be made torpid with fatigue, but all would have leisure to cultivate the kindly and philanthropical affections of the soul and to let loose his faculties in the search of intellectual improvement. What a con-trast does this scene present us with the present state of human so-ciety, where the peasant and the labourer work till their understand-ings are benumbed with toil, their sinews contracted and made cal-lous by being forever on the stretch, and their bodies invaded with infirmities and surrendered to an untimely grave? What is the fruit of this disproportioned and unceasing toil? At evening they return to a family famished with hunger, exposed half-naked to the inclemencies of the sky, hardly sheltered, and denied the slenderest instruction, unless in a few instances where it is dispensed by the hands of osten-tatious charity and the first lesson communicated is unprincipled servility. All this while their rich neighbour—but we visited him be-fore.

How rapid and sublime would be the advances of intellect if all men were admitted into the field of knowledge! At present ninety-nine persons in an hundred are no more excited to any regular exer-tions of general and curious thought than the brutes themselves. What would be the state of public mind in a nation where all were wise, all had laid aside the shackles of prejudice and implicit faith, all adopted with fearless confidence the suggestions of truth, and the lethargy of the soul was dismissed for ever? It is to be presumed that the inequality of mind would in a certain degree be permanent; but it is reasonable to believe that the geniuses of such an age would far surpass the grandest exertions of intellect that are at present known. Genius would not be depressed with false wants and niggardly pa-tronage. It would not exert itself with a sense of neglect and oppres-sion rankling in its bosom. It would be freed from those apprehen-sions that perpetually recall us to the thought of personal emolument, and of consequence would expatiate freely among sentiments of gen-erosity and public good.

From ideas of intellectual let us turn to moral improvement. And here it is obvious that all the occasions of crime would be cut off for ever. . . .

The fruitful source of crimes consists in this circumstance, one man's possessing in abundance that of which another man is destitute. We must change the nature of mind before we can prevent it from being powerfully influenced by this circumstance, when brought strongly home to its perceptions by the nature of its situation. Man must cease to have senses, the pleasures of appetite and vanity must cease to gratify, before he can look on tamely at the monopoly of these pleasures. He must cease to have a sense of justice before he can clearly and fully approve this mixed scene of superfluity and distress. It is true that the proper method of curing this inequality is by reason and not by violence. But the immediate tendency of the established system is to persuade men that reason is impotent. The injustice of which they complain is upheld by force, and they are too easily induced by force to attempt its correction. All they endeavour is the partial correction of an injustice which education tells them is necessary, but more powerful reason affirms to be tyrannical.

Force grew out of monopoly. It might accidentally have occurred among savages whose appetites exceeded their supply, or whose passions were inflamed by the presence of the object of their desire; but it would gradually have died away as reason and civilisation advanced. Accumulated property has fixed its empire, and henceforth all is an open contention of the strength and cunning of one party against the strength and cunning of the other. In this case the violent and premature struggles of the necessitous are undoubtedly an evil. They tend to defeat the very cause in the success of which they are most deeply interested; they tend to procrastinate the triumph of truth. But the true crime is in the malevolent and partial propensities of men, thinking only of themselves and despising the emolument of others; and of these the rich have their share.

The spirit of oppression, the spirit of servility and the spirit of fraud, these are the immediate growth of the established system of property. These are alike hostile to intellectual and moral improvement. The other vices of envy, malice and revenge are their inseparable companions. In a state of society where men lived in the midst of plenty and where all shared alike the bounties of nature these sentiments would inevitably expire. The narrow principle of selfishness would vanish. No man being obliged to guard his little store, or provide with anxiety and pain for his restless wants, each would lose his own individual existence in the thought of the general good. No man would be an enemy to his neighbour, for they would have nothing for which to contend; and of consequence philanthropy would resume the empire which reason assigns her. Mind would be delivered from her perpetual anxiety about corporal support and free to expatiate in the field of thought which is congenial to her. Each man would assist the enquiries of all.

Let us fix our attention for a moment upon the revolution of principles and habits that immediately grow out of an unequal distribution of property. Till it was thus distributed men felt what their wants required and sought the supply of those wants. All that was more than this was regarded as indifferent. But no sooner is accumulation introduced than they begin to study a variety of methods for disposing of their superfluity with least emolument to their neighbour, or in other words by which it shall appear to be most their own. They do not long continue to buy commodities before they begin to buy men. He that possesses or is the spectator of superfluity soon discovers the hold which it affords us on the minds of others. Hence the passions of vanity and ostentation. Hence the despotic manners of them who recollect with complacence the rank they occupy, and the restless ambition of those whose attention is engrossed by the possible future.

Ambition is of all the passions of the human mind the most extensive in its ravages. It adds district to district, and kingdom to kingdom. It spreads bloodshed and calamity and conquest over the face of the earth. But the passion itself, as well as the means of gratifying it, is the produce of the prevailing system of property. It is only by means of accumulation that one man obtains an unresisted sway over multitudes of others. It is by means of a certain distribution of income that the present governments of the world are retained in existence. Nothing more easy than to plunge nations so organised into war. But if Europe were at present covered with inhabitants all of them possessing competence and none of them superfluity, what could induce its different countries to engage in hostility? If you would lead men to war, you must exhibit certain allurements. If you be not enabled by a system, already prevailing and which derives force from prescription, to hire them to your purposes, you must bring over each individual by dint of persuasion. How hopeless a task by such means to excite mankind to murder each other! It is clear then that war in every horrid form is the growth of unequal property. As long as this source of jealousy and corruption shall remain, it is visionary to talk of universal peace. As soon as the source shall be dried up, it will be impossible to exclude the consequence. It is property* that forms men into one common mass and makes them fit to be played upon like a brute machine. Were this stumbling block removed, each man would be united to his neighbour in love and mutual kindness a thousand times more than now; but each man would think and judge for himself. Let then the advocates for the prevailing system at least consider what it is for which they plead and be well assured that they

---

* Second and third editions: "It is accumulation," etc.

have arguments in its favour which will weigh against these disadvantages.

There is one other circumstance which, though inferior to those above enumerated, deserves to be mentioned. This is population. It has been calculated that the average cultivation of Europe might be improved so as to maintain five times her present number of inhabitants.* There is a principle in human society by which population is perpetually kept down to the level of the means of subsistence. Thus among the wandering tribes of America and Asia we never find through the lapse of ages that population has so increased as to render necessary the cultivation of the earth. Thus among the civilised nations of Europe by means of territorial monopoly the sources of subsistence are kept within a certain limit, and if the population became overstocked, the lower ranks of the inhabitants would be still more incapable of procuring for themselves the necessaries of life. There are no doubt extraordinary concurrences of circumstances by means of which changes are occasionally introduced in this respect, but in ordinary cases the standard of population is held in a manner stationary for centuries. Thus the established system of property may be considered as strangling a considerable portion of our children in their cradle. Whatever may be the value of the life of man, or rather whatever would be his capability of happiness in a free and equal state of society, the system we are here opposing may be considered as arresting upon the threshold of existence four fifths of that value and that happiness.

* Ogilvie, Part I, Sect. iii, par. 35.

Robert Owen

1770–1857

The son of a Welsh artisan, Robert Owen was a fascinating mixture of social reformer, utopian planner, and highly successful businessman. By the time he was a young man of thirty, he was already a director of the New Lanark mills. There he introduced a wide variety of technical improvements and organizational changes to the great profit of the stockholders. And there also he erected model dwellings for his workmen, introduced more humane techniques of factory discipline, and educated the children of his employees on progressive theories. These experiments made New Lanark famous and a stream of visitors came to see how Owen operated both his factory and his community.

It was at New Lanark that Owen developed theories that sounded revolutionary to fellow employers: reduction of working hours from seventeen to ten, refusal to employ children under ten, free education in schools built at his expense, and abolition of fines in his workshops. Owen's answer to his critics was a clear common-sense statement of the proposition that humane treatment increases worker productivity:

> *Experience must have taught you the difference between an efficiently equipped factory with its machinery always clean and in good working order and one in which the machinery is filthy and out of repair and working only with the greatest amount of friction. Now if the care which you bestow upon machinery can give you such excellent results, may you not expect equally good results from care spent upon human beings, with their infinitely superior structure? Is it not quite natural to conclude that these infinitely more delicate and complex mechanisms will also increase in force and efficiency and will really be much more economical if they are kept in good working condition and treated with a certain measure of*

320

*kindness? Such kindness would do much to remove the mental fric-
tion and irritation which always results whenever the nourishment is
insufficient to keep the body in full productive efficiency, as well as
to arrest deterioration and to prevent premature death.*

*The successful organization of New Lanark as a model community
under the guidance of a benevolent despot, Owen himself, was only
the first of Owen's careers. In the second of them, he dabbled in the
founding of model communities, organized in imitation of New Lanark
and in extension of its principles. Orbiston in Scotland and New Harmony in Indiana were both Owenite communities begun in the same
year, 1825, and lasting only a few years before dissension and disorder forced their dissolution. Nothing daunted, at the age of sixty-
three Owen turned to the third and the last of his careers, his association with the trade-union movement. His name is also linked with the
Rochdale experiment in co-operation.*

It was a great career, the life of a dedicated crank of genius. His
A New View of Society *dates from his New Lanark period. It is a
triumphant, didactic statement of the principles his experience had
taught him. It was utterly plain to him that character depended entirely upon the appropriate associations that an individual encountered. Hence it was very easy by proper education to train a
child to be a useful citizen of his community. It was even possible, as
Owen himself had demonstrated, to take mature operatives, beset by
the malingering, ignorance, and drunkenness which their previous
associations had exposed them to, and yet make of them decent,
sober, and ambitious artisans. Owen's claim is sweeping:* "Any general character, from the best to the worst, from the most ignorant to
the most enlightened, may be given to any community, even to the
world at large, by the application of proper means, which means are
to a great extent at the command and under the control of those who
have influence in the affairs of men." *Even the world at large!*

The present selection is from A New View of Society *(Everyman
edition, 1927), pp. 137-50.*

Education and Happiness

According to the last returns under the Population Act, the poor and
working classes of Great Britain and Ireland have been found to exceed fifteen millions of persons, or nearly three-fourths of the population of the British Islands.

The characters of these persons are now permitted to be very generally formed without proper guidance or direction, and, in many cases, under circumstances which directly impel them to a course of extreme vice and misery; thus rendering them the worst and most dangerous subjects in the empire; while the far greater part of the remainder of the community are educated upon the most mistaken principles of human nature, such, indeed, as cannot fail to produce a general conduct throughout society, totally unworthy of the character of rational beings.

The first thus unhappily situated are the poor and the uneducated profligate among the working classes, who are now trained to commit crimes, for the commission of which they are afterwards punished.

The second is the remaining mass of the population, who are now instructed to believe, or at least to acknowledge, that certain principles are unerringly true, and to act as though they were grossly false; thus filling the world with folly and inconsistency, and making society, throughout all its ramifications, a scene of insincerity and counteraction.

In this state the world has continued to the present time; its evils have been and are continually increasing; they cry aloud for efficient corrective measures, which if we longer delay, general disorder must ensue.

"But," say those who have not deeply investigated the subject, "attempts to apply remedies have been often made, yet all of them have failed. The evil is now of a magnitude not to be controlled; the torrent is already too strong to be stemmed; and we can only wait with fear or calm resignation to see it carry destruction in its course, by confounding all distinctions of right and wrong."

Such is the language now held, and such are the general feelings on this most important subject.

These, however, if longer suffered to continue, must lead to the most lamentable consequences. Rather than pursue such a course, the character of legislators would be infinitely raised, if, forgetting the petty and humiliating contentions of sects and parties, they would thoroughly investigate the subject, and endeavour to arrest and overcome these mighty evils.

The chief object of these Essays is to assist and forward investigations of such vital importance to the well-being of this country, and of society in general.

The view of the subject which is about to be given has arisen from extensive experience for upwards of twenty years, during which period its truth and importance have been proved by multiplied experiments. That the writer may not be charged with precipitation or presumption, he has had the principle and its consequences examined, scrutinised, and fully canvassed, by some of the most learned, intelligent, and competent characters of the present day: who, on every principle of duty as well as of interest, if they had discovered error in either, would have exposed it—but who, on the contrary, have fairly acknowledged their incontrovertible truth and practical importance.

Assured, therefore, that his principles are true, he proceeds with confidence, and courts the most ample and free discussion of the subject; courts it for the sake of humanity—for the sake of his fellow creatures—millions of whom experience sufferings which, were they to be unfolded, would compel those who govern the world to exclaim —"Can these things exist and we have no knowledge of them?" But they do exist—and even the heart-rending statements which were made known to the public during the discussions upon Negro slavery, do not exhibit more afflicting scenes than those which, in various parts of the world, daily arise from the injustice of society towards itself; from the inattention of mankind to the circumstances which incessantly surround them; and from the want of a correct knowledge of human nature in those who govern and control the affairs of men.

If these circumstances did not exist to an extent almost incredible, it would be unnecessary now to contend for a principle regarding Man, which scarcely requires more than to be fairly stated to make it self-evident.

This principle is, that *"Any general character, from the best to the worst, from the most ignorant to the most enlightened, may be given to any community, even to the world at large, by the application of proper means; which means are to a great extent at the command and under the control of those who have influence in the affairs of men."*

The principle as now stated is a broad one, and, if it should be found to be true, cannot fail to give a new character to legislative proceedings, and such a character as will be most favourable to the well-being of society.

That this principle is true to the utmost limit of the terms, is evident from the experience of all past ages, and from every existing fact.

Shall misery, then, most complicated and extensive, be experienced, from the prince to the peasant, throughout all the nations of the world, and shall its cause and the means of its prevention be known, and yet these means withheld? The undertaking is replete with difficulties which can only be overcome by those who have influence in society: who, by foreseeing its important practical benefits, may be induced to contend against those difficulties; and who, when its advantages are clearly seen and strongly felt, will not suffer individual considerations to be put in competition with their attainment. It is true their ease and comfort may be for a time sacrificed to those prejudices; but, if they persevere, the principles on which this knowledge is founded must ultimately universally prevail.

In preparing the way for the introduction of these principles, it cannot now be necessary to enter into the detail of facts to prove that children can be trained to acquire *"any language, sentiments, belief, or any bodily habits and manners, not contrary to human nature."*

For that this has been done, the history of every nation of which we have records, abundantly confirms; and that this is, and may be again done, the facts which exist around us and throughout all the countries in the world, prove to demonstration.

Possessing, then, the knowledge of a power so important, which, when understood, is capable of being wielded with the certainty of a law of nature, and which would gradually remove the evils which now chiefly afflict mankind, shall we permit it to remain dormant and useless, and suffer the plagues of society perpetually to exist and increase?

No: the time is now arrived when the public mind of this country, and the general state of the world, call imperatively for the introduction of this all-pervading principle, not only in theory, but into practice.

Nor can any human power now impede its rapid progress. Silence will not retard its course, and opposition will give increased celerity to its movements. The commencement of the work will, in fact, ensure its accomplishment; henceforth all the irritating angry passions, arising from ignorance of the true cause of bodily and mental character, will gradually subside, and be replaced by the most frank and conciliating confidence and goodwill.

Nor will it be possible hereafter for comparatively a few individuals, unintentionally to occasion the rest of mankind to be surrounded by circumstances which inevitably form such characters as they afterwards deem it a duty and a right to punish even to death; and that, too, while they themselves have been the instruments of forming those characters. Such proceedings not only create innumerable evils to the directing few, but essentially retard them and the great mass of society from attaining the enjoyment of a high degree of positive happiness. Instead of punishing crimes after they have permitted the human character to be formed so as to commit them, they will adopt the only means which can be adopted to prevent the existence of those crimes; means by which they may be most easily prevented.

Happily for poor traduced and degraded human nature, the principle for which we now contend will speedily divest it of all the ridiculous and absurd mystery with which it has been hitherto enveloped by the ignorance of preceding times: and all the complicated and counteracting motives for good conduct, which have been multiplied almost to infinity, will be reduced to one single principle of action, which, by its evident operation and sufficiency, shall render this intricate system unnecessary, and ultimately supersede it in all parts of the earth. That principle is *the happiness of self, clearly understood and uniformly practised; which can only be attained by conduct that must promote the happiness of the community.*

For that Power which governs and pervades the universe has evidently so formed man, that he must progressively pass from a state of ignorance to intelligence, the limits of which it is not for man himself to define; and in that progress to discover, that his individual happiness can be increased and extended only in proportion as he actively endeavours to increase and extend the happiness of all around him. The principle admits neither of exclusion nor of limitation; and such appears evidently the state of the public mind, that it will now seize and cherish this principle as the most precious boon which it has yet been allowed to attain. The errors of all opposing motives will appear in their true light, and the ignorance whence they arose will become so glaring, that even the most unenlightened will speedily reject them.

For this state of matters, and for all the gradual changes contemplated, the extraordinary events of the present times have essentially contributed to prepare the way.

Even the late Ruler of France, although immediately influenced by the most mistaken principles of ambition, has contributed to this happy result, by shaking to its foundation that mass of superstition and bigotry, which on the continent of Europe had been accumulating for ages, until it had so overpowered and depressed the human intellect, that to attempt improvement without its removal would have been most unavailing. And in the next place, by carrying the mistaken selfish principles in which mankind have been hitherto educated to the extreme in practice, he has rendered their error manifest, and left no doubt of the fallacy of the source whence they originated.

These transactions, in which millions have been immolated, or consigned to poverty and bereft of friends, will be preserved in the records of time, and impress future ages with a just estimation of the principles now about to be introduced into practice; and will thus prove perpetually useful to all succeeding generations.

For the direful effects of Napoleon's government have created the most deep-rooted disgust at notions which could produce a belief that such conduct was glorious, or calculated to increase the happiness of even the individual by whom it was pursued.

And the late discoveries and proceedings of the Rev. Dr. Bell and Mr. Joseph Lancaster have also been preparing the way, in a manner the most opposite, but yet not less effectual, by directing the public attention to the beneficial effects, on the young and unresisting mind, of even the limited education which their systems embrace.

They have already effected enough to prove that all which is now in contemplation respecting the training of youth may be accomplished without fear of disappointment. And by so doing, as the consequences of their improvements cannot be confined within the British Isles, they will for ever be ranked among the most important benefactors of the human race. But henceforward to contend for any new exclusive system will be in vain: the public mind is already too well informed, and has too far passed the possibility of retrogression, much longer to permit the continuance of any such evil.

For it is now obvious that such a system must be destructive of the happiness of the excluded, by their seeing others enjoy what they are not permitted to possess; and also that it tends, by creating opposition from the justly injured feelings of the excluded, in proportion to the extent of the exclusion, to diminish the happiness even of the privileged: the former therefore can have no rational motive for its continuance.

If, however, owing to the irrational principles by which the world has been hitherto governed, individuals, or sects, or parties, shall yet by their plans of exclusion attempt to retard the amelioration of society, and prevent the introduction into PRACTICE of that truly just spirit which knows no exclusion, such facts shall yet be brought forward as cannot fail to render all their efforts vain.

It will therefore be the essence of wisdom in the privileged class to co-operate sincerely and cordially with those who desire not to touch one iota of the supposed advantages which they now possess; and whose first and last wish is to increase the particular happiness of those classes, as well as the general happiness of society. A very little reflection on the part of the privileged will ensure this line of conduct; whence, without domestic revolution—without war or bloodshed—nay, without prematurely disturbing any thing which exists, the world will be prepared to receive principles which are alone calculated to build up a system of happiness, and to destroy those irritable feelings which have so long afflicted society—solely because society has hitherto been ignorant of the true means by which the most useful and valuable character may be formed.

This ignorance being removed, experience will soon teach us how to form character, individually and generally, so as to give the greatest sum of happiness to the individual and to mankind.

These principles require only to be known in order to establish themselves; the outline of our future proceedings then becomes clear and defined, nor will they permit us henceforth to wander from the right path. They direct that the governing powers of all countries should establish rational plans for the education and general formation of the characters of their subjects. *These plans must be devised to train children from their earliest infancy in good habits of every description (which will of course prevent them from acquiring those of falsehood and deception). They must afterwards be rationally educated, and their labour be usefully directed. Such habits and education will impress them with an active and ardent desire to promote the happiness of every individual, and that without the shadow of exception for sect, or party, or country, or climate. They will also ensure, with the fewest possible exceptions, health, strength, and vigour of body; for the happiness of man can be erected only on the foundations of health of body and peace of mind.*

And that health of body and peace of mind may be preserved sound and entire, through youth and manhood, to old age, it becomes equally necessary that the irresistible propensities which form a part of his nature, and which now produce the endless and ever multiplying evils with which humanity is afflicted, should be so directed as to increase and not to counteract his happiness.

The knowledge, however, thus introduced will make it evident to the understanding, that by far the greater part of the misery with which man is encircled *may* be easily dissipated and removed; and that with mathematical precision he *may* be surrounded with those circumstances which must gradually increase his happiness.

Hereafter, when the public at large shall be satisfied that these principles *can* and *will* withstand the ordeal through which they must inevitably pass; when they shall prove themselves true to the clear comprehension and certain conviction of the unenlightened as well as the learned; and when, by the irresistible power of truth, detached from falsehood, they shall establish themselves in the mind, no more to be removed but by the entire annihilation of human intellect; then the consequent practice which they direct shall be explained, and rendered easy of adoption.

In the meantime, let no one anticipate evil, even in the slightest degree, from these principles; they are not innoxious only but pregnant with consequences to be wished and desired beyond all others by *every* individual in society.

Some of the best intentioned among the various classes in society may still say, "All this is *very delightful and very beautiful in theory*, but *visionaries* alone expect to see it *realized*." To this remark only one reply *can* or *ought* to be made; that *these principles have been carried most successfully into practice.*

(The beneficial effects of this practice have been experienced for many years among a population of between two and three thousand at New Lanark, in Scotland; at Munich, in Bavaria; and in the Pauper Colonies at Fredericks-oord.)

The present Essays, therefore, are not brought forward as mere matter of speculation, to amuse the idle visionary who *thinks* in his closet, and never *acts* in the world; but to create universal activity, pervade society with a knowledge of its true interests, and direct the public mind to the most important object to which it can be directed —to a national proceeding for rationally forming the character of that immense mass of population which is now allowed to be so formed as to fill the world with crimes.

Shall questions of merely local and temporary interest, whose ultimate results are calculated only to withdraw pecuniary profits from one set of individuals and give them to others, engage day after day the attention of politicians and ministers; call forth petitions and delegates from the widely spread agricultural and commercial interests of the empire—and shall the well-being of millions of the poor, half-naked, half-famished, untaught, and untrained, hourly increasing to a most alarming extent in these islands, not call forth *one* petition, *one* delegate, or *one* rational effective legislative measure?

No! for such has been our education, that we hesitate not to devote years and expend millions in the *detection* and *punishment* of crimes, and in the attainment of objects whose ultimate results are, in comparison with this, insignificancy itself: and yet we have not moved one step in the true path to *prevent* crimes, and to diminish the innumerable evils with which mankind are now afflicted.

Are these false principles of conduct in those who govern the world to influence mankind permanently? And if not, *how,* and *when* is the change to commence?

THE PRINCIPLES OF THE FORMER ESSAYS APPLIED
TO A PARTICULAR SITUATION.

"Truth must ultimately prevail over error."

At the conclusion of the Second Essay, a promise was made that an account should be given of the plans which were in progress at New Lanark for the further improvement of its inhabitants; and that a practical system should be sketched, by which equal advantages might be generally introduced among the poor and working classes throughout the United Kingdom.

This account became necessary, in order to exhibit even a limited view of the principles on which the plans of the author are founded, and to recommend them generally to practice.

That which has been hitherto done for the community at New Lanark, as described in the Second Essay, has chiefly consisted in *withdrawing some of those circumstances which tended to generate, continue, or increase early bad habits; that is to say, undoing that which society had from ignorance permitted to be done.*

To effect this, however, was a far more difficult task than to train up a child from infancy in the way he should go; for that is the most easy process for the formation of character; while to unlearn and to change long acquired habits is a proceeding directly opposed to the most tenacious feelings of human nature.

Nevertheless, the proper application steadily pursued did effect beneficial changes on these old habits, even beyond the most sanguine expectations of the party by whom the task was undertaken.

The principles were derived from the study of human nature itself, and they could not fail of success.

Still, however, very little, comparatively speaking, had been done for them. They had not been taught the most valuable domestic and social habits: such as the most economical method of preparing food; how to arrange their dwellings with neatness, and to keep them always clean and in order; but, what was of infinitely more importance, they had not been instructed how to train their children to form them into valuable members of the community, or to know that principles existed, which, when properly applied to practice from infancy, would ensure from man to man, without chance of failure, a just, open, sincere, and benevolent conduct.

It was in this stage of the progress of improvement, that it became necessary to form arrangements for surrounding them with circumstances which should gradually prepare the individuals to receive and firmly retain those domestic and social acquirements and habits. For this purpose a building, which may be termed the "New Institution," was erected in the centre of the establishment, with an enclosed area before it. The area is intended for a playground for the children of the villagers, from the time they can walk alone until they enter the school.

It must be evident to those who have been in the practice of observing children with attention, that much of good or evil is taught to or acquired by a child at a very early period of its life; that much of temper or disposition is correctly or incorrectly formed before he attains his second year; and that many durable impressions are made at the termination of the first twelve or even six months of his existence. The children, therefore, of the uninstructed and ill-instructed, suffer material injury in the formation of their characters during these and the subsequent years of childhood and of youth.

It was to prevent, or as much as possible to counteract, these primary evils, to which the poor and working classes are exposed when infants, that the area became part of the New Institution.

Into this playground the children are to be received as soon as they can freely walk alone; to be superintended by persons instructed to take charge of them.

As the happiness of man chiefly, if not altogether, depends on his own sentiments and habits, as well as those of the individuals around him; and as any sentiments and habits may be given to all infants, it becomes of primary importance that those alone should be given to them which can contribute to their happiness. Each child, therefore, on his entrance into the playground, is to be told in language which he can understand, that "he is never to injure his play-fellows; but that, on the contrary, he is to contribute all in his power to make them happy." This simple precept, when comprehended in all its bearings, and the habits which will arise from its early adoption into practice, *if no counteracting principle be forced upon the young mind,* will effectually supersede all the errors which have hitherto kept the world in ignorance and misery. So simple a precept, too, will be easily taught, and as easily acquired; for the chief employment of the superintendents will be to prevent any deviation from it in practice. The older children, when they shall have experienced the endless advantages from acting on this principle, will, by their example, soon enforce the practice of it on the young strangers: and the happiness which the little groups will enjoy from this rational conduct, will ensure its speedy and general and willing adoption. The habit also which they will acquire at this early period of life by continually acting on the principle, will fix it firmly; it will become easy and familiar to them, or, as it is often termed, natural.

Thus, by merely attending to the evidence of our senses respecting human nature, and disregarding the wild, inconsistent, and absurd theories in which man has been hitherto trained in all parts of the earth, we shall accomplish with ease and certainty the supposed Herculean labour of forming a rational character in man, and that, too, chiefly before the child commences the ordinary course of education.

The character thus early formed will be as durable as it will be advantageous to the individual and to the community; for by the constitution of our nature, when once the mind fully understands that which is true, the impression of that truth cannot be erased except by mental disease or death; while error must be relinquished at every period of life, whenever it can be made manifest to the mind in which it has been received. This part of the arrangement, therefore, will effect the following purposes:

The child will be removed, so far as is at present practicable, from the erroneous treatment of the yet untrained and untaught parents.

The parents will be relieved from the loss of time and from the care and anxiety which are now occasioned by attendance on their children from the period when they can go alone to that at which they enter the school.

The child will be placed in a situation of safety, where, with its future school-fellows and companions, it will acquire the best habits and principles, while at meal times and at night it will return to the caresses of its parents; and the affections of each are likely to be increased by the separation.

The area is also to be a place of meeting for the children from five to ten years of age, previous to and after school-hours, and to serve for a drill ground, the object of which will be hereafter explained; and a shade will be formed, under which in stormy weather the children may retire for shelter.

These are the important purposes to which a playground attached to a school may be applied.

Those who have derived a knowledge of human nature from observation, know, that man in every situation requires relaxation from his constant and regular occupations, whatever they be: and that if he shall not be provided with or permitted to enjoy innocent and uninjurious amusements, he must and will partake of those which he can obtain, to give him temporary relief from his exertions, although the means of gaining that relief should be most pernicious. For man, irrationally instructed, is ever influenced far more by immediate feelings than by remote considerations.

Those, then, who desire to give mankind the character which it would be for the happiness of all that they should possess, will not fail to make careful provision for their amusement and recreation.

The Sabbath was originally so intended. It was instituted to be a day of universal enjoyment and happiness to the human race. It is frequently made, however, from the opposite extremes of error, either a day of superstitious gloom and tyranny over the mind, or of the most destructive intemperance and licentiousness. The one of these has been the cause of the other; the latter the certain and natural consequence of the former. Relieve the human mind from useless and superstitious restraints; train it on those principles which facts, ascertained from the first knowledge of time to this day, demonstrate to be the only principles which are true; and intemperance and licentiousness will not exist; for such conduct in itself is neither the immediate nor the future interest of man; and he is ever governed by one or other of these considerations, according to the habits which have been given to him from infancy.

The Sabbath, in many parts of Scotland, is not a day of innocent and cheerful recreation to the labouring man; nor can those who are confined all the week to sedentary occupations, freely partake, without censure, of the air and exercise to which nature invites them, and which their health demands.

The errors of the times of superstition and bigotry still hold some sway, and compel those who wish to preserve a regard to their respectability in society, to an overstrained demeanour; and this demeanour sometimes degenerates into hypocrisy and is often the cause of great inconsistency. It is destructive of every open, honest, generous, and manly feeling. It disgusts many, and drives them to the opposite extreme. It is sometimes the cause of insanity. It is founded on ignorance, and defeats its own object.

While erroneous customs prevail in any country, it would evince an ignorance of human nature in any individual to offend against them, until he has convinced the community of their error.

To counteract, in some degree, the inconvenience which arose from the misapplication of the Sabbath, it became necessary to introduce on the other days of the week some innocent amusement and recreation for those whose labours were unceasing, and in winter almost uniform. In summer, the inhabitants of the village of New Lanark have their gardens and potato grounds to cultivate; they have

walks laid out to give them health and the habit of being gratified
with the ever-changing scenes of nature—for those scenes afford
not only the most economical, but also the most innocent pleasures
which man can enjoy; and all men may be easily trained to enjoy
them.

In winter the community are deprived of these healthy occupations and amusements; they are employed ten hours and three quarters every day in the week, except Sunday, and generally every individual continues during that time at the same work: and experience has shown that the average health and spirits of the community
are several degrees lower in winter than in summer; and this in part
may be fairly attributed to that cause.

These considerations suggested the necessity of rooms for innocent
amusements and rational recreation.

Many well-intentioned individuals, unaccustomed to witness the
conduct of those among the lower orders who have been rationally
treated and trained, may fancy such an assemblage will necessarily
become a scene of confusion and disorder; instead of which, however, it proceeds with uniform propriety; it is highly favourable to
the health, spirits, and dispositions of the individuals so engaged; and
if any irregularity should arise, the cause will be solely owing to the
parties who attempt to direct the proceedings being deficient in a
practical knowledge of human nature.

It has been and ever will be found far more easy to lead mankind
to virtue, or to rational conduct, by providing them with well-regulated innocent amusements and recreations, than by forcing them to
submit to useless restraints, which tend only to create disgust, and
often to connect such feelings even with that which is excellent in
itself, merely because it has been judiciously associated.

Hitherto, indeed, in all ages and in all countries, man seems to have
blindly conspired against the happiness of man, and to have remained
as ignorant of himself as he was of the solar system prior to the days
of Copernicus and Galileo.

Many of the learned and wise among our ancestors were conscious
of this ignorance, and deeply lamented its effects; and some of them
recommended the partial adoption of those principles which can
alone relieve the world from the miserable effects of ignorance.

The time, however, for the emancipation of the human mind had
not then arrived: the world was not prepared to receive it. The history
of humanity shows it to be an undeviating law of nature that man
shall not prematurely break the shell of ignorance; that he must pa-
tiently wait until the principle of knowledge has pervaded the whole

mass of the interior, to give it life and strength sufficient to bear the light of day.

Those who have duly reflected on the nature and extent of the mental movements of the world for the last half-century, must be conscious that great changes are in progress; that man is about to advance another important step towards that degree of intelligence which his natural powers seem capable of attaining. Observe the transactions of the passing hours; see the whole mass of mind in full motion; behold it momentarily increasing in vigour, and preparing ere long to burst its confinement. But what is to be the nature of this change? A due attention to the facts around us, and to those transmitted by the invention of printing from former ages, will afford a satisfactory reply.

From the earliest ages it has been the practice of the world to act on the supposition that each individual man forms his own character, and that therefore he is accountable for all his sentiments and habits, and consequently merits reward for some and punishment for others. Every system which has been established among men has been founded on these erroneous principles. When, however, they shall be brought to the test of fair examination, they will be found not only unsupported, but in direct opposition to all experience, and to the evidence of our senses.

This is not a slight mistake, which involves only trivial consequences; it is a fundamental error of the highest possible magnitude; it enters into all our proceedings regarding man from his infancy; and it will be found to be the true and sole origin of evil. It generates and perpetuates ignorance, hatred, and revenge, where, without such error, only intelligence, confidence, and kindness would exist. It has hitherto been the Evil Genius of the world. It severs man from man throughout the various regions of the earth; and makes enemies of those who, but for this gross error, would have enjoyed each other's kind offices and sincere friendship. It is, in short, an error which carries misery in all its consequences.

This error cannot much longer exist; for every day will make it more and more evident *that the character of man is, without a single exception, always formed for him; that it may be, and is, chiefly, created by his predecessors; that they give him, or may give him, his ideas and habits, which are the powers that govern and direct his conduct. Man, therefore, never did, nor is it possible he ever can, form his own character.*

The knowledge of this important fact has not been derived from any of the wild and heated speculations of an ardent and ungoverned imagination; on the contrary, it proceeds from a long and patient study of the theory and practice of human nature, under many varied circumstances; it will be found to be a deduction drawn from such a multiplicity of facts, as to afford the most complete demonstration.

Had not mankind been misinstructed from infancy on this subject, making it necessary that they should unlearn what they have been taught, the simple statement of this truth would render it instantly obvious to every rational mind. Men would know that their predecessors might have given them the habits of ferocious cannibalism, or of the highest known benevolence and intelligence; and by the acquirement of this knowledge they would soon learn that, as parents, preceptors, and legislators united, they possess the means of training the rising generations to either of those extremes; that they may with the greatest certainty make them the conscientious worshippers of Juggernaut, or of the most pure spirit, possessing the essence of every excellence which the human imagination can conceive; that they may train the young to become effeminate, deceitful, ignorantly selfish, intemperate, revengeful, murderous—of course ignorant, irrational, and miserable; or to be manly, just, generous, temperate, active, kind, and benevolent—that is, intelligent, rational, and happy. The knowledge of these principles having been derived from facts which perpetually exist, they defy ingenuity itself to confute them; nay, the most severe scrutiny will make it evident that they are utterly unassailable.

Is it then wisdom to think and to act in opposition to the facts which hourly exhibit themselves around us, and in direct contradiction to the evidence of our senses? Inquire of the most learned and wise of the present day, ask them to speak with sincerity, and they will tell you that they have long known the principles on which society has been founded to be false. Hitherto, however, the tide of public opinion, in all countries, has been directed by a combination of prejudice, bigotry, and fanaticism, derived from the wildest imaginations of ignorance; and the most enlightened men have not dared to expose those errors which to them were offensive, prominent, and glaring.

Happily for man this reign of ignorance rapidly approaches to dissolution; its terrors are already on the wing, and soon they will be compelled to take their flight, never more to return. For now the knowledge of the existing errors is not only possessed by the learned and reflecting, but it is spreading far and wide throughout society; and ere long it will be fully comprehended even by the most ignorant.

Attempts may indeed be made by individuals, who through ignorance mistake their real interests, to retard the progress of this knowledge; but as it will prove itself to be in unison with the evidence of our senses, and therefore true beyond the possibility of disproof, it cannot be impeded, and in its course will overwhelm all opposition.

These principles, however, are not more true in theory than beneficial in practice, whenever they are properly applied. Why, then, should all their substantial advantages be longer withheld from the mass of mankind? Can it, by possibility, be a crime to pursue the only practical means which a rational being can adopt to diminish the misery of man, and increase his happiness?

These questions, of the deepest interest to society, are now brought to the fair test of public experiment. It remains to be proved, whether the character of man shall continue to be formed under the guidance of the most inconsistent notions, the errors of which for centuries past have been manifest to every reflecting rational mind; or whether it shall be moulded under the direction of uniformly consistent principles, derived from the unvarying facts of the creation; principles, the truth of which no sane man will now attempt to deny.

It is then by the full and complete disclosure of these principles, that the destruction of ignorance and misery is to be effected, and the reign of reason, intelligence, and happiness is to be firmly established.

It was necessary to give this development of the principles advocated, that the remaining parts of the New Institution, yet to be described, may be clearly understood. We now proceed to explain the several purposes intended to be accomplished by the School, Lecture Room, and Church.

It must be evident to those who have any powers of reason yet undestroyed, that man is now taught and trained in a theory and practice directly opposed to each other. Hence the perpetual inconsistencies, follies, and absurdities, which every one can readily discover in his neighbour, without being conscious that he also possesses similar incongruities. The instruction to be given in the School, Lecture Room, and Church is intended to counteract and remedy this evil; and to prove the incalculable advantages which society would derive from the introduction of a theory and practice consistent with each other. The uppermost story of the New Institution is arranged to serve for a School, Lecture Room, and Church. And these are intended to have a direct influence in forming the character of the villagers.

It is comparatively of little avail to give to either young or old "precept upon precept, and line upon line," *except the means shall be also prepared to train them in good practical habits.* Hence an education for the untaught and ill-taught becomes of the first importance to the welfare of society; and it is this which has influenced all the arrangements connected with the New Institution.

The time the children will remain under the discipline of the playground and school, will afford all the opportunity that can be desired to create, cultivate, and establish, those habits and sentiments which tend to the welfare of the individual and of the community. And in conformity to this plan of proceeding, the precept which was given to the child of two years old, on coming into the playground, "that he must endeavour to make his companions happy," is to be renewed and enforced on his entrance into the school: and the first duty of the schoolmaster will be to train his pupils to acquire the practice of always acting on this principle. It is a simple rule, the plain and obvious reasons for which children at an early age may be readily taught to comprehend, and as they advance in years, become familiarized with its practice, and experience the beneficial effects to themselves, they will better feel and understand all its important consequences to society.

Such then being the foundation on which the practical habits of the children are to be formed, we proceed to explain the superstructure.

In addition to the knowledge of the principle and practice of the above-mentioned precept, the boys and girls are to be taught to write expeditiously a good legible hand; and to learn correctly, so that they may comprehend and use with facility the fundamental rules of arithmetic. The girls are also to be taught to sew, cut out, and make up useful family garments; and, after acquiring a sufficient knowledge of these, they are to attend in rotation in the public kitchen and eating rooms, to learn to prepare wholesome food in an economical manner, and to keep a house neat and well arranged.

It was said that the children are to be taught to read well, and to understand what they read.

In many schools, the children of the poor and labouring classes are never taught to understand what they read; the time therefore which is occupied in the mockery of instruction is lost. In other schools, the children, through the ignorance of their instructors, are taught to believe without reasoning and thus never to think or to reason correctly. These truly lamentable practices cannot fail to indispose the young mind for plain, simple, and rational instruction.

The books by which it is now the common custom to teach children to read, inform them of anything except that which, at their age, they ought to be taught; hence the inconsistencies and follies of adults. It is full time that this system should be changed. *Can man, when possessing the full vigour of his faculties, form a rational judgment on any subject, until he has first collected all the facts respecting it which are known? Has not this been, and will not this ever remain, the only path by which human knowledge can be obtained?* Then children ought to be instructed on the same principles. They should first be taught the knowledge of facts, commencing with those which are most familiar to the young mind, and gradually proceeding to the most useful and necessary to be known by the respective individuals in the rank of life in which they are likely to be placed; and in all cases the children should have as clear an explanation of each fact as their minds can comprehend, rendering those explanations more detailed as the child acquires strength and capacity of intellect.

As soon as the young mind shall be duly prepared for such instruction, the master should not allow any opportunity to escape, that would enable him to enforce the clear and inseparable connection which exists between the interest and happiness of each individual and the interest and happiness of every other individual. This should be the beginning and end of all instruction; and by degrees it will be so well understood by his pupils, that they will receive the same conviction of its truth, that those familiar with mathematics now entertain of the demonstrations of Euclid. And when thus comprehended, the all-prevailing principle of known life, the desire of happiness, will compel them without deviation to pursue it in practice.

It is much to be regretted that the strength and capacity of the minds of children are yet unknown; their faculties have been hitherto estimated by the folly of the instruction which has been given to them; while, if they were never taught to acquire error, they would speedily exhibit such powers of mind, as would convince the most incredulous how much the human intellect has been injured by the ignorance of former and present treatment.

It is therefore indeed important that the mind from its birth should receive those ideas only which are consistent with each other, which are in unison with all the known facts of the creation, and which are therefore true. Now, however, from the day they are born, the minds of children are impressed with false notions of themselves and of mankind; and in lieu of being conducted into the plain path leading to health and happiness, the utmost pains are taken to compel them to pursue an opposite direction, in which they can attain only inconsistency and error.

Let the plan which has now been recommended be steadily put in practice from infancy, *without counteraction from the systems of education which now exist,* and characters, even in youth, may be formed, that in true knowledge, and in every good and valuable quality, will not only greatly surpass the wise and learned of the present and preceding times, but will appear, as they really will be, a race of rational or superior beings. It is true, this change cannot be instantaneously established; it cannot be created by magic, or by a miracle; it must be effected gradually—and to accomplish it finally will prove a work of labour and of years. For those who have been misinstructed from infancy, who have now influence and are active in the world, and whose activity is directed by the false notions of their forefathers, will of course endeavour to obstruct the change. Those who have been systematically impressed with early errors, and conscientiously think them to be truths, will of necessity, while such errors remain, endeavour to perpetuate them in their children. Some simple but general method, therefore, becomes necessary to counteract as speedily as possible an evil of so formidable a magnitude.

It was this view of the subject which suggested the utility of preparing the means to admit of evening lectures in the New Institution; and it is intended they should be given, during winter, three nights in the week, alternately with dancing.

To the ill-trained and ill-taught these lectures may be made invaluable; and these are now numerous; for the far greater part of the population of the world has been permitted to pass the proper season for instruction without being trained to be rational; and they have acquired only the ideas and habits which proceed from ignorant association and erroneous instruction.

It is intended that the lectures should be familiar discourses, delivered in plain impressive language, to instruct the adult part of the community in the most useful practical parts of knowledge in which they are deficient, particularly in the proper method of training their children to become rational creatures; how to expend the earnings of their own labour to advantage; and how to appropriate the surplus gains which will be left to them, in order to create a fund which will relieve them from the anxious fear of future want, and thus give them, under the many errors of the present system, that rational confidence in their own exertions and good conduct, without which consistency of character or domestic comfort cannot be obtained, and ought not to be expected. The young people may be also questioned relative to their progress in useful knowledge, and allowed to ask for explanations. In short, these lectures may be made to convey, in an amusing and agreeable manner, highly valuable and substantial information to those who are now the most ignorant in the community; and by similar means, which at a trifling expense may be put into action over the whole kingdom, the most important benefits may be given to the labouring classes, and through them, to the whole mass of society.

For it should be considered that *the far greater part of the population belong to or have risen from the labouring classes; and by them the happiness and comfort of all ranks, not excluding the highest, are very essentially influenced:* because even much more of the character of children in all families is formed by the servants, than is ever supposed by those unaccustomed to trace with attention the human mind from earliest infancy. It is indeed impossible that children in any situation can be correctly trained, until those who surround them from infancy shall be previously well-instructed; and the value of good servants may be duly appreciated by those who have experienced the difference between the very good and very bad.

Henri Comte de Saint-Simon

1760–1825

Saint-Simon was born a nobleman, but discarded his title during the French Revolution. In the course of an adventurous life, he fought in the American Revolution, restored his fortunes briefly by land speculation, ended his life in great poverty, and devoted the last portion of it to the promulgation of a messianic conception of a new society. Inevitably he was to be its Messiah. Although he was little read in his own lifetime, he collected a band of faithful disciples and his doctrine in France, and to some degree in England, had considerable influence. In France, Auguste Comte began his career as an avowed follower of Saint-Simon and in England John Stuart Mill credited the movement with bringing home to him a "new mode of political thinking." While as always Mill was unprepared to accompany the Saint-Simonians all the way, especially in their attacks upon property, he professed himself ". . . greatly struck with the connected view which they for the first time presented to me, of the natural order of human progress; and especially with their division of all history into organic periods and critical periods." In the first of these periods, as Mill understood the doctrine, mankind organized its life by some great set of affirmations, some unifying creed. In the critical periods, ". . . mankind lose their old convictions without acquiring any new ones, of a general or authoritative character, except the conviction that the old are false." Christianity inaugurated an organic period, and the Reformation a critical period. Mankind was now awaiting a new organic period, inaugurated under the auspices of Saint-Simon.

The religious overtones of the new revelation testified to some of the instabilities of Saint-Simon's own character. And many of the features of the ideal society that Saint-Simon and his disciples described were wildly utopian. But there were important differences between

341

Saint-Simon's utopia and the utopias that preceded it. Perhaps the most significant was the Saint-Simonian perception of the central place of industry and those who ministered to industry. In fact, Saint-Simon relied upon the unleashed powers of the new technology to keep proletarians contented and intellectuals interested. By placing industry at the center of his scheme, he radically revaluated the social standings of the professions. The following passage gives the flavor of this performance:

> Let us suppose that France suddenly loses fifty of her first-class doctors, fifty first-class chemists, fifty first-class physiologists, fifty first-class bankers, two hundred of her best merchants, six hundred of her foremost agriculturists, five hundred of her most capable ironmasters, etc. . . . Seeing that these men are its most indispensable producers, makers of its most important products, the minute that it loses these the nation will degenerate into a mere soulless body and fall into a state of despicable weakness in the eyes of rival nations, and will remain in this subordinate position so long as the loss remains and their places are vacant.

Such would be the consequence of losing the industrialists, the scientists, and the farmers: men who operate the levers of the new economic machine. What would happen on the different premise that France lost the major members of her Establishment:

> Imagine that France retains all her men of genius, whether in the arts and sciences or in the crafts and industries, but has the misfortune to lose on the same day the king's brother, the Duke of Angoulême, and all the other members of the royal family; all the great officers of the Crown; all ministers of state . . . all the Privy Councillors . . . all the marshals, cardinals, archbishops, bishops, canons . . . all government employees; all the judges; and on top of that a hundred thousand proprietors, the cream of her nobility. Such an overwhelming catastrophe would certainly grieve the French, for they are a kindly-disposed nation. But the loss of a hundred and thirty thousand of the best-reputed individuals in the State would give rise to sorrow of a purely sentimental kind. It would not cause the community the least inconvenience.

In short, government misconceived its objects. Proper government was the administration of industry, of the economy at large. Much that passed for government was, when not actively harmful, at least useless. To Saint-Simon the appropriate place to lodge political power was in a Chamber of Deputies whose representatives were drawn from trade, fabrication, and agriculture, not from the church, the nobility, and the idle rich. Even superior to this Chamber was to be a second body whose membership was restricted to savants, artists, and engineers.

Echoes of these Saint-Simonian positions are not difficult to hear. Engels's government, which administered things rather than men, and much of Sorel's writings explicitly derive from Saint-Simon. And it is possible to identify in the current English discussion over the virtues and failings of "meritocracy" the concern of a nation which is beginning to choose its leaders according to intellectual merit solely.

The passage that follows contains a somewhat naïve discussion of the natural taste among men for equality as well as a typical argument for Saint-Simon's new hierarchical arrangement in the ideal society. It is reprinted with the permission of The Macmillan Company from Selected Writings of Saint-Simon, *translated by F. M. H. Markham. First published in 1953.*

On Social Organization (1825)

The mechanism of social organization was inevitably very complicated so long as the majority of individuals remained in a state of ignorance and improvidence which rendered them incapable of administering their own affairs. In this state of incomplete intellectual development they were swayed by brutal passions which urged them to revolt and every kind of anarchy.

In such a situation, which was the necessary prelude to a better social order, it was necessary for the minority to be organized on military lines, to obtain a monopoly of legislation, and so to keep all power to itself, in order to hold the majority in tutelage and subject the nation to strong discipline. Thus the main energies of the community have till now been directed to maintaining itself as a community, and any efforts directed to improving the moral and physical welfare of the nation have necessarily been regarded as secondary.

To-day this state of affairs can and should be completely altered. The main effort should be directed to the improvement of our moral and physical welfare; only a small amount of force is now required to maintain public order, since the majority have become used to work (which eliminates disorder) and now consists of men who have recently proved that they are capable of administering property, whether in land or money.

As the minority no longer has need of force to keep the proletarian class in subordination, the course which it should adopt is as follows:

(1) A policy by which the proletariat will have the strongest interest in maintaining public order.

(2) A policy which aims at making the inheritance of landed property as easy as possible.

(3) A policy which aims at giving the highest political importance to the workers.

Such a policy is quite simple and obvious, if one takes the trouble to judge the situation by one's own intelligence, and to shake off the yoke enforced on our minds by the political principles of our ancestors—principles which were sound and useful in their own day, but are no longer applicable to present circumstances. The mass of the population is now composed of men (apart from exceptions which occur more or less equally in every class; who are capable of administering property whether in land or in money, and therefore we can and must work directly for the improvement of the moral and physical welfare of the community.

The most direct method of improving the moral and physical welfare of the majority of the population is to give priority in State expenditure to ensuring work for all fit men, to secure their physical existence; spreading throughout the proletarian class a knowledge of positive science; ensuring for this class forms of recreation and interests which will develop their intelligence.

We must add to this the measures necessary to ensure that the national wealth is administered by men most fitted for it, and most concerned in its administration, that is to say the most important industrialists.

Thus the community, by means of these fundamental arrangements, will be organized in a way which will completely satisfy reasonable men of every class.*

---

* Men are not as bad as they think they are: they are more severe on themselves than they deserve. It is true that theoretically they appear to be strongly inclined to despotism, but, in actual fact, they prefer equality.

If an Englishman obtains a post in India, he goes there with enthusiasm, and in his imagination pictures the delights that despotism will procure for him. He can, if he likes, keep a harem; he will be surrounded by hundreds of servants—some to keep off the flies which might irritate him, others always ready to carry him in a palanquin. The whole population will crawl before him; he will have the power to order a beating for any Indian who does not obey his wishes with enough zeal or intelligence.

Well, this Englishman who in India wallows in the delights of despotism, hastens to return to England, as soon as he has made his fortune, to enjoy again the advantages of equality. The moment he arrives in harbour in Great Britain he finds himself rudely hustled by the people, and yet that

There will no longer be a fear of insurrection, and consequently no longer a need to maintain large standing armies to suppress it; no longer a need to spend enormous sums on a police force; no longer a fear of foreign danger, for a body of thirty millions of men who are a contented community would easily repel attack, even if the whole human race combined against them.

We might add that neither princes nor peoples would be so mad as to attack a nation of thirty millions who displayed no aggressive intentions against their neighbours, and were united internally by mutual interests.

Furthermore, there would no longer be a need for a system of police-spying in a community in which the vast majority had an interest in maintaining the established order.

---

does not make him wish to return to the place where everybody makes way for him.

We see Russians of vast wealth leaving their country to live in western Europe, while western Europeans only go to Russia to make their fortune, and hasten to bring back to their own homes the wealth they have acquired there.

There are good reasons why rich men prefer to live in countries where equality between the members of the community is most far advanced, since these countries are at the same time those where they can most easily and fully satisfy their wants.

In any French town of some importance, a man with money can, at any hour and without previous notice, eat well at a moderate price. In Russia only the great nobles can obtain good food.

If a traveller has a breakdown of his carriage anywhere in England, he can either have his carriage repaired or buy on the spot a carriage as good as the other. In Russia, a traveller whose carriage breaks down on a main road between big towns, is forced to finish his journey in a peasant's cart.

Thus, in fact, the richest and most powerful men have an interest in the growth of equality, since the means of satisfying their wants increases in the same proportion as the levelling of the individuals composing the community.

It is commonly assumed that those who profit by an abuse are strongly attached to it. This is an error; what they are determined on is not to let themselves be deprived of advantages which pass into the hands of others. It was the nobles who in France initiated the suppression of the privileges which they enjoyed, and they regretted this sacrifice only when they saw, first, all the former commoners behave towards them like members of a privileged order, and then a new aristocracy growing up in which the former nobles were only admitted as inferiors.

In conclusion to this note, let me say what perhaps should have been stated first, that the improvement of the lot of the masses secures the welfare of men of every class, and that, to improve the lot of the masses, it is necessary not merely to transfer privilege, but to abolish it. It is necessary not merely to let abuses change hands, but to eliminate them.

The men who brought about the Revolution, the men who directed it, and the men who, since 1789 and up to the present day, have guided the nation, have committed a great political mistake. They have all sought to improve the governmental machine, whereas they should have subordinated it and put administration in the first place.

They should have begun by asking a question the solution of which is simple and obvious. They should have asked who, in the present state of morals and enlightenment, are the men most fitted to manage the affairs of the nation. They would have been forced to recognize the fact that the scientists, artists and industrialists, and the heads of industrial concerns are the men who possess the most eminent, varied, and most positively useful ability, for the guidance of men's minds at the present time. They would have recognized the fact that the work of the scientists, artists, and industrialists is that which, in discovery and application, contributes most to national prosperity.

They would have reached the conclusion that the scientists, artists and leaders of industrial enterprises are the men who should be entrusted with administrative power, that is to say, with the responsibility for managing the national interests; and that the functions of government should be limited to maintaining public order.°

° I propose to explain briefly how the imposition of government on top of administration produces harmful effects at the present day, when the mass of the nation consists of men who no longer require to be closely supervised, since they have shewn themselves capable of administering all kinds of property. To-day the proletarian class can only become dangerous to public order, if the administrators of the national interests are so inept or selfish as to let them become unemployed.

It is easy to convince oneself, and others, that one has the capacity to govern, because the ability or lack of ability to govern can only be proved by experience. Any man can imagine and persuade others that he would govern well, so long as he has not governed already.

It is not the same in the case of mathematics, physics, chemistry, physiology, mechanics, poetry, painting, sculpture, architecture, farming, manufacture, commerce, and banking.

It is easy for any man to judge whether he possesses great ability in the sciences or arts; it is easy to verify whether he has attained great importance in a branch of industry. In any case, errors of this sort would not be serious, since his neighbours would soon open his eyes, if they were blinded by vanity.

It follows from what I have said that the ambition of scientists, artists and industrialists, to participate in the administration of national interests, is not dangerous to the community. It is advantageous rather, since they can only succeed in their ambition through solid achievements; while the ambition which aims at a place in the government is harmful to the community, because the most incapable men may be consumed by such an am-

The reformers of 1789 should have said to themselves as follows:

The kings of England have given a good example to monarchy by agreeing to give no order without the approval and signature of a minister. The magnanimity of the kings of France demands that they show still greater generosity to their people, and that they should agree to make no decision affecting the general interests of the nation without the approval of the men most fitted to judge their decisions—that is to say, without the approval of the scientists and the most eminent artists, without the approval of the most important industrialists.

The community has often been compared to a pyramid. I admit that the nation should be composed as a pyramid; I am profoundly convinced that the national pyramid should be crowned by the monarchy, but I assert that from the base of the pyramid to its summit the layers should be composed of more and more precious materials. If we consider the present pyramid, it appears that the base is made of granite, that up to a certain height the layers are composed of valuable materials, but that the upper part, supporting a magnificent diamond, is composed of nothing but plaster and gilt.

The base of the present national pyramid consists of workers in their routine occupations; the first layers above this base are the leaders of industrial enterprises, the scientists who improve the methods of manufacture and widen their application, the artists who give the stamp of good taste to all their products. The upper layers, which I assert to be composed of nothing but plaster, which is easily recognizable despite the gilding, are the courtiers, the mass of nobles whether of ancient or recent creation, the idle rich, the governing class from the prime minister to the humblest clerk. The monarchy is the magnificent diamond which crowns the pyramid.

---

bition and, in order to satisfy it, strive to overthrow the whole social order.

One of the important effects of this ambition, which inflamed almost all Frenchmen when the government of the unfortunate Louis XVI was overturned, is very extraordinary. It was with the aim of being governed less, and less expensively, that the nation embarked on revolution. Up to the present it has achieved as a result more government, and more expensive government, than it had before the revolution.

The industrialists produce much more than before the Revolution, but a great part of the increased production is used to pay useless military staffs, and a mass of clerks who employ their time for the most part in reading newspapers and sharpening pens—a result which satisfies neither the needs nor the feelings of the producers.

Karl Marx

1818–1883

In the Critique of the Gotha Programme, *Marx allowed himself the luxury of speculation on the shape of the world to be. It was a luxury, for Marx and Engels differentiated their own brand of "scientific" socialism from the utopian musings of Owen, Fourier, Saint-Simon, and Godwin in part by their insistence on close analysis of the society which then existed. From this analysis, and from it alone, was it possible to infer the laws of capitalist development, the movement to socialism, and the ultimate crisis of capitalist economies. Even here, Marx takes pains to demonstrate the connection between the capitalist society of the present and the socialist, and ultimately communist, societies of the future.*

The brief extract that follows distinguishes between socialism and communism in a manner which Lenin later greatly expanded in State and Revolution. *The new socialist society, emerging as it must from the womb of capitalism, is ". . . in every respect tainted economically, morally and intellectually with the hereditary diseases of the old society." This taint makes it necessary to pay workers unequally and to preserve a coercive state, designed to eliminate the remnants of capitalist opposition. It is clear that here as in capitalism this state serves the aims of class domination, but the class which now rules is the proletariat.*

The better society that is at the end of economic change is communist. And here at last the utopian element in Marxist thought manifests itself. The paragraph with which the selection closes is spiritually very close to Godwin and Owen:

> In a higher phase of communist society, after the tyrranical subordination of individuals according to the distribution of labour and thereby also the distinction between manual and intellectual

348

work, have disappeared, after labour has become not merely a means to live but in itself the first necessity of living, after the powers of production have also increased and all the springs of co-operative wealth are gushing more freely together with the all-round development of the individual, then and then only can the narrow bourgeois horizon of rights be left far behind and society will inscribe on its banner: "From each according to his capacity, to each according to his need."

Which is to say that a happy day will come beyond alienation and past scarcity.

The selection is from Critique of the Gotha Programme (*New York: International Publishers, 1933*), *pp. 29-31.*

The Gotha Programme

What we have to deal with here is a communist society, not as if it had *developed on a basis of its own,* but on the contrary as *it emerges from capitalist society,* which is thus in every respect tainted economically, morally and intellectually with the hereditary diseases of the old society from whose womb it is emerging. In this way the individual producer receives back again from society, with deductions, exactly what he gives. What he has given to society is his individual amount of labour. For example, the social working-day consists of the sum of the individuals' hours of work. The individual working-time of the individual producer is that part of the social working-day contributed by him, his part thereof. He receives from society a voucher that he has contributed such and such a quantity of work (after deductions from his work for the common fund) and draws through this voucher on the social storehouse as much of the means of consumption as the same quantity of work costs. The same amount of work which he has given to society in one form, he receives back in another.

Here obviously the same principle prevails as that which regulates the exchange of commodities so far as this exchange is of equal values. Content and form are changed because under the changed conditions no one can contribute anything except his labour and, on the other hand, nothing can pass into the possession of individuals except individual objects of consumption. But, so far as the distribution of the latter among individual producers is concerned, the same principle prevails as in the exchange of commodity-equivalents, i.e. equal quantities of labour in one form are exchanged for equal quantities of labour in another form.

350 THE VARIETIES OF ECONOMICS: VOLUME ONE

The equal right is here still based on the same principle as bourgeois right, although principle and practice are no longer at daggers drawn, while the exchange of equivalents in commodity exchange only exists *for the average* and not for the individual case.

In spite of this advance, this *equal right* is still continually handicapped by bourgeois limitations. The right of the producers is *proportional* to the amount of labour they contribute; the equality consists in the fact that everything is measured by an *equal measure*, labour.

But one man will excel another physically or intellectually and so contributes in the same time more labour, or can labour for a longer time; and labour, to serve as a measure, must be defined by its duration or intensity, otherwise it ceases to be a standard measure. This *equal* right is an unequal right for unequal work. It recognises no class differences because every worker ranks as a worker like his fellows, but it tacitly recognises unequal individual endowment, and thus capacities for production, as natural privileges. It is therefore a right of inequality in its content, as in general is every right. Right can by its very nature only consist in the application of an equal standard; but unequal individuals (and they would not be different individuals if they were not unequal), are only measurable by an equal standard in so far as they can be brought under an equal observation, be regarded from one *definite* aspect only, e.g. in the case under review, they must be considered *only as workers* and nothing more be seen in them, everything else being ignored. Further, one worker is married, another single, one has more children than another and so on. Given an equal capacity for labour and thence an equal share in the funds for social consumption, the one will in practice receive more than the other, the one will be richer than the other and so forth. To avoid all these inconveniences, rights must be unequal instead of being equal.*

* In *Anti-Dühring* (pt. i, chap. x) Engels writes as follows in regard to the demand for equality: "The demand for equality in the mouth of the proletariat has, however, a double meaning. It is either—as was the case at the very start, for example in the peasants' wars—the natural reaction against the crying social inequalities, against the contrast between the rich and the poor, the feudal lords and their serfs, surfeit and starvation; as such it is the simple expression of the revolutionary instinct, and finds its justification in that, and indeed only in that. Or, on the other hand, the proletarian demand for equality has arisen as the reaction against the bourgeois demand for equality, drawing more or less correct and more far-reaching demands from this bourgeois demand, and serving as material for agitation in order to rouse the workers against the capitalists on the basis of the capitalists' own assertions; and in this case it stands and falls with civil

But these deficiencies are unavoidable in the first phase of communist society when it is just emerging after prolonged birth-pangs from capitalist society. Right can never be higher than the economic structure and the cultural development of society conditioned by it.

In a higher phase of communist society, after the tyrannical subordination of individuals according to the distribution of labour and thereby also the distinction between manual and intellectual work, have disappeared, after labour has become not merely a means to live but is in itself the first necessity of living, after the powers of production have also increased and all the springs of co-operative wealth are gushing more freely together with the all-round development of the individual, then and then only can the narrow bourgeois horizon of rights be left far behind and society will inscribe on its banner: "From each according to his capacity, to each according to his need." *

---

equality itself. In both cases the real content of the proletarian demand for equality is the demand for the abolition of classes. Any demand for equality which goes beyond this of necessity passes into absurdity." In his work *Economics and Politics in the Period of the Proletarian Dictatorship* Lenin writes in connection with Engels' statement: "Long ago Engels explained in *Anti-Dühring* that the conception of equality, as the expression of the relations of a trading system of production, becomes a prejudice unless equality is understood in the sense of the *abolition of classes*. This simple truth concerning the distinction between the bourgeois-democratic and the socialist conception of equality is constantly forgotten. But if this is not forgotten, then it becomes clear that the proletariat, having overthrown the bourgeoisie, thereby takes a decisive step towards the abolition of classes, and that to complete this the proletariat must continue its class war, using the apparatus of State power and employing various forms of struggle, coercion and action in relation to the bourgeoisie which has been overthrown and in relation to the hesitating petty-bourgeoisie" (vol. xxiv, p. 515, Lenin's *Works*, Russian edition). Compare the passages in *The State and Revolution* . . . in which Lenin in part quotes, in part summarises and develops the ideas put forward by Marx in the *Critique*.

* . . . In connection with Communist Saturdays Lenin said in December 1919: "If we ask ourselves what distinguishes Communism from Socialism, we must say that Socialism is the society which grows directly out of capitalism, is the first form of the new society. Communism, however, is a higher form of society, and it can only develop when Socialism has been completely consolidated. Socialism implies work without the help of capitalists, social labour with strict accounting, control and supervision by the organised advance guard, the foremost section of the workers; for that reason both the norms of labour and the reward of labour must be laid down. The fixing of these is necessary because capitalist society has bequeathed to us such tendencies and such habits as absence from work, distrust of social economy, old habits of the small farmer which are prevalent in all peasant countries. All of this takes place in spite of an actual Communist

economy. We call Communism the system in which people act in fulfilment of social obligations without any special apparatus of coercion, when unpaid labour for society has become universal" (vol. xxiv, p. 651, Lenin's *Works,* Russian edition). Compare also Lenin's article: "From the Destruction of the Old Order to the Creation of the New" (vol. xxv, p. 151).

Edward Bellamy

1850–1898

Edward Bellamy wrote his utopian novel, Looking Backward, *in 1888. An immediate success, it caused widespread emulation. Perhaps a hundred utopian novels were written between 1888 and 1900, some of them serious efforts in Bellamy's spirit to draw the shape of a more desirable future, others sheer science fiction. Disciples of Bellamy formed 150 Nationalist Clubs designed to put into effect his doctrines. And the effect on perceptive young people is suggested by a recollection of William Allen White:*

> *I remember the tremendous thrill I had from reading the books from the late Eighties and the early Nineties. I was a young man passing out of my teens. I went into life a thoroughgoing conservative but before I had been ten years out of college, I was crossing the deadline into an open-minded attitude about political, social, and economic problems. Probably this was the yeast of Edward Bellamy working in me. I have never been permanently cured. The book had a tremendous influence on my generation.*

No doubt part of Bellamy's appeal was the consequence of a graceful literary style and a rather insipid romantic thread running through the novel. However, there were more important reasons why the novel spoke to its generation. Bellamy wrote at a time when American society was passing through a transformation from a rural, frontier community (in common myth at least) to an industrial society dominated by vast aggregations of capital and darkened by bloody conflict between labor and management. The free lands of the West were gone. Immigrant workers, speaking strange languages and believing in who knew what un-American ideologies, were turbulent elements in a society few understood and many feared. This was the age of

353

Haymarket Riots, of the anarchists, of the South Improvement Company, the meat trust, and the railroad trusts.

It was the strength of Bellamy's utopianism that he did not flee from the industrialism of the present to some rural Arcadia of the past. Instead, he offered a whole series of novelties designed to make use of the powers of production of the new economic system. His demand for absolute equality of all citizens no doubt reflected the socialism of the utopians and their belief that men resemble each other much more than they differ from each other. But even here Bellamy tempers his utopianism with a description of how incentives might be varied to distribute the right numbers of individuals to the right places. And his new Industrial Army is simply an extension of the dominating tendencies toward size and concentration which marked the private economy. Here it is the government which is the single trust. Bellamy made a just estimate of the productive potentialities of the new industrialism, even if he underrated the coercive possibilities that his bureaucratic structure could scarcely avoid. For better or for worse, Bellamy turned his back upon the associationism of the early utopians, upon their preference for the self-contained community, and took the path that organization has since followed—toward size, centralization, and specialization of function.

Bellamy leaves unsolved the great problems of resource allocation and implicit pricing. Nevertheless, it does not strain the facts unduly to observe that there is in him a premonition at least of the allocative mechanism which Oskar Lange later employed to prove the compatibility of public ownership and free consumer choice. This selection is from Looking Backward (New York: Modern Library, 1951), pp. 46-56.

The Industrial Army

'But you have not yet told me how you have settled the labor problem. It is the problem of capital which we have been discussing,' I said. 'After the nation had assumed conduct of the mills, machinery, railroads, farms, mines, and capital in general of the country, the labor question still remained. In assuming the responsibilities of capital the nation had assumed the difficulties of the capitalist's position.'

'The moment the nation assumed the responsibilities of capital those difficulties vanished,' replied Dr. Leete. 'The national organization of labor under one direction was the complete solution of what was, in your day and under your system, justly regarded as the insoluble labor problem. When the nation became the sole employer, all the citizens, by virtue of their citizenship, became employees, to be distributed according to the needs of industry.'

'That is,' I suggested, 'you have simply applied the principle of universal military service, as it was understood in our day, to the labor question.'

'Yes,' said Dr. Leete, 'that was something which followed as a matter of course as soon as the nation had become the sole capitalist. The people were already accustomed to the idea that the obligation of every citizen, not physically disabled, to contribute his military services to the defense of the nation was equal and absolute. That it was equally the duty of every citizen to contribute his quota of industrial or intellectual services to the maintenance of the nation was equally evident, though it was not until the nation became the employer of labor that citizens were able to render this sort of service with any pretense either of universality or equity. No organization of labor was possible when the employing power was divided among hundreds or thousands of individuals and corporations, between which concert of any kind was neither desired, nor indeed feasible. It constantly happened then that vast numbers who desired to labor could find no opportunity, and on the other hand, those who desired to evade a part or all of their debt could easily do so.'

'Service, now, I suppose, is compulsory upon all,' I suggested.

'It is rather a matter of course than of compulsion,' replied Dr. Leete. 'It is regarded as so absolutely natural and reasonable that the idea of its being compulsory has ceased to be thought of. He would be thought to be an incredibly contemptible person who should need compulsion in such a case. Nevertheless, to speak of service being compulsory would be a weak way to state its absolute inevitableness. Our entire social order is so wholly based upon and deduced from it that if it were conceivable that a man could escape it, he would be left with no possible way to provide for his existence. He would have excluded himself from the world, cut himself off from his kind, in a word, committed suicide.'

'Is the term of service in this industrial army for life?'

'Oh, no; it both begins later and ends earlier than the average working period in your day. Your workshops were filled with children and old men, but we hold the period of youth sacred to education, and the period of maturity, when the physical forces begin to flag, equally sacred to ease and agreeable relaxation. The period of industrial service is twenty-four years, beginning at the close of the course of education at twenty-one and terminating at forty-five.

After forty-five, while discharged from labor, the citizen still remains liable to special calls, in case of emergencies causing a sudden great increase in the demand for labor, till he reaches the age of fifty-five, but such calls are rarely, in fact almost never, made. The fifteenth day of October of every year is what we call Muster Day, because those who have reached the age of twenty-one are then mustered into the industrial service, and at the same time those who, after twenty-four years' service, have reached the age of forty-five, are honorably mustered out. It is the great day of the year with us, whence we reckon all other events, our Olympiad, save that it is annual.'

7

'It is after you have mustered your industrial army into service,' I said, 'that I should expect the chief difficulty to arise, for there its analogy with a military army must cease. Soldiers have all the same thing, and a very simple thing, to do, namely, to practice the manual of arms, to march and stand guard. But the industrial army must learn and follow two or three hundred diverse trades and avocations. What administrative talent can be equal to determining wisely what trade or business every individual in a great nation shall pursue?'

'The administration has nothing to do with determining that point.'

'Who does determine it, then?' I asked.

'Every man for himself in accordance with his natural aptitude, the utmost pains being taken to enable him to find out what his natural aptitude really is. The principle on which our industrial army is organized is that a man's natural endowments, mental and physical, determine what he can work at most profitably to the nation and most satisfactorily to himself. While the obligation of service in some form is not to be evaded, voluntary election, subject only to necessary regulation, is depended on to determine the particular sort of service every man is to render. As an individual's satisfaction during his term of service depends on his having an occupation to his taste, parents and teachers watch from early years for indications of special aptitudes in children. A thorough study of the National industrial system, with the history and rudiments of all the great trades, is an essential part of our educational system. While manual training is not allowed to encroach on the general intellectual culture to which our schools are devoted, it is carried far enough to give our youth, in addition to their theoretical knowledge of the national industries, mechanical and agricultural, a certain familiarity with their tools and methods. Our schools are constantly visiting our workshops, and often are taken on long excursions to inspect particular industrial enterprises. In your day a man was not ashamed to be grossly ignorant of all trades except his own, but such ignorance would not be consistent with our idea of placing every one in a position to select intelligently the occupation for which he has most taste. Usually long before he is mustered into service a young man has found out the pursuit he wants to follow, has acquired a great deal of knowledge about it, and is waiting impatiently the time when he can enlist in its ranks.'

'Surely,' I said, 'it can hardly be that the number of volunteers for any trade is exactly the number needed in that trade. It must be generally either under or over the demand.'

'The supply of volunteers is always expected to fully equal the demand,' replied Dr. Leete. 'It is the business of the administration to see that this is the case. The rate of volunteering for each trade is closely watched. If there be a noticeably greater excess of volunteers over men needed in any trade, it is inferred that the trade offers greater attractions than others. On the other hand, if the number of volunteers for a trade tends to drop below the demand, it is inferred that it is thought more arduous. It is the business of the administration to seek constantly to equalize the attractions of the trades, so far as the conditions of labor in them are concerned, so that all trades shall be equally attractive to persons having natural tastes for them. This is done by making the hours of labor in different trades to differ according to their arduousness. The lighter trades, prosecuted under the most agreeable circumstances, have in this way the longest hours, while an arduous trade, such as mining, has very short hours. There is no theory, no *a priori* rule, by which the respective attractiveness of industries is determined. The administration, in taking burdens off one class of workers and adding them to other classes, simply follows the fluctuations of opinion among the workers themselves as indicated by the rate of volunteering. The principle is that no man's work ought to be, on the whole, harder for him than any other man's for him, the workers themselves to be the judges. There are no limits to the application of this rule. If any particular occupation is in itself so arduous or so oppressive that, in order to induce volunteers, the day's work in it had to be reduced to ten minutes, it would be done. If, even then, no man was willing to do it, it would remain undone. But of course, in point of fact, a moderate reduction in the hours of labor, or addition of other privileges, suffices to secure all needed volunteers for any occupation necessary to men. If, indeed, the unavoidable difficulties and dangers of such a necessary pursuit were so great that no inducement of compensating advantages would overcome men's repugnance to it, the administration would only need to take it out of the common order of occupations by declaring it "extra hazardous," and those who pursued it especially worthy of the national gratitude, to be overrun with volunteers. Our young men are very greedy of honor, and do not let slip such opportunities. Of course you will see that dependence on the purely voluntary choice of avocations involves the abolition in all of anything like unhygienic conditions or special peril to life and limb. Health and safety are conditions common to all industries. The nation does not maim and slaughter its workmen by thousands, as did the private capitalists and corporations of your day.'

'When there are more who want to enter a particular trade than there is room for, how do you decide between the applicants?' I inquired.

'Preference is given to those who have acquired the most knowledge of the trade they wish to follow. No man, however, who through successive years remains persistent in his desire to show what he can do at any particular trade, is in the end denied an opportunity. Meanwhile, if a man cannot at first win entrance into the business he prefers, he has usually one or more alternative preferences, pursuits for which he has some degree of aptitude, although not the highest. Every one, indeed, is expected to study his aptitudes so as to have not only a first choice as to occupation, but a second or third, so that if, either at the outset of his career or subsequently, owing to the progress of invention or changes in demand, he is unable to follow his first vocation, he can still find reasonably congenial employment. This principle of secondary choices as to occupation is quite important in our system. I should add, in reference to the counter-possibility of some sudden failure of volunteers in a particular trade, or some sudden necessity of an increased force, that the administration, while depending on the voluntary system for filling up the trades as a rule, holds always in reserve the power to call for special volunteers, or draft any force needed from any quarter. Generally, however, all needs of this sort can be met by details from the class of unskilled or common laborers.'

'How is this class of common laborers recruited?' I asked. 'Surely nobody voluntarily enters that.'

'It is the grade to which all new recruits belong for the first three years of their service. It is not till after this period, during which he is assignable to any work at the discretion of his superiors, that the young man is allowed to elect a special avocation. These three years of stringent discipline none are exempt from, and very glad our young men are to pass from this severe school into the comparative liberty of the trades. If a man were so stupid as to have no choice as to occupation, he would simply remain a common laborer; but such cases, as you may suppose, are not common.'

'Having once elected and entered on a trade or occupation,' I remarked, 'I suppose he has to stick to it the rest of his life.'

'Not necessarily,' replied Dr. Leete; 'while frequent and merely capricious changes of occupation are not encouraged or even permitted, every worker is allowed, of course, under certain regulations and in accordance with the exigencies of the service, to volunteer for another industry which he thinks would suit him better than his first choice. In this case his application is received just as if he were volunteering for the first time, and on the same terms. Not only this, but a worker may likewise, under suitable regulations and not too frequently, obtain a transfer to an establishment of the same industry in another part of the country which for any reason he may prefer. Under your system a discontented man could indeed leave his work at will, but he left his means of support at the same time, and took his chances as to future livelihood. We find that the number of men who wish to abandon an accustomed occupation for a new one, and old friends and associations for strange ones, is small. It is only the poorer sort of workmen who desire to change even as frequently as our regulations permit. Of course transfers or discharges, when health demands them, are always given.'

'As an industrial system, I should think this might be extremely efficient,' I said, 'but I don't see that it makes any provision for the professional classes, the men who serve the nation with brains instead of hands. Of course you can't get along without the brain-workers. How, then, are they selected from those who are to serve as farmers and mechanics? That must require a very delicate sort of sifting process, I should say.'

'So it does,' replied Dr. Leete; 'the most delicate possible test is needed here, and so we leave the question whether a man shall be a brain or hand worker entirely to him to settle. At the end of the term of three years as a common laborer, which every man must serve, it is for him to choose, in accordance to his natural tastes, whether he will fit himself for an art or profession, or be a farmer or mechanic. If he feels that he can do better work with his brains than his muscles, he finds every facility provided for testing the reality of his supposed bent, of cultivating it, and if fit of pursuing it as his avocation. The schools of technology, of medicine, of art, of music, of histrionics, and of higher liberal learning are always open to aspirants without condition.'

'Are not the schools flooded with young men whose only motive is to avoid work?'

Dr. Leete smiled a little grimly.

'No one is at all likely to enter the professional schools for the purpose of avoiding work, I assure you,' he said. 'They are intended for those with special aptitude for the branches they teach, and any one without it would find it easier to do double hours at his trade than try to keep up with the classes. Of course many honestly mistake their vocation, and, finding themselves unequal to the requirements of the schools, drop out and return to the industrial service; no discredit attaches to such persons, for the public policy is to encourage all to develop suspected talents which only actual tests can prove the reality of. The professional and scientific schools of your day depended on the patronage of their pupils for support, and the practice appears to have been common of giving diplomas to unfit persons, who afterwards found their way into the professions. Our schools are national institutions, and to have passed their tests is a proof of special abilities not to be questioned.

'This opportunity for a professional training,' the doctor continued, 'remains open to every man till the age of thirty is reached, after which students are not received, as there would remain too brief a period before the age of discharge in which to serve the nation in their professions. In your day young men had to choose their professions very young, and therefore, in a large proportion of instances, wholly mistook their vocations. It is recognized nowadays that the natural aptitudes of some are later than those of others in developing, and therefore, while the choice of profession may be made as early as twenty-four, it remains open for six years longer.'

Samuel Butler

1835–1902

In this country Samuel Butler is probably best known as the author of a scarifying autobiographical novel, The Way of All Flesh, *which as a comment on clerical hypocrisy, cruelty to children, and intricately unpleasant family relations, yields precedence to few later efforts. He was also a controversialist of vehement and ingenious opinions. He was convinced both that Handel was the greatest of all composers and that the true author of the* Odyssey *was Nausicaa. He wrote a series of volumes attacking Darwinian evolution. His own doctrine of creative evolution gave central place to Charles Darwin's grandfather, Erasmus Darwin, and Lamarck.*

He wrote Erewhon—"nowhere" *spelled backward save for the reversal of the "w" and the "h"—as a young man. While it is an imperfect novel and an incompletely thought-through tract, it is full of charm and sharp comment on English Victorian society. In contrast to Bellamy, Butler's point of view is reactionary. He harks back to a time before industrialism. Indeed, his Erewhonians have destroyed their machines and preserve in museums a few carefully disabled examples of an art that they grew to despise. Much of the amusement in the novel is Butler's reversal of accepted British conventions. In Erewhon, bad health is a crime punished by imprisonment, but embezzlement, assault, and burglary are treated with the greatest sympathy. In Erewhon, one is guilty of a bad cold and ill of theft. The treatment of Erewhonian illness can be very painful, much as English medicine often increased the suffering of the ill.*

Butler's "Musical Banks" can be read as a parody on the high official position of religion and churches in England and the very low opinion that the community genuinely holds of their role. It can be read, as well, as sharp comment on what really counted in English life,

361

commerce, competition, and ruthless self-advancement. For Butler the solution to the results of contemporary capitalism is the elimination of capitalism itself.

The selection comes from Erewhon (New York: Modern Library, 1927), pp. 137-50.

Musical Banks

Now I had already collected that the mercantile affairs of the Erewhonians were conducted on a totally different system from our own; I had, however, gathered little hitherto, except that they had two distinct commercial systems, of which the one appealed more strongly to the imagination than anything to which we are accustomed in Europe, inasmuch as the banks that were conducted upon this system were decorated in the most profuse fashion, and all mercantile transactions were accompanied with music, so that they were called Musical Banks, though the music was hideous to a European ear.

As for the system itself I never understood it, neither can I do so now: they have a code in connection with it, which I have not the slightest doubt that they understand, but no foreigner can hope to do so. One rule runs into, and against, another as in a most complicated grammar, or as in Chinese pronunciation, wherein I am told that the slightest change in accentuation or tone of voice alters the meaning of a whole sentence. Whatever is incoherent in my description must be referred to the fact of my never having attained to a full comprehension of the subject.

So far, however, as I could collect anything certain, I gathered that they have two distinct currencies, each under the control of its own banks and mercantile codes. One of these (the one with the Musical Banks) was supposed to be *the* system, and to give out the currency in which all monetary transactions should be carried on; and as far as I could see, all who wished to be considered respectable, kept a larger or smaller balance at these banks. On the other hand, if there is one thing of which I am more sure than another, it is that the amount so kept had no direct commercial value in the outside world; I am sure that the managers and cashiers of the Musical Banks were not paid in their own currency. Mr. Nosnibor used to go to these banks, or rather to the great mother bank of the city, sometimes but not very often. He was a pillar of one of the other kind of banks, though he appeared to hold some minor office also in the musical ones. The ladies generally went alone; as indeed was the case in most families, except on state occasions.

I had long wanted to know more of this strange system, and had the greatest desire to accompany my hostess and her daughters. I had seen them go out almost every morning since my arrival and had noticed that they carried their purses in their hands, not exactly ostentatiously, yet just so as that those who met them should see whither they were going. I had never, however, yet been asked to go with them myself.

It is not easy to convey a person's manner by words, and I can hardly give any idea of the peculiar feeling that came upon me when I saw the ladies on the point of starting for the bank. There was a something of regret, a something as though they would wish to take me with them, but did not like to ask me, and yet as though I were hardly to ask to be taken. I was determined, however, to bring matters to an issue with my hostess about my going with them, and after a little parleying, and many inquiries as to whether I was perfectly sure that I myself wished to go, it was decided that I might do so.

We passed through several streets of more or less considerable houses, and at last turning round a corner we came upon a large piazza, at the end of which was a magnificent building, of a strange but noble architecture and of great antiquity. It did not open directly on to the piazza, there being a screen, through which was an archway, between the piazza and the actual precincts of the bank. On passing under the archway we entered upon a green sward, round which there ran an arcade or cloister, while in front of us uprose the majestic towers of the bank and its venerable front, which was divided into three deep recesses and adorned with all sorts of marbles and many sculptures. On either side there were beautiful old trees wherein the birds were busy by the hundred, and a number of quaint but substantial houses of singularly comfortable appearance; they were situated in the midst of orchards and gardens, and gave me an impression of great peace and plenty.

Indeed it had been no error to say that this building was one that appealed to the imagination; it did more—it carried both imagination and judgment by storm. It was an epic in stone and marble, and so powerful was the effect it produced on me, that as I beheld it I was charmed and melted. I felt more conscious of the existence of a remote past. One knows of this always, but the knowledge is never so living as in the actual presence of some witness to the life of bygone ages. I felt how short a space of human life was the period of our own existence. I was more impressed with my own littleness, and much more inclinable to believe that the people whose sense of the fitness of things was equal to the upraising of so serene a handiwork, were hardly likely to be wrong in the conclusions they might come to upon any subject. My feeling certainly was that the currency of this bank must be the right one.

We crossed the sward and entered the building. If the outside had been impressive the inside was even more so. It was very lofty and divided into several parts by walls which rested upon massive pillars; the windows were filled with stained glass descriptive of the principal commercial incidents of the bank for many ages. In a remote part of the building there were men and boys singing; this was the only disturbing feature, for as the gamut was still unknown, there was no music in the country which could be agreeable to a European ear. The singers seemed to have derived their inspirations from the songs of birds and the wailing of the wind, which last they tried to imitate in melancholy cadences that at times degenerated into a howl. To my thinking the noise was hideous, but it produced a great effect upon my companions, who professed themselves much moved. As soon as the singing was over, the ladies requested me to stay where I was while they went inside the place from which it had seemed to come.

During their absence certain reflections forced themselves upon me.

In the first place, it struck me as strange that the building should be so nearly empty; I was almost alone, and the few besides myself had been led by curiosity, and had no intention of doing business with the bank. But there might be more inside. I stole up to the curtain, and ventured to draw the extreme edge of it on one side. No, there was hardly any one there. I saw a large number of cashiers, all at their desks ready to pay checks, and one or two who seemed to be the managing partners. I also saw my hostess and her daughters and two or three other ladies; also three or four old women and the boys from one of the neighboring Colleges of Unreason; but there was no one else. This did not look as though the bank was doing a very large business; and yet I had always been told that every one in the city dealt with this establishment.

I cannot describe all that took place in these inner precincts, for a sinister-looking person in a black gown came and made unpleasant gestures at me for peeping. I happened to have in my pocket one of the Musical Bank pieces, which had been given me by Mrs. Nosnibor, so I tried to tip him with it; but having seen what it was, he became so angry that I had to give him a piece of the other kind of money to pacify him. When I had done this he became civil directly. As soon as he was gone I ventured to take a second look, and saw Zulora in the very act of giving a piece of paper which looked like a check to one of the cashiers. He did not examine it, but putting his hand into an antique coffer hard by, he pulled out a quantity of metal pieces apparently at random, and handed them over without counting them; neither did Zulora count them, but put them into her purse and went back to her seat after dropping a few pieces of the other coinage into an alms box that stood by the cashier's side. Mrs. Nosnibor and Arowhena then did likewise, but a little later they gave all (so far as I could see) that they had received from the cashier back to a verger, who I have no doubt put it back into the coffer from which it had been taken. They then began making towards the curtain; whereon I let it drop and retreated to a reasonable distance.

They soon joined me. For some few minutes we all kept silence, but at last I ventured to remark that the bank was not so busy to-day as it probably often was. On this Mrs. Nosnibor said that it was indeed melancholy to see what little heed people paid to the most precious of all institutions. I could say nothing in reply, but I have ever been of opinion that the greater part of mankind do approximately know where they get that which does them good.

Mrs. Nosnibor went on to say that I must not think there was any want of confidence in the bank because I had seen so few people there; the heart of the country was thoroughly devoted to these establishments, and any sign of their being in danger would bring in support from the most unexpected quarters. It was only because people knew them to be so very safe, that in some cases (as she lamented to say in Mr. Nosnibor's) they felt that their support was unnecessary. Moreover these institutions never departed from the safest and most approved banking principles. Thus they never allowed interest on deposit, a thing now frequently done by certain bubble companies, which by doing an illegitimate trade had drawn many customers away; and even the shareholders were fewer than formerly, owing to the innovations of these unscrupulous persons, for the Musical Banks paid little or no dividend, but divided their profits by way of bonus on the original shares once in every thirty thousand years; and as it was now only two thousand years since there had been one of these distributions, people felt that they could not hope for another in their own time and preferred investments whereby they got some more tangible return; all which, she said, was very melancholy to think of.

Having made these last admissions, she returned to her original statement, namely, that every one in the country really supported these banks. As to the fewness of the people, and the absence of the able-bodied, she pointed out to me with some justice that this was exactly what we ought to expect. The men who were most conversant about the stability of human institutions, such as the lawyers, men of science, doctors, statesmen, painters, and the like, were just those who were most likely to be misled by their own fancied accomplishments, and to be made unduly suspicious by their licentious desire for greater present return, which was at the root of nine-tenths of the opposition; by their vanity, which would prompt them to affect superiority to the prejudices of the vulgar; and by the stings of their own conscience, which was constantly upbraiding them in the most cruel manner on account of their bodies, which were generally diseased.

Let a person's intellect (she continued) be ever so sound, unless his body is in absolute health, he can form no judgment worth having on matters of this kind. The body is everything: it need not perhaps be such a strong body (she said this because she saw that I was thinking of the old and infirm-looking folks whom I had seen in the bank), but it must be in perfect health; in this case, the less active strength it had the more free would be the working of the intellect, and therefore the sounder the conclusion. The people, then, whom I had seen at the bank were in reality the very ones whose opinions were most worth having; they declared its advantages to be incalculable, and even professed to consider the immediate return to be far larger than they were entitled to; and so she ran on, nor did she leave off till we had got back to the house.

She might say what she pleased, but her manner carried no conviction, and later on I saw signs of general indifference to these banks that were not to be mistaken. Their supporters often denied it, but the denial was generally so couched as to add another proof of its existence. In commercial panics, and in times of general distress, the people as a mass did not so much as even think of turning to these banks. A few might do so, some from habit and early training, some from the instinct that prompts us to catch at any straw when we think ourselves drowning, but few from a genuine belief that the Musical Banks could save them from financial ruin, if they were unable to meet their engagements in the other kind of currency.

In conversation with one of the Musical Bank managers I ventured to hint this as plainly as politeness would allow. He said that it had been more or less true till lately; but that now they had put fresh stained glass windows into all the banks in the country, and repaired the buildings, and enlarged the organs; the presidents, moreover, had taken to riding in omnibuses and talking nicely to people in the streets, and to remembering the ages of their children, and giving them things when they were naughty, so that all would henceforth go smoothly.

"But haven't you done anything to the money itself?" said I, timidly.

"It is not necessary," he rejoined; "not in the least necessary, I assure you."

And yet any one could see that the money given out at these banks was not that with which people bought their bread, meat, and clothing. It was like it at a first glance, and was stamped with designs that were often of great beauty; it was not, again, a spurious coinage, made with the intention that it should be mistaken for the money in actual use; it was more like a toy money, or the counters used for certain games at cards; for, notwithstanding the beauty of the designs, the material on which they were stamped was as nearly valueless as possible. Some were covered with tin foil, but the greater part were frankly of a cheap base metal the exact nature of which I was not able to determine. Indeed they were made of a great variety of metals, or, perhaps more accurately, alloys, some of which were hard, while others would bend easily and assume almost any form which their possessor might desire at the moment.

Of course every one knew that their commercial value was *nil*, but all those who wished to be considered respectable thought it incumbent upon them to retain a few coins in their possession, and to let them be seen from time to time in their hands and purses. Not only this, but they would stick to it that the current coin of the realm was dross in comparison with the Musical Bank coinage. Perhaps, however, the strangest thing of all was that these very people would at times make fun in small ways of the whole system; indeed, there was hardly any insinuation against it which they would not tolerate and even applaud in their daily newspapers if written anonymously, while if the same thing were said without ambiguity to their faces— nominative case verb and accusative being all in their right places, and doubt impossible—they would consider themselves very seriously and justly outraged, and accuse the speaker of being unwell.

I never could understand (neither can I quite do so now, though I begin to see better what they mean) why a single currency should not suffice them; it would seem to me as though all their dealings would have been thus greatly simplified; but I was met with a look of horror if ever I dared to hint at it. Even those who to my certain knowledge kept only just enough money at the Musical Banks to swear by, would call the other banks (where their securities really lay) cold, deadening, paralyzing, and the like.

I noticed another thing, moreover, which struck me greatly. I was taken to the opening of one of these banks in a neighboring town, and saw a large assemblage of cashiers and managers. I sat opposite them and scanned their faces attentively. They did not please me; they lacked, with few exceptions, the true Erewhonian frankness; and an equal number from any other class would have looked happier and better men. When I met them in the streets they did not seem like other people, but had, as a general rule, a cramped expression upon their faces which pained and depressed me.

Those who came from the country were better; they seemed to have lived less as a separate class, and to be freer and healthier; but in spite of my seeing not a few whose looks were benign and noble, I could not help asking myself concerning the greater number of those whom I met, whether Erewhon would be a better country if their expression were to be transferred to the people in general. I answered myself emphatically, no. The expression on the faces of the high Ydgrunites was that which one would wish to diffuse, and not that of the cashiers.

A man's expression is his sacrament; it is the outward and visible sign of his inward and spiritual grace, or want of grace; and as I looked at the majority of these men, I could not help feeling that there must be a something in their lives which had stunted their natural development, and that they would have been more healthily minded in any other profession. I was always sorry for them, for in nine cases out of ten they were well-meaning persons; they were in the main very poorly paid; their constitutions were as a rule above suspicion; and there were recorded numberless instances of their self-sacrifice and generosity; but they had had the misfortune to have been betrayed into a false position at an age for the most part when their judgment was not matured, and after having been kept in studied ignorance of the real difficulties of the system. But this did not make their position the less a false one, and its bad effects upon themselves were unmistakable.

Few people would speak quite openly and freely before them, which struck me as a very bad sign. When they were in the room every one would talk as though all currency save that of the Musical Banks should be abolished; and yet they knew perfectly well that even the cashiers themselves hardly used the Musical Bank money more than other people. It was expected of them that they should appear to do so, but this was all. The less thoughtful of them did not seem particularly unhappy, but many were plainly sick at heart, though perhaps they hardly knew it, and would not have owned to being so. Some few were opponents of the whole system; but these were liable to be dismissed from their employment at any moment, and this rendered them very careful, for a man who had once been cashier at a Musical Bank was out of the field for other employment, and was generally unfitted for it by reason of that course of treatment which was commonly called his education. In fact it was a career from which retreat was virtually impossible, and into which young men were generally induced to enter before they could be reasonably expected, considering their training, to have formed any opinions of their own. Not unfrequently, indeed, they were induced, by what we in England should call undue influence, concealment, and fraud. Few indeed were those who had the courage to insist on seeing both sides of the question before they committed themselves to what was practically a leap in the dark. One would have thought that caution in this respect was an elementary principle, one of the first things that an honorable man would teach his boy to understand; but in practice it was not so.

I even saw cases in which parents bought the right of presenting to the office of cashier at one of these banks, with the fixed determination that some one of their sons (perhaps a mere child) should fill it. There was the lad himself—growing up with every promise of becoming a good and honorable man—but utterly without warning concerning the iron shoe which his natural protector was providing for him. Who could say that the whole thing would not end in a lifelong lie, and vain chafing to escape? I confess that there were few things in Erewhon which shocked me more than this.

Yet we do something not so very different from this even in England, and as regards the dual commercial system, all countries have, and have had, a law of the land, and also another law, which, though professedly more sacred, has far less effect on their daily life and actions. It seems as though the need for some law over and above, and sometimes even conflicting with, the law of the land, must spring from something that lies deep down in man's nature; indeed, it is hard to think that man could ever have become man at all, but for the gradual evolution of a perception that though this world looms so large when we are in it, it may seem a little thing when we have got away from it.

Huxley's gay anti-utopia of the 1930's, Brave New World, was from an austere economic standpoint an effort to deal with the question of what happens when the problem of scarcity vanishes. Huxley's world is wildly, incredibly wealthy. Consumer goods of unique varieties are available to everybody. Production is so completely organized that an endless flood of goods threatens to overwhelm the consuming capacities of the population. It is the world of the Garden of Eden, equally it is the universe of Al Capp's shmoo. Hence Brave New World is a fantasy of consumption rather than of production. Its scientists have available techniques that the modern advertising agency could only envy. Sleep-teaching in childhood conditions each inhabitant of the Brave New World to play his appropriate role, be it Alpha-Plus intellectual or Epsilon-Minus moron. And an important part of that role is high consumption. Thus the child is conditioned to dislike grass and trees, sources of pleasure that consume no equipment, and to enjoy complicated games that use up quantities of raw materials.

A generation before J. K. Galbraith argued in The Affluent Society *that a large share of industrial output had to be forced down the throats of customers, Huxley envisaged a society organized to accomplish smoothly this very necessity of forced feeding. Thus Huxley's implied comment on the great nineteenth-century utopians— Godwin, Owen, Fourier, and Saint-Simon—denied that human life would truly flower in liberty and amity once the persistent afflictions of scarcity were lightened. The economic moral of the tale suggests instead that for the slavery of poverty, the slavery of abundance will be substituted. Where once slave-masters organized their victims in great gangs of sweated labor, now more benevolent slave-masters organize their happier subjects into masses of incessant consumers.*

The contrast between this vision and Crosland's hopes for new liberty and new gaiety in English life could scarcely be sharper. Theirs are two visions of what a mass society can turn into. For everyone's sake, we must hope that Crosland is nearer to the truth of the future than Huxley is.

The excerpt below is from Brave New World *by Aldous Huxley. Copyright, 1932, 1946, by Aldous Huxley. Reprinted by permission of Harper & Brothers.*

Brave New World

By eight o'clock the light was failing. The loud speakers in the tower of the Stoke Poges Club House began, in a more than human tenor, to announce the closing of the courses. Lenina and Henry abandoned their game and walked back towards the Club. From the grounds of the Internal and External Secretion Trust came the lowing of those thousands of cattle which provided, with their hormones and their milk, the raw materials for the great factory at Farnham Royal.

An incessant buzzing of helicopters filled the twilight. Every two and a half minutes a bell and the screech of whistles announced the departure of one of the light monorail trains which carried the lower caste golfers back from their separate course to the metropolis.

Lenina and Henry climbed into their machine and started off. At eight hundred feet Henry slowed down the helicopter screws, and they hung for a minute or two poised above the fading landscape. The forest of Burnham Beeches stretched like a great pool of darkness towards the bright shore of the western sky. Crimson at the horizon, the last of the sunset faded, through orange, upwards into yellow and a pale watery green. Northwards, beyond and above the trees, the Internal and External Secretions factory glared with a fierce electric brilliance from every window of its twenty stories. Beneath them lay the buildings of the Golf Club—the huge Lower Caste barracks and, on the other side of a dividing wall, the smaller houses reserved for Alpha and Beta members. The approaches to the monorail station were black with the ant-like pullulation of lower-caste activity. From under the glass vault a lighted train shot out into the open. Following its southeasterly course across the dark plain their eyes were drawn to the majestic buildings of the Slough Crematorium. For the safety of night-flying planes, its four tall chimneys were flood-lighted and tipped with crimson danger signals. It was a landmark.

"Why do the smoke-stacks have those things like balconies around them?" enquired Lenina.

"Phosphorus recovery," explained Henry telegraphically. "On their way up the chimney the gases go through four separate treatments. P_2O_5 used to go right out of circulation every time they cremated some one. Now they recover over ninety-eight per cent. of it. More than a kilo and a half per adult corpse. Which makes the best part of four hundred tons of phosphorus every year from England alone." Henry spoke with a happy pride, rejoicing wholeheartedly in the achievement, as though it had been his own. "Fine to think we can go on being socially useful even after we're dead. Making plants grow."

Lenina, meanwhile, had turned her eyes away and was looking perpendicularly downwards at the monorail station. "Fine," she agreed. "But queer that Alphas and Betas won't make any more plants grow than those nasty little Gammas and Deltas and Epsilons down there."

"All men are physico-chemically equal," said Henry sententiously. "Besides, even Epsilons perform indispensable services."

"Even an Epsilon . . ." Lenina suddenly remembered an occasion when, as a little girl at school, she had woken up in the middle of the night and become aware, for the first time, of the whispering that had haunted all her sleeps. She saw again the beam of moonlight, the row of small white beds; heard once more the soft, soft voice that said (the words were there, unforgotten, unforgettable after so many night-long repetitions): "Every one works for every one else. We can't do without any one. Even Epsilons are useful. We couldn't do without Epsilons. Every one works for every one else. We can't do without any one . . ." Lenina remembered her first shock of fear and surprise; her speculations through half a wakeful hour; and then, under the influence of those endless repetitions, the gradual soothing of her mind, the soothing, the smoothing, the stealthy creeping of sleep. . . .

"I suppose Epsilons don't really mind being Epsilons," she said aloud.

"Of course they don't. How can they? They don't know what it's like being anything else. We'd mind, of course. But then we've been differently conditioned. Besides, we start with a different heredity."

"I'm glad I'm not an Epsilon," said Lenina, with conviction.

"And if you were an Epsilon," said Henry, "your conditioning would have made you no less thankful that you weren't a Beta or an Alpha." He put his forward propeller into gear and headed the machine towards London. Behind them, in the west, the crimson and orange were almost faded; a dark bank of cloud had crept into the zenith. As they flew over the Crematorium, the plane shot upwards on the column of hot air rising from the chimneys, only to fall as suddenly when it passed into the descending chill beyond.

"What a marvellous switchback!" Lenina laughed delightedly.

But Henry's tone was almost, for a moment, melancholy. "Do you know what that switchback was?" he said. "It was some human being finally and definitely disappearing. Going up in a squirt of hot gas. It would be curious to know who it was—a man or a woman, an Alpha or an Epsilon. . . ." He sighed. Then, in a resolutely cheerful voice, "Anyhow," he concluded, "there's one thing we can be certain of; whoever he may have been, he was happy when he was alive. Everybody's happy now."

"Yes, everybody's happy now," echoed Lenina. They had heard the words repeated a hundred and fifty times every night for twelve years.

Landing on the roof of Henry's forty-story apartment house in Westminster, they went straight down to the dining-hall. There, in a loud and cheerful company, they ate an excellent meal. *Soma* was served with the coffee. Lenina took two half-gramme tablets and Henry three. At twenty past nine they walked across the street to the newly opened Westminster Abbey Cabaret. It was a night almost without clouds, moonless and starry; but of this on the whole depressing fact Lenina and Henry were fortunately unaware. The electric sky-signs effectively shut off the outer darkness. "CALVIN STOPES AND HIS SIXTEEN SEXOPHONISTS." From the façade of the new Abbey the giant letters invitingly glared. "LONDON'S FINEST SCENT AND COLOUR ORGAN. ALL THE LATEST SYNTHETIC MUSIC."

They entered. The air seemed hot and somehow breathless with the scent of ambergris and sandalwood. On the domed ceiling of the hall, the colour organ had momentarily painted a tropical sunset. The Sixteen Sexophonists were playing an old favourite: "There ain't no Bottle in all the world like that dear little Bottle of mine." Four hundred couples were five-stepping round the polished floor. Lenina and Henry were soon the four hundred and first. The saxophones wailed like melodious cats under the moon, moaned in the alto and tenor registers as though the little death were upon them. Rich with a wealth of harmonics, their tremulous chorus mounted towards a climax, louder and ever louder—until at last, with a wave of his hand, the conductor let loose the final shattering note of ether-music and blew the sixteen merely human blowers clean out of existence. Thunder in A flat major. And then, in all but silence, in all but darkness, there followed a gradual deturgescence, a *diminuendo* sliding gradually, through quarter tones, down, down to a faintly whispered dominant chord that lingered on (while the five-four rhythms still pulsed below) charging the darkened seconds with an intense expectancy. And at last expectancy was fulfilled. There was a sudden explosive sunrise, and simultaneously, the Sixteen burst into song:

> Bottle of mine, it's you I've always wanted!
> Bottle of mine, why was I ever decanted?
>> Skies are blue inside of you,
>> The weather's always fine;
> For
> There ain't no Bottle in all the world
> Like that dear little Bottle of mine.

Five-stepping with the other four hundred round and round Westminster Abbey, Lenina and Henry were yet dancing in another world —the warm, the richly coloured, the infinitely friendly world of *soma*-holiday. How kind, how good-looking, how delightfully amusing every one was! "Bottle of mine, it's you I've always wanted . . ." But Lenina and Henry had what they wanted . . . They were inside, here and now—safely inside with the fine weather, the perennially blue sky. And when, exhausted, the Sixteen had laid by their sexophones and the Synthetic Music apparatus was producing the very latest in slow Malthusian Blues, they might have been twin embryos gently rocking together on the waves of a bottled ocean of blood-surrogate.

"Good-night, dear friends. Good-night, dear friends." The loud speakers veiled their commands in a genial and musical politeness. "Good-night, dear friends . . ."

Obediently, with all the others, Lenina and Henry left the building. The depressing stars had travelled quite some way across the heavens. But though the separating screen of the sky-signs had now to a great extent dissolved, the two young people still retained their happy ignorance of the night.

Swallowing half an hour before closing time, that second dose of *soma* had raised a quite impenetrable wall between the actual universe and their minds. Bottled, they crossed the street; bottled, they took the lift up to Henry's room on the twenty-eighth floor. And yet, bottled as she was, and in spite of that second gramme of *soma*, Lenina did not forget to take all the contraceptive precautions prescribed by the regulations. Years of intensive hypnopaedia and, from twelve to seventeen, Malthusian drill three times a week had made the taking of these precautions almost as automatic and inevitable as blinking. . . .

It was a small factory of lighting-sets for helicopters, a branch of the Electrical Equipment Corporation. They were met on the roof itself (for that circular letter of recommendation from the Controller was magical in its effects) by the Chief Technician and the Human Element manager. They walked downstairs into the factory.

"Each process," explained the Human Element Manager, "is carried out, so far as possible, by a single Bokanovsky Group."

And, in effect, eighty-three almost noseless black brachycephalic Deltas were cold-pressing. The fifty-six four-spindle chucking and turning machines were being manipulated by fifty-six aquiline and ginger Gammas. One hundred and seven heat-conditioned Epsilon Senegalese were working in the foundry. Thirty-three Delta females, long-headed, sandy, with narrow pelvises, and all within 20 millimetres of 1 metre 69 centimetres tall, were cutting screws. In the assembling room, the dynamos were being put together by two sets of Gamma-Plus dwarfs. The two long work-tables faced one another; between them crawled the conveyor with its load of separate parts; forty-seven blonde heads were confronted by forty-seven brown ones. Forty-seven snubs by forty-seven hooks; forty-seven receding by forty-seven prognathous chins. The completed mechanisms were inspected by eighteen identical curly auburn girls in Gamma green, packed in crates by thirty-four short-legged, left-handed male Delta-Minuses, and loaded into the waiting trucks and lorries by sixty-three blue-eyed, flaxen and freckled Epsilon Semi-Morons.

"O brave new world . . ." By some malice of his memory the Savage found himself repeating Miranda's words. "O brave new world that has such people in it."

C. A. R. Crosland

1918–

In the ideological battle within the British Labour Party that followed
the electoral defeat of 1959, C. A. R. Crosland was one of Hugh Gait-
skell's sturdiest intellectual supporters against the Socialist funda-
mentalists on the left wing of the Labour Party. The Future of Socialism, which appeared in 1956, was an eloquent statement of the current necessities of a socialist movement. Among these necessities were
coming to terms with the growing affluence of British society, realizing that to a very substantial degree the struggle for protection of
the weak and economically just income distribution had been won,
reassessing the orthodoxies of traditional socialist thought, and con-
ceiving a new expression of a viable socialist doctrine.

Crosland's attempt to write a program based upon his own prescriptions led him to discard some sturdy Labour Party traditions. In his
book and in later statements, Crosland does not so much discard nationalization of industry as he limits its claims, suggests alternative
modes of public control over private enterprise, and indicates the relative unimportance of nationalization in itself. Also in opposition to the
more intransigent left-wingers of his own party, Crosland obviously
believes that it is possible to work within a capitalist society to promote economic justice, stimulate economic growth, and raise the
quality of human experience.

Crosland is a fair but severe critic of the Puritan tradition in British
socialism which received its great impetus from the austere lives of
the Webbs, who, as Crosland and others have described them, were
paragons of industry—their honeymoon was dedicated to the investigation of Dublin's trade societies—and cultural philistines.
Now that victory is at least in sight, now that material poverty has
been defeated, it is time, Crosland maintains, to cherish different

376

virtues. The *"liberty"* and *"gaiety"* that Crosland advocates are matters of ". . . *more open-air cafés, brighter and gayer streets at night,
later closing-hours for public houses, more local repertory theatres,
better and more hospitable hoteliers and restaurateurs, brighter and
cleaner eating-houses, more riverside cafés, more pleasure-gardens
. . . more murals and pictures in public places, better designs. . . ."*
And it is obvious that good people and loyal socialists are among the
enemies who block the path to these good things.

Crosland is at the end of one important stream of socialist thought
to which he himself refers as the tradition of William Morris. His critics
have, nevertheless, found it difficult to see what is specifically socialist about Crosland's vision. Since he denies the necessity for class war-
fare and the urgency of public ownership, these critics purport to
find Crosland's position indistinguishable from mild, liberal social re-
formism. Crosland's major intellectual antagonist, Richard Crossman,
has taken the position that no major change in economic, social, or
cultural life can take place in a society that is still dominated by the
entrenched power of a capitalist class. This too is an orthodox socialist position. The struggle between these two positions has not yet
been resolved within the British Labour Party.

The passage below is taken from The Future of Socialism, *by* C. A.
R. Crosland *(London: Jonathan Cape, 1956), pp. 517, 521-9.*

Liberty and Gaiety in Private Life; the Need
for a Reaction Against the Fabian Tradition

Society's decisions impinge heavily on people's private lives as well
as on their social or economic welfare; and they now impinge, in my
view, in too restrictive and puritanical a manner. I should like to see
action taken both to widen opportunities for enjoyment and relaxation, and to diminish existing restrictions on personal freedom.

The first of these requires, it is true, a change in cultural attitudes
rather than government legislation. If this were to come about, much
could be done to make Britain a more colourful and civilised country
to live in. We need not only higher exports and old-age pensions, but
more open-air cafés, brighter and gayer streets at night, later closing-
hours for public houses, more local repertory theatres, better and
more hospitable hoteliers and restaurateurs, brighter and cleaner eating-houses, more riverside cafés, more pleasure-gardens on the Bat-
tersea model, more murals and pictures in public places, better designs for furniture and pottery and women's clothes, statues in the

centre of new housing-estates, better-designed street-lamps and tele-phone kiosks, and so on *ad infinitum*. The enemy in all this will often be in unexpected guise; it is not only dark Satanic things and people that now bar the road to the new Jerusalem, but also, if not mainly, hygienic, respectable, virtuous things and people, lacking only in grace and gaiety.

This becomes manifest when we turn to the more serious question of socially-imposed restrictions on the individual's private life and lib-erty. There come to mind at once the divorce laws, licensing laws, prehistoric (and flagrantly unfair) abortion laws, obsolete penalties for sexual abnormality, the illiterate censorship of books and plays, and remaining restrictions on the equal rights of women.* Most of these are intolerable, and should be highly offensive to socialists, in whose blood there should always run a trace of the anarchist and the libertarian, and not too much of the prig and the prude. If we really attach importance to the 'dignity of man,' we must realise that this is as much affronted by a hypocritical divorce law which, as Matthew Arnold once wrote, neither makes divorce impossible nor makes it decent, as by the refusal to establish a joint production council in a factory.† A time will come, as material standards rise, when divorce-law reform will increase the sum of human welfare more than a rise in the food subsidies (though no doubt the party managers will be less enthusiastic for it). Socialists cannot go on indefinitely professing to be concerned with human happiness and the removal of injustice, and then, when the programmes are decided, permitting the National Executive, out of fear of certain vocal pressure-groups, to become more orthodox than the bench of bishops.

Much of this can at least claim the sanction of one powerful stream of socialist thought—that stemming from William Morris; though other, Nonconformist and Fabian, influences wear a bleaker and more for-bidding air. For one brought up as a Fabian, in particular, this inevitably means a reaction against the Webb tradition. I do not wish

---

* Though if we remove these last, we should in fairness also remove unequal responsibilities from men. Women cannot claim equal rights, and at the same time continue to bring breach-of-promise or alienation-of-affec-tion cases.

† Indeed many of these reforms can be justified by the simple moral judgment that hypocrisy is bad. There is something nauseating about the shocked outcry which greets any proposal to amend the licensing laws or to allow plays to be performed on Sundays, and the sanctimonious assumption of superiority over the immoral and godless Continentals, when we con-sider that public prostitution is tolerated in Britain on a scale which amazes visitors from more 'godless' countries. Let us at least have a little consistency.

to be misunderstood. All who knew the Webbs have testified to their personal kindliness, gentleness, tolerance, and humour; and no one who reads *Our Partnership* can fail to be intensely moved by the deep unaffected happiness of their mutual love. But many of their public virtues, so indispensable at the time, may not be as appropriate to-day. Reacting as they were against an unpractical, Utopian, sentimental, romantic, almost anarchist tradition on the Left, they were no doubt right to stress the solid virtues of hard work, self-discipline, efficiency, research, and abstinence: to sacrifice private pleasure to public duty, and expect that others should do the same: to put Blue Books before culture, and immunity from physical weakness above all other virtues.

And so they spent their honeymoon investigating Trade Societies in Dublin. And so Beatrice could write that 'owing to our concentration on research, municipal administration and Fabian propaganda, we had neither the time nor the energy, nor yet the means, to listen to music and the drama, to brood over classic literature, to visit picture galleries, or to view with an informed intelligence the wonders of architecture.' * And so Sidney withheld approval from the Soviet experiment until workers' control had been suppressed, and Beatrice until the anti-abortion law had been enacted, and she could write with approval of the serious, youthful Comsomols with their passion for self-discipline and self-improvement: and of the emphasis on personal hygiene and self-control—'there is no spooning in the Parks of Recreation and Rest.' † And historically, without a doubt, this insistence on austerity was a vital service to a young and growing opposition movement.

But now we surely need a different set of values. Permeation has more than done its job. To-day we are all incipient bureaucrats and practical administrators. We have all, so to speak, been trained at the L.S.E., are familiar with Blue Books and White Papers, and know our way around Whitehall. We realise that we must guard against romantic or Utopian notions: that hard work and research are virtues: that we must do nothing foolish or impulsive: and that Fabian pamphlets must be diligently studied. We know these things too well. Posthumously, the Webbs have won their battle, and converted a genera-

* *Our Partnership*, p. 14.
† From a document privately circulated on her return from Russia in 1932 (quoted in *The Webbs and Their Work*, p. 226). And she goes on to relate with approval a warning said to have been given by Stalin to a high-placed Commissar: 'I do not want to enquire into your private affairs, but if there is any more nonsense about women, you go to a place where there are no women.'

tion to their standards. Now the time has come for a reaction: for a greater emphasis on private life, on freedom and dissent, on culture, beauty, leisure, and even frivolity. Total abstinence and a good filing-system are not now the right sign-posts to the socialist Utopia: or at least, if they are, some of us will fall by the wayside.

V Cultural and Amenity Planning; and the Declining Importance of Economic Problems

In the field of cultural values, what is mainly, indeed desperately, needed is determined government planning—to preserve what beauty we still have left in Britain, and to help create a little more. With personal consumption rising by 2-4% a year and likely to double in 20 years, it will really not much matter a decade from now whether we plan to produce rather more of this and less of that, or exactly what prices are charged for this commodity or that. The level of material welfare will soon be such that marginal changes in the allocation of resources will make little difference to anyone's contentment. If they wish, let the violent economic planners and anti-planners battle the matter out. The rest of us will grow progressively more indifferent.

But we shall grow progressively less indifferent, or so it is to be hoped, to the question of town and country, and architectural, planning. It is hard to discuss this without a tinge of melancholy. It was always obvious that profit-maximisation and market forces would be inimical to the preservation of beauty—the ribbon-building of the 1930s, the speculative housing estates, the steady destruction of London's Georgian squares, made us sufficiently aware of that. And to jog our memories we have only to see the new and utterly pedestrian commercial buildings now beginning to dwarf the City churches, and soon St. Paul's: or to read of cases such as that recently reported, where the English Electric Company, enjoying annual profits measured in millions of pounds, rejected the highly-commended winning design in a competition for its new head office, in favour of a mediocre but commercially more convenient structure.

The melancholy comes from the gradual fading of the post-war hopes of public planning. The post-war era was to be, in this respect, a brave new world. Brilliant, imaginative town-plans were to re-create our major cities. The new towns were to bring an end to London's urban sprawl, and to provide the greatest social and architectural experiment for centuries past. National Parks, the Land Fund, and in a different sphere the Arts Council, symbolised what was to be a new attention to beauty and culture. Above all the Town and Country Planning Act was to be a sure defence against the vulgarities and atrocities of the past.

And public planning in fact has much to its credit. The new towns have been a brave, and abundantly worthwhile, experiment. Post-war housing estates have, on the average, reached a better architectural standard than their predecessors (though seldom a very high one). The blitzed cities have not grown up wholly messy and haphazard, but with at least an element of design and spaciousness. National Parks are slowly (but so slowly) creeping from theory to reality. Some atrocities have been prevented by the Town and Country Planning Act. One public enterprise, the Forestry Commission, as the Kielder in particular shows, has added something new and imaginative to British life not only in its splendid forests, but in the design of forest villages. Nor has the State been backward, as the Festival of Britain demonstrated, as a direct patron of the arts.

But progress has been terribly slow; and the results terribly patchy. And now the impetus seems to be going out of the whole movement; and a middle-aged, apathetic disillusionment is setting in. A Conservative Minister of Works will not take the trouble to save Coleshill, though all the experts told him that he could. High Paddington is abandoned on grounds of cost. The design and adequacy of council-houses has deteriorated appallingly since 1951. The Government itself all but demolished Colcutt's Imperial Institute campanile. The City of London is almost past saving from second-rate mediocrity; even the limited New Barbican project was turned down time and again by the City Corporation. The new towns are compelled to skimp their amenity building through lack of funds. The Board of Trade, always the enemy of both social and economic enlightenment, by relaxing its licensing controls, is once more permitting industry to expand in London and Birmingham, and making it inevitable that these cities, against all our post-war hopes, will spread inexorably into the countryside again. And this is only part of the problem which overshadows all others in this field: the relentless invasion of the countryside by 'Subtopia,' and the gradual obliteration of the distinction between town and country.*

This is not a book about architecture, or town and country planning; I am not, in any event, expert enough to go into detail. But detail in fact is hardly necessary, since the enemies to be overcome are attitudes of mind; if they can be conquered, the detailed policies will follow. These enemies are first parsimony, secondly indifference, and

* *v.* Ian Nairn, *Outrage* (Architectural Press, 1955).

thirdly anarchistic selfishness. The parsimony can be overcome by a recognition that the total sums involved are a minute fraction of total consumers', or even total Budgetary, expenditure. It is literally true that an annual increase in 'cultural' spending of £30 millions for the next 10 years, out of an annual increase in output of some £300 millions and a Budget of over £3,000 millions, would revolutionise the situation. It only needs a little, and so little, firmness in the face of the Beaverbrook Press.*

The indifference can be countered only by a display of savagery on the part of the minority who care for these matters—though it may, in the end, not be a minority at all, once the issues are put and the votes collected; this is a sphere in which determined leadership might yield generous dividends. The selfishness, often dressed up in the plausible language of complaints against bureaucracy or compulsory purchase or inadequate compensation, and fortified by a vulgar philistinism amongst those who articulate it in Parliament and the Press, will never be eradicated by argument or debate. We have here a simple, but deep, dividing line at once of principle and temperament; a clash of values to be resolved, not by verbal compromise, but simply by struggle.

Although this emphasis on culture, and that in the previous section on personal liberty, cannot claim the label socialist, they do provide a justification for supporting the Labour in preference to the Conservative Party. Not that the former's record on cultural or libertarian issues is immaculate—far from it. But it is at least significantly better than the Conservative record. A higher proportion of Labour than Tory Members of Parliament has consistently voted for enlightenment on issues such as the Festival of Britain, town and country planning, divorce-law reform, the censorship of plays and books, the abolition of hanging, and the Arts Council; socialists have even shown more practical interest in the preservation of historic private houses; while post-war Labour Chancellors, under Mr. Dalton's lead, initiated the Land Fund and showed unexampled generosity to the Universities. The mood of the Party is therefore mildly encouraging. But one grows too hopeful. By the time we next come back to power, many opportunities will have been lost irretrievably; as this is written, innumerable pygmies, presented with an opportunity that only Wren

---

* Personally I should be prepared, to take one concrete example, to pay any subsidy necessary to encourage more high building in cities in the interests of preserving the countryside—whatever the *Sunday Express* said about government waste, or the *Economist* about the 'distortion' of resources.

has ever before enjoyed, are busy spawning their ugly rectangles all over the City of London.

Nevertheless, I hope and believe that the Labour Party may come to take the lead in this struggle. It would, in the judgment of history, do more for Britain by planning the City of London than by planning the chemical industry, and infinitely more by abolishing hanging than by abolishing the tied cottage. It has a favourable background and tradition for assuming this role—the influence of William Morris, its long-standing belief in social as opposed to private values, and the tender, respectful feeling for culture that characterises the educated working class. And it certainly has the opportunity—not merely because the need is so urgent, but because material standards are rising to the point where we can spare more energy, and more resources, for beauty and culture.

Indeed this is a sphere in which the original co-operative ideal is directly relevant. I discussed this ideal in Chapter V, and concluded that although it was both obviously unfulfilled and historically part of socialism, yet it was hard to see how it could be realised in practice, and on a national scale, in terms of personal motives or industrial relations. But in the cultural field, such an ideal, which demands that social should be placed above private interests, is practicable as well as relevant; though recent experience has taught us that 'private' in this context has little to do with private profit, and must be defined as 'sectional'—to include city corporations, local councils, nationalised industries, and even government departments, as well as private business. But if we pursue this ideal vigorously, and even savagely, we might make Britain not only a more prosperous, not only a more just and equal and contented, but also a more beautiful and civilised country to live in.

In so doing, and with the aid of rising material standards, we might find that another aspect of this ideal, the weakening of the motive of personal gain, was also being insensibly and imperceptibly realised. 'When the accumulation of wealth,' Keynes once wrote, 'is no longer of high social importance, there will be great changes in the code of morals. . . . I see us free to return to some of the most sure and certain principles of religion and traditional virtue—that avarice is a vice, that the exaction of usury is a misdemeanour, and the love of money is detestable, that those walk most truly in the paths of virtue and sane wisdom who take least thought for the morrow. We shall once more value ends above means and prefer the good to the useful. We shall honour those who can teach us how to pluck the hour and the day virtuously and well, the delightful people who are capable of taking direct enjoyment in things.'*

It is no doubt too early yet to relax into these more humane ways, hemmed in as we still are by squalor and distress, especially in under-privileged lands abroad; and all our hopes may yet be blasted by a failure to resolve the competitive struggle known as the Cold War. But even now, as Keynes went on to say, 'there will be no harm in making mild preparations for our destiny, in encouraging, and ex-perimenting in, the arts of life as well as the activities of purpose.' We do not want to enter the age of abundance, only to find that we have lost the values which might teach us how to enjoy it.

* *Essays in Persuasion* (Macmillan, 1931), pp. 371-2.